Young
HOLLYWOOD

Young
HOLLYWOOD

JAMES CAMERON-WILSON

MADISON BOOKS
LANHAM, MARYLAND

Published by Madison Books
4720 Boston Way
Lanham, Maryland 20706

3 Henrietta Street
London WC2E 8LU England

Distributed by National Book Network

The paper used in this publication meets the minimum
requirements of American National Standard for
Information Sciences – Permanence of Paper for
Printed Library Materials, ANSI Z39.48-1984.
Typeset by
Colorcraft, Hong Kong
and printed in Great Britain

Library of Congress Cataloging-in-Publication Data

Cameron-Wilson, James.
    Young Hollywood/James Cameron-Wilson.
        p.   cm.
    Includes bibliographical references and index.
    ISBN 1-56833-038-3
    I. Motion picture actors and actresses – United
    States – Biography.
I. Title.
PN1998.2.C36   1994
791.43'028'092273 – dc20
[B]   94-19583
                                                 CIP

Title page: the original Brat Pack (left to right): Emilio Estevez, Rob Lowe,
C. Thomas Howell, Matt Dillon, Ralph Macchio, Patrick Swayze, Tom Cruise.
The movie is Francis Ford Coppola's trend-setting 1983 release *The Outsiders*.

Dedication

To Frances, my wife –
for her spiritual support
and understanding.

ACKNOWLEDGEMENTS

The author would like to thank the following for their assistance in the preparation of this book.

My endless gratitude must go to Virginia Palmer, Nigel Mulock and Karen Baldwin for supplying me with so much useful material. Also, my thanks to the actors and directors who talked to me, so that I might gain a greater perspective of my subject. But, most of all, I must thank my mother for furnishing me with office space, and my wife, Frances, for supplying the moral nourishment.

The author and publisher also make grateful acknowledgement to the following organizations for the reproduction of the promotional stills which illustrate this book: Amblin Entertainment, Blue Dolphin Films, Buena Vista Pictures Distribution, Cannon Film Distributors, Castle Premier Releasing, Columbia Pictures, Curzon Film Distribution, DC Comics Inc., De Laurentiis Entertainment Group, Electric Pictures, First Independent Films Ltd, The Geffen Film Company, Guild Film Distribution, Hemdale Film Distribution, Hollywood Pictures, Lorimar Distribution International, Mainline Pictures, Metro Goldwyn Mayer, Miracle Films, New Line Cinema Corporation, New World Pictures, Odyssey, Orion Pictures Corporation, Palace Pictures, Paramount Picture Corporation, Polygram Filmed Entertainment, Pony Boy Inc., Rank Film Distributors Ltd, The Samuel Goldwyn Company, Touchstone Pictures, Tri-Star Pictures, Twentieth Century Fox, United International Pictures (UK), Universal City Studios, Vestron Pictures (UK) Ltd, Virgin Vision, Warner Brothers Inc., Westmount Communication Film Joint Ventures.

Introduction

It all started in 1983 with Francis Ford Coppola's *The Outsiders*. A modestly budgeted fable based on a cult novel, the film was a refreshing antidote to the director's financially troubled, overblown productions *Apocalypse Now* and *One From the Heart*. Back in 1972, following an unremarkable liaison with the box-office, Coppola had been employed to make a low-budget gangster movie for Paramount. He was hired, it was said, because he would 'be easy to control,' having no track record to swell his head nor a reputation as trouble-maker. However, as soon as he had signed along the dotted line, Coppola began to contest Paramount's casting choices for the leading role of Mafia chieftain Don Corleone. The studio had Burt Lancaster, George C. Scott and Orson Welles in mind, but the yound director wanted Marlon Brando, who hadn't had a hit in eons. Coppola also insisted on casting a stage actor called Al Pacino to play Corleone's son, Michael, in preference to such established names as Warren Beatty, Dustin Hoffman and Jack Nicholson.

He got his way. Brando was paid the measly sum of $50,000 for his part (and a cut of the profits), and was supported by a largely unknown cast that included Pacino, James Caan, Robert Duvall and Diane Keaton. The movie went on to win the Oscar for best film and best actor and became the highest grossing picture in history. It was called *The Godfather*.

Coppola was now unstoppable, but his subsequent career turned out to be an obstacle course of escalating budgets and troubled shoots, and when he later turned to the actors that he had transformed into household names he found that he could no longer afford them. Turning his back on the star system, the director signed up a cast of young unknowns for his self-consciously poetic adaptation of S.E. Hinton's best-selling novel *The Outsiders*. In retrospect, it's hard to conceive that the film was not a box-office success (it actually lost money), but it struck a big enough chord to help its young actors into commercially healthier projects. The cast in question comprised C. Thomas Howell, Ralph Macchio, Matt Dillon, Patrick Swayze, Rob Lowe, Emilio Estevez, Tom Cruise and Diane Lane, all of whom are included in this book.

If not a blockbuster, *The Outsiders* was at the very least a potent audition tape for the next generation of movie luminaries. To a lesser degree, Coppola went on to discover more stars (also featured in this tome), casting his nephew Nicolas Cage in *RumbleFish, The Cotton Club* and *Peggy Sue Got Married*, D.B. Sweeney in *Gardens of Stone*, Christian Slater in *Tucker: The Man and His Dreams* and Andy Garcia and Bridget Fonda in *The Godfather Part III*.

He had sown the seeds. A year after *The Outsiders* opened, a 34-year-old screenwriter called John Hughes directed his first film, a teenage comedy entitled *Sixteen Candles*. This was considerably more successful, and featured more adolescent would-be household names, namely Molly Ringwald, Anthony Michael Hall, John Cusack and Jami Gertz. Meanwhile, Tom Cruise had hit pay dirt with *Risky Business*, Matt Dillion was winning excellent reviews for his goofy comedy *The Flamingo Kid*, and Emilio Estevez had become a minor cult in the decidedly quirky *Repo Man*. Before long, teenage stars were emerging at the rate of one a month, and a new cinemagoing audience was born. Statistics revealed that movie punters were getting younger by the year and Hollywood could barely keep up. You only had to amble into your local newsagent to see the number of posters, postcards and fanzines dedicated to the worship of the new celluloid elite, all of whom seemed barely out of their school blazers. Older stars like Robert Redford, Burt Reynolds and Jane Fonda were patently losing their box-office grip.

This book chronicles the careers and lives of one hundred actors and actresses who have emerged since *The Outsiders*. Of course, there are many more that could have been included in these pages. Some names that have emerged since 1983 have already hit the vaults of obscurity, while others are too old to be classified as part of the 'Young Hollywood' phenomenon (i.e. Kathy Bates and John Malkovich). Many stars made my short list but, for one reason or another, failed to make the top one hudnred. No doubt their omission will infuriate some readers, their careers will flourish and I will be plagued by sleepless nights. My apologies, then, to Kevin Anderson, Jim Carrey, Rae Dawn Chong, Jennifer Connelly, Macaulay Culkin, Sherilyn Fenn, Balthazar Getty, Annabeth Gish, Crispin Glover, Jennifer Grey, Lukas Haas, Kelly Lynch, Penelope Ann Miller, Mike Myers, Judd Nelson, Martha Plimpton, Jason Priestley, Helen Slater, Meg Tilly, Marisa Tomei, Mare Winningham and Daphne Zuniga.

For the record, I have used the year 1955 as the book's cut-off point – i.e. actors born before that date are not included. The sole exception to the rule (and rules were invented to be broken) is the inclusion of Patrick Swayze. Not only does he look as if he was born after 1955 (he was actually born in 1952), but he has appeared in many films in the Brat Pack canon, such as *Red Dawn, Youngblood*, and, most notably, *The Outsiders*. Thus, he is this tome's honorary member, a sort of grandfather of the Brat Pack. Other borderline stars have been excluded because their careers

seem to belong elsewhere. Even though Melanie Griffith was born in 1957, her very first leading man was Gene Hackman (in *Night Moves;* 1975), followed by Paul Newman (in *The Drowning Pool*) a year later. Since then her co-stars have included such hardy veterans as Harrison Ford, Michael Douglas and her frequent husband Don Johnson.

Likewise, you will not find such recent, but older names as Kevin Costner, Michael Keaton, Steven Seagal or Bruce Willis within, whose careers have been chronicled exhaustively elsewhere. There are, however, a few anomalies. Jodie Foster was a star long before 1983, but by dint of her age she is included (she is, after all, younger than Tom Cruise). Other former child stars such as Tatum O'Neal and Brooke Shields are bypassed as their subsequent careers have been of minimal interest. Also, in an effort to keep the book bang up to date, I have included a few performers who may be more famous tomorrow than they are today: Patricia Arquette, William Baldwin, Brendan Fraser, Juliette Lewis, Samantha Mathis, Dermot Mulroney and Mary-Louise Parker. These talented actors are already receiving considerable attention and a growing legion of fans. It will be interesting to see if they are still around in five years' time. Then there are the entries who fit no particular pigeon-hole but are, nevertheless, stars working in Hollywood: the Australian-born Nicole Kidman, the Belgian Jean-Claude Van Damme and the music industry's (and several other industries') Madonna.

And so to the matter of ground rules. Unless otherwise specified, dates before films indicate the year of their American release. As for titles, I have opted to enter films under the name of their American release. However, it should be pointed out that some films are privy to several name changes in their exotic transition from country to country and then on to video and TV. Where a title has been altered for its UK release, I have listed this in brackets. Ditto any other alternative titles – all in an effort to save researchers from the embarrassment of confusing one film for two or even three (you will be surprised how many reference books list alternative titles as two separate films). For a laugh, you can turn to the filmography of Lou Diamond Phillips to see the sort of headache that awaits potential scholars of this sort of thing. The filmographies themselves are as complete as they can be, and include all cinema, TV and video titles – however brief the entrant's appearance may be in them.

Due to the public interest in stars' birth dates, I have included as many as I could find and have placed them in the main body of the text immediately following the introductory paragraphs. But in spite of the tireless help of learned colleagues, I have been unable to unearth every single birthday. The likes of Phoebe Cates, Nicole Kidman and Mary Stuart Masterson have successfully kept their special days secret from the media. So if a godparent of any of the above should read this, please drop me a line so that I can include the date in future editions of this book.

In the meantime, I hope *Young Hollywood* proves to be a readable and informative answer to many film buffs' prayers.

Patricia ARQUETTE

Five feet two and as pretty as an Alpine meadow, Patricia Arquette displayed a considerable range in a very short career. She showed a winning aptitude for comedy, and was equally adept at drama, playing a teenage mother in the acclaimed TV movie *Daddy* and a young woman plagued by horrific dreams in *A Nightmare On Elm Street 3 – Dream Warriors*. For a while she was known as the younger sister of Rosanna Arquette (which she is), although the only thing they seemed to have in common was beauty and talent. 'If there were a similarity between us,' Patricia says, 'I would accept it gladly. But we have totally different personalities.' She admits that she was wary of following in her famous sister's footsteps: 'When I told Rosanna I wanted to be an actress, I was really afraid about it because she was doing so well. I was going through a really insecure time in my life, but she said, "Look, I really believe in you. I know you can do it."'

And she did.

The latest bud from a theatrical dynasty that was appearing in vaudeville four generations ago, Patricia was born in 1968, the middle child of five. She admits, 'I never exactly trained as a little kid, but we did do all these little shows ...' She made her professional debut in a children's version of Paul Sill's *Story Theatre*, and did voice-overs

and radio commercials on America's east coast. Then, in 1974, she moved with her family to Los Angeles. During her early teens, she worked as a model in Portugal, France and Italy, and later trained with the famous drama coach Milton Katselas.

She returned to Europe as an actress, playing 'Zero' in the film *Pretty Smart*, a routine sex-in-high-school malarkey, set in an all-girls academy on a Greek island. There, she graduated high school herself, and returned to America to star in *A Nightmare On Elm Street 3 – Dream Warriors*. She played Kristen Parker, a girl suffering from a sleeping disorder, who battles Freddie Krueger through a series of stunning special effects. Most famously, it was young Patricia who was swallowed by Krueger in a legendary, jaw-dropping sequence. She was offered *Nightmare 4*, but declined, explaining, 'I was very honoured, but I didn't want to get stuck doing horror for the rest of my life.'

Meanwhile, she won glowing reviews (*The Los Angeles Times* called her 'superb') for the TV movie *Daddy*, in which she played a teenage girl encumbered with a child nobody (including boyfriend Dermot Mulroney) wanted her to have. Ironically, a year later she was pregnant herself and, barely out of her teens, gave birth to Enzo, a son she named after a character in *The Godfather*. But, in contrast to the conclusion in *Daddy*, she went on to rear the child by herself. She says, 'On the one hand I was really happy, but on the other I was very afraid and scared. I was given a part in *Last Exit to Brooklyn*, but it was a very dark and violent film and I didn't want to take that into me when I was

pregnant, because I absorb so much when I work. I just couldn't do it.' Later, she revealed, 'I'm so glad I'm young having a kid. My body bounced back. And I have the energy.'

In 1988 her 'life-long dream' came true when she was cast in Sam Shepard's film *Far North*. 'I had an English teacher who made us read *Curse of the Starving Class*,' she explained, 'and I was totally blown away. I took out all of Sam's plays and read each one and was completely taken by his writing.' Unfortunately, *Far North* – in which she played Jilly, the rebellious and highly-sexed teenage niece of Jessica Lange – was a stagey, mannered piece that only came alight when Arquette was on screen.

She was also marvellous in *Prayer of the Roller Boys*, a confused futuristic yarn with only occasional glimpses of comic invention, in which she played a sexy undercover cop; she then went up for the role of Dorothy, the pregnant girlfriend of Viggo Mortensen, in Sean Penn's *The Indian Runner*. Penn explains: 'I was exhausted, but I had finally found someone who could play Dorothy well, and I just did not want to see another actress.' But Arquette was already booked for an audition, and Penn was forced to go through the paces. 'She was Dorothy,' he marvelled. 'We all knew the minute she came into the room. It was that simple.'

On TV, she was directed by Diane Keaton

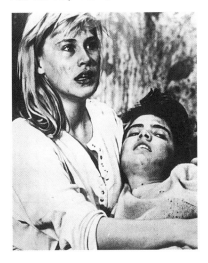

We all have to start somewhere: Patricia Arquette cradles Heather Langenkamp in her arms in *A Nightmare On Elm Street 3: Dream Warriors*

Patricia Arquette (on the horse) watches as Jessica Lange and Tess Harper argue – in Sam Shepard's *Far North*

in a CBS Schoolbreak Special called *The Girl With the Crazy Brother*, which led to the TV movie *Wildflower*, also directed by Keaton. In the latter, she played Alice Guthrie, a teenage epileptic, and was simply sensational. Liam Neeson caught the movie and was stunned. 'For the first time in ten years, I saw a performance by an actress that made me think, "Oh my God."' When he heard that Arquette was to be in the film version of Edith Wharton's ironic novella *Ethan Frome*, he agreed to join her. 'Liam had just seen *Wildflower* and was writing me a note,' the actress recalled, 'and it all came together.' She played Mattie Silver, the spirited young woman who brings brief light into the drab existence of the disfigured Ethan (Neeson). The film, directed by John Madden, was a loving, beautifully crafted version of the novel, although some critics found it a trifle stiff.

Meanwhile, she was excellent as a dignified lesbian in the charming comedy *Inside Monkey Zetterland*, also starring Martha Plimpton and Rupert Everett, and then, in *Trouble Bound*, played a Mafia princess who falls in with an ex-con on the run from the Mob (Michael Madsen). Next, she was running from the Family again in Tony Scott's *True Romance*, this time hitched to Christian Slater and a suitcase full of stolen contraband. This was the Big One. From the director of *Top Gun* and *Beverly Hills Cop II*

Patricia with Corey Haim in the loopy *Prayer of the Roller Boys*

Patricia Arquette with Steven Weber in the 1993 TV movie *Betrayed by Love*

As Alabama, the heroine of Tony Scott's lyrical, hard-hitting *True Romance*

(Tony Scott), and a hot, hot script by Quentin Tarantino (of *Reservoir Dogs* esteem), *True Romance* was a mouth-watering property for any actress. But with a supporting cast that included Dennis Hopper, Gary Oldman, Brad Pitt, Val Kilmer and Christopher Walken, Ms Arquette was in the money. Indeed, she reputedly pocketed a cool million for the lead in *Beyond Rangoon*.

Filmography

1987: *Pretty Smart*; *A Nightmare On Elm Street 3: Dream Warriors*; *Daddy* (TV). 1988: *Time Out*; *Far North*. 1991: *Dillinger* (TV); *Prayer of the Rollerboys*; *The Indian Runner*; *Wildflower* (TV). 1992: *Inside Monkey Zetterland*. 1993: *Ethan Frome*; *Trouble Bound*; *True Romance*; *Betrayed By Love* (TV). 1994: *Holy Matrimony*; *Ed Wood*; *The Gold Cup*; *Beyond Rangoon*; *Infinity*.

Rosanna ARQUETTE

Rosanna Arquette suffered from the celebrity syndrome. Her films were seldom as well known as she was, but still fame followed her like an obedient puppy. In 1983 she had a song named after her (Toto's No. 2 hit *Rosanna*), two years later she top-billed in *Desperately Seeking Susan* whose unknown co-star – Madonna – turned the comedy into a sensational cult. She then moved in with rock star Peter Gabriel, formerly of Genesis who, when she posed naked for Playboy, reportedly threw a fit and terminated their relationship. Instantaneously, the media scrambled for crumbs of scandal.

The tabloids regaled their readers with stories of the actress's unorthodox up-bringing, her flower power childhood, the rallies she attended (with 'Stop the war' painted across her infant chest), her drug addiction at 13, her cohabitation with a man at 15, her marriage at 17 . . .

But Rosanna Arquette was a better actress than her press would have us believe. It was just that her timing was bad. From the start she was typecast. 'I played every pregnant teenage runaway, hooker, addict, that was ever on the planet,' she recalls. Then, when she broke that mould, 'I did *Desperately Seeking Susan*, *After Hours* and *Nobody's Fool* and they all came out within a year of each other. Those are the films that stuck in people's minds – but I'm an actor, not a little ingenue chickie,' she insists.

And, to her credit, Rosanna Arquette was attracting the attention of some top level directors: not least Martin Scorsese, Lawrence Kasdan and John Sayles. Sayles, who directed her in his '1960s' high school romance *Baby, It's You*, ventured, 'When I cast Rosanna, I knew she was the only person who could play the innocent in the first half of the movie and bring out the emotional depth for the second part.' Mike Hodges, who guided her performance as a travelling clairvoyant in his *Black Rainbow*, volunteered, 'Rosanna played the toughness any entertainer on the road would have, but she was extra wonderful because a little-girl-lost emerged above my original inentions.'

But soon her career was to stumble. Her leading role in John Milius's *Flight of the*

Rosanna Arquette

Rosanna Arquette, with Tommy Lee Jones, in the 1982 *The Executioner's Song*

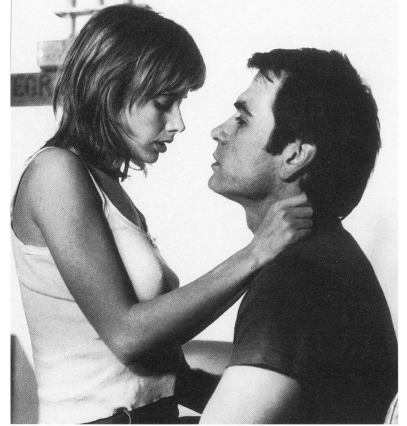

Intruder was hacked back to a romantic subplot in order to accommodate her male co-stars (Danny Glover, Willem Dafoe and Brad Johnson). Then, when she landed the lead in *Radio Flyer*, Columbia Pictures's $30 million sci-fi fantasy, the film was shut down after two weeks of shooting. First time director David Mickey Evans (who had written the script) was replaced by Richard Donner, the latter taking it upon himself to recast the movie, supplanting Arquette in favour of Lorraine Bracco.

The actress's next two movies – *The Linguini Incident*, with David Bowie, and *Father & Sons*, with Jeff Goldblum – were both bombs.

Rosanna Arquette was born into theatrical tradition. Her great-grandfather was an actor, as was her grandfather, Cliff Arquette, who became immortalised on American radio and television as the beloved bumpkin Charles Weaver (on *Dave and Charley*, *The Charles Weaver Show*, etc). Rosanna's father, Lewis Arquette, is an actor-producer and her mother, Mardi, a poet and playwright. Even three of her four siblings have gone into acting, namely sometime drag queen Alexis

(*Last Exit to Brooklyn*), David (TV's *The Outsiders*) and Patricia (*Far North*, *True Romance*).

Rosanna herself was born on 10 August 1959 in Manhattan and made her theatrical debut aged eight in *Story Theatre*, directed by her father. Between the ages of 11 and 13 she lived in 'this spiritual brotherhood – an actor's and musician's commune. And I was going to school in this town in Virginia where it was like the Civil War was still going on. Most of my friends were black, so I was always writing B-L-A-C-K P-O-W-E-R on my hands and flashing the rednecks.'

At 14, she moved to New Jersey on her own and attended South Orange Junior High where she first became interested in drama. She rejoined her family in Chicago a year later and then, with her parents' blessing, hitchhiked to San Francisco where she studied acting for a year.

Winning a part in a play in Los Angeles, she was spotted by a casting director who recommended her to an agent. This in turn led to a number of small parts on television, including a role in NBC's *Shirley*, in which she played Shirley Jones's daughter Debra. On the big screen, she had a walk-on in *More American Graffiti* and then landed a good role opposite Bette Davis in the well-received TV film *The Dark Secret of Harvest Home*, a gothic tale set in New England. She then appeared in the awful *Gorp*, with fellow unknown Dennis Quaid, and played a topless hitchhiker in Blake Edwards's showbiz spoof *S.O.B.*

But it wasn't until NBC's scorching TV movie *The Executioner's Song* that critics woke up. Rosanna played Nicole Baker, the girlfriend of convicted killer Gary Gilmore (Tommy Lee Jones), who famously asked for his own death sentence. The film was a compelling portrayal of real-life crime, scripted by Norman Mailer from his own best-seller, and was released theatrically in Europe.

This led to another star-making performance in the TV movie *Johnny Belinda*, with Quaid and Richard Thomas, and then the lead in John Sayles's *Baby, It's You*, co-starring Vincent Spano as Rosanna's 'Sheik'. The latter was a sensitive, credible tale of a schoolgirl exploring her centre of gravity through sex and amateur dramatics and, turning in an affecting, naturalistic performance devoid of mannerisms, Arquette has seldom been better since. More TV films followed, and a tedious vehicle for Christopher Reeve, *The Aviator*, in which the actress was at her annoying worst as the latter's reluctant passenger. Then, thankfully, came *Desperately Seeking Susan*..

Rosanna as Roberta in Susan Seidelman's charmingly idiosyncratic *Desperately Seeking Susan*

Rosanna as the mixed-up, alluring Marcy in Martin Scorsese's unpredictable comedy *After Hours*

Rosanna played Roberta, an inept, bored housewife ignored by her husband and reduced to following the personal ads in the paper for entertainment. Gradually, she becomes intrigued by a recurring entry headed 'DESPERATELY SEEKING SUSAN' and follows it up incognito. Soon, she finds herself following Susan (Madonna) on a shopping spree, buys the latter's jacket from a second-hand clothes shop and then becomes mistaken for her after she loses her memory. It transpires that Susan was one in-demand dame and everybody is after her – now unwittingly impersonated by Roberta.

Farce is one of the most difficult forms of comedy to pull off on film, but director Susan Seidelman had the good sense to inject it with a decent shot of realism, making this a credible, hilarious ride. Rosanna was never better as the housewife with dreams above her station, transformed by fate at its most bizarre. Madonna was better than anybody expected, but it was still Rosanna Arquette who carried the film.

And so the next bout of typecasting set in. She played another New York kook in Scorsese's *After Hours*, leading a hapless Griffin Dunne into a night of chaos, but left the picture all too soon. For Lawrence

As the talented fake medium Martha Travis in Mike Hodges's *Black Rainbow*

Kasdan's starry western *Silverado*, she spent five months in preparation, only to find her part virtually discarded in the editing room. She played a gangster's moll in Hal Ashby's *8 Million Ways To Die*, but the film was so bad it didn't even get a release in Britain – even with Jeff Bridges top-billed. *Nobody's Fool*, a bizarre romantic comedy, saw her as an eccentric looking for Mr Right (Eric Roberts), but the film was a flop; as was the omnibus turkey *Amazon Women on the Moon*.

Luc Besson's *The Big Blue*, a magical, unusual aquatic epic, had all the potential to be a hit, but was too offbeat for most tastes (and Rosanna was in a particularly irritating mood). She was much better as the clairvoyant in Mike Hodges's *Black Rainbow*, a serious, intriguing examination of the paranormal which fell apart when it turned into a routine thriller. The role was actually suggested to the actress by Scorsese, who had just directed her in his *Life Lessons* segment from *New York Stories*, an unsuccessful trio of short films depicting life in the Big Apple.

There were more TV movies and a couple of box-office stiffs: the Australian romantic comedy-fantasy *Wendy Cracked a Walnut* (and laid an egg); and *The Linguini Incident*, another oddball comedy about eccentric New Yorkers.

More recently, she played the female interest in *Nowhere To Run*, a timeworn action-packed vehicle for Belgian muscleman Jean-Claude Van Damme. Oddly, Rosanna shed her clothes (twice) for the under-written role of a widow and mother who seduces Van Damme on her farm. For many years Rosanna had protested against nudity in films, explaining, 'I don't like the way it feels. I'm not going to do that again. Fuck that!' She disrobed again in *The Wrong Man*. At the end of 1993, the actress married for a third time, to the restaurateur Johnny Sidel.

FILMOGRAPHY

1977: *Having Babies II* (TV). 1978: *Zuma Beach* (TV); *The Dark Secret of Harvest Home* (TV). 1979: *More American Graffiti*. 1980: *Gorp*. 1981: *S.O.B.*; *A Long Way Home* (TV); *The Wall* (TV). 1982: *The Executioner's Song* (TV; UK: theatrical); *Johnny Belinda* (TV). 1983: *Baby, It's You*; *Off the Wall*; *One Cooks, the Other Doesn't* (TV). 1984: *The Parade* (TV); *The Aviator*. 1985: *Survival Guides* (TV); *Desperately Seeking Susan*; *After Hours*; *Silverado*. 1986: *8 Million Ways To Die*; *Nobody's Fool*; *Amazon Women On the Moon*. 1988: *The Big Blue*; *Promised a Miracle* (TV). 1989: *New York Stories* (episode: *Life Lessons*); *Black Rainbow*. 1990: *Wendy Cracked a Walnut*; *Sweet Revenge* (TV); *Separation* (TV). 1991: *Flight of the Intruder*; *Son of the Morning Star* (TV). 1992: *The Linguini Incident*; *Father & Sons*; *In the Deep Woods* (TV). 1993: *Nowhere To Run*; *The Wrong Man*. 1994: *Fear City: A Family-Style Comedy* (cameo); *Pulp Fiction*; *Search and Destroy*.

Kevin BACON

The features are unmistakeable. The famous upturned nose, the impish smile, the small demonic eyes and those wicked, wicked dimples. If Kevin Bacon was to try Shakespeare, he would be typecast as Puck. Or Caliban.

And yet, in a medium obsessed with killing, Bacon has avoided psycho typecasting. At least, until *Criminal Law*, his 18th picture. But then, he was originally approached to play the good guy. When Gary Oldman was signed up to play the lead, Bacon jumped at the chance of playing the serial killer Oldman defends and then brings to justice. But of course Bacon's character is meant to look innocent - at first. Then, two years later, the actor went on to win some of the best notices of his career as the homosexual prison inmate in *JFK*.

But, more often than not, Kevin Bacon was the clean-cut good guy. On a few occasions he even got to play the romantic lead. But Bacon is a better actor than that, and *has* displayed a remarkable range, both in the types of films he has appeared in, and the

Kevin Bacon

roles he has played. He also has a roguish sense of humour, admitting, 'I judge whether or not I can be in line with someone's sense of humour based on whether or not they enjoyed *This is Spinal Tap*. I've seen it no less than 20 times.'

The son of an architect and a mother involved in child education, Kevin Bacon was born on 8 July 1958, in Philadelphia. At an early age he started taking drama lessons with a church group and later became the youngest member of the Manning Street Actor's Theatre. 'From the moment I started drama,' he says, 'I knew that I wanted to be an actor. It was just something I knew I had to do.'

With the endorsement of his parents, he moved to New York at the age of 17 and spent a year with the Circle in the Square Theatre. He then appeared in a number of off-Broadway productions and did time in TV appearing in the daytime soap *Search For Tomorrow* (which had previously boasted Robert De Niro, Jill Clayburgh and Kevin Kline in its ranks) and *The Guiding Light*, as the runaway T.J.

In 1978 he made his film debut as Chip Diller in the phenomenally successful, anarchic comedy *National Lampoon's Animal House*, a film which blessed a number of its cast members' futures (newcomers John Belushi, Tom Hulce, Karen Allen, Peter Riegert, et al). He had a small part as a young husband in *Starting Over*, with Burt Reynolds and Jill Clayburgh, and had a bigger role in the well-received TV movie *The Gift*, starring Glenn Ford.

In the original *Friday the 13th* he played Jack, an unhappy camper who is ceremoniously butchered immediately after making love (he was the guy who got an arrow through the throat). The film was another enormous success, and spawned seven frightful sequels which, thankfully, Bacon had nothing to do with. Instead, he got into into a much better ensemble piece, *Diner*, which

Kevin as the deviant serial killer Martin Thiel (with Gary Oldman in the background) in *Criminal Law*

Kevin as small-time filmmaker in *The Big Picture*

was to set new standards for cinema aimed at and about young people. Bacon had the flashiest role, as Fenwick, an immature, ghoulish alcoholic who opens the film by staging his own death in a car wreck. Written and directed by Barry Levinson, *Diner* also starred Steve Guttenberg, Daniel Stern, Mickey Rourke and Ellen Barkin, and was a critical triumph.

After that, Bacon played a teenage hustler in *Forty Deuce*, based on the off-Broadway play by Alan Bowne (in which the actor had starred). This was followed by the so-so TV movie *The Demon Murder Case* and then a three-part omnibus production, *Enormous Changes at the Last Minute*, also featuring Ellen Barkin and co-scripted by John Sayles.

Then came the biggie: *Footloose*. Kevin Bacon was at his most appealing as 'Ren', the city boy who turns up at a small Mid-Western town to discover that dancing has been outlawed. Rather good at moving his feet, Ren objects to this terpsichorean censorship and strives to set matters straight. After putting his foot in it, he dances up a storm and even wins the affections of the stern preacher's daughter (Lori Singer). The director Herbert Ross, who started out as a dancer and choreographer, brought an enormous zing to the proceedings and helped the film to a healthy box-office run.

With this commercial success under his belt, Kevin Bacon saw his career nosedive. He was a star, but his films didn't measure up. He tamed the wildnerness in *White Water Summer* and played a bicycle messenger boy in *Quicksilver*, neither of which gained a theatrical release in Britain. There was also a mediocre, stagey TV movie, *Lemon Sky* which, although it left the critics cold, did introduce him to the actress Kyra Sedgwick, whom he married a year later (in 1988).

Next, he took a cameo in John Hughes's *Planes, Trains and Automobiles* (in which he steals a taxi from Steve Martin), and then accepted a supporting role in the whimsical *End of the Line*, produced by and co-starring Mary Steenburgen. He was at his charismatic best as the young husband burdened by domesticity in Hughes's *She's Having a Baby* (Elizabeth McGovern was having it), but the film went nowhere. *Criminal Law* did little better, but was a good-looking, atmospheric attempt at *film noir*, with Bacon the serial killer gleefully tormenting his own lawyer (Gary Oldman).

He had the lead in *The Big Picture*, a winning, occasionally hilarious spoof on Hollywood, pre-empting *The Player* by three years. Bacon was Nick Chapman, a scrupulous film student who believes in black-and-white, simple camera moves and heterosexual relationships. In an industry devoted to the quick buck, Chapman is eventually forced to contemplate a movie called *Beach Nuts*. A stalwart supporting cast included Martin Short (superb as Chapman's agent), Jennifer Jason Leigh, Roddy McDowall, Elliott Gould and John Cleese.

An even better picture turned up in the form of *Tremors*, a hugely entertaining comic-thriller with Bacon and Fred Ward as a pair of tough, wiry handymen encountering giant worms in the Nevada desert. Again, Bacon was top-billed, and made an engaging leading man, complete with a no-bull, off-kilter sense of humour.

He was offered the starring role in *Flatliners*, but instead opted for the straighter part of the idealistic David Labraccio, who initially resists the idea of experimenting with death (in order to sample after-life experiences). Kiefer Sutherland took the part Bacon rejected, Julia Roberts and William Baldwin also starred, and the film was a hit.

His next one, *He Said, She Said*, a romantic comedy with Elizabeth Perkins, wasn't. Neither was *Queens Logic*, a 'reunion' picture in the tradition of *The Big Chill*, which also starred John Malkovich, Joe Mantegna and Jamie Lee Curtis. Next came *JFK*, Oliver Stone's much-publicised conspiracy thriller, with Kevin Costner top-billed as a crusading DA sifting through the red herrings surrounding Kennedy's assassination. Although Bacon only had a small role, he got better notices than Costner.

In *Pyrates*, he and Kyra Sedgwick played a sexually active couple who caused fires whenever they made love. Although occasionally amusing, this bizarre sex comedy strived *too* hard to be original and failed to catch on. Then it was back to the ensemble ranks to play a hard-edged Navy lawyer in *A Few Good Men*. With a cast that included Tom Cruise, Jack Nicholson and Demi Moore, Bacon had to struggle to make an impression, but succeeded in holding his own in the courtroom. In fact, he was one of the best things in the film.

He then journeyed to Africa to play a basketball coach looking for his dream player in *The Air Up There*, for director Paul Michael Glaser.

FILMOGRAPHY

1978: *National Lampoon's Animal House.* **1979**: *Starting Over; The Gift* (TV). **1980**: *Friday the 13th; Hero At Large.* **1981**: *Only When I Laugh* (UK: *It Hurts Only When I Laugh*). **1982**: *Diner; Forty Deuce.* **1983**: *The Demon Murder Case* (TV); *Enormous Changes*

The star and his wife: Kevin Bacon and Kyra Sedgwick pose on the set of *Pyrates*

at the Last Minute. **1984**: *Footloose.* **1986**: *Quicksilver.* **1987**: *White Water Summer* (aka *Rites of Summer*) (filmed in 1985); *Lemon Sky* (TV); *Planes, Trains and Automobiles; End of the Line.* **1988**: *She's Having a Baby.* **1989**: *Criminal Law* (filmed in 1987); *The Big Picture.* **1990**: *Tremors; Flatliners.* **1991**: *He Said, She Said; Queen's Logic; JFK.* **1992**: *Pyrates; A Few Good Men.* **1993**: *The Air Up There.* **1994**: *The River Wild; Murder in the First.*

Alec BALDWIN

Alec Baldwin is an exceptionally talented actor with charisma to spare. He's also as good looking as they get: six-foot-tall, with a strong jawline and pale-blue, fluorescent eyes that female journalists are prone to swoon over. He's been described as a ladies' man, and has been involved with Michelle Pfeiffer, Ally Sheedy, Cynthia Gibb, and was briefly engaged to Janine Turner in 1983. He's had his bad press, too, thanks largely to a high-profile liaison with Kim Basinger, but more often than not has shown an integrity rare in a burgeoning film star. Once, he turned down a $1 million offer from a Japanese tobacco company to promote their product. With typical candour, he explained, 'I could make a fortune if I wanted to. But doing a piece of acting is like making love to somebody. I say to myself, "Can I get it up for this? Can I make love to this every day?".'

Baldwin is also courageous enough to express his political (or otherwise) views in

at George Washington University, but became disillusioned with electoral politics and, following the break-up of a two-year relationship, moved to New York University and studied drama under Lee Strasberg. He was yet to finish his course when he landed the role of the odious Billy Allison Aldrich in the daytime TV soap *The Doctors*, a role he played for two-and-a-half years. 'I thought, "I'll do this for a while, make some money, be able to pay for a year or two of law school, and then get out of this business".'

Instead, Baldwin followed the advice of his agent, moved to Los Angeles and got another TV series, *Cutter To Houston*. Baldwin played internist Dr Hal Wexler, one of three physicians working at a Texas community hospital (the other two were Jim Metzler and Shelley Hack). There was another soap, *Knot's Landing*, but enough was enough and Baldwin fled to New York in 1986 after his character, a disturbed evangelist, was killed off. He made his stage debut in a Broadway revival of Joe Orton's *Loot* and won a Theatre World Award for best performance by a newcomer. Hollywood took note.

His big screen debut came with the the male lead in *Forever, Lulu*, a picture he describes as, 'one of the worst films ever committed to celluloid'. He then played Kevin Bacon's smarmy best friend in *She's Having a Baby* and Michelle Pfeiffer's husband in *Married To the Mob* – after Ray Liotta turned the role down. He was a friendly ghost in Tim Burton's hit *Beetlejuice*, a talk show producer in *Talk Radio*, and Melanie Griffith's cheating boyfriend in *Working Girl*. He was superb as the exuberant evangelist Jimmy Swaggart in *Great Balls of Fire!*, and was even better as the amoral ex-con in *Miami Blues*, produced by Jonathan Demme. Next, he landed the role of Jack Ryan (turned down by Harrison Ford) in *The Hunt For Red October*, and made a dynamic, hugely appealing hero. The film grossed $200 million worldwide and Baldwin was declared the biggest new male star of 1990.

But then things went badly wrong. After he dropped out of Philip Kaufman's prestigious *Henry and June* – due, he contends, to 'exhaustion' – he lost the showy role of Vincent Mancini in Francis Ford Coppola's *The Godfather Part III* (Andy Garcia got it). Some even say he dropped the first film to get the second. He was, however, looking forward to playing the David Janssen part in the $30 million film version of TV's *The Fugitive*, for director Walter Hill. But this, too, failed to materialise, and was put on hold due to script difficulties. Two years later, Harrison Ford walked off with the part.

public, and pulls no punches. He's unafraid to take a supporting role if the film merits it (*Glengarry Glen Ross* did), and if a big movie conflicts with a previous commitment, he's been known to jettison the better offer. And even before he was a star, the cream of Hollywood came begging for his services.

'He is so eminently gifted,' offered Jonathan Demme, who cast Baldwin as Mafia hitman Frank 'Cucumber' DeMarco in *Married To the Mob*. 'We were very fortunate to get Alec to play a relatively small part, one that required tremendous presence.'

'I'd call him a working-class Cary Grant,' added Oliver Stone, who directed the actor in *Talk Radio*. 'I thought he did us a big favour, because he was getting hot then, and it was a small budget movie in which he took a supporting role. But he approached it as an actor wanting to be part of a team, not a star.'

'Some people you will find are very good actors, and some have that indefinable screen charimsa,' continued James Foley, director of *Glengarry Glen Ross*. 'But Alec Baldwin is one of those rare people who have both. That's what makes him a movie star.'

Baldwin himself has said that, 'If I have one stupid, childish thing I wish for, I'd like to win a Tony award. That would really, really make me happy.' Ironically, when he was cast as Jack Ryan in the $42.5 million movie *Patriot Games* (with a series of lucrative sequels attached), Baldwin jumped boat. *Games* was running behind schedule, and the actor had promised his services to the play *A Streetcar*

Alec Baldwin in an early role, as the bible-thumping Jimmy Swaggart in *Great Balls of Fire!*

Named Desire on Broadway. So, he turned down the biggest star-making part of his career and was replaced by Harrison Ford. Still, Baldwin got rave reviews for his role as Kowalski in *Streetcar* and, come 4 May 1992, was nominated for a Tony – alongside Alan Alda, Brian Bedford and Judd Hirsch. A month later, the prize was presented to Judd Hirsch for his performance in *Conversations With My Father*, and a week after that *Patriot Games* opened across America to gross a staggering $25 million in seven days. Baldwin's own movie that year, *Prelude To a Kiss*, only made $19 million in its entire run. Still, the critics loved it.

He was born Alexander Rae Baldwin III on 3 April 1958, the second oldest of six children. Three of his younger brothers have gone on to successful acting careers of their own, namely William (*Backdraft*, *Sliver*), Daniel (*Harley Davidson and the Marlboro Man*, *Knight Moves*) and Stephen (*Crossing the Bridge*, TV's *Young Riders*). Alec, or Xander as his family knew him, grew up in Massapequa, on Long Island, New York, where his father taught riflery at the local high school. Xander dreamed of a career in public service, but enjoyed acting enough in school productions. Maybe acting could lead him to bigger things, he figured.

For three years he studied political science

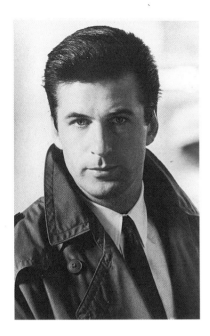

Alec Baldwin as CIA analyst Jack Ryan in the box-office smash *The Hunt For Red October*

Criminal charm: Alec Baldwin as the immoral crook Frederick J. Fender Jr in George Armitage's *Miami Blues*

Alec Baldwin with the love of his life, Kim Basinger, in Disney's troubled *The Marrying Man*

Baldwin took a cameo in Woody Allen's *Alice* (playing another ghost) and then landed the title role in Disney's *The Marrying Man*, with Kim Basinger. The on-set troubles on the latter are now part of Hollywood legend. Basinger and Baldwin, playing on-again, off-again lovers, fell for each other hard, and apparently declared war on Disney in the process. Basinger reportedly fired cameraman Ian Baker and forced the film's writer – Neil Simon, no less – off the set. Baldwin admitted, 'It was a terrible, terrible experience,' and the film turned out to be both a critical and box-office disaster. However, Baldwin and Basinger proved their love was for real when they tied the knot on 19 August 1991.

Next came the romantic fantasy *Prelude To a Kiss*, with Baldwin repeating his stage role to fine effect, and then a powerhouse cameo in *Glengarry Glen Ross* – as a ruthless company spokesman. He then joined Nicole Kidman in the corkscrew thriller, *Malice*, for director Harold Becker.

FILMOGRAPHY

1984: *Sweet Revenge* (TV). 1985: *Love On the Run* (TV). 1986: *Forever, Lulu*. 1987: *She's Having a Baby; The Alamo: 13 Days to Glory* (TV). 1988: *Married To the Mob; Beetlejuice; Talk Radio; Working Girl*. 1989: *Great Balls of Fire!* 1990: *Miami Blues; The Hunt For Red October; Alice*. 1991: *The Marrying Man* (UK: *Too Hot To Handle*). 1992: *Prelude To a Kiss; Glengarry Glen Ross*. 1993: *Malice*. 1994: *The Getaway; The Shadow; Heaven's Prisoners*.

William BALDWIN

The Baldwin brothers came in all shapes and sizes. Alec, the eldest, was the handsome one, a could-be Cary Grant. Daniel was stockier, tougher-looking, and played bad guys and aggressive cops. The youngest, Stephen, was the mischievous baby of the family, always ready with a wicked grin and a prank. And then there was William – or Billy – lanky, 6'4", sensitive, more beautiful than his brothers, in a love-me-or-step-on-me sort of way. While the twentysomething generation was swooning over the antics of Alec Baldwin in *The Hunt For Red October*, teenage girls were revving up their pulses for Billy in *Flatliners*, *Backdraft* and *Three of Hearts*.

Ironically, Billy got his first break playing a killer in the TV movie *The Preppie Murder*, based on the true case of ladies' man Robert Chambers. Co-star Tuesday Knight was impressed by the actor's ability to immerse himself in the role. 'His eyes go so blank,' she explained. 'Yet in other scenes he shows a vulnerable, gentle side like Chambers must have had. Even though you know he's a murderer, you can see why girls like him.'

Veteran actor Danny Aiello, who played the policeman interrogating Chambers, had a major emotional scene with Baldwin. 'It was one of the greatest scenes I've ever been involved in,' Aiello says. 'Billy had a very tough role. He had to stay flat the entire time before he finally broke down and cried . . . He's wonderful. I never had so much pleasure working with a kid.'

William Baldwin was born on 21 February 1963 in Massapequa, Long Island, New York, the fourth child (of six) to high school coach Alexander Rae Baldwin Jr. Billy's mother, Carol, recalled, 'Their father gave the kids enormous drive. He instilled in them the feeling that they could do anything. All the children set goals for themselves.'

Billy's goal was law school and he graduated from the State University of New York with a degree in political science.

William Baldwin

However, inspired by his brother's success in showbusiness, he abandoned law and tried drama himself, signing up with the renowned Ford model agency to pay for acting class. From TV commercials (in particular his endorsement of Levi's 501 jeans), he landed the role of a Vietnam soldier in Oliver Stone's *Born On the Fourth of July* (interestingly, both Stephen and Daniel Baldwin had roles in the same movie). This led to the starring role in *The Preppie Murder*, for which he won excellent reviews as the smarmy, ruthless Chambers, luring Jennifer Levin (Lara Flynn Boyle) to her death in Central Park.

In Mike Figgis's *Internal Affairs*, he played corrupt cop Richard Gere's emotionally unhinged and ultimately ill-fated partner, and then teamed up with Kiefer Sutherland, Julia Roberts and Kevin Bacon as one of five

William Baldwin as firefighter Brian McCaffrey in Ron Howard's incendiary *Backdraft* with Kurt Russell

Just a gigolo: William Baldwin with Kelly Lynch in Yurek Bogayevicz's *Three of Hearts*

medical students experimenting with death in Joel Schumacher's MTV thriller *Flatliners*. Baldwin played Joe Hurley, a somewhat smarmy ladies' man whose past sexual conquests literally come back to haunt him. The film was a hit and Baldwin was instantly in demand.

. He was offered the part of the young hitchhiker who seduces Geena Davis in *Thelma and Louise*, and accepted it, when he landed the key role in Ron Howard's big-budget, all-star *Backdraft*. He walked off the former (and was replaced by an unknown Brad Pitt) and joined Kurt Russell, Scott Glenn, Jennifer Jason Leigh, Rebecca De Mornay, Donald Sutherland and Robert De Niro for the latter, playing the son of a heroic

With Sharon Stone in the box-office disappointment *Sliver*

Chicago firefighter who cannot accept his father's death. Russell was his big brother and determined to teach him a few life lessons. In spite of the spectacular cast, it was the fire-fighting scenes that stole the acting honours, although the film's $76 million box-office gross in the States hardly damaged any careers.

Indeed, Baldwin was next signed up to play the romantic male lead in *Three of Hearts*, winning top-billing over Kelly Lynch and Sherilyn Fenn. Long in pre-production, the film was originally destined as a vehicle for Robert Downey Jr. Then Baldwin won the role of Sharon Stone's enigmatic boyfriend in the erotic thriller *Sliver*, described by director Phillip Noyce as 'the *Rear Window* of the 1990s? In order to skewer the part over a roster of potential leading men, Baldwin had to screen test with Ms Stone to establish their sexual chemistry. He emerged triumphant.

He was also announced to play the notorious 1930s outlaw George R. Kelly in the long-awaited gangster movie *Machine Gun Kelly*.

FILMOGRAPHY

1989: *Born On the Fourth of July; The Preppie Murder* (TV). **1990:** *Internal Affairs; Flatliners.* **1991:** *Backdraft.* **1993:** *Three of Hearts; Sliver.* **1994:** *A Pyromaniac's Love Story.*

Drew BARRYMORE

Many scenes from the highest-grossing film of all time, *E.T. The Extra-Terrestrial*, stand out in the memory. But one of the most poignant and unforgettable must be the one in which little Gertie, her hair in pigtails, presents E.T. with a pot of flowers and then kisses him on the nose. As screen kisses go, it is one of the most indelible.

At the time, Drew Barrymore was only seven years old, the youngest in the cast. It was inconceivable then, back in 1982, that *E.T.* – described as the best film Disney never made – would a) become the biggest money-maker of all time, and b) that a decade later the most famous member of its cast would be the kid sister.

Drew Barrymore's fame rests on a number of factors. She is the youngest member of one of Hollywood's most prestigious acting dynasties. Her grandfather is the legendary actor, matinee idol and writer John Barrymore; her great-aunt the Oscar-winning actress Ethel Barrymore; her great-uncle the Oscar-winning actor Lionel Barrymore. Even her father, the actor-turned-poet John Jr, courted some fame, although his drug busts and failed marriages earned the lion's share of public attention.

Drew herself became a tabloid favourite when she took to drinking at nine, became a cocaine addict at 12, and entered rehab at 13 – all of which she chronicled in her 1990 book, *Little Girl Lost*.

She is also one of the few child actresses who has managed to make a successful transition to adult star, winning special kudos for her role as a psychotic nympho in the 1992 *Poison Ivy*. While *Playboy* singled out her 'emphatic screen presence,' *Rolling Stone* raved, 'as the teen fatale of this low-budget,

Drew Barrymore, aged seven, flanked by screen siblings Henry Thomas and Robert MacNaughton, in *E.T. – The Extra-Terrestrial*

It started with a hiss: child star and pyromaniac Drew Barrymore in *Firestarter*, from the Stephen King bestseller

Posing seductively as Amy Fisher in *Beyond Control – The Amy Fisher Story*

high-style find, Drew Barrymore kicks her *E.T.* image over the rainbow. Now little Gertie rivals Sharon Stone in indulging basic instincts . . . Barrymore nails every carnal, comic and vulnerable shading in her role; she's a knockout.'

Drew herself is a little more philosophical. Although in 1992 she admitted, 'everybody's all over me,' she was quick to add, 'but I know that next month the hype might not be there.'

Born Andrew Blyth Barrymore on February 22 1975, in Los Angeles, the actress made her professional debut at eleven months, doing a dog food commercial. Eighteen months after that she appeared in the TV movie *Suddenly, Love*, with Cindy Williams and Joan Bennett, played William Hurt's daughter, Margaret, in *Altered States*, and did another TV movie, *Bogie*, a poor biog of Humphrey Bogart. Then came *E.T.*

When Drew was cast as Henry Thomas's cute kid sister (who screams the house down

on encountering the alien and then dresses him in drag), her formidable lineage was unknown to Spielberg. However, she had enough professional confidence that the director allowed her to 'let me do what I wanted . . . as long as I knew my lines.'

In *Irreconcilable Differences* she played Ryan O'Neal and Shelley Long's daughter, Casey, who sues her insufferable parents for divorce; and landed the title role in *Firestarter*, as a 'pyrokinetic' nine-year-old on the run. In the latter she was supported by no less than George C. Scott, Martin Sheen, Art Carney and Louise Fletcher.

Stephen King, on whose novel *Firestarter* was based, was so impressed with the little actress that (with a little encouragement from Dino De Laurentiis), he wrote *Cat's Eye* especially for her. This was the story of a little girl whose cat protects her from a menacing moll hiding in her bedroom wall. Two other segments based on Stephen King short stories completed the movie, with the likes of James Woods and Robert Hays filling out an impressive cast. Drugs, booze and rehab followed, and the little child star with the heart-breaking gaze vanished.

Four years later, aged 14, Drew Barrymore

returned with a vengeance. In *Far From Home* she played her first sexy adolescent, Joleen Cross, who is struggling to put away childish things while fighting off an insane killer in a trailer park. The film tried to be more than just another slasher movie, bringing in themes of father-daughter bonding (Matt Frewer, who top-billed, played her old man), but was hardly par for the course.

She faired better, in a supporting role, in Alan J. Pakula's classy, semi-autobiographical *See You In the Morning*, the story of musical families. Psychiatrist Jeff Bridges had two children by model Farrah Fawcett and falls for photographer Alice Krige, who has three kids of her own. Barrymore played the eldest, Cathy, and improvised her scenes with Krige. Particularly memorable is the episode in which mother and daughter lie in bed talking. Looking at her child's blossoming form, Krige remarks wistfully, 'How I longed to be big-breasted.' To which Barrymore answers smartly, 'It's no fun, believe me.'

Neither *Far From Home* nor *See You In the Morning* did well at the box-office, and Ms Barrymore threw herself into a flurry of work – before her options could run out. She burned up the screen in *Poison Ivy* (French-kissing co-star Sara Gilbert, coming on to her best friend's father, making love on the bonnet of a Mercedes) and won the reviews of her career. If 1992 didn't give her any commercial breaks, it was her most visible year since *E.T.* phoned home.

Besides the widely-publicized release of *Poison Ivy*, she had a cameo in the road movie *Motorama*; played a victimised eyewitness in *Sketch Artist*, with Jeff Fahey, was haunted by her own malevolent spirit in *Doppelganger*, was nominated for a Golden Globe award as a man-eating killer in *Guncrazy* (a teenage version of *Bonnie and Clyde*); and played the actress tenant of a prostitute in the TV movie *2000 Malibu Road*. She also starred in *Ectopia*, with her then–boyfriend Balthazar Getty, and played the title role in the timid TV movie *Beyond Control: The Amy Fisher Story*, based on journalists' accounts and court records of the notorious case surrounding the 17-year-old would-be murderess. In early 1994 she married club owner Jeremy Thomas.

FILMOGRAPHY

1978: *Suddenly, Love* (TV). 1980: *Altered States; Bogie* (TV). 1982: *ET – The Extra-Terrestrial.* 1984: *Irreconcilable Differences; Firestarter.* 1985: *Cat's Eye.* 1986: *Babes in Toyland* (TV). 1989: *Far From Home; See You In the Morning; No Place To Hide; Baby Doll Blues.* 1992: *Poison Ivy; Motorama; Sketch*

Artist; *Doppleganger; Guncrazy; 2000 Malibu
Road* (TV); *Ectopia.* 1993: *Beyond Control: The
Amy Fisher Story* (TV); *Bad Girls; Wayne's
World 2* (cameo). 1994: *Inside the Goldmine;
Boys on the Side; Mad Love.*

Annette BENING

Annette Bening's rise to stardom was so swift
that no one saw her coming. From virtual
obscurity, she played Dan Aykroyd's wife in a
John Hughes movie, then took the female
lead in a Milos Forman epic, worked
opposite Meryl Streep in *Postcards From the
Edge*, won an Oscar nomination, played
leading lady to Robert De Niro and Harrison
Ford, bagged the coveted role of Catwoman
in *Batman Returns* and then snared
Hollywood's most famous and unattainable
bachelor, Warren Beatty, giving birth to his
daughter and leading him to the altar. And all
this in the space of three years.

Born in Topeka, Kansas, on 29 May 1958,
Annette was the daughter of an insurance
salesman and the youngest of four children.
In the 1960s, the Benings moved west and
Annette grew up in San Diego where her
passion for acting developed. For a short
while she studied at the San Francisco State
University (earning a bachelor's degree in
theatre arts), and then spent five years at San
Francisco's American Conservatory Theatre.
It was there that she met her husband,

Annette Bening

**Annette Bening as the conniving Marquise
de Merteuil in Milos Forman's sumptuous
*Valmont***

Steven White, who was then directing her in
a production of *Romeo and Juliet.*

To further her career in theatre and film,
Mr and Mrs White moved to New York in
1986. There, Annette landed a small bit
part in *Miami Vice*, did a TV commercial for
Arrid-deodorant (which was never aired),
and appeared in a pilot for the sitcom *It Had
To Be You*, with Tim Matheson (which went
on without her). Her luck changed when she
was cast in her first play, Tina Howe's *Coastal
Disturbances*, as Holly Dancer, a photographer burned by romance. The play
transferred to Broadway and for her performance Annette was nominated for a Tony
and won the Clarence Derwent Award.

When the run of *Coastal Disturbances* ran
its natural course, the actress was offered the
role of Dan Aykroyd's sexually frustrated wife
in *The Great Outdoors*, written and produced

by John Hughes. Unfortunately, the comedy was both predictable and overly familiar, borrowing plot elements from such earlier Hughes pictures as *National Lampoon's Vacation* and *Planes, Trains and Automobiles*.

The TV movie *Hostage* was better, in which she portrayed Carol Burnett's bitter daughter, shortly before the latter is held hostage by an escaped con (played by Burnett's real-life daughter, Carrie Hamilton) who ultimately replaces her in her mother's affections. Bening then auditioned for the role of Madame de Tourvel in Stephen Frears' *Dangerous Liaisons*. At the same time, Milos Forman was casting *Valmont*, his version of the Choderlos De Laclos story of sexual corruption in 18th century France. Michelle Pfeiffer won the part in Stephen Frears' production, but Frears was impressed enough with Annette that he wanted her to play the courtesan whose naked derrière is used as a writing desk by John Malkovich. Tough luck. Forman cast Annette in the even bigger role of the Marquise de Merteuil in *Valmont* (which Glenn Close played in *Liaisons*). Of the two versions, Forman's made more sense as his characters were substantially younger (and consequently more sympathetic), their games of cruel seduction attributed to the hot-headed conceit of youth. Bening was nothing short of superb, eschewing the mannered nuances of evil that Glenn Close laid on with a trowel. By refusing to underline her character's roguery, Bening's performance was all the more credible and chilling.

After this, she had an effective cameo as Dennis Quaid's jilted lover in Mike Nichols' *Postcards From the Edge*, spilling the beans to an indignant Meryl Streep. Catty, beautiful and short on brain cells, Bening was a delight, and the film went on to become a resounding hit. Meanwhile, Stephen Frears returned to her door, offering her the role of the libidinous con artist Myra Langtry in *The Grifters* (after Geena Davis had turned it down). This time she said yes, and acted her co-stars – John Cusack and Anjelica Huston – off the screen. The film was a critical success and earned Bening an Oscar nomination and the best actress award from the National Society of Film Critics.

She was Robert De Niro's neglected wife in *Guilty By Suspicion*, an absorbing, authentic account of the Communist witchhunt in 1950s Hollywood, and then played Harrison Ford's better half in Mike Nichols's *Regarding Henry*. The latter was unfairly knocked by the critics, as it was a moving, thought-provoking look at a hot-shot lawyer (Ford) who's reduced to an infantile state when shot in the

Trick or treat? Annette Bening as con artist Myra Langtree in Stephen Frears's *The Grifters*

Vegas Virginia: Annette Bening as *Bugsy* Siegel's wilful mistress Virginia Hill

head. With his career wiped out, Henry/Ford finds his better instincts revitalized as he starts life anew, with the fresh viewpoint of a child. The film had plenty to say, and did so with a maturity and insight that went straight for the heart. Nichols, considered by many in Hollywood as the consummate actor's director, was bowled over by his leading lady. 'She's got this unique combination of sexiness and intelligence,' he ventured. 'It's what you dream of: someone beautiful and sexy who's also a character actor. We were in the middle of shooting when I saw *The Grifters*; and I was really shocked, because it was someone I didn't know at all. I have no idea how she does it.'

Her next leading man starred opposite her in real life, following his stormy relationship with Madonna and the tabloids. He was Warren Beatty and he cast her in his next picture, *Bugsy*, which he also co-produced. A romanticized look at Benjamin 'Bugsy' Siegel, the prince of gangsters, the film concentrated on Bugsy's romance with society hostess

Virginia Hill (Bening), a cookie as tough as Bugsy was ruthless. Bening won equal billing to Beatty above the title (a rare honour, Madonna note), and held her own in a very strong cast (Ben Kingsley, Joe Mantegna, Harvey Keitel). Her brush-off line to Beatty at the beginning of the film became a classic of its kind, as she belittled the gangster with a withering, 'Why don't you run outside and jerk yourself a soda?' This time the critics approved, and the film stormed off with no less than ten Oscar nominations (although it only won two).

Next, Bening was to play an unmarried mother in the rural Irish drama *The Playboys*, but changed her mind at the last minute. The film's production company was not amused, and sued the actress to the tune of $1 million for breach of oral contract (Robin Wright took over the part, and was brilliant). Meanwhile, Ms Bening had more important things to occupy her, as she had won the most coveted role of the year, beating out Julia Roberts, Cher and Michelle Pfeiffer to play Catwoman in *Batman Returns*.

Batman himself, Michael Keaton, explained, 'Annette has this really great off-centre quality, and I'd just seen her in *The Grifters*. So when [director] Tim [Burton] said to me, "We've got to think about Catwoman," I mentioned Anette and he said, "What a good idea." No one else was discussed.'

Then the impossible happened: she conceived Warren Beatty's child. For the second time, Michelle Pfeiffer took a part Bening had hoped to make her own and, again, Bening's replacement turned out to be ideal. In both the case of *The Playboys* and *Batman Returns*, it's hard to imagine that Annette Bening could have been as effective, and yet she has been so good in everything else. Anyway, she gave birth to all eight pounds 11 ounces of Kathlyn Beatty in January of 1992 and married the child's father in March.

In 1993 she and Beatty were announced to star in *Love Affair*, a re-make of the 1939 romantic comedy starring Irene Dunne and Charles Boyer – from a new script by Robert Towne.

FILMOGRAPHY

1988: *The Great Outdoors; Hostage* (TV). 1989: *Valmont.* 1990: *Postcards From the Edge; The Grifters.* 1991: *Guilty By Suspicion; Regarding Henry; Bugsy.* 1994: *Love Affair; Lilah.*

Michael BIEHN

For a man so conventionally handsome, Michael Biehn is surprisingly adept at playing villains. His cut-glass bone structure, muscular physique and controlled intensity give him a nervy edge and an aura that he might explode at any time. As the good guy (in *The Terminator*) he was gung-ho and heroic, as the villain (in *The Abyss*) he was vulnerable, unpredictable and pretty frightening. Maybe it's all in the eyes. One moment they can look soulful and puppy-doggish, the next they

are burning with menace. Or maybe Michael Biehn is just a good actor.

He was born in Anniston, Alabama, on 31 July 1957, and grew up in Lincoln, Nebraska, and then, aged 14, moved with his family to Lake Havasu, Arizona. It was there that he won a drama scholarship to the University of Arizona thanks to a noteworthy reading in a high school speech tournament. Two years later he left prematurely to pursue an acting career in Los Angeles, studying with the drama coach Vincent Chase.

There, he had two lines in the pilot for the sci-fi TV series *Logan's Run*, and had a walk-on in the hit movie musical *Grease*. Although *The Fan* was cited as his first film, Michael Biehn was a leading man before then. It was just that the movies weren't memorable. He was the male lead in *Coach*, a feeble high school basketball saga with Cathy Lee Crosby in the title role, and he had a decent part in the TV beach movie *Zuma Beach*, in which his little-known co-stars included Rosanna Arquette, Timothy Hutton and Tanya Roberts. He also skewered top-billing in the moronic Canadian comedy *Hog Wild*, co-starring Patti D'Arbanville.

Next, he won the coveted title role in *The Fan*, as the psychotic, handsome admirer of Broadway star Lauren Bacall, and the film was timely enough to open two months after

Michael Biehn as Russell Quinn, husband of Demi Moore, in *The Seventh Sign*

Biehn as Lt Coffey in James Cameron's exhilarating *The Abyss*

John Hinckley Jr shot President Reagan. Also in its commercial favour, *The Fan*'s shock factor was amplified to capitalize on such current high grossers as *Friday the 13th*. This fact, and the removal of the original director Warris Hussein, caused friction on the set, and upset Bacall.

Biehn was then up for the leading role in Franc Roddam's military school drama *The Lords of Discipline*. But, the actor relates, 'Paramount told Franc he couldn't cast any of his choices, as they wanted David Keith, who'd just done *An Officer and a Gentleman*. Franc ended up giving me a small role as a bad guy, and I'll tell you, it wasn't hard to work up the motivation to hate the David Keith character.'

He had better luck in James Cameron's superb, gripping sci-fi thriller *The Terminator*, playing Kyle Rees, a guerrilla agent transported back in time to combat ruthless cyborg Arnold Schwarzenegger. Shot for a modest $6.4 million, *The Terminator* recouped $40 million, making it one of the most profitable movies of all time. It also established a healthy working relationship between Biehn and Cameron, a liaison that *should* have propelled Biehn to international stardom.

He was the lead in a two-part TV movie, *Deadly Intentions* (as another psychopath), and then saved Sigourney Weaver from the acid-spitting bitches in Cameron's *Aliens*, an exhilarating roller-coaster ride of horror and special effects. Cameron, sagely, knew he

Michael Biehn (*right*) with Charles Sheen in the dire *Navy SEALS*

Biehn (*left*) with Matt Craven in *K2*

could not top Ridley Scott's original *Alien*, so he made an entirely different movie, avoiding the pitfalls of sequeldom. The result was a picture that set new standards in the horror/sci-fi genre and went on to make more money than the first film.

Unwisely, Biehn accepted the role of a lawyer (prosecuting a serial killer) in *Rampage* because, he says, he wanted to work with director William Friedkin; and then played a Vietnam vet in *In a Shallow Grave*, so disfigured he cannot face his girlfriend (or his life). Both films bombed. Carl Schultz's *The Seventh Sign*, a stylish, apocalyptic thriller was better, but Biehn had little to do as Demi Moore's concerned husband. Then James Cameron came to the rescue again with *The Abyss*. As he did with *The Terminator* and *Aliens*, Cameron turned on the testosterone and special effects, proving himself the master of epic macho thrillers. Again, Biehn was at his most charismatic, this time playing the violent, unstable Lieutenant Coffey, a Navy Seal who cracks under the strain of being submerged 25,000 feet beneath sea level. In a film with enough peril to keep the cast of *The Poseidon Adventure* unhappy, Biehn added another level of panic as a very nasty piece of work.

'I like playing bad guys,' the actor admitted, 'but I don't want to be pigeonholed. As

much as I like Bruce Dern, I wouldn't want *his* career. I'd like to play romantic leading men. I'd like to go back and forth.'

He was another Navy Seal, but a nice one, in, er, *Navy SEALS*, which Biehn summarized as, 'a *Top Gun* rip-off. (Co-star) Charlie Sheen ended up rewriting most of the action stuff.' He then rejoined director Franc Roddam for the exciting mountaineering drama *K-2*, this time playing the lead, as a climber 'too dumb to let reality stand in the way of success.' Unfortunately, mountaineering films were not the rage in 1992, and it was a tough box-office climb for the movie. Had it been released the following year, in the wake of Sylvester Stallone's *Cliffhanger*, it could have done much better.

Next, Michael Biehn starred in the above-average thriller *Timebomb*, as a hallucinating Vietnam vet (remember *Jacob's Ladder*?), with Patsy Kensit; and then played another bad guy in the fast-moving TV movie *A Taste For Killing*, with Jason Bateman and Henry Thomas as his prey. After that he starred in *Deadfall*, alongside James Coburn, Charlie Sheen, Peter Fonda and Nicolas Cage, under the direction of the last named's brother, Christopher Coppola. Neither films secured wide releases, although *Tombstone* did. As Johnny Ringo, arch-enemy of Doc Holliday and Wyatt Earp (played by Val Kilmer and Kurt Russell), Biehn was a colourful, wild-eyed villain complete with spectacular moustache. But it was his sensational sleight of hand with a gun that stood Biehn apart from the other (numerous) villains in the western.

A practitioner of the martial arts, Michael Biehn is the father of three sons and is married to a former English model, Gina.

FILMOGRAPHY

1978: *Grease* (walk-on); *Zuma Beach* (TV); *Coach*. 1980: *Hog Wild*. 1981: *The Fan*. 1983: *The Lords of Discipline*. 1984: *The Terminator*. 1985: *Deadly Intentions* (TV). 1986: *Aliens*. 1987: *Rampage*. 1988: *In a Shallow Grave*; *The Seventh Sign*. 1989: *The Abyss*. 1990: *Navy SEALS*. 1992: *K-2*; *Timebomb*; *A Taste For Killing* (TV). 1993: *Strapped*; *Deadfall*; *Tombstone*. 1994: *Blood of the Hunter*.

Lara Flynn BOYLE

Long, lanky and lovely, Lara Flynn Boyle was not a new Rita Hayworth nor a modern Marilyn Monroe nor a budding Bardot. She was a science unto herself. One minute she could be sophisticated and alluring, and the next a comic goofball. Clint Eastwood, who directed her in *The Rookie*, attempted to

Lara Flynn Boyle with Charlie Sheen in Clint Eastwood's *The Rookie*

pigeonhole the actress as 'being in the Katharine Hepburn mould,' but his perception is open to argument. No, Lara Flynn Boyle is a one-off.

Created an overnight star on the designer-weird TV serial *Twin Peaks*, Lara Flynn hurled herself into the sort of workload that could short circuit a computer bank. And yet in each role she managed to be different, whether playing a self-assured showgirl in *Mobsters*, the accident-prone girlfriend of Mike Myers in *Wayne's World* or a seductive runaway in *Where the Day Takes You*. And yet one always had the feeling there was even more to come.

The only child of a middle-class Irish family, Lara was born on 24 March 1970 in Davenport, Iowa. When she was six, her parents divorced and her mother took her to a Chicago suburb and shouldered three jobs to pay the bills. 'We lived in this decrepit two-story building,' Lara recalls, 'and I remember how Mom would put out bait for the rats, and how I would have to shovel them up afterwards.'

To help combat her daughter's shyness, Mrs Boyle enrolled her in an improvisation class which nurtured the all-too-familiar acting bug. Later, Lara won a scholarship to the Chicago Academy for the Arts and in her second year (aged 15) she landed her first professional role. This was the part of

Robert Urich's daughter in the epic TV mini-series *Amerika*, which was filmed over a period of nine months in Nebraska and Toronto.

In 1988, Lara returned to Chicago to make her big screen debut in *Poltergeist III*, and demonstrated a powerful set of lungs. Encouraged by this turn of events, she moved to Los Angeles and found the going tough. At the time, she complained, 'When I audition for things they say, "If Winona Ryder doesn't get it, you will." I used to think I would never work, but Hollywood makes so many movies, Winona Ryder can't possibly do all of them. Besides, last week they thought I looked like Elizabeth McGovern.'

She secured a small part in *Dead Poets Society* (as Josh Charles' love interest) and picked up the female lead in *How I Got Into College*, which was a start, even if the film was a non-starter. In the latter she played the dream date of school nerd Corey Parker, and was the inspiration for the latter's spirited attempts to get into an exclusive college that only accepted a grade-point average of 3.5. The film averaged 0.5, but Lara was both gorgeous and credible. She had an even bigger part in the TV movie *The Preppie Murder*, playing real-life victim Jennifer Levin, whose murder in New York's Central Park (in 1987) provoked outraged headlines. William Baldwin played the killer.

Fame arrived for sure with David Lynch's *Twin Peaks*, in which Lara played Donna Hayward, the sweet, innocent best friend of Laura Palmer or, in the words of producer

Mark Frost, 'the girl next door – but it's a pretty weird neighbourhood.' The show was an instantaneous cult phenomenon and catapulted Lara Flynn Boyle into the eye of Hollywood. She also landed in the lap of her leading man, Special Agent Dale Cooper, aka Kyle MacLachlan. To show willing, he followed her to Paris where she was filming *May Wine* – a Gallic comedy with Joanna Cassidy – and she gushed: 'It's so great. We're very happy. We're both goofy and it's hard to find someone you can be silly with.' They remained together until, in the autumn of 1992, Kyle began dating the Canadian supermodel Linda Evangelista. Lara started seeing another actor, but she refused to divulge his name.

Next, she played Charlie Sheen's law student girlfriend in Clint's *The Rookie*, and was about the only character that made any sense. *The Dark Backward* was an experimental mistake, with Judd Nelson, James Caan and Rob Lowe, and *Mobsters* a glossy

Lara Flynn Boyle as the duplicitous Suzanne Brown in John Dahl's enthralling *Red Rock West*

With Matthew Modine in Alan Rudolph's complex, riveting *Equinox*

shoot-up for the boys, with Christian Slater and Patrick Dempsey as, respectively, 'Lucky' Luciano and Meyer Lansky. Lara played Mara Motes, Luciano's red-headed moll. 'Mara was kind of a mesh between a diva and Bambi all rolled together,' the actress explained. 'She was a showgirl, but pure of heart and sweet, plus she was still a lady – *and* paid her own rent.' Again, Lara Flynn gave more than the part demanded which, as the filmmakers had originally confused her with Sherilyn Fenn, was an act of extreme magnanimity.

Where the Day Takes You followed, a starry and rather *too* chic look at the homeless in and around Hollywood Boulevard, and then the phenomenally successful *Wayne's World*. Although the laughs in the latter were allotted to *Saturday Night Live* alumni Mike Myers and Dana Carvey, Lara stole a load of her own as Stacy, Wayne's psychotic former girlfriend. 'Stacy thinks she and Wayne are destined to be together and she's going to prove it whether he likes it or not,' the actress clarified. 'Of course, it always backfires on her.'

Again, she changed tack dramatically with her role in Alan Rudolph's *Equinox*, as the painfully shy Beverly who enters into a tenuous romance with a nerdy Matthew Modine. This was love as it really often is, and Ms Boyle captured the moment beautifully. In *Eye of the Storm*, an intriguing German-American thriller, she portrayed the sexy young wife of Dennis Hopper, and was a target of the same in *Red Rock West*. In the latter, Hopper played a hitman hired by Lara's spouse (J.T. Walsh), but is constantly distracted by Nicolas Cage's hapless drifter. The film was an ingenious thriller, splashed with dark comedy, and Lara Flynn made a seductive, unpredictable heroine. 'What attracted me most to the role,' she says, 'was that it was basically a man's part – very strong and multi-dimensional. Nobody in the film, least of all me, takes much crap from anyone.'

Next, the actress had the title role in the *very* temporary *The Temp*, playing the efficient but lethal secretary to company executive Timothy Hutton, and then snared top-billing in *Finnegans Wake*, inspired by the indecipherable literary work by James Joyce, co-starring F. Murray Abraham, Martin Sheen, Martin Landau and Glenn Ford.

FILMOGRAPHY

1988: *Poltergeist III*. 1989: *Terror on Highway 91* (TV); *How I Got Into College*; *Dead Poets Society*; *The Preppie Murder* (TV). 1990: *May Wine*; *The Rookie*. 1991: *The Dark Backward* (UK: *The Man With Three Arms*); *Mobsters* (UK: *Mobsters – The Evil Empire*). 1992: *Where the Day Takes You*; *Wayne's World*; *Equinox*; *Eye of the Storm*. 1993: *Red Rock West*; *The Temp*; *Finnegans Wake*. 1994: *Past Tense*; *Threesome*; *Baby's Day Out*; *The Road to Wellville*.

Matthew BRODERICK

Neil Simon, Broadway's favourite son, selected Matthew Broderick to play his alter ego in his autobiographical hits *Brighton Beach Memoirs* and *Biloxi Blues*. Sidney Lumet, who has directed the likes of Paul Newman, Dustin Hoffman and Al Pacino in his time, has called Broderick, 'one of the two best young actors in the United States. There's just this profundity to his work that you rarely, if ever, see in actors that young. He's totally involved, and he's incapable of being a cliche.' Matthew Broderick can also boast such enormous hits as *WarGames*, *Ferris Bueller's Day Off* and *Biloxi Blues* to his name, as well as such superb films as *Torch Song Trilogy* and *Glory*. At the age of 20, he was an award-winning stage actor and a movie star. Furthermore, he remained faithful

to the theatre, developing a working relationship with the dramatist Horton Foote and appearing in the latter's plays *On Valentine's Day* and *The Widow Claire*. But, in spite of two tragedies – his father's death in 1982 and a fatal car accident in 1987 – Broderick could not seem to shed his boyish, good-natured persona, and he became branded the eternal teenager. Even when he tackled the bravest role of his career – Colonel Robert Gould Shaw in *Glory* – it was his older co-stars Denzel Washington and Morgan Freeman who rode off with the acting honours.

Matthew Broderick was born on 21 August 1962 in New York, the third child and only son of playwright/painter Patricia and actor James Broderick (*Five Easy Pieces*, *Dog Day Afternoon*). When he was eight years old, 'my father said he was doing a play that had two parts for kids,' Broderick recalls. 'The idea of actually going on the stage scared me so much that I started crying. I thought I didn't want to be an actor after that, and I didn't get back into it until high school.'

Even then, it took a whole year before he could summon up enough courage to audition for a minor role in *A Midsummer Night's Dream* at Manhattan's Walden School, an establishment famous for its theatre programme. Still, once started, he appeared in a total of ten plays in three years, prompting his drama coach to reveal, 'It was pretty clear to me that he had it. Matthew had an incredible ability to be natural, to be warm. He had this magnetism.'

Shortly after graduation, Broderick made his professional stage debut in Horton Foote's *On Valentine' Day*, starring his father, and then won the young male lead in the film *No Small Affair*, to be directed by the formidable Martin Ritt and to co-star Sally Field. The young actor was ecstatic, rehearsed his Oscar speech and then watched in horror as the film collapsed, due to – in the euphemism of the film industry – 'creative differences.'

With his self-confidence buffeted, Broderick failed to capitalize on a string of auditions and, in desperation, accepted a commercial for an anti-itch cream. There was a small part in a gay play at a minor, sleazy New York theatre, and Broderick's agent advised him against it, explaining that 'there's no money in it, and you'll be typecast as a gay for the rest of your life'. Still, it was work, and Broderick was in no position to be worried about typecasting. The play was Harvey Fierstein's *Torch Song Trilogy* and Broderick played David, a troubled, streetwise teenager adopted by Arnold Beckoff, a drag queen played by

Matthew Broderick as he looked in 1988

A 23-year-old Matthew Broderick in the medieval fantasy *Ladyhawke*

Fierstein himself. *Newsweek* raved, 'Matthew Broderick gives one of the most original, witty and touching performances I've ever seen from a young actor,' while *The New York Times* praised him for his 'naturalness and spontaneity.' The play later transferred to a bigger theatre, did excellent business and Broderick won the Outer Critics' Circle and Village awards for his performance. He was on the way.

'Herbert Ross, the director, saw me in the show and asked me to come audition,' Broderick remembers. 'He was directing Neil Simon's play *Brighton Beach Memoirs* and his own movie, *Max Dugan Returns*. I read for both. Later, when I was putting on my coat to leave, the casting director said, 'You had a good day.' I said, 'I got the movie, didn't I?' She said, 'No, you got them both.'

In *Brighton Beach* he played the 15-year-old Eugene Morris Jerome and won the Tony award for his performance, Broadway's highest honour. In *Max Dugan Returns*, also written by Simon, he starred alongside Marsha Mason, Jason Robards and Donald Sutherland. Immediately afterwards, he landed the starring role in *WarGames*, the highly entertaining story of a computer whiz-kid who thinks he's playing sophisticated video games, when in fact he's locked into the government's Norad missile-defence system, prompting the escalation of World War III. Broderick lent the film an added boost with his boyish zest and charm, and the movie went on to make a mint at the box-office.

Sadly, Matthew's father didn't live long enough to witness his son's overnight celebrity. Aged 55, James Broderick died on 1 November 1982. Consequently, young Matthew failed to fully appreciate his new-found success. Even when he won both auditions for *Max Dugan* and *Brighton Beach*, it wasn't until his father's enthusiasm that he fully appreciated the significance of his triumph.

After *WarGames*, things slowed down a bit as Broderick agonized over future roles. Besides his stage work, he appeared in the film version of Horton Foote's *1918*, for a fraction of his normal fee (which was now considerable). He played Brother Vaughn, a restless Texas teenager, a supporting part he did in honour of his father who had appeared in the original stage production. Next, he was engaging but miscast as a medieval thief in the romantic fantasy *Ladyhawke*, aiding and abetting the romance of Rutger Hauer and Michelle Pfeiffer; and then starred in a TV edition of Athol Fugard's *Master Harold . . . and the Boys*. There was a video version of *Cinderella*, with Jennifer Beals, and he then recreated his stage role (Brother Vaughn) in Horton Foote's *On Valentine's Day*, a prequel to *1918*. But it wasn't until *Ferris Bueller's Day Off*, written, produced and directed by John Hughes, that

Matthew Broderick came into his own as a movie star.

Combining an impish charm with a rebellious in-the-face bonhomie, Broderick was perfect as the resourceful, 17-year-old truant, even though he was now 24 himself. The film was an enormous hit at the box-office, and Broderick's grinning, cheeky mug was all over the media. Under the sly direction of Hughes, Broderick became a contemporary anti-hero for downtrodden teens, and was launched into the popularity polls, just above Michael Douglas and Harrison Ford. *Ferris Bueller* also introduced him to Jennifer Grey, who played his sister Jeanie, and the couple became a couple – for three years.

Ironically, his next film, a dud, was to co-star his future girlfriend Helen Hunt. This was the ambitious *Project X*, a well-researched tear-jerker for animal lovers and anti-nuke

protesters. Broderick played a demoted airman, relegated to a top-secret military training programme to look after simian guinea pigs, that is, chimpanzees. Naturally, Broderick finds his loyalties divided – between his professional duty and the call of his own heart. A sort of *Short Circuit* gone ape, but without the laughs, *Project X* was a noble, sober effort, and for the most part avoided sentimentalizing its subject.

After that, Broderick returned to the off-Broadway stage to star in Horton Foote's *The Widow Claire*, and then repeated his turn as Eugene Morris Jerome in the film version of *Biloxi Blues*, the second leg of Neil Simon's autobiographical trilogy. This time Eugene found himself in a steaming Mississippi boot camp, pitted against drill sergeant Christopher Walken and falling in love with Penelope Ann Miller. Superbly written by Simon and sensitively directed by Mike

Matthew as Jimmy Garrett in Jonathan Kaplan's *Project X*

Broderick (*centre*) as Colonel Robert Shaw with his troops in Edward Zwick's outstanding *Glory*

Broderick with Marlon Brando in Andrew Bergman's *The Freshman*

Nichols, the film further benefited from Matthew Broderick's endearing, funny performance as the gauche wit discovering the complexities of adult life. Unlike the screen adaptation of the first play *Brighton Beach Memoirs* (in which the Simon/Broderick/Eugene role was played by Jonathan Silverman), *Biloxi Blues* was a resounding hit.

But the movie's success was tinged with tragedy. On 5 August 1987, following the film's completion, Broderick and Grey were holidaying in Ireland, just outside Enniskillen, when their rented BMW 316 collided with a Volvo, killing both occupants – 28-year-old Anna Gallagher and her 63-year-old mother, Margaret Dohetty. Broderick himself suffered several broken ribs, a fractured thigh, a collapsed lung, concussion and facial cuts, while Jennifer was let off with minor bruises.

Today, Broderick admits that he may have been driving on the wrong side of the road, and faced a five-year prison sentence for reckless driving. On 15 February 1988, the actor pleaded guilty *in absentia* to careless driving and was fined £100, prompting the headline FERRIS BUELLER'S LET OFF in *The New York Post*. After the accident, the star spent a year in physiotherapy and underwent extensive psychotherapy. And, while he endured his first month in hospital, Jennifer Grey told the press, 'Matthew and I held hands and read together for hours. An accident like that means you never again take a single day for granted. I feel so lucky to be alive and to have Matthew beside me.' Nevertheless, their relationship failed to survive the trauma and the couple separated in 1988.

Now older and wiser, Broderick found himself being more picky when it came to selecting roles. He was announced to star in *Chances Are*, with Cybill Shepherd, but the part went to Robert Downey Jr. He took a supporting role in the film version of *Torch Song Trilogy*, now playing Alan, the gay boyfriend of drag queen Arnold Beckoff, again essayed by Harvey Fierstein. The play lost none of its bite nor humour in its transfer to the screen, but the accolades were slapped squarely on Fierstein's shoulders.

Broderick's next three films also gave freer range to his co-stars, and not surprisingly so. In Sidney Lumet's limp crime comedy *Family Business*, Broderick was improbably cast as the son of Dustin Hoffman and grandson of Sean Connery (!), and the film was a box-office stiff. He was much better in *Glory*, playing a character roughly his own age, the 25-year-old Colonel Robert Gould Shaw, who leads a regiment of negro soldiers on a heroic charge on a Confederate stronghold in the American Civil War. Broderick was superb as the confused, obstinate Bostonian officer, but was criticized for being too young for the role. Ironically, the actor was actually two years older than his real-life counterpart. However, it was Denzel Washington, as a rebellious slave who signs up with the 54th Regiment, who won an Oscar that year (for best supporting actor). Broderick then returned to more familiar terrain with *The Freshman*, as a film student pressed into the services of a Mafia don, played by Marlon Brando with an uncanny resemblance to Vito Corleone in *The Godfather*. *The Freshman* was an amiable enough caper, but it is Brando's cameo that people remember.

It was to be another two years until Broderick returned to cinema screens, and then he must have regretted it. In the unbelievably bad *Out On a Limb*, he played a city Yuppie who drops a $140 million take-over bid to rescue his sister in a backwater town called Buzzsaw. The trade paper *Variety* was uncharacteristically charitable when, in September of 1992, it described it as a 'moronic comedy' and 'the worst film of the year so far.'

Next, Broderick appeared with Max Von Sydow in Philip Borsos's *Cider House Rules*, and was then very good as a love-lost gourmet cook in the ensemble New York comedy *The Night We Never Met*, co-starring Annabella Sciorra and Kevin Anderson. In the meantime, his romance with Helen Hunt had foundered, and he took up with the actress Sarah Jessica Parker (*LA Story*, *Honeymoon in Vegas*).

FILMOGRAPHY

1983: *Max Dugan Returns; WarGames*. 1984: *1918*. 1985: *Ladyhawke; Master Harold . . . and the Boys* (TV); *Cinderella* (video). 1986: *On Valentine's Day; Ferris Bueller's Day Off*. 1987: *Project X*. 1988: *Biloxi Blues; Torch Song Trilogy*. 1989: *Family Business; Glory*. 1990: *The Freshman*. 1992: *Out On a Limb*. 1993: *The Cider House Rules; The Night We Never Met*. 1994: *The Lion King* (voice only); *Mrs Parker & the Vicious Circle; A Life in the Theatre* (TV); *The Road to Wellville; Infinity* (also dir.).

Nicolas CAGE

The same year that Ralph Macchio (born in 1961) was portraying the wide-eyed, teenage Daniel in *The Karate Kid Part II*, Nicolas Cage (born in 1964), was playing Kathleen Turner's middle-aged husband in *Peggy Sue Got Married*. Such is Cage's brawny, hairy and weathered physique, that he has been able to play a wide range of characters – mostly older than himself. With his drooping eyes and unruly nose, he displays the appearance of a permanently offended bloodhound. He is the first to admit that, 'I don't think I really look like a romantic leading man,' and has capitalized on the fact. Richard Benjamin, who directed him in *Racing With the Moon*, suggests that he does have, 'movie looks. Look at Bogart. Look at Cagney. They weren't conventionally handsome either.'

Actually, there's nothing conventional about Nicolas Cage. 'He's a little *Addams Family*,' admits Joel Coen, who directed the actor in *Raising Arizona*. 'He likes to promote that image, anyway. He's a strange guy.' Indeed, *The Los Angeles Times* once described him as 'the crown prince of the darker realms of absurdity.' While Cage himself confides, 'I get turned on by craziness.' His problems with drugs and alcohol have been no state secret, either. Neither have his one-night stands with loose-mouthed women.

And there's no pretence at movie star urbanity when you meet him. His hair disarranged with the finesse of a hurricane, he'll as likely be unshaven, half-dressed and resentful of the intrusion. Yet, broach the subject of acting, and he'll happily pass an afternoon with you. And does Nicolas Cage take his acting seriously. But more of that anon.

Born Nicolas Coppola on 7 January 1964, in Long Beach, California, the actor was the youngest of three sons. His father, August Coppola, taught comparative literature at California State University and went on to become dean of the School of Creative Arts at San Francisco State University; his mother, Joy Vogelsang, was an interpretive dancer and choreographer from New York. More famously, his uncle is the film director Francis Ford Coppola, his aunt the actress Talia Shire (Adrian Balboa in the *Rocky* films) and his cousin Sofia Coppola, who played Mary Corleone in *The Godfather Part III*.

Nic was 12 when his parents divorced and, after his mother was hospitalized for a nervous breakdown, he moved to San Francisco with his father. There are various theories surrounding his ambition to become an actor; one that he was inspired after seeing James Dean in *East of Eden*, another that he thought it was an easy way 'to get laid.' Anyhow, at 15 he enrolled in San Francisco's Young Conservatory, part of the American Conservatory Theatre, where he appeared in a production of *Golden Boy*. He then moved on to the Beverly Hills High School, when, at 16, he won a small role as a surfer in the pilot TV movie *The Best of Times* – which he described as 'probably the worst TV show on the air.'

Encouraged by this propitious start, he dropped out of school in his senior year and immediately got a job in the cinema – selling popcorn. He played a larger part in the history of movies when he won his first role, as Bud, in the enormously popular *Fast Times at Ridgemont High*, playing Judge Reinhold's sidekick. He then auditioned for his uncle.

'I auditioned for him for the role of Dallas in *The Outsiders*,' he recalls. 'I was there for nine hours. But I was so nervous, I didn't know what I was doing.' He says that to prepare for this ordeal, he locked himself in his room for two weeks, downed a quantity of beer and contemplated a poster of Charles Bronson – hoping to become a hooligan through osmosis. Come the big day, Uncle Francis changed his mind and asked Nic to read for the role of Two-Bit instead. 'I couldn't change gear and everything fell apart,' the actor complains. 'I was in hospital for a while after that and decided I didn't want to act anymore.' The role of Dallas went to Matt Dillon and Emilio Estevez got the part of Two-Bit. Nicolas Coppola changed his name to Nicolas Cage.

However, his uncle persuaded him to take a part in *RumbleFish*, as Smokey, the hunk in

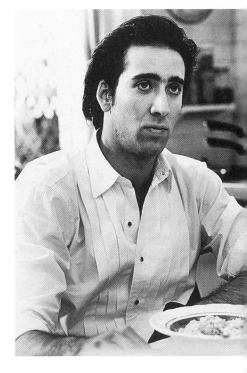

Cage as the passionate, one-handed baker Ronny Cammareri in Norman Jewison's Oscar-winning *Moonstruck*

Nicolas Cage in Alan Parker's *Birdy*

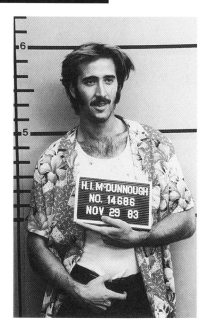

Cage as inveterate inmate H.I. McDunnough in the Coen brothers's phenomenal *Raising Arizona*

Wild thing: Nicolas Cage at his absolute coolest in David Lynch's strange tribute to *The Wizard of Oz:* the Lynchian *Wild at Heart*

the black cutaway T-shirt who steals Diane Lane from Matt Dillon. He then landed the lead in Martha Coolidge's surprising romantic comedy, *Valley Girl*, as the down-market slob who wins the heart of a preppy beauty (Deborah Foreman). It was a small film, but the critics warmed to it and it was a moderate success.

He played Sean Penn's best buddy in Richard Benjamin's tasteful, aesthetically composed *Racing With the Moon*, but the actor dismisses it in retrospect. 'I didn't think it was that good,' he insists. 'Richard Benjamin, who is really an actor, was too new at his craft. The film looked great because he spent more time on the technical aspects of it, rather than on the actors. Consequently, my character was terribly incomplete.' Others in the cast included Elizabeth McGovern and Nic's close friend from high school, Crispin Glover.

He was Richard Gere's hoodlum brother (Mad Dog Dwyer) in Francis Coppola's spectacular gangster/jazz epic *The Cotton Club*, a splendid film but a box-office flop; and then he segued into Alan Parker's *Birdy*.

For the last-named, Nicolas Cage went hog wild in his preparation to play a disfigured Vietnam vet. Not only did he wear facial bandages on and *off* the set for a total of five weeks, but had a tooth on either side of his jaw removed.

'It was my idea to have the teeth pulled and to wear the bandages,' he explains, as if to shift the blame from an invisible culprit. 'It gave me the right "feel." If you work honestly in one direction, you'll find that other directions are taken care of on their own. Because of the bandages my jaw always hurt, which in turn made it difficult for me to eat, so I lost 15 pounds. My mental attitude to the part had helped me to alter physically.' Previewed at Cannes, *Birdy* prompted a 12 minute standing ovation and flew off with the Grand Prix Jury prize.

He then played real-life Canadian rowing champion Ned Hanlan in *The Boy in Blue*. This, too, required some preparation. The actor trained furiously on weights, rowed himself silly, and revealed: 'I couldn't begin to explain how painful it was.' He was due to star in the apocalyptic thriller *Miracle Mile*, and was already casting his co-stars when the picture was delayed. Instead, he played Kathleen Turner's loutish husband in Coppola's sweet time-travelling fantasy, *Peggy Sue Got Married*. His performance was wild and unpredictable, and annoyed the heck out of Ms Turner, who reputedly wanted him fired.

'Can you blame her?,' he proposes. 'I was basically working without regard for anyone in the movie, just doing whatever I wanted and hijacking the movie, for better or worse.' His own notices were not good, and he never worked with his uncle again.

He then hit on a golden streak that was to transform him overnight from underground punk to pretty well-known punk. The brothers Joel and Ethan Coen who, together, wrote, produced and directed the cult thriller *Blood Simple*, cast him as the dishevelled hero, H.I. (Herbert I. McDonnough), in their magical, hilarious and truly inspired comedy nightmare *Raising Arizona*. The story of an ill-matched couple (Cage and Holly Hunter) who live in a trailer and dream of acquiring a baby (any which way they can), the film was one of the most original and best honed comedies of the 1980s. But if *Raising Arizona* failed to nail the kudos of the establishment, Norman Jewison's *Moonstruck* gained more than its fair share.

A heavily Italian-American comedy about a widow (Cher) caught between her affections for a sincere, overweight Danny Aiello and his one-handed, younger brother (Cage), *Moonstruck* was skillfully written, directed and acted, and won a handful of Oscars, including a best actress nod for Cher. Jewison admired Cage's total immersion into the role of the love-lorn, one-handed slob, even if, on this occasion, Cage kept his real limb intact. However, the actor's love-drenched outpourings to Cher were more than a little kindled

by the break-up of his four-year relationship with the actress Jenny Wright (*Young Guns II*, *The Lawnmower Man*). 'I was kind of hoping that Jenny would be out there somewhere to hear my romantic pleading,' he admitted sheepishly.

Nic Cage was now an established leading man, but his choice of films was anything but orthodox. He accepted the part of a seedy literary agent who's convinced he's a vampire, in *Vampire's Kiss*, a stylish psychological black comedy. Again, he took his quest for realism to unnatural lengths. He tried to persuade his director, the London-born Richard Bierman, to introduce a real bat (to no avail), and then switched the raw egg he had to eat for a live cockroach. 'I wanted there to be a moment of something so *real*,' he explains. 'When I saw the film with an audience, the reaction was so intense. All I had done was eat a cockroach.'

He then starred in an Italian war film, *Time to Kill*, and the poorly received *Top Gun* clone *Fire Birds*, with Sean Young. *Wild at Heart* was all the rage at Cannes (it won the Palme d'Or), and became a must-see attraction for the seriously alternative. Cage was Sailor Ripley, a parole-jumping eccentric on the road with Laura Dern, with Mother (Diane Ladd) in hot pursuit. Directed by David Lynch with the self-indulgence of a disturbed teacher's pet, the film was an uneven mix of fantasy, gore and parody.

Even worse was Sam Pillsbury's erotic melodrama *Zandalee*, with Cage a libidinous rogue who has to utter such dialogue as, 'I want to shake you naked and eat you alive, Zandalee.' It wasn't a hit.

However, Andrew Bergman's *Honeymoon in Vegas* was. Cage was back in his *Raising Arizona* mode, playing a likeable goofball afraid to commit to marriage. However, when he loses his fiancee (Sarah Jessica Parker) to big-time gambler James Caan in a poker game, he is transformed into a raving romantic. Harking back to the madcap comedies of the 1930s, *Honeymoon* displayed some charm, a good deal of slapstick and its fair share of belly laughs. It also won Cage a 'best actor in a comedy or musical' Golden Globe nomination.

He was then top-billed in the 'cowboy *noir* thriller' *Red Rock West*, in which he played an honest Joe mistaken for a hit man – and who attempts to cash in on the error (to his downfall). A deliciously offbeat tale, the film kept one guessing until the final reel, and was even then dishing out surprises. In the black comedy *Amos & Andrew* he was another blue-collar slob, this time an underdog who ends up in an exclusive island jail. And then he joined the all-star cast (Michael Biehn, James Coburn, Charlie Sheen, Peter Fonda, auntie Talia Shire) of *Deadfall*, directed by his older brother, Christopher Coppola – the story of two men caught in a dangerous con game. He then starred opposite Shirley MacLaine in Hugh Wilson's *Guarding Tess*, and was announced as the star of Andrew Bergman's comedy *It Could Happen To You* (after Billy Crystal bowed out). He was also due to star in *Cash Out*, the story of two men who go to Vegas to win the money of their dreams.

FILMOGRAPHY

1981: *The Best of Times* (TV). 1982: *Fast Times at Ridgemont High*. 1983: *RumbleFish*; *Valley Girl*. 1984: *Racing With the Moon*; *The Cotton Club*; *Birdy*. 1986: *The Boy in Blue*; *Peggy Sue Got Married*. 1987: *Raising Arizona*; *Moonstruck*. 1988: *Vampire's Kiss*. 1989: *Time to Kill* (aka *Short Cut/Tempo di Mecidere*). 1990: *Fire Birds* (UK: *Wings of the Apache*); *Wild at Heart*. 1991: *Zandalee*. 1992: *Honeymoon in Vegas*; *Red Rock West*; *Amos & Andrew*. 1993: *Deadfall*; *Guarding Tess*. 1994: *It Could Happen To You*; *It Happened in Paradise*; *Kiss of Death*.

Blood silly: Nicolas Cage as the deranged literary agent in Richard Bierman's profoundly unusual *Vampire's Kiss*

Phoebe CATES

Unlike most models who turned to acting, Phoebe Cates hit a lucky streak. Not only was her second film, *Fast Times at Ridgemont High*, a highly visible launching pad for the careers of many of today's finest actors (Sean Penn, Jennifer Jason Leigh, Eric Stoltz, Forest Whitaker, Nicolas Cage, etc), but two years later she found herself at the centre of a colossal hit: Joe Dante's *Gremlins*. She also had a knack for knowing the right people: like her father, the TV producer-director Joseph Cates, her uncle the director Gilbert Cates, her good friend Bridget Fonda, and not least her husband, Kevin Kline.

Born in 1962 in New York City, Phoebe dreamed of becoming a prima ballerina. Winning a scholarship to the School of American Ballet, she studied hard to qualify for the New York City Ballet when, at 14, a knee injury forced her to abandon her vocation. Instead, she embarked on an extremely successful modelling career, gracing the covers of magazines worldwide and appearing in lucrative commercials. Yet, in

Phoebe Cates (*left*) with Jennifer Jason Leigh in the groundbreaking *Fast Times*

Cates (*left*) with Annabeth Gish, Page Hannah and Bridget Fonda in *Shag*

spite of her success, she found modelling nothing more than 'bookings, getting made up, getting pinned into clothes and being in front of a camera and hot lights all day.' Although, she admits, 'I did get to go to some great locations throughout the world. That was fun, but it wasn't enough. The second I started getting bored with it, I simply stopped.'

She then attended The Professional Children's School in Manhattan and, inevitably, the movies followed. Her first film, *Paradise*, is invariably excluded from her biographies, and it is easy to see why. A blatant rip-off of *The Blue Lagoon*, it starred Phoebe and William Aames as a pair of sparsely clad lovers on a tropical island and it couldn't have been more silly. Still, Phoebe did have the starring role and looked lovely without her fashion accessories.

Next came the trend-setting *Fast Times at Ridgemont High*, in which she played Linda, the less-than-innocent schoolgirl who dates older men. This led to the title role in an abysmal TV movie, *Baby Sister*, with Ted Wass; and the lead in an even worse sex comedy, *Private School*, co-starring Matthew Modine.

The following year, 1984, things looked up. She made her theatrical debut off-Broadway in Joseph Papp's *The Nest of the Wood*

With Zach Galligan in a race against time in Joe Dante's delirious *Gremlins 2: The New Batch*

Grouse, and landed the female lead in *Gremlins*, executive produced by Steven Spielberg. Although the film's success sprang from the engineering effects of the cute-but-dangerous Gizmo (*never* feed him after dark), Phoebe was a pleasant enough human presence. She was also in the successful mini-series *Lace*, based on Shirley Conran's best-selling tome.

On the last-named she befriended co-star Brooke Adams, who was then dating Kevin Kline. Not to jump to any conclusions, but

Phoebe is now Kevin's wife. . . Five years later the couple married privately in New York and managed to keep their nuptials secret for more than two weeks. This is particularly surprising as the media had been predicting the event for more than four years.

After *Lace* came a bout of stage work and *Lace II*. There was an instantly forgettable movie in 1987, the 'comic' fantasy *Date With an Angel*, and it wasn't until *Bright Lights*, *Big City* a year later that the actress emerged from relative obscurity. Based on the landmark novel by Jay McInerney, *Bright Lights* was a tortured production that saw stars and directors come and go, before landing in the unlikely lap of Michael J. Fox (and director James Bridges). Ms Cates wasn't exactly stretched on her part, as she was cast as Fox's wife, a high-fashion model. Although a prestigious production, it wasn't a hit.

Neither were the next two, a pair of nostalgic Southern tales with strong female casts. In *Shag*, Phoebe was joined by Bridget Fonda, Annabeth Gish and Page Hannah (Daryl's sister), and in *Heart of Dixie* by Ally Sheedy and Virginia Madsen. She had a cameo in *I Love You To Death* (in which she is briefly courted by a libidinous Kevin Kline), and then did another TV movie, *Largo Desolato*, with F. Murray Abraham.

She reprised her role as Kate Beringer in *Gremlins 2: The New Batch* which, although a

Ignore my nightmare: Phoebe Cates with Rik Mayall in *Drop Dead Fred*

box-office disappointment, was far more entertaining and funnier than its predecessor. Then, from her best film she plopped into the worst of her career yet: *Drop Dead Fred*. A grossly infantile romp starring Rik Mayall as Phoebe's imaginary childhood 'friend', the film depended heavily on snot and excrement to win laughs. Needless to say, it didn't get any.

Next, Ms Cates segued into her most demanding role yet – as mother – and then co-starred to little effect in the romantic comedy *Bodies, Rest and Motion*, playing Bridget Fonda's best friend and former girlfriend of Tim Roth.

FILMOGRAPHY

1982: *Paradise*; *Fast Times at Ridgemont High*. 1983: *Baby Sister* (TV); *Private School*. 1984: *Gremlins*; *Lace* (TV). 1985: *Lace II* (TV). 1987: *Date With an Angel*. 1988: *Bright Lights, Big City*; 1988: *Shag*. 1989: *Heart of Dixie*. 1990: *I Love You To Death* (cameo); *Largo Desolato* (TV); *Gremlins 2: The New Batch*. 1991: *Drop Dead Fred*. 1992: *Bodies, Rest and Motion*. 1993: *My Life's in Turnaround* (cameo as herself). 1994: *Princess Caraboo*.

Tom CRUISE

Tom Cruise was the determined pup who broke away from the Brat Pack and ended up king of the jungle. Like his cohorts Matt Dillon, Emilio Estevez, Rob Lowe, et al, he emerged from Francis Coppola's cult movie *The Outsiders*, but then steadily moved up the cinematic ranks, transforming himself from young puck to the most expensive buck in the business.

Tom Cruise in *A Few Good Men*

In a 1992 feature on the millionaire's club, *Movieline* magazine wrote, 'If you're going to pay anybody too much to star in the movie you're spending too much to make, pay Tom Cruise. He's the only *bona fide* movie star of his generation.'

In 1986 and 1987, Tom Cruise was the number one top box-office attraction in America, bigger than Eddie Murphy, Sylvester Stallone or Clint Eastwood. In '88 he dropped one place, but only after Jack Nicholson had nudged his way into the top spot. However, Cruise was to have the last laugh: in 1992 he not only walked away with $12 million for *A Few Good Men*, but also

top-billed Nicholson, who only received $8m.

Tom Cruise, who was also (reportedly) paid somewhere between $10m and $12m for *Far and Away* – plus a percentage of the gross profits – was quick to point out that, 'I don't have a set price. To me each film is different. The people who own studios didn't get to where they were by being dumb businessmen. They aren't going to pay me one penny more than I'm worth, especially in this marketplace. They wouldn't pay me if I wasn't worth it. And the day I'm not, they won't.'

In spite of his price, Tom Cruise was in demand. So much so, that everybody thought they were working with him. In 1990 he was reputedly making *China Maze*, James Ivory's *An Innocent Millionaire*, *Out West*, *Top*

The early days: Tom Cruise (centre), flanked by C. Thomas Howell and Emilio Estevez in *The Outsiders*

Gun II and *What Makes Sammy Run?* – none of which saw the light of day. He was also due to star in *Backdraft*, *Edward Scissorhands*, *Prelude To a Kiss*, *Rush* and *Till There Was You*, all of which were filmed with other actors.

As Hollywood's *Top Gun*

Cool pool: Tom Cruise in *The Color of Money*

Instead, Cruise made *Days of Thunder* and met his future wife, the 5'10", flaming-haired Nicole Kidman from Australia.

Very little about Tom Cruise is not known to his public. They know he is 5'9", a devout Scientologist, an ardent environmentalist, was married to Mimi Rogers for three years, divorced her, and then wed Nicole. They know he is the top gun, the leading star of his generation, the handsome, determined actor who fought and planned his way to the top, taking risks, working with the best.

Paul Newman, who played Cruise's

mentor in *The Color of Money*, described him as, 'This kid [who had] the head and the balls to be one of the great ones. . . the next Hollywood legend.'

Dustin Hoffman, who co-starred with Cruise in Barry Levinson's *Rain Man*, said of him: 'There's no sense of a crest in Tom. His talent is young, his body is young, his spirit is young. He's a Christmas tree – he's lit from head to toe. He's the biggest star in the world.'

But Barry Levinson believes 'Tom is at a disadvantage. He's got a pretty face, so his abilities are underestimated. And he's not working a rebel image, which is associated with being a good actor.'

Indeed, far from being the sullen, paparazzi-punching rebel, Cruise is endearing in his eagerness to please. In person, he is surprisingly boyish, polite and modest. The cocky bravura that accompanies so many of his screen characters evaporates as he – ever so courteously – explains his case. Maybe Cruise is still covering his tracks, knowing that overnight superstardom can vanish as quickly as it materializes. He appears to be terrified of putting a foot wrong. Like Mitchell Y. McDeere, the character the actor so closely mirrors in *The Firm*, Cruise is a high-achiever, a success story who has overcome insurmountable odds to make it to the top. For a start, he's dyslexic and never went to college, a drawback he surmounts by carrying a dictionary with him wherever he goes.

Born Thomas Cruise Mapother IV in Syracuse, New York, on July 3 1962, the actor grew up surrounded by women. There was his mother, Mary Lee, and then his three

sisters, Lee Anne, Marian and Cass. His father, Thomas Cruise Mapother III, was an electrical engineer and moved the family from Canada to New Jersey, from Missouri to New York. At kindergarten, Tom was forced to become right-handed, and by the age of 12 had attended 12 schools in as many cities. At one academy his classmates voted him the boy least likely to succeed.

When he was young, his mother explained, 'Tom used to create skits and imitate Donald Duck and Woody Woodpecker and W.C. Fields – all when he was just a tiny tot. I guess I was his greatest audience. He had it in him then, but as he got older, he was more into sports, and it stopped completely.'

Tom was 11 when his father walked out and Mary Lee Mapother took the family back to Louisville, her Kentucky hometown. Five years later, she re-married and the family finally settled down in Glen Ridge, New Jersey.

For a while Cruise contemplated becoming a priest and spent a year in a Franciscan seminary. He was also a keen wrestler, but when a leg injury forced him off the school team he auditioned for a play out of boredom. The part was Nathan Detroit in Guys and Dolls. It was his. 'It felt just right,' he explains. 'It felt like I had a way to express myself. I decided then and there that this was what I wanted to do. I packed my bags and went to New York. I didn't even attend my high school graduation.'

Master Mapother shortened his name to Tom Cruise, waded through auditions during the day and waited on tables at night. When there was time, he attended classes at the Neighbourhood Playhouse, honing his craft. Within five months, he landed a small role in Franco Zeffirelli's Endless Love, 18th-billed, as Billy.

He had another bit, playing the sidekick of headstrong military cadet David Shawn in Taps, an army drama starring George C. Scott, Timothy Hutton and Sean Penn. When the actor playing Shawn was considered too weak for the part, Cruise stepped in. Sean Penn recalls, 'Cruise was so strong that the other guy didn't have a chance. Cruise was overwhelming. And we'd all kind of laugh, because he was so sincere.'

Cruise next joined the cast of The Outsiders, playing the high-spirited buddy of C. Thomas Howell and Emilio Estevez,

revealing his sculptured torso in an open shirt and brandishing the tattoo of an eagle on his considerable biceps. It was a negligible role, but he was in the right place at the right time.

He lost the part of Paul Newman's son in Harry & Son (because he was too young – the role went to Robby Benson), and then landed his first lead, playing the retiring, gauche, yet enterprising Joel Goodsen in Risky Business. Co-starring Rebecca De Mornay as the prostitute who conspires with Joel to run a one-night brothel in his parents' house, the film was a critical and popular hit, grossing $65 million in the US. To this day, the scene people remember best is the one in which Cruise mimes to Bob Seger belting out Old Time Rock & Roll, wearing nothing but his socks, Y-fronts and shirt tails. It was the most sensational piece of beefcake posturing since John Travolta donned his white suit in Saturday Night Fever. On a famous occasion Ron Reagan Jr parodied it in an episode of Saturday Night Live, TDK cassettes copied it for their magazine ads and Campbell's Soup likewise borrowed it for a commercial.

'In the script, the scene was one line that said, "Joel dances in underwear through the house,"' Cruise explains. 'But I had tried it a couple of ways where it didn't work. Finally, I put on socks, waxed the floor, and then put dirt around the area so I could slide right out to the centre of the frame. Then we did the

thing with the candlestick – using it as a microphone? – and made it into this rock and roll number. And we just kept going, trying different things. [Paul] Brickman [the director] would say, "I want something crazy here," so I'd jump onto the couch and, you know, just let loose. I saw Brickman after he saw the rushes on that scene and he said, "It's the most hysterical scene in the movie."'

Cruise was a star. He dated Rebecca De Mornay in the glare of the paparazzi's flash bulbs and won top-billing in his second movie, All the Right Moves. The story of a steel town jock who tries to win a football scholarship to make something of himself, the film was another hit.

However, the star's next film, Ridley Scott's Legend, was less popular. Actually, it was a disaster. A misconceived fairy tale that failed to rise above its stunning 'look', the film proved to be a troubled shoot, aggravated by the set being burned down mid-shoot. Also, Cruise's father had just died. It was a rough time for the actor, who spent a year marooned in London while nursing filial guilt. And, to add injury to insult, he put his back out.

In future, Cruise promised himself, he would have more control over the films he accepted. On his return from England he broke up with Rebecca. It was the actor's lowest point – moments before he turned from star to superstar.

When Cruise was offered a project about

With an Oscar-winning Paul Newman in Martin Scorsese's The Color of Money

an elite navy pilot, he liked the sound of it, but wouldn't commit immediately. Instead, he insisted on working on the script with producers Don Simpson and Jerry Bruckheimer before consenting to do the picture. Simpson and Bruckheimer agreed, in spite of the box-office failure of *Legend*.

'He was terrific,' Simpson offered. 'Tom would show up at my house, grab a beer, and we'd work for five or six hours on the script. Sometimes we'd act scenes out. The guy doesn't see things from just a couple of perspectives, he can really wrap his arms around something and see it from all angles. We had a lot of fun.'

Again, Cruise took his research to the extreme, studying and flying with real pilots. Sheepishly, he divulged, 'I came close to getting my licence, but didn't really have enough time.'

The film, called *Top Gun*, was the biggest money-making picture of 1986. Recruitment into the navy escalated. A song from the picture, Berlin's 'Take My Breath Away', held the number one spot in Britain for four weeks. Other actors in the movie – Kelly McGillis, Val Kilmer, Anthony Edwards, Meg Ryan and Tim Robbins – all went on to greater glory.

Having made the ultimate pop movie, Tom Cruise was now ready to prove his mettle as a Serious Actor. Working with Martin Scorsese, the most highly acclaimed filmmaker in America, seemed the next logical step.

The Color of Money was Paul Newman's film, everybody knew that. It was a sequel to 1961's *The Hustler*, which starred Newman as 'Fast' Eddie Felson, pool shark *extraordinaire*. In the sequel, Newman is 25 years wiser, and acts as mentor to Vince Laurie, a hotshot hustler who reminds Felson of what he used to be: raw, hungry, brilliant. Cruise won equal billing to Newman – *and* his friendship (it was the latter who introduced him to motor racing).

'He's got a lot of actor's courage,' Newman conceded. 'He doesn't mind climbing up there and jumping off. It's nice to watch that.'

Although it was Newman who ultimately won the Oscar, Cruise revealed a new edge to his acting, exhibiting an innocence and vulnerability overlayed with a stylish, steely braggadocio. His pool playing, too, brought a fresh athleticism and flamboyance to the game. Needless to say, *The Color of Money* broke box-office records for Touchstone Pictures, eventually grossing $47 million in the US.

After this Cruise took some time off to pace himself and to wait for *Rain Man* to happen. The story of a flash, young salesman who discovers he has an autistic savant older brother, *Rain Man* was a project Cruise and Dustin Hoffman desperately wanted to do together. Whatever it took. Martin Brest, who was hoisted on to the Hollywood A-list after directing *Beverly Hills Cop*, walked off *Rain Man* after fearing that it was turning into

a two-man road movie. Next, Steven Spielberg battled with the screenplay, and then Sydney Pollack. They both walked away.

Meanwhile, Cruise was fielding other offers, became obsessed with motor racing and, on the morning of 9 May 1987, married the actress Mimi Rogers. He admired her strength and intelligence and after eight months revealed, 'Mimi helps me. She was there with me whenever she could be on *Rain Man*. Yet she's got her own career, which is just as important as mine. I just really enjoy our marriage.'

While still waiting for *Rain Man* to happen, the actor segued into *Cocktail*, a glossy, lightweight beefcake vehicle in which he played a womanizing, super-slick barman. Characteristically, he worked hard on his performance, and toiled undercover in a couple of New York bars, learning to juggle bottles while he served up potent cocktails. According to the film's director, Roger Donaldson, 'When Tom and I decided to make this movie, we said, "Well, it might not make any money, but at least it'll get good reviews."' However, the critics dismissed the film – but the public turned up in their droves, earning *Cocktail* a handsome $75 million in the US.

Eventually, Barry Levinson came on board the runaway train that was *Rain Man* and kicked the film into production.

As it happens, the wait was worth it. Cruise was paid $3 million for his part, and *Rain Man* went on to gross over $171 million in the States alone. It also won the Oscar for best film, best actor (Hoffman), director and screenplay. Cruise himself didn't get a nomination, but his co-star – who has been called exacting by his kindest critics – had nothing but praise for him: 'I don't usually meet people with my work habits,' Hoffman admitted, 'but Tom and I both like to get up before dawn and exercise. We'd drive to the set together, using the time to rehearse. Neither of us much like lunch; [so] we both stayed in the trailer and worked on the material. At night, Tom was constantly knocking on my door. He'd say, "Why don't we do it this way?" And he'd do my lines so well he could have played my part.'

It must have been an odd sensation for Tom Cruise to see his last two co-stars both walk off with an Oscar. So, having already served time with Coppola and Scorsese, he hitched up with America's other great

With an Oscar-winning Dustin Hoffman in Barry Levinson's *Rain Man*

celluloid maestro, Oliver Stone. Their film together was *Born On the Fourth of July*, based on Ron Kovic's harrowing real-life story, a project Al Pacino had previously walked off. Stone accused the latter of getting 'cold feet', but Cruise had anything but. This was to be his Big One. Not only did the actor befriend Ron Kovic, but insisted on riding around in a wheelchair on *and off*-set. At nights he would wheel himself right up to bed, and allow Mimi to help him into his sheets.

'It was very difficult getting up on curbs,' he recalls. 'In fact, it was exhausting. Every day that I was in that chair, I built up different muscles – but I was still tired.'

Cruise also grew his hair long, cultivated a spindly moustache and totally turned himself over to the role, frequently enduring the most humiliating of scenes. The end result was nothing short of gut-wrenching and the film went on to lasso eight Oscar nominations, including a nod for Cruise as best actor. The odds were in his favour for winning the statuette, but to most people's surprise, another chair-bound actor wheeled off with the award – Daniel Day-Lewis, for *My Left Foot*. Still, Cruise is obviously here for the duration and, like his old friend Paul Newman, will probably see many more Oscar nominations slip by before the award is his.

Next, he practised his skills on the circuit with *Days of Thunder*, a motor racing drama based on his own idea, which was produced by Don Simpson and Jerry Bruckheimer and

As crippled Vietnam vet Ron Kovic in Oliver Stone's gut-wrenching *Born on the Fourth of July*

Top wheel: Tom Cruise in *Days of Thunder*, based on his own story

directed by Tony Scott – all of whom had previously worked on *Top Gun*.

'It's not *Top Gun* on wheels,' Cruise defended his high octane venture. 'The characters have depth. It's about America and America's sons, really. Cars symbolise to me creative greatness. These drivers are artists. It's not just about going out there and putting your foot on the pedal.'

Whatever else the film was, it was a well-oiled machine that moved with the precision of a turbo engine. And the racing sequences were sensational. The preliminary advertising

played up Cruise's power as a household name. Full page ads devoted three quarters of their space to six letters: C – R – U – I – S – E , followed by LIKE THUNDER in smaller capitals. Although *Days of Thunder* was considered a box-office 'disappointment', it grossed $82m in the States and $230m (including video sales) worldwide – which was nothing to cry about.

This time his leading lady was Nicole Kidman, who had made an enormous impression in the Australian thriller *Dead Calm*. She didn't receive the kindest reviews for her role in *Days of Thunder*, but her love scenes with Cruise must have packed some punch as the couple became engaged – even before the actor's divorce from Mimi Rogers was final. They married – secretly – in Telluride, Colorado, on Christmas Eve, 1990. Like Mimi before her, Nicole is a keen disciple of Scientology, Cruise's chosen religion.

The tabloids moved in, and vicious stories circulated around Hollywood's latest spot-lit couple. One rumour suggested that Cruise married Kidman because his first wife couldn't give him children. Another story, much publicized, claimed that the star forced his new girlfriend to have fertility tests before he'd marry her. Another announced Kidman's pregnancy.

'It's very strange reading about your life and thinking it's not true,' Kidman offered. 'It's *not* true, I don't know where they get it from. What's unbelievable is how the stories get out of control. They spread all over the world to Australia . . .'

Meanwhile, Mimi Rogers could not contain her bitterness: 'I can complain about it now,' she confessed, 'but when you marry somebody, you love them and you realise the association is part of the deal. But you get to a point where it's enough already . . . I'm waiting for the moment when I don't have to talk about that fucking name anymore. I've had it welded onto mine for years now.'

When Tom Cruise was signed up to play a brash, illiterate Irish farmhand opposite Kidman's rebellious aristocrat in *Far and Away*, director Ron Howard swears he didn't know they were an item. Cruise defends Howard by saying, 'You know, he lives in Connecticut – and he doesn't read the *National Enquirer*. Not that they ever get it right.'

Far and Away was a very personal project for Howard, who based the screenplay on stories from his own family's Irish background. Shot in Panavision Super 65mm, the film was a sweeping, old-fashioned romance, in which Cruise and Kidman bickered at each other across their respective class barriers until the final, sun-lit smooch. Budgeted at $42 million, the project was a sizeable gamble for Universal Pictures and, when it opened in the summer of 1992, it couldn't compete against *Lethal Weapon 3* and *Alien³*. However, the film did exhibit some staying power and two months later was making more money than either of the aforementioned. The reason for this was that cinemagoers were going back to see it *again*. Eventually, it clocked up $59 million in the States – which was $4m more than *Alien³* made.

In *A Few Good Men*, Tom Cruise played Lt Daniel Kaffee, in the words of his superior, 'a fast food, slick-assed' Navy lawyer. However, Kaffee is forced to re-examine his legal ethics when he teams up with Demi Moore to defend two Marines accused of murder. Slouching around Washington DC in jeans and sports jacket, Cruise looked uncannily like Joel Goodsen in *Risky Business*, until,

done up to the nines in full military uniform, he is dressed to kill. The problem with Cruise in the film is that he is so readily associated with his role as the crusading good guy, that it was hard to believe he could be such an irresponsible cad (dishing out plea bargains in order to find time to play softball). Equally, it was predictably obvious that he was going to pull his socks up before the film's end. Still, the film was the biggest box-office hit over the 1992 Christmas period, which helped refuel Cruise's standing as a bankable legend. Indeed, he was voted the biggest box-office star of 1992 by America's cinema managers.

He then landed another Big Movie, *The Firm*, based on John Grisham's number one bestseller of 1991. Robert Towne scripted, Scott Rudin produced and Sydney Pollack directed, with Cruise playing a hotshot law student signed up by a questionable – nay, *lethal* – law firm in Memphis. Gene Hackman, Jeanne Tripplehorn, Holly Hunter and Ed Harris co-starred. In January of 1993, Cruise took a brief leave of absence from the set to join his wife for a few days to bond with the daughter they adopted in Miami. In spite of the secrecy surrounding the occasion, the *National Enquirer* turned up to take the first pictures of the happy trio, and the world was let in on the secret.

Future aspirations include the mandatory stab at directing, something many think Cruise has the focus to pull off – including Ron Howard. 'Can Tom Cruise direct a movie? Without a doubt,' the filmmaker conceded. 'Whether he will like it or not, that's another story. But as an actor who became a director myself, I can see that Tom thoroughly understands the process. . . It's easy for him to shift and see the big picture. Most actors can't do that, even highly skilled, experienced ones.'

Sure enough, in the spring of '93, Cruise was announced as the director of an episode of TV's *Fallen Angels*. It was a start.

FILMOGRAPHY

1981: *Endless Love; Taps.* 1983: *Losin' It* (aka *Tijuana*); *The Outsiders; Risky Business; All the Right Moves.* 1985: *Legend.* 1986: *Top Gun; The Color of Money.* 1988: *Cocktail; Rain Man.* 1989: *Born On the Fourth of July.* 1990: *Days of Thunder* (also co-story). 1992: *Far and Away; A Few Good Men.* 1993: *The Firm.* 1994: *Interview with the Vampie.*

The body *Perfect*: Jamie Lee displays her famous leotard

Jamie Lee CURTIS

Jamie Lee Curtis has gone through a number of transformations. At first, she was known as the daughter of Hollywood royalty, the offspring of former hearthrob Tony Curtis and actress Janet Leigh. Then, when she became an actress herself, she was dubbed 'the Queen of Scream', thanks to her vocal roles in such shockers as *Halloween, Prom Night* and *Terror Train*. She graduated from teenage victim to a full blown woman in *Trading Places*, and became famous for her breasts. Two years later, vacuum-sealed into a leotard in *Perfect*, she was the girl with the

legs. She was about to be labelled a has-been when, in 1988, she returned with a bang in the surprise hit *A Fish Called Wanda*, playing a big-time crook sexually turned on by foreign languages. And, finally, she became famous as a TV star; in the highly-acclaimed sitcom *Anything But Love* – as Chicago scribe Hannah Miller.

Jamie Lee Curtis was born on 22 November 1958 in Los Angeles, and was three-years old when her parents divorced. When she was 11, her father was arrested in England for possession of marijuana. A gawky and flat-chested teenager, she was educated at Beverly Hills High School, Westlake School for Girls and Choate Rosemary Hall in Connecticut. She went on to attend the University of the Pacific, and as part of one of her courses there, auditioned for Universal Studios and won a seven-year contract. Aged 18, she dropped out of college and took small roles in such TV fare as *Quincy*, *Columbo* and *The Nancy Drew Mysteries*. Six months into her career, she won the part of Lt Barbara Duran in the TV movie *Operation Petticoat*, a re-make of her father's 1959 comedy classic and a pilot for a new TV show. She recreated her role in the series, playing the part for 13 months. 'For somebody who was not a beauty, and had no discernible talent,' she says, 'I had amazing success very quickly. I was 18! I knew nothing!' And, 'I was playing a woman who was supposed to be in her thirties. I had all this make-up and hair, but it didn't matter how dressed up I was, I was the "kid".' The actress is quick to point out, too, that she got her roles without the aid of nepotism: 'I always felt the need not to go to the people closest to me,' she insisted.

The month *Operation Petticoat* went off the air, John Carpenter's *Halloween* opened in America and changed the face of the horror film. Jamie Lee played Laurie Strode, an innocent teenager stalked by a psychotic killer known as Michael Myers. Donald Pleasence was top-billed as Myers's anxious psychiatrist, but it was Jamie Lee's screaming heroine that the public remembered. The film was decidedly Hitchcockian in tone, and the press played up the comparison between Jamie Lee's character and her mother's in *Psycho* (in which the latter was famously stabbed to death in the shower).

Halloween led to more horror, but of lesser pedigree. There was Carpenter's mediocre *The Fog*, with Janet Leigh; the Canadian slasher *Prom Night*, with a serious Leslie Nielsen; and another Canadian entry in the genre, *Terror Train*, starring Ben Johnson.

If the actress's career was failing to make

Jamie Lee Curtis in 1980

inroads into art, her personal life was suffering, too. Now in her early twenties, she went on a three-year spree of substance abuse and drinking, a spell she later blamed on her father's influence. She recovered, but her career was still in the doldrums. There was a so-so TV movie, *She's In the Army Now*, with Melanie Griffith; an intriguing thriller with Stacy Keach, *RoadGames*, which failed to catch on; the disappointing *Halloween II* (although Curtis was now top-billed above Pleasence); and another TV outing, *Death of a Centerfold: The Dorothy Stratten Story* (in which she played the real-life, tragic Playboy centrefold), a story which was better told two years later in Bob Fosse's *Star 80*.

Her favourite movie up to this time was Amy Jones's low-budget romantic drama *Love Letters*, in which she played a woman who takes up with a married man (James Keach). However, in spite of good notices, the public stayed away. Nevertheless, they turned up in droves to see her play a golden-hearted hooker in *Trading Places*, a hilarious comedy with Dan Aykroyd and Eddie Murphy. Although she'd indulged in some steamy sex scenes in *Love Letters*, nobody had noticed, so when she took off her shirt in *Trading Places*, everybody went hog wild.

'All of a sudden I was "a sex girl",' she

muses. 'All of a sudden people discovered that I had breasts. I mean, it was wild. To this day it's the topic of conversation when people meet me. So, I bared my breasts. Everybody does it. I don't want to start listing all the actresses that have done nudity in movies . . . I was playing a hooker, and there was no question that nudity was in the movie. It turned out to be my avenue into a more mainstream audience. It took six seconds.'

For Jamie Lee, 1984 was an even more important year. In *Grandview, USA*, she played the owner of a demolition derby romantically wedged between C. Thomas Howell and Patrick Swayze but, more importantly, she picked up a copy of *Rolling Stone*. In it, she found a photograph of the chameleonic actor and writer Christopher Guest. 'He was wearing a plaid shirt, he had a smirk on his face, and I thought he was just the most beautiful man,' she remembers. 'I called up his agent and sort of fumbled for words, trying to find out if he was single, and would he want to go out with me? I had never, *ever* done this before.

'Anyway, he never called. But, about two months later, I was having dinner in a restaurant, and he was there. We looked at each other, and he sort of signalled that he'd gotten the message by waving at me. He called me the next day. That was June 28. We went out July 2 and were married December 18.'

The following year she paid her debt to *Rolling Stone* by starring in *Perfect*, opposite John Travolta. She played an aerobics instructor (in those famous leotards) and Travolta was the reporter from *Rolling Stone* who romanced her. Columbia Pictures invested a small fortune in promoting the picture, but the critics retaliated with bile, and the movie was a box-office bomb. Still, the attendant publicity had served Jamie Lee well. Now she was even more famous. And more cautious. 'When *Perfect* bombed, I made a personal decision that I would let the script dictate my choices finally. I would only do things that appealed to me. It's what most good actors do.'

While Jamie Lee weighed up her career,

she and her new hubby adopted a 12-hour-old baby, Annie, as Curtis was unable to have children of her own. And while Annie brought new joy into her parents' lives, her mother's career stumbled. Four films in three years failed to make an impression with critics or public alike, until a small comedy from England upped Jamie Lee's ante. This was the oddly titled *A Fish Called Wanda*, starring and written by the oddly proportioned English TV comedian John Cleese, with the unlikely supporting cast of Jamie Lee, Kevin Kline and Michael Palin. However, the *Fish* had one thing in its favour – it was hysterically funny.

A superbly structured crime caper with beautifully realised characters, *A Fish Called*

Scream queen: Jamie Lee Curtis in *Halloween*

Jamie Lee with her co-stars from *A Fish Called Wanda* Michael Palin, John Cleese and Kevin Kline

Wanda was loaded with canny observations of the love- hate bridge between America and Britain. It also boasted a cracking pace and priceless dialogue. All the actors on hand were on the top of their form, with Jamie Lee a particularly engaging temptress (Wanda Gershwitz) who seduces all three of her co-stars – in the name of greed. The film was a smash box-office success, and everybody's favourite comedy of the year.

Jamie Lee was on a roll. She next starred as Hannah Miller in the ABC sitcom *Anything But Love*, playing a journalist on the *Chicago Weekly*, platonically involved with co-writer Marty Gold (Richard Lewis). Although successful, the series suffered a bumpy ride, which included three separate pilot shows, alternative time slots, conceptual shifts and even cancellation, until popular demand brought the series back. It also won Curtis a Golden Globe and the People's Choice Award as 'America's favourite female performer in a new TV series.' The former honour reduced her to tears, and prompted her to write a thank you note to each of the judges. 'It's taken me 12 years for people to recognize my work,' she declared.

In the hard-hitting crime thriller *Blue Steel*, the actress was top-billed as a rookie cop pursued by a psychotic killer (Ron Silver), and

Jamie Lee poses with Mel Gibson for *Forever Young*

Summers Die (TV). 1987: *Amazing Grace and Chuck* (UK: *Silent Voice*); *A Man in Love*. 1988: *Dominick and Eugene* (UK: *Nicky and Gino*); *A Fish Called Wanda*. 1990: *Blue Steel*. 1991: *Queens Logic*; *My Girl*. 1992: *Forever Young*. 1993: *Mother's Boys*. 1994: *My Girl 2*; *True Lies*.

John CUSACK

John Cusack is the most unusual of leading men. A hive of contradictions, his gangly 6'2" frame is capped by a boyish face, itself stamped with a wisdom beyond its years. Look closer, and you notice an army of freckles washed back though countless nights in darkened cinemas and smoky clubs. Cusack, who paid his acting dues alongside the likes of Rob Lowe, Molly Ringwald and Demi Moore, boycotted Hollywood's glitzier parties in favour of the seclusion of blues bars in his native Chicago, preferring to soak up a nocturnal atmosphere with non-actors. He *is* a dedicated film buff, but his taste is decidedly non-mainstream, favouring 'great classics like *Plan 9 From Outer Space*. I love things that you can laugh at, but also things that are piercing and fierce that take on the establishment,' he professes.

His own, early, films, were hardly in the same league as *Plan 9*, and when he swore he'd never do another 'teen pic', he played love-struck high school student Lloyd Dobler in his best film to date, *Say Anything*. In his defence, Cusack explains, 'I really didn't want to graduate high school again. But then I thought, I'm 22, I'm only going to be this young once, I might as well close that part of my career on a good note.'

It was a very good note indeed, and led to the lead in Stephen Frears's critically saluted, hard-boiled film noir thriller *The Grifters*, in which the actor played a sleazy con man with an Oedipus complex. Frears volunteered, 'John is like a jazz musician. He zones off into these dark moods, then zaps out of it with no warning and goes on. There's a light blackness to his talent that I found extraordinary. Someone once described John to me as being Jimmy Stewart with an edge, and I think that description is quite accurate.'

Cusack's next big break was to be signed up by James Cameron (*Terminator 2*, *Aliens*) to play real-life, multi-schizophrenic Billy Milligan in the eagerly-awaited film version of *The Crowded Room*. Virtually every star under 45 in Hollywood was after the part, but Cameron held out for Cusack. However, due to financial problems afflicting Cameron's production company, the film was put on hold. At the time of going to press, *The*

John Cusack in 1989

won more good reviews (her old ally, *Rolling Stone*, glowed, 'Curtis must be praised for a great performance filled with ferocity and feeling'). She was lost in the all-star cast of *Queens Logic* (Kevin Bacon, Joe Mantegna, John Malkovich, Tom Waits), a labour of love which virtually sank without trace, and then bounced back in the excruciating *My Girl*. A sugary vehicle for the photogenic allure of an 11-year-old Anna Chlumsky and Macaulay Culkin, the film apparently appealed to American family audiences and strolled away with $58 million in the bank (in the US alone). Jamie Lee Curtis, decked out in a trampy 1960s wardrobe, looked too old to be convincing, and her attraction to Chlumsky's overweight father (Dan Aykroyd, as a mortician) was inexplicable.

Next, she was cast in the romantic, old-fashioned *Forever Young*, as a single mother with the hots for Mel Gibson, unaware that he is actually old enough to be her grandfather. Hers was a beautifully judged performance, an adroit mix of humour and pain.

She then starred in *Mother's Boys*, from the novel by Bernard Taylor, with Vanessa Redgrave and Joanne Whalley-Kilmer in support.

FILMOGRAPHY

1977: *Operation Petticoat* (TV). 1978: *Halloween*. 1980: *The Fog*; *Prom Night*; *Terror Train*. 1981: *She's In the Army Now* (TV); *RoadGames*; *Halloween II*; *Death of a Centerfold: The Dorothy Stratten Story* (TV). 1982: *Money On the Side* (TV). 1983: *Love Letters* (aka *Passion Play*); *Trading Places*. 1984: *Grandview, USA*. 1985: *Perfect*. 1986: *As*

Crowded Room still had a green light, but it was a flickering one. If or when the film does get made, it should turn Cusack's career around. Meanwhile, the actor bided his time with a string of surprising cameos, in no less than five consecutive movies: *Roadside Prophets*, *The Player*, *Shadows and Fog*, *Map of the Human Heart* and *Bob Roberts*.

John Cusack, one of five children, was born on 28 June 1966 in Evanston, Illinois, an affluent suburb of Chicago. His father is the Emmy Award-winning documentary filmmaker Richard Cusack, and his older sister, Joan, an appealing and successful actress, who won an Oscar nomination for *Working Girl* and has also appeared in *Broadcast News*, *My Blue Heaven* and *Toys*. John himself was encouraged to act at the age of nine and took classes at the Piven Theatre Workshop in Evanston. At 12, he was already an old hand at commercials, promoting the joys of McDonald's on TV and the advantages of Heinz Tomato Ketchup on radio. While still in high school he wrote and staged two

Cusack with Meredith Salenger in the delightful wilderness yarn *The Journey of Natty Gann*

Cusack as George 'Buck' Weaver in John Sayles's baseball thesis, *Eight Men Out*

Cusack with Ione Skye in Cameron Crowe's *Say Anything*

musical comedies, which were later broadcast on local TV.

He was 16 when he breezed into the office of Chicago agent Ann Geddes and told her that he'd win any audition she set him up for. Impressed by his chutzpah, Ms Geddes put him up for a role as Rob Lowe's bright sidekick in *Class*. He got it.

A slew of 'teen pics' followed, but Cusack kept his dramatic focus by periodically returning to Chicago. In 1984 (aged 18), he wrote and directed an award-winning programme for NBC TV and produced a stage production of *The Day They Shot John Lennon*. He later formed his own theatrical company, New Criminals, and won a local prize for best director.

On screen, he starred in Rob Reiner's sleeper hit *The Sure Thing*, playing a 19-year-old Ivy League student who dreams of an easy lay. On a cross-country journey to find his 'sure thing', he's thrown together with fellow student Daphne Zuniga, whose patience has been frazzled by Cusack's chat-up lines on astronomy. Inevitability wins out, but not before we have warmed to these two sweet teenagers, misled by society to behave out of character. Cusack was an unlikely yet irresistible romantic hero, replacing beefcake swagger with a touching credibility.

The Sure Thing not only introduced Cusack to a new public, but to his best friend Tim Robbins, who played Gary. The pair soon became inseparable, and on one famous occasion set out to find Elvis Presley. 'We went from New York to Memphis before we found out that Elvis was actually dead, that he'd mated with a female bear, and their son – a half-man bear-child – was alive and heir to the throne,' he recalls. 'But it wasn't until we ended up in Vegas twisted drunk that the trip really got dark.'

Back on film, he played a hobo in Disney's surprisingly distinguished outdoor adventure *The Journey of Natty Gan*, but then succumbed to more teenage drivel. 'I must have been asleep,' he reveals reluctantly. 'I guess I had to learn that holes in scripts don't fix themselves.' The only decent title in the lot was Reiner's *Stand By Me*, in which the actor made a brief appearance as Whil Weaton's older brother. He was offered a pile of money to play Molly Ringwald's live-in boyfriend in *For Keeps*, but turned it down to escape to Africa. 'I had to get away,' he explains.

He was good as the principled baseball player George 'Buck' Weaver in John Sayles's *Eight Men Out*, but the film was terribly dreary; and then he turned down, then accepted, the lead in *Say Anything*. Although a box-office disappointment, the film was fresh, funny and achingly honest, and put a new zing in Cusack's career.

He took a supporting role in Roland Joffé's *Fat Man and Little Boy*, a film he's deservedly proud of, in which he played a young scientist who works on the atomic bomb; and then

With Anjelica Huston in Stephen Frears's acclaimed exercise in film noir, *The Grifters*

Willem DAFOE

Thanks to a number of controversial movies, Willem Dafoe found himself the actor to be written about in those fashionable glossies that like to think of themselves as champions of fashion. Dafoe was not a name to Joe Smith on the street, but the films he appeared in were tabloid-famous: *Platoon*, *The Last Temptation of Christ*, *Misssissippi Burning* . . .

As a leading man, he was for the most part uninteresting, but as a character actor he was dynamite. Who could forget his snarling, malevolent gangleader in Walter Hill's *Streets of Fire?* Or the quietly menacing killer in William Friedkin's *To Live and Die in LA?* The tragic, proud Auschwitz pugilist in *Triumph of the Spirit?* Or the devoutly evil, repugnant Bobby Peru in David Lynch's *Wild at Heart?* His countenance, too, is unforgettable. Although the skin is tightly stretched over his cheekbones, his lips have the rubber generosity of loose dough. His eyes are deep-set, yet his face is surprisingly flat. The nose is hooked like a barb, the forehead unexpectedly high. For an actor, it was a visage to be proud of, a face that could project pathos, sexuality or evil. Above all, evil.

William Dafoe was born on 22 July 1955 in Appleton, Wisconsin, the seventh of eight children. The son of a surgeon (his father) and a nurse, Dafoe was the black sheep of the family and dropped out of high school in his senior year. He also rebelled against his name, because he hated the moniker 'Billy'. 'The name Willem made me feel funny for a while,' he admits, 'because I don't like the idea of having a stage name. But I guess I'm used to it now; I've been Willem longer than I've been Billy.'

At the University of Wisconsin-Milwaukee he became disillusioned with his drama classes which, he concluded, 'had very little to do with theatre,' so enlisted in an experimental theatre group, Theatre X, instead, touring America, France, Germany, Italy and Holland. In 1978 he decided to dabble in more mainstream theatre and moved to New York, but found, 'I didn't like the commercial work that was being done on or off-Broadway.' He was, however, impressed by a production performed by the avant-garde Wooster Group. 'I couldn't make head or tails of it,' he says, 'but it was so exciting

heavyweight players as Mandy Patinkin and Richard Widmark.

The actor then went on the cameo trail, proving most effective of all in Tim Robbins' *Bob Roberts*, in which he played a recalcitrant TV host who refuses to kowtow to the ingratiating charm of political candidate Bob (Robbins). He was a star again in *Money For Nothing*, a flop.

FILMOGRAPHY

1983: *Class*. 1984: *Sixteen Candles*; *Grandview USA*. 1985: *The Sure Thing*; *The Journey of Natty Gann*. 1986: *Better Off Dead*; *One Crazy Summer*; *Stand By Me*. 1987: *Tapeheads*; *Hot Pursuit*; *Broadcast News* (cameo). 1988: *Eight Men Out*; *Say Anything*. 1989: *Shadow Makers* (US: *Fat Man and Little Boy*). 1990: *The Grifters*; *True Colors*. 1991: *Roadside Prophets*. 1992: *The Player* (cameo); *Shadows and Fog*; *Map of the Human Heart*; *Bob Roberts*. 1993: *Money for Nothing*; 1994: *The Badger*; *The Road to Wellville*; *Bullets Over Broadway*; *Floundering*.

came *The Grifters*. Cusack was surprisingly at home in the sleazy milieu of author Jim Thompson's novel, as a small-time con artist who plays the sexual affections of his mother (Anjelica Huston) off on his scheming girlfriend (Annette Bening). Both actresses were honoured by America's National Society of Film Critics, but Cusack came away empty-handed.

He then starred in Herbert Ross's *True Colors*, as a treacherous, social-climbing politician who clashes with his former law school buddy James Spader. Cusack struggled manfully with the implausibilities of his role, but in the end the obvious plot strands and character manipulation capsized the film, Cusack and the entire cast (including such

that I desperately wanted to work with them.'

Uninvited, he dropped in on the group's director, Elizabeth LeCompte, who threw him out. He admits, now, that he was an intrusion on her work, but the director soon relented and gave birth to his son, Jack, five years later.

While working alongside LeCompte (who was 11 years his senior), Dafoe looked for work in the cinema. 'If I had any aspirations,' he says, 'it was to be a great B-movie actor.' His first film, *Heaven's Gate*, was far from B-movie terrain (at a cost of $40 million), although Dafoe was un-billed in a spit-and-a-cough appearance. However, he had the lead in *The Loveless*, an insipid, low-budget tale of a marauding gang of bikers which showed no promise for its star – Dafoe – or its director, Kathryn Bigelow. Both went on to inordinately better things.

In *The Hunger* he and John Pankow played 'phone booth youths', 17th and 16th billed respectively, and then he had another bit in the soft-porn *New York Nights*, 'loosely based on Arthur Schnitzler's play *Reigen*.' Things looked up with the starring role (as a hitchhiker) in *Roadhouse 66*, co-starring Judge Reinhold, but the film was dreadful. He had a good part in Walter Hill's electric rock 'n' roll fable *Streets of Fire*, as Raven, the flamboyant and ruthless biker who kidnaps Diane Lane, and he then did an obscure picture for The Wooster Group, *The Communists Are Comfortable*, shot on 16mm and shown virtually nowhere. He was then another memorable villain in William Friedkin's gritty

Dafoe (*right*) – with Robert Gordon – in his first starring role, in Kathryn Bigelow's *The Loveless*

urban thriller To *Live and Die in LA*, playing a laid-back killer with more style than moral fibre – co-starring William Petersen, John Pankow and John Turturro.

Dafoe was fast becoming Hollywood's favourite bad guy when he won the heroic lead in Oliver Stone's violent Vietnam epic *Platoon*. '*Platoon*,' the actor says, 'offered me a role reversal. For once I got to play the good guy.' And then, characteristically, he added,

'Anyway, I think the only thing that defines a villain and a hero is which way the gun is pointing.' To prepare for the role of Sergeant Elias, Dafoe endured weeks of gruelling training. He and his co-stars slept in two-man fox holes (which they dug themselves), lived off cold, unappetizing provisions, and lugged full military gear up and down hills for miles. Still, the hard work paid off. *Platoon* grossed over $134 million in the US and won Oscars for best film, direction, editing and sound. Dafoe himself was nominated for an Academy Award as best supporting actor, but was beaten to the podium by Michael Caine (for *Hannah and Her Sisters*).

With his new standing, Dafoe won top-billing as a hard-nosed undercover cop in *Off Limits*, a fast-paced crime thriller set in 1968 Saigon, and admitted he was a sucker 'for inhabiting those mythological roles – cowboys, cops, soldiers. There's a little boy in me who wants to come up against those images, try them on and see how they feel.'

However, he changed tack dramatically when he was cast as Jesus in Martin Scorsese's long-awaited *The Last Temptation of Christ*, based on the controversial 1955 novel by Nikos Kazantzakis. If *Platoon* had sparked criticism for its realistic violence, that was nothing compared to the outrage that greeted *Last Temptation*. Public figures denounced the film sight unseen and protesters showered paint on cinemagoers as they left the theatre. The film was actually an intelligent, deeply-felt portrayal of Christ

Dafoe as Salamo Arouch in Robert M. Young's harrowing *Triumph of the Spirit*

as a man, and did more for the rediscovery of Jesus than a million sermons. Dafoe himself was quietly affecting as a mortal with an impossible burden, who understandably questions his role in God's plan.

More controversy followed with the release of Alan Parker's powerful racial drama *Mississippi Burning*. This, too, provoked outrage, public chastisement and a *Time* magazine cover story. Inspired by real events,

The role he wished he hadn't taken: Dafoe as Defence Attorney Frank Dulaney in the laughable *Body of Evidence*

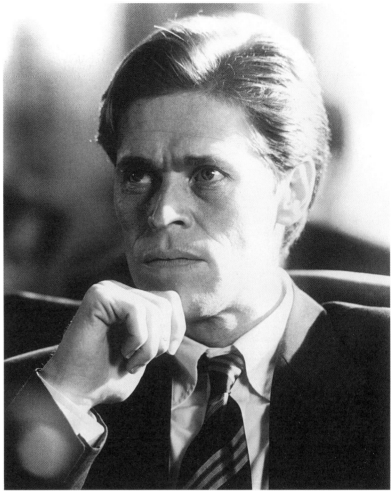

Willem Dafoe as FBI agent Alan Ward in Alan Parker's *Mississippi Burning*

the film focused on a small Mississippi town where two Jewish whites and a negro were executed by members of the Ku Klux Klan. Dafoe and Gene Hackman played FBI men sent to investigate, and it was their (white) perspective that angered many blacks. Still, *Mississippi Burning* was undeniably a distinguished, thought-provoking production, superbly acted by its two leads, and backed by outstanding direction from Parker.

Triumph of the Spirit was another disturbing study of real events, in which Dafoe played Greek middleweight boxer Salamo Arouch who literally fights to stay alive in the Auschwitz concentration camp. Filmed on actual locations, the film boasted an authenticity that numbed the senses. In Oliver Stone's harrowing *Born On the Fourth of July*, Dafoe took a supporting role as a bitter paraplegic who befriends Tom Cruise on a nightmarish trip to Mexico. He then took a cameo in John Waters' *Cry-Baby*, and a

supporting – but unforgettable – role in David Lynch's *Wild at Heart*. In the latter, he was the lizard-like Bobby Peru, an unsavoury figure who molests Laura Dern and meets a graphically violent end that had cinemagoers diving between their knees.

He was less effective in John Milius's *Flight of the Intruder*, as veteran, gung-ho bombardier Virgil Cole. Danny Glover, Brad Johnson and Rosanna Arquette also starred, and in spite of some worthy special effects, *Intruder* turned out to be the most boring film about Vietnam yet. A thriller, *Arrive Alive*, with Joan Cusack, fell through, as did Dafoe's stab at romantic comedy. He auditioned for the Richard Gere role in *Pretty Woman*, but failed to appreciate the subtext. The stand-up comedienne Kathy Najimy was there at his audition: 'It was hysterical. Willem Dafoe was like a scary guy picking up a prostitute – I don't think he got it. Believe me, it would've been a whole different movie.'

He played a New York drug dealer in Paul Schrader's excessively dull *Light Sleeper*, and was no luckier in *White Sands*, a leaden crime melo. Cast against type, Dafoe played an honest, small-time sheriff who takes on the identity of a corpse in order to track down its killer. In spite of some lovely scenery, and a cast that included Mary Elizabeth Mastrantonio, Mickey Rourke and Samuel L. Jackson, the film failed to generate any dramatic sparks.

Continuing his run of bad luck, Dafoe teamed up with Madonna to play her defence attorney in *Body of Evidence*. Accused of using her body as a deadly weapon, Madonna has Dafoe arguing in court that, 'It's not a crime to be a great lay.' This, and other ludicrous scenes, were met with raucous laughter from cinemagoers.

FILMOGRAPHY

1980: *Heaven's Gate*. 1981: *The Loveless*.

1982: *The Hunger; New York Nights*. 1984: *Roadhouse 66; Streets of Fire; The Communists Are Comfortable (And Three Other Stories)*. 1985: *To Live and Die in LA*. 1986: *Platoon*. 1987: *Dear America* (voice only). 1988: *Off Limits* (UK: *Saigon*); *The Last Temptation of Christ; Mississippi Burning*. 1989: *Born On the Fourth of July; Triumph of the Spirit*. 1990: *Cry-Baby* (cameo); *Wild at Heart*. 1991: *Flight of the Intruder*. 1992: *Light Sleeper; White Sands*. 1993: *Body of Evidence; Faraway, So Close*. 1994: *Tom and Viv; The Night and the Moment; Clear and Present Danger*.

Geena DAVIS

Facially, she is not perfect. Her eyes are too small, her teeth too pronounced, her jaw too square. Her lips, though, are volcanic, and when she smiles her mouth explodes. Her body, too, shatters thermometers. Six foot tall, she flows in all the right places and her legs go all the way to China. But it's her ebullient personality, comedy timing, business acumen and above all her acting talent, that has made Geena Davis a star to reckon with. Such combinations of intelligence, sex appeal and genuine wit are virtually unheard of in Hollywood.

Following her Oscar for *The Accidental Tourist*, then the furore and critical plaudits surrounding *Thelma and Louise* (it made the

cover of *Time* magazine) and the colossal box-office success of *A League of Their Own*, Geena Davis was one of the hottest properties in America.

Of course, she had already been famous, but was famous for all the wrong reasons. Famous for her eccentric marriage to Jeff Goldblum (they showered bizarre gifts on each other), famous for ·her collection of strange gadgets and tacky bric-a-brac and famous for her unconventiuonal leading men. In a relatively short career, Geena Davis had starred opposite Bill Murray in a clown's costume, Dustin Hoffman in drag, a rocketful of aliens, a ghost with halitosis, a disobedient corgi, a vampire, a fly, Susan Sarandon and Madonna. This, some may say, was fitting for Hollywood's zaniest actress. But just don't say it to Geena.

'It is irritating to be perceived as kooky, or whacky, or zany, or whatever it is,' she complains. 'It's very limiting and somehow disapproving and certainly not how I perceive myself. I am not Pee-wee Herman; I'm a serious actor, a serious person doing something serious.'

True. She is a member of Mensa, the international society whose members' intelligence exceeds that of 98 per cent of the population. She can also speak fluent Swedish, is a talented cartoonist, small-time inventor and accomplished musician, able to

play the drums, flute, organ and piano. She also runs her own production company, Genial Pictures, on the lot at Twentieth Century Fox, with whom she has a production deal. In 1992, Genial had 12 films in pre-production – all due to star Ms Davis. Not bad for an ex-model.

Virginia Elizabeth Davis was born on 21 January 1957 in Wareham, Massachusetts (near Cape Cod), the daughter of William Davis, a civil engineer, and Lucille, a teacher's assistant. Her one brother is a geotechnical engineer living in Las Vegas. Geena recalls that, 'I knew when I was five or something that I wanted to be an actress. I can remember parts of my life where I was thinking, "Well, I'll be an actress, and I'll be a clothing designer, and an inventor, and a graphic artist." I thought, "I'll be each thing for ten years, and I'll switch professions, because there are so many things I want to be."'

She studied acting at Boston University and moved to New York in 1979 where she initially worked as a waitress. Lying about her height (she wore high heels and said she was 5'10'' without them), she got signed up by the prestigious Zoli modelling agency. In between catwalk assignments she took a job as a sales assistant in a dress shop and to combat boredom posed with the mannequins in the window to confuse passers-by. The prank was a crowd-puller, and she was consequently hired to stand in the window every Saturday. She also married the manager of the store's restaurant, a liaison which lasted two years.

Before embarking on a modelling trip to Paris, she auditioned for a small role in the

Geena Davis

Come on baby, light my fire: Geena Davis in *Beetlejuice*, seen here with Alec Baldwin and a supernatural manicure

film *Tootsie* and, in France, received a telegram telling her she had won the part. Essentially her role was a visual joke, but she carried it off with aplomb. Wearing nothing but the skimpiest underwear, she played a TV starlet who shares a dressing room with Dustin Hoffman (5'6''), the latter disguised as an actress. Her naked innocence was charming, Hoffman's embarrassment hilarious, the film an enormous success.

After terminating her marriage, Ms Davis moved to Los Angeles to pursue her career as movie star. Almost instantly she landed the role of Dabney Coleman's naive researcher Wendy Killian in the TV sitcom *Buffalo Bill* (Coleman had played her director in *Tootsie*), for which she contributed to the show as writer. The following year she starred in her own series, *Sara*, as single San Francisco attorney Sara McKenna.

In the Chevy Chase comedy *Fletch*, she played a newspaper morgue chief, a role originally written for a man, and then joined Linda Hamilton as a Russian seductress trained by Sally Kellerman to be a spy – in the dreadful TV movie *Secret Weapons*. In NBC's *Family Ties* she was Karen, the mixed-up housekeeper, and then played a horny vampire in the horror spoof *Transylvania 6-5000*. The latter was nothing to write home about, but it did introduce her to Jeff Goldblum, who seemed to share her lop-sided view of life and, at 6'4'', was a physically suitable date. They returned to the world of the unreal in David Cronenberg's *The Fly*, a Beauty and the Beast tale in which Davis loved Goldblum in spite of his strange buzzing noise. The film was distinguished by some remarkable special effects, was very frightening (and often revolting), yet never lost sight of its sense of humour. Goldblum and Davis made an attractive, offbeat couple, and *The Fly* went on to become a sizeable hit.

In 1987, on the appropriate night of Hallowe'en in the appropriate place of Las Vegas, Jeff Goldblum and Geena Davis exchanged wedding vows on a whim. A year later, Geena was in another hit, and back in the world of the unreal, in Tim Burton's fantastical *Beetlejuice*. This time she was a ghost, the ordinary kind who doesn't believe in tricks and has impeccable taste in interior design. But she and her spectral hubby – Alec Baldwin – are pushed to their limit by an obnoxious human family who move into their home. Enough is enough, and so Geena and Alec call on Peoplebuster Betelgeuse (Michael Keaton) to rid them of their mortal pests. A nice twist on a familiar tale, *Beetlejuice* was consistently hilarious, and

Geena and Susan Sarandon as *Thelma & Louise*

Geena made the most appealing spook in recent memory.

Now typecast as weird and wonderful, she played Valerie Dale in *Earth Girls Are Easy*, a dizzy manicurist who believes Finland is the capital of Norway. She also plays host to three furry extraterrestrials who take over her home and her libido. It was pure Goldblum-Davis territory (he co-starred as one of the aliens), but *too* wacky for most tastes.

She beat out a host of A-list actresses for the role of Muriel Pritchett in *The Accidental Tourist*, Lawrence Kasdan's film version of Ann Tyler's best-seller. Muriel, on the surface a zany scatterbrain, is in fact an extraordinarily complex character, a woman damaged by men but still in desperate need of them. It would have been easy to play Muriel's goofy physicality and to ignore the pain underneath, but Geena dissected her character with the precision of a surgeon and the tenacity of a bull terrier. She was also hilarious, as she forced her way into the affections of William Hurt's emotionally numb writer, only gradually revealing to him the truth about her troubled past. Kasdan, who at one stage had considered casting Melanie Griffith in the part,

marvelled, 'Geena is like a lot of people with whom I've worked, in that it is impossible for them to lie. It's just absolutely impossible for them to do the cheap thing, so there is an enormous sense of integrity.'

Thankfully, Geena's fellow actors recognized this talent, and she was awarded the Oscar for best supporting actress – beating out such rival nominees as Michelle Pfeiffer and Sigourney Weaver. Although she said at the time that Goldblum, 'wasn't jealous for a second, only totally happy for me,' some contribute the break-up of their marriage to Geena's Academy Award. A year later – 1990 – the actress filed for divorce from her husband. Since then, the tabloids have been full of gossip, exposing Geena's relationships with Brad Pitt, security specialist Gavin de Becker – and Jeff Goldblum (!). In the summer of 1993 she announced her engagement to the film director Renny Harlin. Ironically, Harlin had previously dated the actress Laura Dern, who was seeing Goldblum at the time of Davis's engagement. They married in September of 193.

After turning down the Annette Bening role in Stephen Frears's *The Grifters*, she starred opposite Bill Murray in one of the funniest films of 1990, *Quick Change*. Murray played a cynical and brilliant bank robber, with Davis his accomplice who steals for love. While Murray finds robbing the bank a cinch, getting out of New York is another matter

(UK: *Accidental Hero*). 1993: *Angie*. 1994: *Speechless; Cutthroat Island*.

Rebecca De MORNAY

Rebecca De Mornay's career started with a bang (literally) and then virtually evaporated. Nine years later she came back with a bang, and was a bigger star than she'd ever been. In *Risky Business*, her first movie to speak of, she won equal billing to Tom Cruise and defeated air conditioners in cinemas throughout the country. Who could forget her slinky entrance in that film? Wearing nothing but a skimpy lavender dress and high heels, she strolls into the living room of Tom Cruise and, ignoring him, walks straight up to the window. She then raises her leg onto the window seat, exposing an inviting stretch of thigh. Turning to her spectator for the first time, she asks seductively, 'Are you ready for me?' Yes he is. After pulling the aforementioned dress over her naked body, he makes love to her – in front of the window, on the stairs, in a chair, in front of the TV . . . As far as first appearances go, it was a career maker.

Nine years later, De Mornay was back. In *The Hand That Rocks the Cradle* she played the nanny from hell, a sweet, troubled soul who turns on a sweet middle-class family, wet nurses the baby and rigs up the greenhouse to kill people. The film was a superb piece of emotional engineering and was the first big money-maker of 1992, clocking up $88 million in the US and staying in cinemas for a phenomenal 26 weeks.

Rebecca De Mornay was born in Los Angeles on 29 August 1961, the daughter of TV personality Wally George. Her parents divorced when she was two, her mother remarried, and her stepfather died when Rebecca was still only five. With the money from his will, she and her mother travelled to Jamaica, Bermuda, Turkey, France, then to England for five years, where Rebecca attended Summerhill School in Suffolk. Later, they lived in a small town in the Austrian Alps for a further seven years, where Rebecca received her high school degree. She graduated in philosophy, mathematics and Latin. By the time she moved back to California, in 1980, she could speak French and German fluently.

In Los Angeles, she studied acting at the Lee Strasberg Institute and attended workshops with Geraldine Page in New York. She made her film debut in Francis Ford Coppola's ill-fated musical *One From the Heart* (briefly spotted in a restaurant sequence), and then landed the role of Lana

entirely. Murray and Davis made a delightfully zany team, with the former on particularly good form, while the dialogue, plot and comic improvisation all conspired to create a hilarious treat.

Then came Ridley Scott's *Thelma and Louise*, one of the most acclaimed and talked-about films of 1991. Davis was Thelma Dickinson, a brow-beaten housewife who's persuaded to go on a weekend fishing trip by her waitress friend Louise (Susan Sarandon). When Thelma is accosted by a redneck rapist, Louise shoots him dead, leading to a cross-country escapade in which the women discover their true identities. *Rolling Stone* magazine raved that *Thelma and Louise* was, 'movie dynmaite, detonated by award-calibre performances,' and, indeed, both Davis and Sarandon were nominated for best actress Oscars. In truth, they both deserved the award, but probably cancelled each other out, letting Jodie Foster win the prize in their place.

Geena was next offered the Sharon Stone part in *Basic Instinct*, but considered the script 'objectionable', instead accepting the central role of Dottie Hinson in the sentimental baseball comedy *A League of Their Own*, co-starring Tom Hanks and Madonna. While *Basic Instinct* went on to gross $117 million in the States in 1992, *A League of Their Own* didn't do too badly itself, clocking up a handsome $107m. She had less luck with *Hero*, a bright, provocative comedy from Stephen Frears in which she played a ruthless TV reporter. Saved from a plane

Geena as Dottie Hinson, catcher for the Rockford Peaches – in Penny Marshall's top-of the league hit *A League of Their Own*

crash by an unidentified figure (Dustin Hoffman), she starts a crusade to find the hero of the hour, and settles on saintly imposter Andy Garcia. A satirical take on the media and the marketability of false heroism, the film elicited favourable reviews (the American critic Scott Patrick called her performance, 'sexy, bright and charming'), but failed to find favour with the public. Maybe the film's biting parody of American patriotism was too bitter a pill to swallow, or possibly Dustin Hoffman's grouchy anti-hero too unsympathetic. But *Hero* was an extremely funny, well-made and moving piece, and was yet another jewel in Geena's crown.

Next, she was announced as the star of Martha Coolidge's *Angie*, as a vulnerable Italian woman from Brooklyn, a part reportedly written for Madonna. Although the latter was filming *Dangerous Game* at the time and couldn't do it, she publicly exhibited her distaste for Davis's casting.

FILMOGRAPHY

1982: *Tootsie*. 1985: *Fletch*; *Secret Weapons* (TV); *Transylvania 6-5000*. 1986: *The Fly*. 1988: *Beetlejuice*; *The Accidental Tourist*. 1989: *Earth Girls Are Easy* (filmed in 1988). 1990: *Quick Change*. 1991: *Thelma and Louise*. 1992: *A League of Their Own*; *Hero*

Rebecca DeMornay

Scharf, the direct, business-minded prostitute in *Risky Business*. The film was a hit, and Rebecca and co-star Tom Cruise embarked on a two-and-a-half year relationship.

In the grim, but highly accomplished *Testament*, she played a young mother coping with the aftermath of nuclear war, and she broke the heart. She was equally good in *The Trip to Bountiful*, as a prim Texas wife accompanying Geraldine Page on an sentimental bus ride, but it was Hal Ashby's big-budget *The Slugger's Wife* that offered her a real shot at stardom.

'After *Risky Business*,' she explained, 'the creme de la creme role for my generation of actress was the female lead in *The Slugger's Wife*. It ended up being one of the biggest bombs that you could ever be a part of, in every respect. It was truly terrible. No one came out of that movie alive.'

De Mornay played the wife of the title, a rock singer married to baseball superstar Michael O'Keefe. Surprisingly – for such an unmitigated mess – the screenplay was by none other than Neil Simon. She was passed over for the role of the gutsy, tomboyish mechanic in Andrei Konchalovsky's *Runaway Train* because, the actress relates, the director had 'watched me in *Risky Business* and told a colleague, "I want a train mechanic, not a call

girl." When I was told that, I decided to make damn sure he hired me.' So she dyed her hair brown, rubbed off her make-up, donned jeans and forced him to meet her. The part was hers.

The film, an exciting thriller set on board a locomotive hurtling through Alaska without a driver, won Oscar nominations for its two male stars, Jon Voight and Eric Roberts, and good notices for De Mornay.

The following year she endured 'an explosive breakup' with Cruise, which she put down to 'professional rivalry', and then starred opposite George C. Scott in an excellent TV version of Edgar Allan Poe's *The Murders in the Rue Morgue*. She was the good-looking one in a low-budget version of *Beauty and the Beast*, with John Savage, and then took the Brigitte Bardot role in Roger Vadim's re-make of his own 1956 erotic classic *And God Created Woman*. This was arguably the worst film of her career, although she was never less than gorgeous, with or without her clothes. She played a Marine dreaming of being an FBI agent in the mirthless comedy *Feds*, and then a tough,

high-powered stockbroker in the *British Dealers*, a sort of cut-price *Wall Street*.

It was while she was plugging *Dealers* at the Cannes Film Festival that she bumped into screenwriter Bruce Wagner, who was there promoting his film, *Scenes from the Class Struggle in Beverly Hills*. Returning to Los Angeles, they married and were divorced within ten months. 'We collided, and the collision was called love and marriage,' she reveals ruefully. 'It was very painful, very explosive. Luckily, we are both still alive.'

By now her career was in such a low gear, that she found herself sixth-billed in Ron Howard's action-thriller *Backdraft*, playing the negligible role of fireman Kurt Russell's estranged wife. Still, the film's producer Richard Lewis was charitable enough to comment, 'She was somebody Ron and I wanted to work with. I couldn't imagine anybody else playing the role.'

She then took on her favourite part to date, that of the 'unbelievably sweet and deep' Flo March in the TV miniseries *An Inconvenient Woman*. As Jason Robards's troublesome mistress, she delivered a neat

DeMornay with Tom Cruise in *Risky Business*, the film that made her name

51

Borrowing Bardot: DeMornay as Robin Shay in Roger Vadim's risible *And God Created Woman*

With Paul McGann in *Dealers*

Maternal instinct: Rebecca DeMornay (with Madeline Zima) in the enormous hit *The Hand That Rocks the Cradle*

line in Judy Holliday mimicry. Not entirely coincidentally, she had previously played the Holliday part of Billie Dawn in a Los Angeles stage production of *Born Yesterday*.

Then came *The Hand Rocks the Cradle*. As Peyton Flanders, every father's dream of the perfect babysitter (and every mother's nightmare), De Mornay was also sweet and deep, but her hidden depths revealed more than maternal yearnings. In a year bursting at the sprockets with memorable female villains (Sharon Stone in *Basic Instinct*, Jennifer Jason Leigh in *Single White Female*, Michelle Pfeiffer's Catwoman), De Mornay's smart, sexy and scheming nanny elicited more

sympathy than most, no small feat for an actress who saw her character as 'really sick.' Peyton had, De Mornay explains, 'a very deep need to be a mother, a very deep need for a family. It's moving when you see the sickening manipulation she's willing to go through to get it.'

She was then seen in the HBO movie *Blind Side*, with Rutger Hauer and Ron Silver and, thanks to *Cradle*, won the lead role in Sidney Lumet's cat-and-mouse thriller *Guilty as Sin*. In the latter she played a criminal defence attorney hired to defend slick killer Don Johnson. At last, at 32, Rebecca De Mornay had a major film she could call her own, complete with a first-rate director and a famous co-star billed *after* her.

In 1993 she was romantically linked with the Canadian songwriter and novelist Leonard Cohen, who is 29 years her senior.

FILMOGRAPHY

1982: *One From the Heart*. 1983: *Risky Business*; *Testament*. 1985: *The Trip to Bountiful*; *The Slugger's Wife*; *Runaway Train*. 1986: *The Murders In the Rue Morgue* (TV). 1987: *And God Created Woman*; *Beauty and the Beast*. 1988: *Feds*. 1989: *Dealers*. 1991: *Backdraft*; *An Inconvenient Woman* (TV). 1992: *The Hand That Rocks the Cradle*. 1993: *Blind Side* (TV); *Guilty as Sin*; *The Three Musketeers*. 1994: *Getting Out* (TV).

Patrick DEMPSEY

Patrick Dempsey was one of the most incongruous leading men of the 1980s and 1990s. Small, wiry and overtly Jewish, he was neither physically suited to romantic comedies nor action adventures. And yet he ploughed through a succession of movies in a notably short period of time. Even more remarkable was that he was invariably the star. Patrick Dempsey's ace card was that he had talent to burn.

He was also an ambitious, determined young man who venerated De Niro and Pacino, and pushed himself hard. Maybe his childhood struggle against dyslexia laid the groundwork for his bull-headed drive and tenacious professionalism. It is no secret that he believed he was often better than the material offered him, and, indeed, he frequently transcended it.

Christian Slater, who played Charles 'Lucky' Luciano to Dempsey's Meyer Lansky in *Mobsters*, noted, 'Patrick is a very concentrated actor. Very, very concentrated and very . . . *extreme*, I think is the word. It was

Patrick Dempsey

Dempsey with Jennifer Connelly in Michael Hoffman's *Some Girls*

fascinating watching him and seeing what he does. It was always a surprise when the camera started rolling. Which made for an . . . interesting atmosphere. A *very* interesting atmosphere.'

Patrick Dempsey was born on 13 January 1966 in Lewiston, Maine, the youngest of three children. Raised in the rural community of Turner and Buckfield, the actor discovered a passion for skiing. In order to improve his skills on the piste, he learned to juggle and ride a unicycle, but such was his expertise that, at 15, he developed his own act. Soon, he was touring the New England vaudeville circuit as a juggler-cum-unicyclist-cum-comedian-cum-magician. Subsequently, he not only won the State of Maine Downhill Racing competition, but also came second in an international juggling event. And, at 17, he won a Talent America contest into the bargain. It was clear from the start that Patrick Dempsey was determined to succeed.

Spotted by an agent, he was invited to audition for a role in a touring production of

Dempsey and the women: Patrick surrounded by Kirstie Alley, Kim Miyori and Carrie Fisher – in Joan Micklin Silver's *Loverboy*

Sibling rivalry: Dempsey and Daniel Stern differ in Joe Roth's most enjoyble *Coup de Ville*

Torch Song Trilogy. He won the part, and spent four months with the company in San Francisco, cementing his interest in acting. He followed this with another tour, playing Eugene in *Brighton Beach Memoirs*, and then made his film debut in *Heaven Help Us*, playing a Catholic schoolboy alongside Andrew McCarthy, Mary Stuart Masterson and Kevin Dillon.

This was followed by a Disney TV movie, *A Fighting Choice*, starring Beau Bridges, in which his portrayal of an epileptic won him a special award from the Epilepsy Foundation. Bearing a passing resemblance to Sean Penn, he seemed the obvious choice to play the dopey surfer Jeff Spicoli in the TV version of *Fast Times at Ridgemont High*. But no, that honour went to Dean Cameron, while Dempsey played the role of the posturing Mike Damone (originated by Robert Romanus in the film). Anyway, the series was a stiff.

So was the ghastly *Meatballs III*, in which Dempsey landed the starring role as a 14-year-old geek trying to lose his virginity. Sally Kellerman played the dead porno star who helped him out. Much better was *In the Mood*, a beguiling comedy in which Dempsey played real-life womanizer Sonny Wisecarver who, at 15, courted and married two older (already married) women. Dempsey really came into his own as the Californian kid

whose combination of innocence and good nature won the hearts of Beverly D'Angelo and Talia Balsam and the front pages of the 1944 tabloids. The director, incidentally, was none other than Phil Alden Robinson, who went on to make *Field of Dreams* and *Sneakers*.

Dempsey was another romantic nerd in *Can't Buy Me Love*, coughing up $1,000 for cheerleader queen Amanda Peterson to pose as his girlfriend for one month. The film was predictable, sentimental, but not without its diverting moments. The actor broached similar ground with *Happy Together*, another romantic comedy about a love-struck geek paired with an impossibly beautiful roommate (Helen Slater this time).

There was a change of pace with the World War II drama *In a Shallow Grave*, a grim, limping affair with Dempsey the bizarre go-between for a disfigured war veteran (Michael Biehn) and his girlfriend (Maureen Mueller). Yet another romantic comedy surfaced with *Some Girls*, in which Dempsey was improbably pursued by a family of aberrant women, a film most notable in that it was produced by Robert Redford. As *Loverboy*, the actor went one better, seducing Kirstie Alley, Carrie Fisher, Barbara Carrera and other Beverly Hills housewives in order to pay for his college tuition.

In *Coup de Ville*, an engaging road movie, Dempsey left romance behind to play the hard-edged, bullying brother of Daniel Stern and Arye Gross, who is forced to share a car journey with them at the behest of their father (Alan Arkin). Based on a true incident, the film courted the predictable but always managed to swerve away in time. A most enjoyable outing.

Then there was *Run*, in which he played an impudent law student chased by the Mob after accidentally killing a don's son. Kelly Preston was the requisite decoration. In *Mobsters* (cruelly nicknamed *Young Buns With Tommy Guns* during production), he joined the other side, portraying true-life gangster Meyer Lansky. 'When you play a real live character,' the actor declared, 'there's a certain honour and respect you must bring to the character in order to portray him in a light that is true to what he did.' Although *Mobsters* was savaged by the critics, it was not without its merits, was well acted by a formidable cast (Christian Slater, Lara Flynn Boyle, Anthony Quinn, F. Murray Abraham, Michael Gambon) and was stunningly flimed.

Next, Dempsey teamed up with Kelly Lynch for *R.S.V.P.* and then went to Paris to *Face the Music*, his umpteenth romantic comedy, in which he played a songwriter at

loggerheads with Molly Ringwald. He had the title role in the inept crime comedy *Bank Robber*, co-starring Lisa Bonet, Judge Reinhold and Forest Whitaker; and then played a frail John Kennedy in the acclaimed TV mini-series *JFK: Reckless Youth* (TV).

FILMOGRAPHY

1985: *Heaven Help Us* (UK: *Catholic Boys*). **1986:** *A Fighting Choice* (TV). **1987:** *Meatballs III*; *In the Mood* (UK: *The Woo Woo Kid*); *Can't Buy Me Love*. **1988:** *Happy Together*; *In a Shallow Grave*; *Some Girls* (UK: *Sisters*). **1989:** *Loverboy*; *Coup de Ville*. **1990:** *Run*. **1991:** *Mobsters* (UK: *Mobsters: The Evil Empire*). **1992:** *R.S.V.P.*; *Face the Music*. **1993:** *Bank Robber*; *JFK: Reckless Youth* (TV). **1994:** *With Honors*.

Johnny DEPP

In 1989, Johnny Depp was getting $45,000 an episode for the TV series *21 Jump Street*. He was being paid $1 million to star in John Waters's *Cry-Baby*. He was receiving 10,000 fan letters a month. And yet he refused to live up to his celebrity. In March of 1989 he was arrested and jailed (for one night) in Vancouver on assault charges. He sported a tattoo on each arm and dressed in torn jeans (prompting Waters to eulogize, 'Nobody looks better in rags'). Stranger still, Depp didn't own an apartment, a house or even a car. Later, when he moved in with Winona Ryder, it was into a series of hotel rooms. And if his address lacked permanency, so did his love life. He was married to his first wife, musician Lori Anne Allison, for two years (1983–5); was engaged to the actress Sherilyn Fenn for three (1985–88); and broke off an engagement to Jennifer Grey a year later. But to prove that his love for Winona was the real thing, Depp added a third tattoo to his collection, a double banner curling down his right deltoid: FOREVER WINONA. And yet that engagement was broken, too.

OK, so Johnny Depp was weird. But then he had an unusual childhood. Part Cherokee, he was born John Christopher Depp II on 9 June 1963 in Owensboro, Kentucky, the youngest of four children (he has two sisters and a brother). His father was a city engineer, his mother a waitress, and when Johnny Jr was seven, the family moved to Miramar, Florida. It was there that he began his life of rebellion. Once, he was suspended from school for exposing his buttocks to a teacher, and was into drugs by 11. He was also known as a vandal and a thief and, at 13, had his first sexual experience. By 14 he had kicked his drug habit, but suffered terribly when his parents divorced a year later. Shortly afterwards, he dropped out of school (in his junior year) and joined a rock group, The Kids, which was a minor sensation locally and opened for such big-name acts as the B-52's, Iggy Pop and Talking Heads. At 20, Depp married Lori Anne, the 25-year-old sister of a fellow musician, and the group upped sticks to try their luck in LA.

Nothing doing. To support himself and his wife, Depp became a biro telephone-salesman, but was divorced from Lori in 1985. Still, they remained amicable and when she started dating actor Nicolas Cage, the guys became friends. Cage suggested Depp talk to his agent with a view to becoming an actor, and so Depp went up for his first audition – for a low-budget horror film called *A Nightmare On Elm Street*. The director, Wes Craven, was getting bleary-eyed viewing the same old posturing studs, when Depp ambled in. The filmmaker immediately saw something different. 'Johnny really had sort of a James Dean attraction,' Craven recalled '– that quiet charisma that none of the other actors had.'

Johnny Depp got the part – as Glenn, the boy who's literally swallowed by a bed in a torrent of blood – and the film was a hit, spawning five sequels (at the last count). Depp then won the lead in the dreadful sex comedy *Private Resort* and, with The Kids disbanded, decided to take this acting thing seriously. He started attending drama classes, but found the parts weren't exactly queuing up at his door. There were a couple of spots on TV, and then the cable movie *Slow Burn*, a dreary thriller starring Eric Roberts. However, he was inspired working with Oliver Stone on *Platoon*, in which he played the interpreter Lerner. *Platoon* went on to become an enormous hit and won the Oscar for best film.

Thinking that he was made, Depp turned down the lead in the TV series *21 Jump Street* ('I wasn't ready for that kind of commitment'), and then took it when his replacement (Jeff Yagher) was excused. Depp played undercover high school cop Tom Hanson and, when the series was a success, became a household name – at least in those households that contained teenage girls. However, for a new face in town, Depp was surprisingly candid in his views on the show. He was happy with the first season, with the series' willingness to tackle such issues as AIDS, juvenile crime, sex, child molestation and the like, but later became disenchanted. He started questioning the direction of his character, the story-lines, the show's moral viewpoint. Soon, his 'high-handed' behaviour

Scarfacial innocent: Johnny Depp lends an ethereal air to Tim Burton's wonderful *Edward Scissorhands*

leaked out to the press, and Depp was branded 'difficult.' After four seasons, he left the show.

Still, he had his fans and the revisionist filmmaker John Waters wrote the part of the delinquent biker Wade Walker in *Cry-Baby* especially for him (Waters also cast such unlikely icons as Iggy Pop, Traci Lords and Troy Donahue in the film). Explaining why he wanted Depp, Waters declared, 'First of all, he's a good actor, but secondly, he's handsome in a real way. He's just got that *thing* that makes a star.'

On the heels of *Cry-Baby*, Depp landed the title role in *Edward Scissorhands*, another very personal vision from a highly idiosyncratic filmmaker. Tim Burton was one of the hottest names in Tinseltown thanks to his direction of *Beetlejuice* and *Batman*, and was now in a position to realize his own fairy

story. This was the occasionally hilarious, always wondrous and surprisinglyly touching tale of a man-boy-machine cursed with 12-inch blades for fingers. Facially scarred by his own hand gestures, and dressed in black leather and studs, his was a fearsome presence, hiding the pathos and love underneath. Edward is desperate to give and to receive affection, but is unable to touch others without hurting them. Reportedly, the role was first offered to Tom Cruise, but he insisted on a cosmetically happy ending. So Depp stepped in, and studied the silent films of Charlie Chaplin to bring a wordless expression and body movement to his role. He says, 'I think the script was one of the best things I'd ever read, so of course I jumped at the opportunity to play him. Because Edward is not human, and not a robot, I didn't think he would talk a lot. He would cut through everything and have the most honest, pure answer with all the clarity in the world.'

Burton was pleased with the result. 'He's great in it,' the director acknowledged. 'I

Johnny Depp at the top of his form as the boy who would be Chaplin – in *Benny & Joon*

summoned to Arizona to serve as best man at his uncle's marriage to a bride thirty years his junior. Jerry Lewis played the uncle, supermodel Paulina Porizkova the latter's bride, while the rest of an unlikely cast included Faye Dunaway, Lili Taylor and Michael J. Pollard. Depp received top-billing, and again proved he was more than just a pretty face.

Next, he played a dyslexic eccentric in love with black-and-white movies and Mary Stuart Masterson in the romantic drama *Benny and Joon*, and then starred in *What's Eating Gilbert Grape*, as a young man from a 'dyslexic family' who falls for the older, married Mary Steenburgen. The latter was directed by the Swedish filmmaker Lasse Hallstrom (*My Life as a Dog*), whom Depp describes as, 'a very sweet, incredibly, amazingly sensitive guy – but also kinda nuts.' He was then reunited with Tim Burton on *Ed Wood*, biography of the cult B-movie director Edward D. Wood Jr.

At the time of going to press Depp was dating English Supermodel Kate Moss.

FILMOGRAPHY

1984: *A Nightmare On Elm Street.* **1985:** *Private Resort.* **1986:** *Slow Burn* (TV); *Platoon.* **1990:** *Cry-Baby*; *Edward Scissorhands.* **1991:** *Freddy's Dead: The Final Nightmare* (cameo). **1992:** *Arizona Dream.* **1993:** *Benny & Joon*; *What's Eating Gilbert Grape.* **1994:** *Ed Wood*; *Don Juan and the Centrefold.*

Laura Dern in David Lynch's *Blue Velvet*

really admired his performance very much. He just risked being – *simple*, you know? Like Edward, Johnny really is perceived as something he is not. Before we met, I'd certainly read about him as the Difficult Hearthrob. But you look at him and you get a feeling. There is a lot of pain and humour and darkness and light. I think it's a very mature and risky performance.' Playing the girl who sees beyond Edward's blades, Winona Ryder made the perfect fairy tale heroine (albeit a product of America's suburban barbecue set). She was also Johnny Depp's girlfriend. The couple met through a friend, and Winona admits, 'I thought maybe he would be a jerk. I didn't know. But he was really, really shy.' They discovered a mutual fixation for J.D. Salinger and the soundtrack album of *The Mission*, and the rest was plain sailing. Burton, not entirely seriously, has called them 'an evil version of Tracy and Hepburn.' In fact, despite a hint of rebellion and a love of the offbeat, they were an intelligent, loving couple just trying to survive in the glare of the spotlight.

Career-wise, Depp took a cameo (seen briefly on a TV) in *Freddy's Dead: The Final Nightmare*, and then worked with another highly individual filmmaker on *Arizona Dream*. This was the weirdest of movies, an oddly lyrical combination of whimsy and slapstick from Emir Kusturica, the Sarajevo-born director, rock musician and Columbia University lecturer. Depp played Axel Blackmar, a New York game warden

Laura DERN

For somebody so inextricably associated with sex, Laura Dern appears refreshingly normal. Sure, she can look ravishing, a sensual stream of hair, legs and arms. But she is not a Hollywood goddess in the sense that Michelle Pfeiffer, Sharon Strone and Julia Roberts are. At 5'10", Laura Dern can be both gawky and goofy. She reminds one of a frisky young foal – not entirely sure of its balance, but nonetheless full of the joys of spring. Her attraction is her spirit, her youth, her acting skills. For one so young, she has been bestowed with an exceptional number of honours. The Los Angeles Film Critics gave her their New Generation Award for her performance in *Smooth Talk*. For *Rambling Rose* she was nominated for an Oscar and won the best actress award at the Montreal Film Festival. And for her role as a crusading widow in the TV film *Afterburn*, she won the Golden Globe award.

Laura Dern specialises in playing innocents, and yet has become associated with cinematic sex. In *Smooth Talk*, she was a

teenage virgin seduced by Treat Williams; in David Lynch's *Blue Velvet* she was the virtuous counterbalance in a plot full of depravity; in the same director's *Wild at Heart*, she was a lustful runaway sexually humiliated by Willem Dafoe; in *Rambling Rose*, she was a nymphomaniac who introduces a 13-year-old boy to the mysterious pleasures of her body . . . Off-screen, too, she had a succession of suitors, some of them famous. For four years she was partnered with Kyle MacLachlan ('a tough but good' relationship); was linked with Peter Horton, of TV's *thirtysomething*; and dated the Finnish filmmaker Renny Harlin (*Die Hard 2, Cliffhanger*).

She was born on 10 February 1967 in Santa Monica, California, the second of two daughters (her older sister drowned as an infant). And the theatre was in her blood. Her parents, Bruce Dern and Diane Ladd, are both actors and Oscar nominees, no less. Tennessee Williams was a cousin, and Laura's great uncle was the poet/playwright Archibald MacLeish. And, for a show of versatility, her great-grandfather was a governor of Utah. However, her parents split up when she was two and Laura became estranged from her father (one of her earliest memories of him was on TV in *Hush*

. . . *Hush, Sweet Charlotte*, in the scene in which his severed head bounces down the stairs). However, she revealed later, 'now we're the best of friends.'

At first, Laura's parents discouraged her desire to become an actress. 'They thought I should be something like a psychologist or a doctor,' she recalls. 'They used to take me to the set hoping I'd get bored and hate it – but it didn't turn out that way.' Indeed, at the age of five, she appeared in an episode of the daytime soap *The Secret Storm* with her mother, and, at six, had a bit in the Burt Reynolds actioner *White Lightning*, also with mum. The following year she consumed nine banana-flavoured ice creams in nine takes in a scene from Martin Scorsese's *Alice Doesn't Live Here Anymore*. Recalls Ladd, 'I said, "She's gonna get sick," and Marty said, "No, she's not. She's gonna be an actress."' Ladd played Flo, the tough-talking waitress in the latter, and won her first Oscar nomination for the part.

When Laura was 11, she dolled herself up to look like a precocious 14-year-old, and nabbed a small role in Adrian Lyne's *Foxes*. At 13, she played a punk rock groupie in *Ladies and Gentlemen, The Fabulous Stains*, with Diane Lane; and a year after that began taking children's classes at the Lee Strasberg Theatre Institute. At school, she attained top grades, and even found time to be class president and homecoming princess. At 16, she enrolled at RADA in London, and cut her teeth on Shakespeare, appearing in productions of *Hamlet* and *A Midsummer Night's Dream*. Back in America, she continued her career in movies, popping up in the TV films *Happy Endings* and *The Three Wishes of Billy Grier*. In *Teachers*, with Nick Nolte, she played a 16-year-old student who decides to have an abortion; and in Peter Bogdanovich's *Mask*, was the blind girl unperturbed by Eric Stoltz's hideous deformity. She then took a dramatic U-turn, and registered at UCLA to study child psychology. Two days into her course she won the starring role in Joyce Chopra's *Smooth Talk* – and turned her back on academia forever.

In the latter she played Connie, a teenage girl coming to terms with her sexuality, and ran away with glowing reviews. When Molly Ringwald was maternally advised against participating in David Lynch's *Blue Velvet*, 'about S & M and bugs,' she lost the most interesting film of her career. Laura Dern stepped in as the sweet, questioning Sandy Williams, and when the film became an enormous cult success, her future seemed assured.

With John Cusack in Roland Joffe's underrated *Fat Man and Little Boy*

Simmering nicely as Lula Pace Fortune in David Lynch's *Wild at Heart*

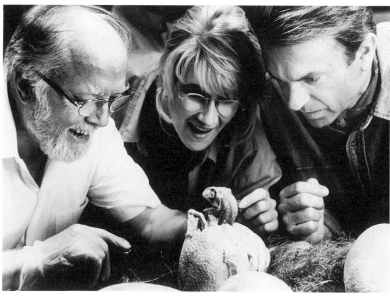

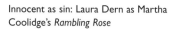

Innocent as sin: Laura Dern as Martha Coolidge's *Rambling Rose*

Laura Dern flanked by Richard Attenborough and Sam Neill in the biggest money-making movie of all-time, *Jurassic Park*

She was re-teamed with Eric Stoltz in *Haunted Summer*, an unconvincing take on the famous get-together between Lord Byron, Percy Shelley and Mary Godwin (with Dern as Claire Clairmont), and took a supporting role in *Fat Man and Little Boy*, Roland Joffe's distinguished drama about the making of the atom bomb. In the latter she played the fictional Nurse Kathleen Robinson, who has an affair with scientist John Cusack, and then has to look on as he slowly dies from radiation. In a display of directorial generosity, David Lynch called on Ms Dern again, this time to play a part diametrically opposed to Sandy in *Blue Velvet*. This time he cast her as Lulu Pace Fortune in *Wild at Heart*, a free spirit fleeing across America's South with her parole-jumping boyfriend Nicolas Cage. Cage and Dern were on the run from Lulu's crazed mother – played with manic glee by none other than Diane Ladd – while Dern summed up the spirit of the enterprise with her famous declaration, 'The whole world's wild at heart and weird on top.' Indeed. The movie grabbed armies of devout followers by the throat, and even nabbed a second Best Supporting Actress Oscar nomination for Ms Ladd.

The latter's luck continued a year later when she won a *third* nomination for *Rambling Rose*, proving that she acts best under the influence of her daughter. Laura

played the rambling Rose of the title, a 19-year-old waif taken into the home and hearts of the genteel Hilliar family. Once rooted, Rose blossoms into an ingenuous nymphomaniac, seducing Mother (Ms Ladd), corrupting Father (Robert Duvall) and showing their young son (Lukas Haas) a thing or two. Based on Calder Willingham's autobiographical novel, the film was a superbly crafted, well-acted drama in the tradition of *Driving Miss Daisy*, but with enough ruffled taboos to give the British censor apoplexy. Although uncut in America, the film fell victim to the scissors in Britain.

Laura Dern was now very hot news indeed – helped, no doubt, by an Oscar nomination for *Rambling Rose*. She turned down the role of Andy – John Lithgow's wife – in the ecological epic *At Play in the Fields of the Lord* (replaced by Daryl Hannah), a wise decision as it turned out, and decided to make a TV movie instead. This was HBO's *Afterburn*, the true story of an American airman's widow who sets about clearing her husband's name after his death is blamed on pilot error. Again, Dern turned in a first-class performance as a strong, sympathetic woman, and won the Golden Globe award as best actress.

After that, she was signed on by Steven Spielberg to play the female lead in *Jurassic*

Park, the biggest grossing movie of all time, and teamed opposite Clint Eastwood for *A Perfect World*. What a year.

FILMOGRAPHY

1973: *White Lightning*. 1974: *Alice Doesn't Live Here Anymore*. 1980: *Foxes*. 1982: *Ladies and Gentlemen, The Fabulous Stains*. 1983: *Happy Endings* (TV). 1984: *The Three Wishes of Billy Grier* (TV); *Teachers*. 1985: *Mask*; *Smooth Talk*. 1986: *Blue Velvet*. 1988: *Haunted Summer*. 1989: *Fat Man and Little Boy* (UK: *Shadow Makers*). 1990: *Wild at Heart*. 1991: *Rambling Rose*. 1992: *Afterburn* (TV). 1993: *Jurassic Park*; *A Perfect World*.

Matt DILLON

More than any other actor of his generation, Matt Dillon epitomized urban cool. Physically tough, emotionally vulnerable, streetwise, brooding, intelligent and ingenuous, Dillon displayed a persona of James Dean intensity without ever appearing to act. He just *was* this really cool guy who wound up in the movies because he couldn't get a job as a mechanic.

In the opening scene of *The Outsiders*, Dillon is seen in long-shot leaning against a traffic light igniting a cigarette. Nonchalant, wise-beyond-his years, he instantly conveys the image that he is a product and a survivor of the streets. Approached by C. Thomas Howell, he is asked, 'What do you want to do?' Dillon's reply is typical: 'Nothing legal, man.'

However, Kelly Lynch, Dillon's co-star in

Matt Dillon

Drugstore Cowboy six years later, claims, 'People don't know how intelligent and gracious an actor he is. He's always the cool guy: cowboy hat, tight jeans, cigarette in the mouth, leaning on a wall, smoking and snarling. That's *not* Matt's energy. There's an innocence and ingenuousness, too. He's a comedian like you wouldn't believe.'

He's also a natural. 'The camera really

does love him,' offers James Dearden, who directed the star in *A Kiss Before Dying*. 'It's extraordinary. I mean, every time he steps in front of the lens – *pow!*'

Matt Dillon was a natural. Born on 18 February 1964 in New Rochelle, New York, the second oldest of five boys and a girl, he was spotted in the corridor of his junior high school by a talent scout. He was 14 and sneaking out of school but ended up in his first movie instead. Until then, Dillon, the son of a salesman, had uttered one line in a play in fourth grade. Sports and shoplifting were more his line – and killing time with the boys. A former classmate volunteers, 'He hung out with a tough crowd – sort of desperadoes. He always wore his jacket collar turned up, and he had a black German shepherd.'

His first film was Jonathan Kaplan's *Over the Edge*, a gritty, unsettling view of rebellious youth, with Dillon cast as Richie White, an ill-fated ruffian with an attitude. His performance was frighteningly authentic for one so young, but it was his face that caught the attention of casting directors. In *Little Darlings* he played a boy called Randy, an underage stud who is pursued by Kristy McNichol at summer camp. It was this performance that really got young hearts fluttering, aided by pin-up portraits in teen magazines and a spontaenous fan club.

After playing two variations on his persona of street tough, Dillon was the school bully in Tony Bill's *My Bodyguard*, forcing puny Chris Makepeace to hire brawny Adam Baldwin. He then turned to romance in *Liar's Moon*, a film that inspired so much confidence in its

distributor that two versions were released, each with a different ending. He then sequed into a PBS TV special, *The Great American Fourth of July and other Disasters*, before embarking on his S.E. Hinton trilogy.

Susan Hinton was the guru scribe of disenchanted youth, whose slim novels suddenly gripped the imagination of filmmakers. The first to go before the cameras was *Tex*, the story of a teenage kid (Dillon) struggling to grow up under trying circumstances. It was directed by Tim Hunter, who had co-scripted *Over the Edge*, and co-starred Meg Tilly and Emilio Estevez.

Next came *The Outsiders*, directed by Francis Coppola and starring a who's who of future stars. Dillon played Dallas Winston, a social underdog looked up to by the likes of C. Thomas Howell and Ralph Macchio. The film was a hit, although not as popular as hindsight would suggest. *RumbleFish* was even less successful, but has earned itself a place as one of the most written-about movies of the 1980s. In this, Dillon played Rusty James, an outsider obsessed by his older brother, biker boy Mickey Rourke. Typically, Rusty is defined (by co-star Nicolas Cage) as 'a very cool dude', in spite of his propensity for getting beaten up and knifed and treating his girlfriend (Diane Lane) like trash.

Next, Dillon won critical raves for the title role in *The Flamingo Kid* and displayed an unexpected gift for comedy. Instead of lording it over impressionable younger kids, Dillon this time was the youngster striving to make it in an adult world. He was top-billed as Jeffrey Willis, a gauche hustler who plays

Matt Dillon with Kim Kliner in Jonathan Kaplan's gripping *Over the Edge*

Dillon with S.E. Hinton in Francis Coppola's adaptation of the latter's cult novel *The Outsiders*

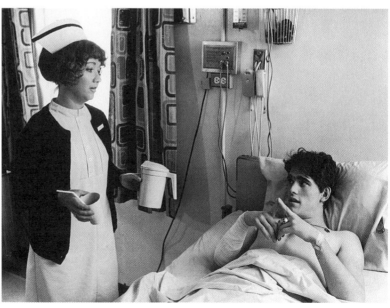

a while he dated a girl from one of his acting classes, and later frequented public events with a blonde model from London called Emma Woollard. He also spent some time with his family, which included his younger brother Kevin, who has followed his famous brother's footsteps, starring in such films as *The Blob*, *War Party* and *The Rescue*.

According to Kaplan, who directed *Over the Edge*, the Dillon brood were 'close, but not cloying.' Adding, 'how many times do we have to hear about Drew Barrymore and Corey Feldman going through another dope treatment? Not the Dillon kids. That stuff doesn't interest them. They'd rather hang out with friends and family.'

The closest Matt Dillon came to serious drug taking was with his role as a junkie and thief in a small, low-budget picture called *Drugstore Cowboy* (set in 1971). Although stark and realistic in its depiction of pharmacy ghouls, the film did have a well-developed sense of humour that made it one of the most perversely irresistible independent American films of 1989. Dillon in particular received raves for his performance, and was subsequently re-embraced by the media.

He off-set this return with a dreadful re-make of the 1956 Robert Wagner thriller *A Kiss Before Dying*. The film's lack of conviction, though, was due less to Dillon's portrayal of a charming serial killer, as to Sean Young's double performance as twin sisters. River Phoenix had turned this one down, and so should have Matt Dillon.

He then made a rare appearance on TV in the three-part, deftly-titled *Women & Men 2: In Love There Are No Rules*. He and Kyra Sedgwick (who previously played his girlfriend in *Kansas*) starred in the segment titled 'Return to Kansas City' – from a short story by Irwin Shaw – in which Dillon portrayed a boxer with marital problems.

In *Singles*, a beautifully written look at Seattle youth, he accepted a supporting role, as Cliff Poncier, a would-be rock star who fails to appreciate his loving girlfriend (Bridget Fonda). Next, he teamed up with Danny Glover in *The Saint of Fort Washington*, a drama focusing on the plight of the homeless in New York, which took nine years to bring to the screen. Dillon played Matthew, an emotionally disturbed schizophrenic who has only his battered camera for company, until he is befriended by Glover. After that, he took the lead in Anthony Minghella's *Mr Wonderful*, the story of a divorcee (Dillon) who tries to find Mr Right for his ex (Annabella Sciorra) – in order to relieve his alimony payments. William Hurt co-starred as a contender.

As the low-life with a poet's heart: Dillon with Max Perlich in Gus Van Sant's idiosyncratic *Drugstore Cowboy*

Dillon with Bridget Fonda in Cameron Crowe's *Singles*

on his charm and angelic looks to make good at a Long Island beach club.

Dillon admits that comedy comes unnaturally to him, but proved surprisingly good at it, aided no doubt by the adroit direction of Garry Marshall (who went on to win even greater acclaim with *Pretty Woman* and *Frankie & Johnny*). 'I believe there was once somebody famous,' the actor points out, 'I don't remember who it was – that said on his deathbed, "Dying's easy, but comedy's hard." And I think that's true.' Next came a string of flops that almost extinguished the actor's career. In *Target*, a run-of-the-mill spy thriller, he played Gene Hackman's son in search of his kidnapped mother; in the Australian *Rebel*, he was miscast as a 1940s GI in love with a cabaret singer; and in the disastrous 1930s-set *Native Son* (based on the celebrated novel by Richard Wright) he played the Communist boyfriend of Elizabeth McGovern.

On paper, *The Big Town* looked like a prestigious star vehicle for the actor, with a supporting cast comprising Diane Lane, Tommy Lee Jones, Tom Skerritt, Lee Grant

and Bruce Dern. In fact, it was another turkey, featuring Dillon as a crap shooter with a lucky streak courting notoriety in 1950s' Chicago. He seemed considerably more at ease as a charismatic, gun-toting psychopath in the entertaining *Kansas* (with Andrew McCarthy), but nobody turned up to witness the event. The public also stayed away from *Bloodhounds of Broadway*, an ill-advised adaptation of a 1928-set Damon Runyan story, with Madonna, Jennifer Grey, Rutger Hauer and Randy Quaid also in the cast.

Off screen, Dillon kept a quiet profile, indulging his love of drawing and painting, and refusing to talk about his private life. For

And then, in a slightly more romantic vein, Dillon played the Caucasian contingent in *Golden Gate*, an interracial love story co-starring Joan Chen.

FILMOGRAPHY

1989: *Over the Edge*. 1980: *Little Darlings*; *My Bodyguard*. 1981: *Liar's Moon*. 1982: *The Great American Fourth of July and Other Disasters* (TV); *Tex*. 1983: *The Outsiders*; *RumbleFish*. 1984: *The Flamingo Kid*. 1985: *Target*; *Rebel*. 1986: *Native Son*. 1987: *The Big Town*; *Dear America* (voice only). 1988: *Kansas*; *Bloodhounds of Broadway*. 1989: *Drugstore Cowboy*. 1991: *A Kiss Before Dying*; *Women & Men 2: In Love There Are No Rules* (TV). 1992: *Singles*; *Malcolm X* (cameo); *The Saint of Fort Washington*; *Mr Wonderful*. 1994: *Golden Gate*; *To Die For*.

Robert DOWNEY Jr

Everybody in Hollywood knew Robert Downey Jr had the talent. James Woods, who co-starred with him in *True Believer*, vouchsafed: 'Bob is the finest of the young actors. He really has that magic gift. I think I'm going to adopt him.' Dan Grodnik, producer on Downey's *1969*, went further: 'Robert's gonna be a big star. He's got the face, he's got the talent, and he's got the style.' Producer Scott Rudin echoed: 'I think of all his peers, Robert seems to be the one with the widest range and the most natural electricity. Very few actors have that combination of mercurial energy and emotional depth. He's now the guy that everybody in Hollywood wants.'

And yet Robert Downey Jr was at a standstill. He had paid his dues in a rollcall of dud movies, playing flash young punks. He had shown his comedic prowess on the cult TV revue *Saturday Night Live*. He had a semi-famous girlfriend, Sarah Jessica Parker, and he lived in a big house in Hollywood Hills built specially for Charlie Chaplin. And yet . . .

In 1989 he told one journalist, 'I'm not going to work again until there's something that I'm really passionate about. I don't want to be thought of as someone who does progressively less good work because he's sort of just caught up in the flow.' He also acknowledged that, 'I'm just in the foetal stages as an actor.'

In 1990, Downey Jr slowed his workaholism down to a walking pace. He made one film: *Air America*. It had 'hit' written all over it. Not only did it have a blockbusting budget, it was a two-hander which gave Downey an opportunity to bounce off one of the most popular men in Christendom

Robert Downey Jr

Downey Jr with Mel Gibson in *Air America*

(Mel Gibson). It also took him to Cannes, where he got to meet other big stars and where Arnold Schwarzenegger introduced him to Maria Shriver as Rob Lowe. All in all, it was a sobering experience. And, when the film opened on August 10, it couldn't compete against *Flatliners* and *Ghost*, and quickly vanished from cinemas. He then resigned himself to another dud, *Into the Sun*, and a supporting role in *Soapdish*, which failed to produce much of a lather.

Then Richard Attenborough cast him in the title role of *Chaplin*, the part of a lifetime. Attenborough, who described Downey as 'an extraordinary boy,' predicted, 'he'll be a world figure as an actor within a month of the film opening. 'Boasting a budget of more than $30 million, *Chaplin* had a supporting cast to die for: Dan Aykroyd, Geraldine Chaplin, Anthony Hopkins, Kevin Kline, Diane Lane, Penelope Ann Miller, James Woods and more. However, Downey, in spite of 22 films to his credit, was still considered an 'unknown'. And Attenborough wanted it that way. 'If you bring in a star, someone with other connotations,' the director argued, 'you start with a disadvantage.' But, Downey countered, 'My worry is – what do I do after this?'

Robert Downey Jr was born on 4 April

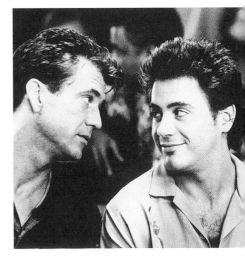

1965, in New York City, the son of an actress/singer and the independent filmmaker Robert Downey. At the age of five, he made his screen debut playing a puppy in his father's bizarre *Pound*. His first words on celluloid were: 'Got any hair on your balls?' The experience was not a happy one, and the child swore he would never act again, and appeared two years later in Downey Snr's *Greaser's Palace*. He also popped up in his father's *Jive* and *Up the Academy*, moved to Los Angeles at 15, and then dropped out of school (Santa Monica High) in the eleventh grade. Moving back to New York, he waited tables, worked as a shoe salesman

Downey Jr showing his flare for comedy with Cathy Moriarty in Michael Hoffman's hilarious *Soapdish*

Robert Downey Jr as Charlie Chaplin

and filled in as 'living art' in a SoHo nightclub (in an orange space suit). He then landed his first film without a parent, John Sayles's *Baby, It's You.*

'I think I had three weeks' work on it,' the actor recalls. 'I had scenes with Rosanna Arquette and I talked wild shit to everyone about how I was the next Dustin Duvall. Then they cut those scenes out, and I was in only one scene, being blocked by a very eager young actress leaning across the lens. So you can see me for just a second. My friends called it *Maybe It's You.'*

There was then a string of small parts in small movies, before Downey Jr made an impact in the Rodney Dangerfield hit *Back to School*, playing Keith Gordon's whacky sidekick. He was also honing his comedic skills (and writing sketches) on *Saturday Night Live*, alongside his pal Anthony Michael Hall (they met on *Weird Science*), Joan Cusack, Jon Lovitz, Randy Quaid and Damon Wayans. Then he gave his best performance yet in the title role of the Warren Beatty-produced *The Pick-Up Artist.* As the wise-cracking womanizer who chases Molly Ringwald, he was the best thing in a very bland movie.

He also won the kindest reviews in the poorly received *Less Than Zero*, a story of everyday alienated Yuppies, based on the cult novel by Brett Easton Ellis. Downey was the Beverly Hills cocaine addict, Julian, and gave a bravura performance of naked despair. There were two more disappointments – the execrable teen comedy *Johnny Be Good*, with Anthony Michael Hall; and Downey Snr's

virtually unreleased *Rented Lips*, a porno spoof. There was also the self-indulgent *1969*, a nostalgic tale of disenchanted youth with Kiefer Sutherland and Winona Ryder, followed by the highly entertaining *True Believer.* In the latter, Downey played an idealistic lawyer assisting James Woods in a murder case, but the film failed to secure a theatrical release in Britain. So did *Chances Are*, a romantic fantasy with Downey as the reincarnated love of Cybill Shepherd. Still, he won billing over Ryan O'Neal and Mary Stuart Masterson, which was some indication of his growing stature in the industry.

This led to *Air America*, an enjoyable action-adventure set in South-East Asia. Downey co-starred as an LA traffic cop transported to Laos to illegally airlift heroin on behalf of the CIA. Essentially a buddy-buddy movie, with Downey and Mel Gibson a charismatic duo, the film ultimately failed to exploit its explosive subject matter. Following the farcical *Too Much Sun*, he was hilarious as David Barnes, the unctuous, libidinous TV producer in *Soapdish*, a riotous comedy.

Wearing dark-rimmed glasses and a lustful stare, he more than held his own in the midst of a top-notch cast: Sally Field, Kevin Kline, Whoopi Goldberg, Cathy Moriarty, Kathy Najimy et al. The film should have been an enormous hit. It wasn't. Then came *Chaplin.*

Downey, a controversial choice for the title role in the long-awaited biog, exceeded all expectations. Thanks to an uncanny make-up job, he was the spitting image of Chaplin, complete with the mournful, lazy eyes and fleshy cheeks. He had the physical grace, the elastic motion, the melancholy stare. Even his accent was consistently English, even though, on occasions, it slid across a few London streets (in one sentence). But even so, it was hard to picture *anybody* who could have been so perfect. The critics agreed, and in a year (1992) replete with stellar perfor-mances, Robert Downey Jr was nominated for an Oscar.

He then joined the all-star cast in *Short Cuts*, Robert Altman's ensemble piece based on the short stories of Raymond Carver. After that, he took the lead in Ron Underwood's *Heart and Souls*, supported by Charles Grodin, Kyra Sedgwick and Alfre Woodard.

1992 was also the year that Downey married the actress Deborah Falconer, whom he had known for some years. The wedding was quick, quiet and painless, just the way Downey wanted it.

There is one story that sums up the street savvy and smarts of Robert Downey Jr. He was visiting the set of the vampire spoof *Buffy the Vampire Slayer* and was introduced to its star, Luke Perry (whose fan mail was then a serious threat to the American postal system). Surveying Perry from head to toe, Downey looked up, much impressed, and said, 'So, you're *the* man in town now – *the* guy.' Then, pausing for a second to let this praise sink in, Downey snapped, 'Get *over* it.' To this day Perry is a fan.

FILMOGRAPHY

1970: *Pound.* 1972: *Greaser's Palace.* 1976: *Jive.* 1980: *Up the Academy.* 1982: *Baby, It's You.* 1984: *Firstborn.* 1985: *Weird Science*; *To Live and Die in LA*; *Tuff Turf.* 1986: *America* (filmed in 1982); *Back to School.* 1987: *Dear America* (voice only); *The Pick-Up Artist*; *Less Than Zero.* 1988: *Johnny Be Good*; *Rented Lips*; *1969*; *True Believer* (UK: *Fighting Justice*). 1989: *Chances Are*; *That's Adequate.* 1990: *Air America.* 1991: *Too Much Sun*; *Soapdish.* 1992: *Chaplin.* 1993: *The Last Party* (documentary); *Short Cuts*; *Heart and Souls.* 1994: *Natural Born Killers*; *Just In Time*; *Restoration.*

teenage son of Richard Crenna and Patty Duke Astin, and then established himself as the chief geek in *Revenge of the Nerds*. 'We all knew the *Nerds* film was shameless,' the actor owns up. 'It was a really silly script, but the reason it was successful was because we were all honest about it.' It was so successful, in fact, that it spawned a sequel, in which Edwards took a guest role.

He played the best friend (John Cusack's) in Rob Reiner's delightful teen romance *The Sure Thing*, and then, on TV, took the title role of the champion downhill skier in *Going For the Gold — The Bill Johnson Story*, with Dennis Weaver and Sarah Jessica Parker in support. But it was the next two films that sealed his stardom.

In *Gotcha!* he skewered top-billing as the amiable college kid who finds himself embroiled in an espionage plot in Paris — thanks to femme fatale Linda Fiorentino. The movie was no masterpiece, but it was an enjoyable bit of hokum that was well played.

Anthony EDWARDS

Anthony Edwards was a likeable, all-purpose leading man who bore a passing resemblance to a young Jeff Bridges. He could appear witty without being obvious, and made a passable hero when the occasion called for it. However, few of his films won a theatrical release in Britain.

Born on 19 July 1963 in Santa Barbara, California, Anthony Edwards was the youngest of five children. His maternal grandfather was an artist who worked for Cecil B. De Mille at Paramount in the 1930s and who helped design Walt Disney's new studio. His mother was also an artist and his father an architect, but Anthony himself became frustrated whenever he tackled a pencil.

Instead, he submerged himself into the theatre programme at Santa Barbara High and at the Santa Barbara Youth Theatre. By the time he emerged from high school he had appeared in 30 shows, mostly musicals. His idols were Gene Kelly and Joel Grey (and, apparently, hardware shops). 'From the time I was 11 until I was 17, I did theatre,' he swears. 'It was all I ever wanted to do.' At 16 he started acting professionally, swatting up on camera technique from his appearances in

Anthony Edwards as cancer victim Decker (with Camille Coduri) in the disappointing *Hawks*

Apocalypse 1989: Anthony Edwards in *Miracle Mile*

dozens of commercials. He also hung out with fellow future star Eric Stoltz, the pair of them ducking into movie theatres and paying children's admission prices due to their short statures (later, he climbed to 6'2").

A fan of Olivier, Richardson and O'Toole, Edwards took a 1980 summer workshop at RADA and followed it up with two years at the University of Southern California. After that he won a small role in the acclaimed, true-life TV movie *The Killing of Randy Webster* (playing Webster's friend), alongside other budding stars Jennifer Jason Leigh and Sean Penn. The three of them re-united for Cameron's Crowe's successful *Fast Times at Ridgemont High* (in which Edwards played Penn's dopehead sidekick), after which he followed with a bigger part in another celebrated movie, *Heart Like a Wheel*.

He turned to television with 23 episodes of the sitcom *It Takes Two*, playing Andy, the

Edwards then took fourth-billing in a film dedicated more to fighter jets than actors, but stole the notices while the film soared into box-office heaven. Edwards played the easy-going Lieutenant Nick Bradshaw – 'Goose' to his friends – the ultimately tragic pilot who valued his wife and son above his testosterone level. The film was *Top Gun* – the highest grosser of 1986 – and the actress

who played his wife was an unknown called Meg Ryan. She was also his girlfriend at the time.

The film's success naturally led to more leading roles, but the next three were all disappointments. *Summer Heat* was a turgid rural drama with Lori Singer; *Hawks* a misguided black comedy with Timothy Dalton, shot in London and Amsterdam; and *Miracle Mile*, an overly sincere romance set during nuclear panic. However, Edwards was invariably good value for money.

His next picture, *Mr North*, was another box-office flop, but a delightful curio for all that. Based on Thornton Wilder's novel *Theophilus North*, the film was shot for under $4 million by Danny Huston, whose illustrious father, John, served as co-scripter and executive producer. Sadly, the elder Huston was to die before completion of the film, but a wonderful cast rallied round to show support: Robert Mitchum (replacing Huston Snr), Lauren Bacall, Anjelica Huston, Mary Stuart Masterson, Virginia Madsen . . . Edwards was totally engaging in the title role, playing a young academic whose surplus of personal electricity leads the community of Newport, Rhode Island, to mistake him for a faith healer. Enchanting whimsy.

Unfortunately, it was downhill from there. Over the ensuing years Anthony Edwards found himself in a roster of pictures that saw

Edwards in one of his best roles, as *Mr North*

Edwards with Anjelica Huston in *Mr North*

little light of day: the teen comedy *How I Got Into College*; *Downtown*, a police melodrama with Forest Whitaker; *El Diablo*, a TV western with Louis Gossett Jr; and a TV fable about the sins of lying, *Hometown Boy Makes Good*.

In 1992, the star reached a new low when he accepted second-billing to child actor Edward Furlong in the horror sequel *Pet Sematary Two*. Still, it wasn't as bad as its predecessor (which wasn't hard) – although nobody turned up to find out. He then starred in the one-hour TV special *Sexual Healing*, as a lonely man who falls in love with an unhappily married woman (Mare Winningham) through a telephone sex line.

FILMOGRAPHY

1981: *The Killing of Randy Webster* (TV). 1982: *Fast Times at Ridgemont High*; *Heart Like a Wheel*. 1984: *Revenge of the Nerds*. 1985: *The Sure Thing*; *Going For the Gold – The Bill Johnson Story* (TV); *Gotcha!*. 1986: *Top Gun*. 1987: *Revenge of the Nerds II: Nerds in Paradise*; *Summer Heat*. 1988: *Hawks*; *Miracle Mile*; *Mr North*. 1989: *How I Got Into College*. 1990: *Downtown*; *El Diablo* (TV); *Hometown Boy Makes Good* (TV). 1992: *Delta Heat*; *Pet Sematary Two*. 1993: *Sexual Healing* (TV). 1994: *The Client*.

Emilio ESTEVEZ

As the phenomenon of the Brat Pack gathered momentum, three seminal films were held responsible: *The Outsiders*, *The Breakfast Club* and *St Elmo's Fire*. Emilio Estevez was in all of them.

In the space of two years Estevez was seen on screen wrestling with Tom Cruise, defending Molly Ringwald's honour and knocking back beers with Rob Lowe. Although he vehemently rejected the Brat Pack label, he was the living embodiment of it. He established considerable notoriety as a ladies' man, his best friends included fellow Packers Cruise, Lowe and Sean Penn, he was engaged to Demi Moore, and he spent more hours at LA's Hard Rock Cafe than was good for him. He was, in the words of the media, a hellraiser.

Later, the star rationalised, 'We were just guys being guys. We'd meet to let off a little steam, that was all. We all have to grow up.' His father, the actor Martin Sheen, took up the defence: 'They were just kids with a sense of humour.' Cruise was more succinct: 'It was just something the press made up.'

Nevertheless, the overt carousing helped keep Emilio's name in the papers – and, subsequently, in the public's mind. He was,

The star as a young writer: Emilio Estevez on the set of *That Was Then, This is Now*

Young man with a gun: Emilio with co-star Richard Dreyfuss in one of his biggest hits, *Stakeout*

Same man, more guns: Emilio as Billy the Kid in Geoff Murphy's *Young Guns II – Blaze of Glory*

however, an unlikely star. He was short (5'6"), he lacked the drop-dead good looks of Rob Lowe, the bravura acting talent of Tom Cruise and the innate sex-appeal of Matt Dillon. He was more often surly than smouldering, and was hardly charismatic. Also, he had the misfortune (or poor judgement) to star in an impressive chain of box-office stiffs (*Nightmares*, *Maximum Overdrive*, *Wisdom*, *Men at Work*, *Freejack*).

He was equally unlucky with films that never materialized. For instance, he was due to play the man who organized the 1969 Woodstock rock festival – in Warner Brothers' *Young Men With Unlimited Capital*. But, according to leaked reports, the film never got made because of billing disputes between Estevez and his co-star, Ralph Macchio. He was then announced to direct *Clear Intent*, from his own screenplay – but, apparently, good intentions did not a movie make. Other projects – *El Nino*, with Martin Sheen directing; *Ask the Dust*, for French filmmaker Daniel Vigne; and *Secret Society*, again with father – all fell through.

Emilio Estevez's personal life was no more successful. The model Carey Salley sued the actor for palimony and child support, claiming he was the father of her two children, Taylor and Paloma. At the time, Emilio publicly denied his paternity, although court records revealed that he had been paying Salley $3,000 a month. She wanted more like $15,000. Meanwhile, Martin Sheen arranged for Taylor's baptism and provided extra financial support for his daughter-out-

law. Estevez refused to talk about 'this personal stuff,' but that was then. Now, he acknowledges, 'You turn your back on your kids and eventually you're going to regret it.'

There was also the Demi Moore situation. The couple met while filming *St Elmo's Fire*, fell in love, set the wedding date for 6 December 1986, and sent out the invitations. Demi then had second thoughts, claiming that 'we were at two different junctures of our internal lives.' After a four-month courtship, she married Bruce Willis.

Emilio's romance with make-up artist Sheryl Berkoff was equally ill-fated. She ended up marrying Rob Lowe. Says Estevez: 'There's an unwritten rule between guys who are friends – you *don't* go out with your buddy's ex-girlfriend. And you certainly don't marry her.'

On a positive note, Emilio Estevez does go down in the history books as the youngest Hollywood star to write his own script – for *That Was Then, This is Now*. The film also showcased his most powerful, bravura performance to date (and one of the best of the year, 1985), playing a rebel without a pause who competes with his best friend (Craig Sheffer) for the affections of a girl (Kim Delaney).

On the strength of this, he entered the history books again as the youngest writer-

director-star of a movie, but this time found himself a victim of the critics. The trade paper *Variety* wrote, '*Wisdom* marks 23-year-old actor Emilio Estevez's directorial debut – and it shows,' adding that the film suffered from 'a completely implausible script and unending sophomoric dialogue.' Estevez countered this with, 'fuck the critics – because they tried to really break me down, and the only thing it did was make me stronger.' Nevertheless, he also admits, 'after *Wisdom*'s release, I was devastated. If I'm watching TV now and the movie comes on, the first thing I do is change the channel to CNN.' Incidentally, the film co-starred Demi Moore.

Emilio's relationship with the press has never been an easy one. He has seemed easy prey. The media had a field day in 1992 when the star allegedly fired actress-model Kathy Ireland from his film *National Lampoon's Loaded Weapon 1* – because, it was reported, she was five inches taller than he. The story goes that he was invited to stand on a box, but turned the offer down. As it happens, the entire scenario was made up by the tabloids.

His loathe-hate relationship with the media is an old battle. When *Life* magazine presented a lavish feature on showbusiness families, he refused to endorse the article, leaving his father and siblings (Charlie Sheen, Ramon and Renee Estevez) to frolic happily for the camera on their own. Emilio Estevez is reluctant to acknowledge any debts.

'I'm much more ambitious than my father,' he has said. 'What I've got from him is the idea that, if I kept my feet firmly planted on the ground, I could achieve whatever I wanted. Everything that's come to me I've earned. I haven't been given stardom. I'm not a pretty boy who was told, "We're going to make you a star." '

Born Emilio Sheen on May 12 1962, in New York City, the actor adopted his father's original (Spanish) surname as his first statement of independence. He wanted to act for as long as he could remember, and as a young teen made Super 8 films with his two brothers and boyhood friends Sean and Christopher Penn and Rob and Chad Lowe.

At the age of 20 he starred opposite his father in the highly-acclaimed TV movie *In the Custody of Strangers*, playing a 16-year-old imprisoned on a charge of drunken behaviour. He then made his theatrical debut in *Tex*, based on the cult novel by S.E. Hinton. On the set, he met the author, who suggested he would make the perfect Mark Jennings, the protagonist of her book *That Was Then, This is Now*. So he optioned the rights.

After he made his name in the surreal *Repo Man* (playing an uncharismatic punk who repossesses cars) – and did time on the Brat Pack trilogy – he embarked on *That Was Then . . . .* 'I thought I'd hire a writer to adapt the novel,' he explained, 'but I had some time on my hands, so I wrote a draft.'

It was a good draft, but it was the fourth adaptation of a Hinton novel and the public

had tired of the familiar tale of the outsider fighting for his rights. The film was not a success.

Success *did* arrive, although belatedly, with John Badham's *Stakeout*, a ferociously entertaining buddy-cop saga strong on romance, laughs and action. Richard Dreyfuss and Estevez played the cops, who stakeout the girlfriend (Madeleine Stowe) of a vicious killer (Aidan Quinn). Estevez's role was originally intended for an older actor ('they were thinking of a James Garner type,' he says) but, per the film's producer, Cathleen Summers, 'once we had decided to play around with their ages, we immediately thought of Emilio.'

Comedy was certainly a change of pace for the actor, and the practical jokes he and Dreyfuss got up to were a joy to behold. Nevertheless, it *was* Dreyfuss's picture.

Another success was the 'Brat Pack' Western *Young Guns*, with Estevez top-billed as a nauseatingly cocky Billy the Kid. But, again, the actor was diluted by his co-stars (Kiefer Sutherland, Lou Diamond Phillips, Charlie Sheen, Terence Stamp, Jack Palance). He had the lead in an excellent TV movie, *Nightbreaker*, as a naive doctor who witnesses government atomic testing (Martin Sheen played the same character in later years), and then directed (and scripted) himself and Charlie Sheen in the risible comedy *Men at Work* (they played garbagemen who stumble on a murder). *Young Guns II – Blaze of Glory*, directed by Geoff Murphy, turned out to be better than the original, although Estevez was even *more* irritating as the cackling outlaw.

In Geoff Murphy's big-budget *Freejack*,

Armed to the teeth: Emilio takes on a volley of bad jokes in *National Lampoon's Loaded Weapon 1*

based on Robert Sheckley's notable sci-fi novel *Immortality, Inc.*, Estevez proved he was not the stuff of macho heroism, and the film's limited glory went to co-star Mick Jagger as the heavy. He was more appealing as an arrogant lawyer forced to coach a children's ice hockey team in *The Mighty Ducks*, but the film was predictable and bland – albeit his biggest solo commercial success. In the US, *The Mighty Ducks* went on to gross over $50 million. Estevez then tried comedy again, playing the 'Mel Gibson' part in *National Lampoon's Loaded Weapon 1*, a spoof of *Lethal Weapon*, *The Silence of the Lambs* and *Basic Instinct*. Samuel L. Jackson co-starred as 'Danny Glover', with such ready hams as Tim Curry and William Shatner in support. The film opened well, grossing $11m in its first week, but quickly lost steam. After that, Estevez continued his spate of workaholism and went straight on to star in *Judgment Night*, a tough thriller about four young guys who witness a mob killing (have you noticed that there are *always* witnesses at a mob killing?). He then rejoined Richard Dreyfuss and director John Badham for *Another Stakeout*.

If, on the whole, Emilio Estevez's career

Still trigger-happy, Emilio top-bills in Geoff Murphy's futuristic flop, *Freejack*

looks like a disaster area, it is not through lack of talent. He demonstrated his potential with the complexity and power of his performance in *That Was Then, This is Now*. He was also excellent as the pressurized jock in *The Breakfast Club*, and showed some flair for comedy in *St Elmo's Fire*. Personally, he now seems more at ease with himself, and is less outspoken in front of the press. By all accounts, he is also a committed father to Taylor and Paloma.

On April 29 1992, at the ripe old age of 29, Emilio Estevez finally declared his conjugal vows to Paula Abdul, the rock star one year his junior (and four inches shorter). The couple, who had been dating for five months and were engaged that February, married spontaneously and secretly in Santa Monica, California, surprising their friends, the media and even Paula's mother. On September 19 they splashed out on a second ceremony (reportedly costing $200,000), and invited the whole family and their intimates (although Tom Cruise and his wife Nicole Kidman chose not to show up, much to the amusement of the media).

FILMOGRAPHY

1982: *In the Custody of Strangers* (TV); *Tex*. 1983: *The Outsiders*; *Nightmares*. 1984: *Repo Man*. 1985: *The Breakfast Club*; *St Elmo's Fire*; *That Was Then, This Is Now* (also scripted). 1986: *Maximum Overdrive*; *Wisdom* (also directed and scripted). 1987: *Stakeout*. 1988: *Young Guns*. 1989: *Nightbreaker* (TV). 1990: *Men at Work* (also directed and scripted); *Young Guns II – Blaze of Glory*. 1992: *Freejack*; *The Mighty Ducks* (UK: *Champions*). 1993: *National Lampoon's Loaded Weapon 1*; *Judgment Night*; *Another Stakeout*. 1994: *D2: The Mighty Ducks*; *The War at Home* (also directed).

Jeff FAHEY

In the late 1980s and early 1990s, Jeff Fahey displayed the hottest matinee idol looks around. With a chiselled jawline and pale blue eyes to die for, he was your prototypical leading man – albeit without a hit movie. Ironically, in his most successful film yet – the 'virtual reality' thriller *The Lawnmower Man* – he played a chap with the mental age of a six-year-old saddled with a fright wig. Not the sort of role to launch next year's heartthrob. In fact, it was co-star Pierce Brosnan who probably benefited most from the film's high profile (another irony: Fahey and Brosnan look remarkably alike, and could easily swap careers).

The man with the see-through eyes: Jeff Fahey in Clint Eastwood's *White Hunter, Black Heart*

Jeff Fahey in *Iron Maze*

Jeff Fahey (pronounce that Fay-hee), one of 13 children of Irish-American parents, was born on 29 November 1956 in Olean, New York. When he was ten, the family moved to Buffalo and Jeff attended two local schools until graduation in 1972. After hitchhiking to Alaska, he travelled round the world – backpacking in Europe, working on a kibbutz in Israel and celebrating his 19th birthday in

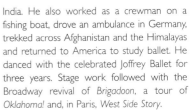

India. He also worked as a crewman on a fishing boat, drove an ambulance in Germany, trekked across Afghanistan and the Himalayas and returned to America to study ballet. He danced with the celebrated Joffrey Ballet for three years. Stage work followed with the Broadway revival of *Brigadoon*, a tour of *Oklahoma!* and, in Paris, *West Side Story*.

On TV, he played Gary Corelli for two and a half years in the daytime soap *One Life To Live*, and made his film debut in Lawrence Kasdan's epic western *Silverado* – as Tyree – whom he later named his own production company after. Back on TV, he starred in *The Execution of Raymond Graham*, playing the convicted killer of the title, and a year later began his film career in earnest.

In the jokey *Psycho III* he was the young male lead, as Duane, an aspiring musician holed up at the Bates Motel, and then starred in *Backfire*, a classy film noir thriller. In the latter he played Donny McAndrew, a Vietnam vet plagued by recurring nightmares and Keith Carradine. In *Split Decisions*, he was Gene Hackman's son, an arrogant boxer; won top-billing (for the first time) in *True Blood*, a routine crime drama with Fahey falsely accused of killing a cop; and then

Jeff Fahey in his biggest hit yet, as *The Lawnmower Man*

starred in *Out of Time*, a British-Egyptian romantic adventure in which he played a zealous archaeologist who discovers a rare bust of Alexander the Great. In the Australian family western *Outback* he portrayed a mysterious American business-man, and then joined Brian Dennehy as one of *The Last of the Finest*, honest LA cops battling a government conspiracy (borrowing its plot from the Iran-Contra affair).

In *Impulse*, directed by Clint Eastwood's former actress girlfriend Sondra Locke, he played an assistant DA who teams up with undercover cop Theresa Russell; and then won good reviews in the TV movie *Parker Kane*, as a gutsy ex-policeman uncovering a toxic waste-dumping scam. In spite of his obvious demand, Jeff Fahey was still a star without a hit picture. This finally arrived with Clint Eastwood's *White Hunter, Black Heart*, a critically revered look at the making of John Huston's *The African Queen*. A success at Cannes, the film starred Eastwood (who also directed) as a recalcitrant filmmaker more interested in shooting elephants than film. Fahey played Pete Verill, the director's biographer, from whose point of view the story is told. Eastwood made a brave stab at character acting, but lacked the vocal depth needed to capture the charisma of the man. Ironically, it was Fahey himself who supplied the movie's greatest magnetism, the actor's weathered good looks making him an ideal candidate for any John Huston movie.

It was back to low-budget mediocrity with the Japanese-produced whodunit *Iron Maze*, with Bridget Fonda, and then a better-than-average TV movie, *Iran: Days of Crisis*, an impressive co-production from America, Britain and France. Fahey co-starred as presidential aide Hamilton Jordan, on whose book the film was based, observing the Iranian revolution through American eyes. *Body Parts* was not good, a tired re-working of the old killer limb routine (remember Michael Caine in *The Hand*?), but then *The Lawnmower Man* saved the day. At least, the latter was a box-office success, thanks to some spectacular computer graphics. Jeff Fahey had the title role, a gardener and village idiot who becomes a supernatural threat when a game of 'virtual reality' unleashes hidden powers in his brain.

This was followed by *Sketch Artist*, another 'B-movie', but one deserving more attention than it received. Fahey had the title role, an LA police artist who sketches suspects from eye-witness memory. Things hot up considerably when witness Drew Barrymore describes Fahey's wife (Sean Young) as the suspect leaving the scene of a brutal murder. Fahey was never better as a man descending into a personal hell, a hero with demons to hide. If the actor's prospects were based on *Sketch Artist* alone, Fahey should be a major star very, very soon.

Next, he was joined by Bo Derek and Robert Mitchum aboard a luxury yacht in the erotic mystery-thriller *Woman of Desire*, and then popped up in Rick King's *Quick*, with Martin Donovan. After that, he played a bodyguard in the thriller *The Hit List*, co-starring James Coburn.

FILMOGRAPHY

1985: *Silverado*; *The Execution of Raymond Graham* (TV). **1986:** *Psycho III*. **1987:** *Backfire*. **1988:** *Split Decisions*. **1989:** *True Blood* (aka *Edge of Darkness*); *Out of Time*; *Outback*. **1990:** *The Last of the Finest* (UK: *Blue Heat*); *Impulse*; *Parker Kane* (TV); *White Hunter, Black Heart*. **1991:** *Iron Maze*; *Iran: Days of Crisis* (TV); *Body Parts*. **1992:** *The Lawnmower Man*; *Sketch Artist*. **1993:** *Woman of Desire*; *Quick* (UK: *Crossfire*); *The Hit List*; *In the Company of Darkness*; *Freefall*. **1994:** *Wyatt Earp*; *Temptation*.

Bridget FONDA

Just because your father is Peter Fonda, your aunt is Jane Fonda and your grandfather is Henry Fonda doesn't mean you're going to be a star. Just because you're beautiful and you don't have to go through aerobic hell to own a lissom body doesn't mean you're going to be a star. Just because you're surrounded by artistic forces with all the right contacts doesn't mean you're going to be a star. Of course, it helps.

Bridget Fonda's lineage, she admits, 'may have affected me slightly, but only because I grew up around creative people.' But, 'in high school I got into a play, and I *knew*. I felt it right away.'

Sometimes, however, she admits, 'I wish my dad was maybe a bum actor or something like that. It would have made it a lot easier for me.' And, on the subject of her famous aunt, Bridget asks, 'Wouldn't you be insecure if she were *your* aunt? I saw her one Christmas and she told me that I have no

Bridget Fonda practices her art in Zelda Barron's *Shag*

muscle tone in my thighs!' Adding: 'I've never worked out to any of Jane's videos. I have a hole in my heart, so I have to be careful.'

Bridget Fonda has all the credentials to be another overnight, flash-in-the-pan flavour-of-the-month. She's pretty, well connected and, well, she lives in Los Angeles. But Fonda has transcended all that, taken risks, down-played her heritage. Hell, if she's going to become a star, she's going to do it on her own terms and her decisions are going to be intelligent ones.

Turning her back on Hollywood, La Fonda honed her craft in British movies, opposite British stars (frequently John Hurt), and working with British intellects. When she was ready, she returned to LA to steal some of the plummest parts on offer.

Born in LA on 27 January 1964, Bridget had an enchanted childhood, living a carefree life of hippie liberation. Her mother, Susan (nee Brewer), was the daughter of an industrialist; her father, Peter Fonda, the star and producer of *Easy Rider*, the hippest movie of the Sixties. Until her parents' divorce in 1972, Bridget lived in California's Coldwater Canyon, and then divided her remaining formative years in Los Angeles (with Peter) and in Montana (with her mother and common-law stepfather). She and Peter would also hang out in New Mexico, letting their hair down with Dennis Hopper and *his* kid, Marin. Bridget was, the latter says, 'a tomboy in beat-up sneakers,' and was happiest riding bikes or sitting around listening to Monty Python records.

At school she appeared in a production of *Harvey* and decided to act professionally. She then moved to the East Coast to study acting at New York University and with the Lee Strasberg Theatre Institute. She also studied cinema and played the lead role in *PPT*, a graduate student film.

For a while Bridget worked in the theatre and then made her film debut (not counting a cameo in *Easy Rider*) in the British-produced *Aria*, a ten-part collection of cinematic interpretations of famous operatic pieces. John Hurt tied the pieces together as an anonymous character wandering around the deserted streets of Cremona in Italy, while Bridget made a striking impression in the seventh segment, *Tristan and Isolde*. Directed by Franc Roddam, the episode featured Fonda and James Mathers as teenage lovers who slash their wrists in a Las Vegas bathroom after a very explicit coupling.

The film was not well-received, but Bridget had turned enough heads to land the female lead in the perfectly awful *You Can't Hurry Love*, a romantic-comedy set in the LA

Fonda (*right*) with Joanne Whalley-Kilmer in *Scandal*

Bridget Fonda as Amy in David Hare's *Strapless*

singles' scene. She was better served by the British-produced *Shag*, a rites-of-passage comedy set in 1963 in Myrtle Beach, South Carolina, where four girlfriends sow their wild oats before moving on to university and/or marriage. Phoebe Cates won top-billing, but Fonda caught the spotlight as the brash, all-over erogenous zone who enters a Miss Sun Queen Pageant wearing nothing but a bikini and the American flag.

She remained in 1963 for Michael Caton-Jones's *Scandal*, the controversial, seedy take on the Profumo affair – replacing Emily Lloyd in the role of show girl and key witness Mandy Rice-Davies. John Hurt starred as the fall guy Stephen Ward, with Ian McKellen as Profumo and Joanne Whalley-Kilmer as the catalytic Christine Keeler. Although Fonda made a brave stab at her English accent, she was, on this occasion, upstaged by her British co-stars. Still, she *was* nominated for a Golden Globe award as best supporting actress.

It was her role in *Shag*, however, that caught the attention of playwright-filmmaker David Hare, who cast her in his third and best film *Strapless*. It was also Fonda's best screen performance to date. Hare's American girlfriend, Blair Brown, played a London radiotherapist courted by an

enigmatic German (Bruno Ganz), while Fonda co-starred as her rebellious younger sister, Amy. It was a plum part and Fonda executed it with verve.

'It was a strange film,' the actress concedes. 'The more you see it, the more you see. Each time there's an extra layer. I loved that movie.'

She returned to America – at least, to Rome's Cinecitta studios – to join the all-star

Trend-setting: Bridget Fonda with Matt Dillon in *Singles*

Victim of the small ads: Fonda in Barbet Schroeder's chilling *Single White Female*

For the first time with her name solo above the title: Bridget Fonda as *The Assassin*

cast of Francis Coppola's *The Godfather Part III*, playing Andy Garcia's ill-fated photo-journalist girlfriend. She stayed in Italy (in and around Milan) to play Mary Godwin Shelley opposite a time-travelling John Hurt – in Roger Corman's preposterous, heavy-handed *Frankenstein Unbound*.

Considering her European schedule, it's hard to believe that Fonda was actually living in New York at the time with her British fiancé, actor-writer Lee Drysdale (they have since separated). For him, she co-starred in *Leather Jackets* – alongside English actor Cary Elwes; and then played an incest victim-turned-murderess in Gary Winick's *Out of the Rain*; and joined Jeff Fahey as a murder suspect in *Iron Maze*, a tiresome, *Rashomon*-style whodunnit. And for her good friend Phoebe Cates she did a one-day cameo on *Drop Dead Fred* (as the girlfriend who discovers Rik Mayall staring up her skirt).

The major Hollywood studios had yet to take Jane's niece to their collective bosom, although the actress did have a neat part as a predatory Southerner in *Doc Hollywood*, opposite Michael J. Fox – but, then, it was directed by her old *Scandal* colleague Michael Caton-Jones.

The star-making turn arrived with *Single White Female*, a prestigious thriller from

Columbia Pictures with Fonda top-billed as Allison Jones, a smart, sexy computer software expert. Let down by her boyfriend, Allison advertises for a flatmate, the latter arriving in the homely shape of Hedra Carlson, played by Jennifer Jason Leigh. At first the two girls get on famously, but gradually Allison sees that Hedra is not all she says she is. Although Jason Leigh had the meatier role, it was Fonda who hogged centre stage, deftly blending her character's vulnerability with a steely inner resolve.

She played a flighty young thing in *Singles*, Cameron Crowe's perceptive look at twentysomething life in Seattle, with Fonda gooey-eyed over would-be rock star Matt Dillon. She had a guest spot in Sam Raimi's

Army of Darkness: Evil Dead 3 ('she absolutely *loves* Raimi's films,' explained Fonda's agent), and then landed the starring role (wrestling the part from Kim Basinger) in John Badham's *Point of No Return*, the Americanisation of the French hit *Nikita*. With Gabriel Byrne, Harvey Keitel and Anne Bancroft in support, Bridget Fonda was no longer the decorative sex kitten in the corner. She was a major star.

Next, she was excellent in the 'existential romantic comedy' *Bodies, Rest and Motion*, with England's Tim Roth as the boyfriend who leaves her to find a better life in Montana, only to return to wrest her from the arms of Eric Stoltz (her real boyfriend, who also produced the movie). She was then announced to star in *Camilla*, a road movie about two unlikely women (Fonda, Jessica Tandy) who set out on a journey in search of their dreams. She also took a supporting role in Bernardo Bertolucci's *Little Buddha*, with Keanu Reeves.

FILMOGRAPHY

1969: *Easy Rider* (bit). 1987: *Aria*. 1988: *Light Years*; *You Can't Hurry Love*; *Shag*. 1989: *Scandal*; *Strapless*. 1990: *The Godfather Part III*; *Leather Jackets*; *Roger Corman's Frankenstein Unbound*. 1991: *Drop Dead Fred* (cameo); *Out of the Rain*; *Iron Maze*; *Doc Hollywood*. 1992: *Singles*; *Single White Female*; *Army of Darkness: Evil Dead 3* (cameo). 1993: *Point of No Return* (UK: *The Assassin*); *Bodies,*

Rest and Motion; Little Buddha; Camilla. 1994: *It Could Happen To You; Rough Magic; The Road to Wellville.*

Jodie FOSTER

She made her professional debut aged three. At eight, she appeared in her first film. At 12, she won an Oscar nomination. At 27, an Oscar. Three years later, she won a second. At 28, she turned film director. A former child star, Jodie Foster was famous before anybody else in this book. But not only did she survive her pre-adolescent celebrity, she surpassed it. Today, she is better known and more respected than ever.

Evelyn 'Brandy' Foster was three months pregnant when she was divorced from Lucius Foster III and, on 19 November 1962, gave birth to her fourth child, Jodie, in the Bronx, New York. Strapped for money, Brandy helped pay the bills by finding advertising assignments for her son, Lucius 'Buddy' Foster IV. On one occasion, Buddy was waiting to audition for a Coppertone sun tan commercial, when Jodie, aged three, was spotted. 'Well, they decided to change the campaign,' Jodie reveals. 'They called up and said they wanted me as the Coppertone girl.' As commercials went, it was one of the most visible of the decade, showing a sun-tanned little girl with her knickers pulled down by a dog to reveal a white bottom. Ten years later that same little girl had appeared in nearly 50 commercials, eight movies and had starred in the TV series *Paper Moon*. But Jodie almost didn't make it.

She was eight when she made her film debut (as Samantha) in Disney's *Napoleon and Samantha*. Her co-stars included Michael Douglas, Will Geer and a lion called Major. Jodie recalls, 'I got too close. His mane sort

of reached around my body, he took me up by my hip, turned me sideways, and started shaking me. I thought it was an earthquake. And everybody ran away!' To this day she has the scars to remind her of the ordeal, but after a spell in hospital, she returned to work two weeks later. 'It was smarter for me to go back,' the actress rationalizes now, ' – you know, to get back on the horse that bucked me.'

On TV, she was a regular on the sitcoms *The Courtship of Eddie's Father* and *Bob and Carol and Ted and Alice*, and popped up in episodes of *Gunsmoke* and *The Partridge Family*. Also, thanks to her appearance in a number of Disney films, she had gained a reputation as a rather sweet, wholesome thing. She changed this popular view of herself when, at the age of 11, she played a streetwise, wine-guzzling ne'er-do-well in Martin Scorsese's *Alice Doesn't Live Here Anymore*. Her performance marked the arrival of a remarkably natural, major character actress and Scorsese, obviously delighted, signed her up to play a 12-year-old hooker in *Taxi Driver*.

'I had never thought of making movies as anything but a nice little hobby that I would probably give up when I was 15,' Jodie explained, ' – until *Taxi Driver*. It was the first time that someone didn't say to me, "OK, now be yourself." I was asked to create a character.'

But before she could play the part, she was submitted to four hours of psychological tests at the insistence of the California State Welfare Department as, in her words, 'they had to see if my morals would hold up during filming.' Adding: 'Kids talk like sailors today – and adults just don't want to know.'

1976 was a good year. *The Washington Post* declared her 'a prodigious movie talent in the making,' and for her role in *Taxi Driver* she was voted best supporting actress by The National Society of Film Critics and The Los Angeles Film Critics. She was also bestowed with an Oscar nomination.

Taxi Driver was just one of three Jodie Foster films screened at the Cannes Film Festival that year. There was also Alan Parker's kid musical *Bugsy Malone*, in which she played Tallulah, a sexy nightclub singer; and the Canadian thriller *The Little Girl Who Lives Down the Lane*, in which she portrayed a pint-sized killer. For the latter she was

Jodie Foster with Robert De Niro in *Taxi Driver* for which she was nominated for an Oscar

Jodie Foster with Rob Lowe in Tony Richardson's *Hotel New Hampshire*

required to undress for the camera, but the idea so repulsed her that her older sister, Connie, supplied the flesh. Jodie carped, 'I didn't think people wanted to see a girl my age naked.'

Her mother disagreed. As Jodie returned to the Disney stable to make such routine family pictures as *Freaky Friday* and *Candleshoe*, Evelyn Foster was pushing her daughter for the role of Vickie La Motta in Scorsese's *Raging Bull*. She decided that Jodie needed to prove her sex appeal, and so signed up photographer Emilio Lari to take some revealing pictures. According to Lari the actress 'was dead set against doing it. But she was only 15, after all. And she only came round after a lot of persuasion from her mother. But I thought, "Oh, my God, I'm in trouble." You see, Jodie was just a small fat baby, not very attractive or sexy.'

Nevertheless, the photographs were taken, and years later came back to haunt the actress as they circulated the tabloids and girlie magazines. But she didn't win the role in *Raging Bull*, a film that was later voted best picture of the decade by the critics.

In 1980, Jodie Foster gave up acting to go to college. No ordinary college, of course. She went to Yale University, where she studied literature (in particular, African-

But her career was in a slump. In the virtually unseen *O'Hara's Wife*, she was billed beneath Ed Asner and Maritte Hartley; she turned producer with an absurd Anglo-Australian-New Zealand costumer *Mesmerized*, another dud; and had a meagre role in the dreadful *Siesta*. In the last-named she played a lascivious English socialite, and was required to lick Julian Sands all over. He later became her boyfriend.

She was good in *Five Corners*, an unusual British-financed drama set in the Bronx in 1964, with Tim Robbins and John Turturro; but was wasted in the wordy, muddled *Stealing Home*, as Mark Harmon's dead girlfriend (but she was great in the flashbacks).

When Kelly McGillis turned down the role of Sarah Tobias, the rape victim in Jonathan Kaplan's *The Accused*, Foster moved in for the kill. 'I did everything I could to get it,' the actress reveals. The film's producers, Stanley Jaffe and Sherry Lansing, could not see Foster in the role, but after gentle nudging from Kaplan agreed to let her screen test. She got it. And she got the part.

The Accused was the film Jodie Foster had been waiting for. Although second-billed to McGillis (who played Sarah's icy attorney), Foster dominated the drama as the real-life good-time Charlene who flirts the night away in a seedy bar and then gets gang-raped on a pin-ball machine. The scene was harrowing to watch, and a nightmare to play. Kaplan reported that, 'it was horrendous and really traumatized people. Actors were breaking down in tears. What Jodie said to me was, "Look, I'm going to be upset, OK, but don't worry about me. Your job is to take care of everyone else."' The scene took five days to film, but Jodie remembered little of the ordeal, with only her cuts and bruises to remind her.

On 29 March 1989, Jodie Foster ran up to the podium at the Hollywood Academy Awards, and, grasping her Oscar, relayed, 'This is such a big deal – and my life is so simple. There are very few things. There is love, and work, and family . . .' She praised her mother and thanked her for 'making all my finger paintings seem like Picassos.'

Next, she starred in the wildly entertaining, eccentric thriller *Backtrack*, and was excellent as a sexy, doughty 'neon artist' hunted down and then romanced by Mafia hitman Dennis Hopper. Hopper also directed, but had his name removed from the credits when the producers re-cut his finished product. Foster ducked behind the camera herself and wrote and directed a short piece called *Hands of Time*, which was

American works). 'I always thought all actresses were stupid,' she confessed, 'and believed if I went to college I wouldn't turn out that way. But I realised what I really wanted was to be an actress and there was nothing stupid about it at all. It's like going to another country – you learn about chopsticks and all that, but what you really learn about is yourself.'

Her self-knowledge was pushed to the limit when, on 30 March 1981, John Hinckley Jr shot President Ronald Reagan outside the Hilton Hotel in Washington. He did it, he said, to impress the love of his life – Jodie Foster. He had sent countless letters to the star, followed by death threats, and claimed he had seen *Taxi Driver* 15 times. She was on campus when the news broke, and in hours she became a media sensation. Her new celebrity, and inadvertent notoriety, unearthed fresh weirdoes and one crazed fan, Michael Richardson, threatened to end her life. After an extensive search, the Secret

Jodie in her first Oscar-winning role, as rape victim Sarah Tobias in Jonathan Kaplan's disturbing *The Accused*

Service picked him up in New York City and found a loaded gun on him.

Jodie Foster was shell-shocked and retreated inside herself. Security guards followed her round campus, as did reporters and fellow students looking for a scoop. The actress resorted to drinking and on one occasion was arrested for possession of cocaine. But, in spite of these distractions, Jodie earned her BA from Yale and graduated with honours. She could also now speak Italian, and – thanks to her mother enrolling her at the Los Angeles Lycee Francaise – was fluent in French. In 1984, when she starred in Claude Chabrol's *Le Sang des Autres*, she recorded all her own dialogue.

With Charlie Sheen in Dennis Hopper's insanely enjoyable *Backtrack*

Jodie Foster in her second Oscar-winning role, as FBI trainee Clarice Sterling – in Jonathan Demme's *The Silence of the Lambs*

shown as part of the Time-Life/BBC documentary series *Americans*. This whet her appetite for bigger things, and she set about preparing her first full-length feature to direct – *Little Man Tate*. But first she needed to capitalize on her new kudos as an Oscar-winning actress.

Michelle Pfeiffer was first choice for the role of FBI trainee Clarice Sterling in Orion's *The Silence of the Lambs*, but turned it down on the grounds that she felt it 'too chilling.' Once again, Foster went into action. She tracked down the director Jonathan Demme in New York and told him she wanted to be his 'second choice.' She also revealed that, 'It's not a flashy part, not the Oscar kind of part. But I don't make movies for flashy, juicy performances. I have to find something in the story that's part of my progress, part of this little train I'm on. In order for me to spend three months on something, to understand it, it has to speak to me personally.'

In order for Clarice Sterling to hold her own against the evil charisma of the film's other major character – top psychiatrist and serial killer Dr Hannibal Lecter, played by Anthony Hopkins – the film needed a strong actress, and Foster threw herself into the role. Adopting a Southern accent, she displayed an admirable mix of steel and brain, but never lost sight of her character's human centre. Demme noted it was, 'the first part Jodie's ever played in which she hasn't had to mask her intelligence.'

In the summer of 1990, Foster buckled down to directing and starring in *Little Man Tate*, and revealed a new talent. She played

Dede Tate, a struggling waitress and single mother who finds she is rearing a seven-year-old child prodigy. Foster, a former child star and prodigy herself, knew her subject well, and produced a mature, thought-provoking work.

Following completion of the film, Orion Pictures signed the actress to a two-year, first-look agreement to star in, direct and produce films for them. Sadly, the company's subsequent cash-flow problems stymied the deal. But Jodie wasn't finished yet.

The Silence of the Lambs opened to ecstatic reviews in 1991 and went on to gross a phenomenal $130 million at the US box-office alone. 1991 also saw the actress, aged 28, receive a lifetime achievement award from the Boston Film Festival. And, later in the year, *Little Man Tate* also opened to favourable reviews.

In the spring of 1992, Jodie Foster won her second Oscar (for *Lambs*), much to the surprise of insiders, who had predicted an incontestable win for Susan Sarandon in *Thelma and Louise*. And to cement the film's victory, it went on to win Oscars for best film, best director, best actor (Hopkins) and best screenplay.

Taking to the stage for a second time, Jodie laughed loudly before announcing, 'This has been such an incredible year! I'd like to thank all of the people in this industry who have respected my choices and who have not been afraid of the power and the dignity that that entitled me to.' And, after much distribution of gratitude, the actress glowed, 'And most of all I'd like to thank my mother Brandy, my friend, the person who has loved me so much and so well that she taught me

in inimitable *Little Man Tate* fashion to fly away. Thank you.'

She then starred opposite Richard Gere in *Sommersby*, an elegant, gut-wrenching romantic drama based on the 1982 Gerard Depardieu film *The Return of Martin Guerre*. Foster played Laurel Sommersby, a woman who falls in love with her own husband (Gere) when he returns from the American Civil War after an absence of six years. However, he is so changed by his experience (for the better), that he is charged with being an imposter. Foster and Gere generated considerable chemistry during their love scenes, and in spite of its pastoral background (a box-office no-no), *Sommersby* performed well commercially.

FILMOGRAPHY

1972: *Napoleon and Samantha*; *Kansas City Bomber*; *Menace On the Mountain* (TV). 1973: *Rookie of the Year* (TV); *Tom Sawyer*; *One Little Indian*. 1974: *Smile, Jennie – You're Dead* (TV). 1975: *Alice Doesn't Live Here Anymore*. 1976: *Echoes of a Summer*; *Taxi Driver*; *Bugsy Malone*; *The Little Girl Who Lives Down the Lane*. 1977: *Freaky Friday*; *Il Casotto* (UK: *The Beach Hut*); *Moi, fleur bleue* (US: *Stop Calling Me Baby!*); *Candleshoe*. 1980: *Carny*; *Foxes*. 1983: *O'Hara's Wife*; *Svengali* (TV). 1984: *The Hotel New Hampshire*; *Le Sang des Autres* (aka *The Blood of Others*) (TV). 1986: *Mesmerized* (also co-produced). 1987: *Siesta*. 1988: *Five Corners*; *Stealing Home*; *The Accused*. 1989: *Backtrack* (UK: *Catchfire*). 1991: *The Silence of the Lambs*; *Little Man Tate* (also directed). 1992: *Shadows and Fog* (cameo). 1993: *Sommersby*. 1994: *Maverick*; *Nell* (also produced).

Michael J. FOX

In John Badham's *The Hard Way*, Michael J. Fox played an extremely successful, very popular and unimaginably rich film star who wants to be taken seriously. And so he teams up with a real-life cop (James Woods) to find out what it's *really* like on the streets of the Bronx, in order to prepare for a role that will change his image. *The Hard Way* was a fast-paced, funny and thoroughly enjoyable action-comedy full of in-jokes. In fact, it was a typical Michael J. Fox movie. Fox, who was an extremely successful, very popular and unimaginably rich film star, had himself been trying to change his image by starring in such gritty, dramatic films as *Light of Day*, *Bright Lights, Big City* and *Casualties of War*. But they had all bombed at the box-office. In short, Michael J. Fox needed to return to the genre for which he was known.

Also, *The Hard Way* surfaced during the Gulf War and at the time Fox felt, 'people desperately needed to laugh.' And, with the birth of his son Sam Michael on May 30 1989, his priorities had changed. He had a family to provide for, a new life to live. As he put it, 'To be a happy, healthy, family-orientated person is more important than trying to be the Boy Prince of Hollywood.'

But his fame was hard to escape. His Vermont wedding to actress Tracy Pollan on 16 July 1988 turned into a media circus. A *National Enquirer* journalist attempted to abduct the bride's grandparents by car to quiz them on their wedding plans. Dozens of reporters offered bribes to locals, and disguised themselves as tourists. Others camouflaged themselves in nearby woods. Six press helicopters hovered over the 'secret' ceremony. One security specialist estimated that the tabloids invested almost $250,000 in covering the wedding, but thanks to a decoy car, 'complete with tin cans tied to the fender and a slip of wedding gown caught in the door,' said Fox, they failed to get their story. Shortly afterwards, Michael J. and his new bride were recovering from the media onslaught on a private beach at Martha's Vineyard. Unbeknownst to them, a frogman emerged from the sea with a waterproof telephoto lens and took a series of photographs. The pictures appeared in publications throughout the world. The media had won after all.

But why all the attention? Well, Fox was one of those rare personalities who had successfully crossed over from TV celebrity to Hollywood glory. For seven years he starred in the sitcom *Family Ties*, for which he won three Emmy awards, the highest accolade TV can bestow. On film, he was equally successful (if not more so), starring in the highest-grossing movie of 1985, *Back to the Future*, as well as its two sequels and such hits as *Teen Wolf* and *The Secret of My Success*. In 1985 he was voted the fourth biggest box-office draw in America, and two years later was placed third (after Eddie Murphy and Michael Douglas). For the period 1989–90, according to *Forbes* magazine, he earned $33 million. Ironically, Fox was only paid $250,000 for the first *Back to the Future*, but was able to ask $5 million for each sequel. He also had a lucrative deal with Pepsi, the joys of which he promoted in a number of TV and cinema ads. Asked why he undertook such an artistically demeaning enterprise, he answered with typical self-deprecation, 'I drink it. They give it to me free, so it'd be stupid not to.'

On top of that, Fox cut a deal with

Michael J. Fox with Susan Ursitti in the 1985 *Teen Wolf*

Michael J. Fox in his most famous role, Marty McFly, in the phenomenally successful *Back to the Future*

Universal Pictures which enabled him to make his own films and to move into television production. Indeed, in 1991 he directed a segment ('The Trap') of the HBO horror omnibus *Tales From the Crypt*, which featured Bruce McGill, Bruno Kirby, Teri Garr and Carroll Baker. Later, he was due to direct the theatrical feature *Thirty Wishes*, in collaboration with Universal and his own production company, Snowback Productions. In his spare time he acted as National Chairman of Public Awareness for the Spina Bifida Association and worked on his skills as a modern father.

Michael Andrew Fox was born on 9 June 1961 in Edmonton, Canada, the fourth son (of five children) of an army officer and a payroll clerk. His childhood was fragmented, as his family moved from one army base to another, and young Michael dreamed of becoming a professional hockey player and/or a rock guitarist. While living in Vancouver, he played rhythm guitar in a local band and discovered acting. At 15, he was cast as a ten-year-old in the Canadian TV series *Leo and Me*, and more or less remained typecast for the rest of his career as a younger man than himself (he is, after all, 5'4").

At 17, he dropped out of school and started working regularly in local TV, theatre and radio. He made his film debut in the critically celebrated TV movie *Letters From Frank*, the story of a newspaper man replaced by a computer. It was his veteran co-stars, Art Carney and Maureen Stapleton, who suggested he try his luck in Hollywood and, in 1980, aged 18, Michael Fox headed south. Not long after his arrival in LA, he secured a small part in a dire Disney film, *Midnight Madness*, and became a regular on the TV series *Palmerstown USA*, playing Willie-Joe. He also auditioned for the Timothy Hutton role in *Ordinary People*, but

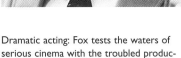

Dramatic acting: Fox tests the waters of serious cinema with the troubled production of *Bright Lights, Big City*

Fox (*left*) with Don Harvey and Sean Penn in Brian De Palma's brutal, if simplistic *Casualties of War*

clashed with the film's director, Robert Redford.

A fan of the character actor Michael J. Pollard, Fox adopted the J in his name, and started popping up in such TV fare as *Trapper John, MD* and *Lou Grant*. However, following the Screen Actors' Guild strike of 1981, he found himself in debt to the tune of $10,000. Salvation arrived in the shape of NBC's sitcom *Family Ties*, the story of caring liberal parents played by Michael Gross and Meredith Baxter Birney. Fox played their Nixon-worshipping son Alex P. Keaton, and stole the show from them.

Gary David Goldberg, the series' creator, volunteered: 'Even if Michael was onstage for just a few minutes, it was electric. We'd look around and say, "Why is the audience leaning forward?" Michael has an ability to let the audience in, to get people to breathe with him. I don't want to say we were fighting his stardom, but it wasn't what we had in mind.'

The show had been going for three years when Eric Stoltz was fired from *Back to the Future*. Although Fox was already up to his eyes in TV work, he signed on to play Marty McFly in the movie, produced by Steven Spielberg and directed by Robert Zemeckis. During the day, he worked on *Family Ties* between 10am and 6pm, and then rushed off to film *Back to the Future* until two in the morning. His schedule was exhausting, but Fox was determined not to miss out on the

opportunity of playing McFly, the affable all-American teenager transported back in time to his parents' courting days of 1955.

The film was a deserved success (it grossed $350 million worldwide) and coincided with the release of *Teen Wolf*, a low-budget comedy about a high school student who becomes a success with the girls when they discover he's a werewolf. The film's concept was more imaginative than its delivery, but Fox's amiable performance made it a hit. So much so, that it spawned an animated TV series and a sequel.

Tired of his image as a lightweight comic actor, Fox next tried something heavier – Paul Schrader's *Light of Day*, a tough Cleveland-set story of rock 'n' roll and domestic blues. However, the film was neither a critical nor a box-office success, and the only good reviews going went to co-stars Joan Jett and Gena Rowlands.

'I did *Light of Day* for the wrong reasons,' Fox admits now. 'I did it because I wanted to do something that wasn't expected of me, and I wanted to do a dramatic film and goof around and play the guitar for five months.'

He returned with a bang in *The Secret of My Success*, playing a country Kansas boy who makes good on Wall Street, defeats his crooked uncle and runs away with the heart of the drop-dead gorgeous Helen Slater. This was designer slapstick at its slickest, with all its commercial ingredients polished to a high shine. Fox himself performed with such joyful energy that one couldn't help but sit back and enjoy the proceedings.

Then, again, the actor tried to be taken seriously. He played Yuppie cocaine addict Jamie Conway in *Bright Lights, Big City*, a Big

Movie based on Jay McInerney's Important Novel about alienated New York youth. Tom Cruise had originally been sought for the starring role and, quite frankly, would have made a more convincing Conway. Fox retaliated that, 'my natural response after I do something successful, is to do the antithetical thing. Because if you only do what you do best and you fail, you're screwed. But if you do something that you're not sure about and you succeed, it's from heaven.'

He was serious again in Brian De Palma's brutal, but simplistic *Casualties of War*, playing a real-life combat GI who brings his unit to court martial for the kidnap, rape and murder of a Vietnamese village girl. Sean Penn co-starred as Fox's commanding officer, and was about as mean as Fox's private was saintly. Frankly, *Casualties of War* just didn't seem convincing, even if the carnage was.

In 1989, Fox filmed the two sequels to *Back to the Future* back-to-back, reuniting him with director Zemeckis and producer Spielberg. In the first, McFly and his faithful companion Doctor Emmett Brown (Christopher Lloyd) are transported into the year 2015, where McFly confronts his own future. Fox had extra fun playing McFly at 47, as well as his own son and daughter! In *Part III*, he and Brown find themselves shuttled back to 1885, where Fox dons a stetson, buckles on his guns and adopts the appropriate nom-de-plume of 'Clint

Sending himself up rotten, Fox plays a movie star researching the role of a cop in John Badham's entertaining *The Hard Way*

Eastwood'. Audiences quibbled over which was the better of the two sequels, but which ever way you looked at it they were both first-rate exercises in escapism.

Next came *The Hard Way*, a box-office disappointment, and then Fox used his clout to get *Doc Hollywood* off the ground. 'It was the first movie I was able to con a studio into making,' the actor revealed proudly. 'It's very low key, there are no car chases and it's just a sweet story. I told them, "Trust me."'

Indeed, *Doc Hollywood* was a delightful romantic comedy with buckets of charm to spare, in which a would-be plastic surgeon finds himself waylaid in a South Carolina backwater. Fox was agreeable as ever, finding true love with a feisty local ambulance driver (Julie Warner) while getting his values fine-tuned. Also, with a domestic gross of $52 million, it showed that with the right star a gentle comedy like this could make money.

Next, he took the title role in Barry Sonnenfeld's *For Love or Money*, as the ambitious employee of a grand New York hotel asked to 'babysit' a beautiful young woman (English actress Gabrielle Anwar) in return for a loan to start his own business. He then returned to Canada for James Lapine's *Life With Mikey*, co-starring Cyndi Lauper.

FILMOGRAPHY

1979: *Letters From Frank* (TV). 1980: *Midnight Madness*. 1982: *Class of 1984*. 1983: *High School USA* (TV). 1984: *Poison Ivy* (TV). 1985: *Back To the Future; Teen Wolf*.

1986: *Family Ties Vacation* (TV). 1987: *Light of Day; The Secret of My Success; Dear America* (voice only). 1988: *Bright Lights, Big City; Casualties of War*. 1989: *Back to the Future Part II*. 1990: *Back To the Future Part III*. 1991: *The Hard Way; Tales From the Crypt* (TV; also directed); *Doc Hollywood*. 1993: *For Love or Money*; (UK: *The Concierge*); *Homeward Bound – The Incredible Journey* (voice only); *Where the River Flows North; Life With Mikey*. 1994: *Greedy; Thirty Wishes* (also directed).

Brendan FRASER

It was not the most auspicious of cinematic breakthroughs, but was a breakthrough nonetheless. *Encino Man* was designed as a vehicle for Pauly Shore, the nerdy, ultra-hip Californian comic (of MTV's *Totally Pauly*), but it was Brendan Fraser, in the title role, who captured the hearts of American girls. The film was as calculating and moronic as they get, being the inane tale of a caveman who comes to life in the suburban community of Encino, California. Fraser was the icon from the Ice Age, who is taught to party by his discoverers, and turns into the coolest dude on campus. The joke is, he proves to be more popular with the local babes than his guardians, who behave like Neanderthals. The film, which was understandably thrashed by the critics, went on to become a minor box-office success and grossed over $40 million in the US.

Having proved his broader comic capabilities, Fraser next turned to drama, and landed the starring role in *School Ties*. Although also situated on campus, the film could not have been further removed from *Encino Man*. Set in 1955, *School Ties* was an intelligent and moving look at anti-Semitism and classism in America's elite prep school system, in which a young Jew is forced to compromise his family and religion in order to benefit from the best education available to him. Fraser was simply superb as the star quarterback who tries to lead a normal life against mounting odds, and with a combination of undiluted charm and acting smarts created one of the most winning cinematic characters of 1992.

The son of a Canadian tourism official, Brendan Fraser was born in 1969 in Indianapolis, Indiana, and grew up in Holland,

Switzerland and Canada. After attending the Upper Canada College preparatory school in Toronto, he enrolled at the Actors' Conservatory, Cornish College of the Arts in Seattle and received a BFA in acting. There, he held an internship at the Intiman Theatre, and was a member of the Laughing Horse Summer Theatre in Ellensburg, Washington State. While in the northwest area he appeared in over 20 plays, including productions of *Waiting For Godot, Arms and the Man* and *Romeo and Juliet*. He made his movie debut with a small role in Nancy Savoca's *Dogfight* – starring River Phoenix and shot in Seattle – and then moved to Los Angeles to further his film career.

On TV, he appeared in the pilot *My Old School* and the highly acclaimed NBC film *Guilty Until Proven Innocent*, with Martin Sheen, before winning the role of *Encino Man*. The part of caveman 'Linkovitch Chomofsky' – 'Link' for short, as in 'Missing Link' – was originally earmarked for Pauly Shore. However, director Les Mayfield felt the largely mute character was unsuited to Shore's vocal talents, and so a new actor had to be found. Mayfield relays, 'We videotaped over 125 candidates for the role and I can honestly say there was only one person who could do it. That was Brendan Fraser. He did an interview with us and he was so intelligent, and so able to manipulate his body and comically move, that I knew we just had to have him.' Fraser himself revealed, 'I just jumped around and wrestled with the plants in the office.' Any which way, he made an endearing caveman in an unendurable movie.

In 1981, Stanley Jaffe and Sherry Lansing

Fraser showing his enthusiasm for the opposite sex (Wanda Acuma) – in *Encino Man*

Brendan Fraser as the young dude 10,000 years' long in the tooth in *Encino Man*. Seen here with Pauly Shore and Sean Astin

Fraser as David Greene in Robert Mandel's outstanding *School Ties*

produced *Taps*, an ensemble picture set in a military academy which nudged Timothy Hutton, Tom Cruise and Sean Penn on their way to stardom. Eleven years later, Lansing and Jaffe selected an equally promising cast for *School Ties*. Besides Brendan Fraser, the film starred Randall Batinkoff, Matt Damon and Chris O'Donnell, all of whom exhibited enormous potential. But of them all, Fraser seemed the one most destined for celebrity.

Unlike his caveman, David Greene in *School Ties* was closer to Fraser's own experience. 'Filming on the Middlesex School campus brought back strong memories of jackets and ties, trees and lush green playing fields, and anxieties over academia – the emphasis on achievement, the weightiness of the workload,' the actor reveals. 'Something I shared with David was that I was willing to do anything to be included in a group, even if it meant denying myself who I was. I think that, in some shape or form, that's a part of all of us.'

Sadly, *School Ties* was not the commercial success it should have been, and made $26 million *less* than *Encino Man*. But Brendan Fraser was in demand. He played a disillusioned young man in another ensemble piece, *Twenty Bucks*, the bizarre story of a 20-dollar note passing through innumerable hands (including those belonging to Linda

Hunt, Gladys Knight, Elisabeth Shue and Christopher Lloyd). But the film was an empty exercise that failed to capitalise on its potential. Fraser then played Donald Sutherland and Lolita Davidovich's son in Percy Adlon's *Younger & Younger*, the strange story of a man who keeps the ghost of his late wife in storage, and then teamed up with Joe Pesci and Moira Kelly for Alek Keshishian's *With Honors*.

FILMOGRAPHY

1991: *Dogfight*. **1992:** *Guilty Until Proven Innocent* (TV); *Encino Man* (UK: *California Man*); *School Ties*; *Twenty Bucks*. **1993:** *Younger & Younger*; *With Honors*. **1994:** *Airheads*; *The Scout*; *Batto* (voice only).

Andy GARCIA

Andy Garcia has been on the brink of stardom for more years than he'd care to remember. After *The Untouchables*, he was on everybody's lips as the next Al Pacino. Then came *Black Rain*, whose producer, Sherry Lansing, promised would make him, 'a major, major star'. *The Godfather Part III*, though, was the film that would discharge him into the stellar stratosphere. Well, almost. And then of course there was Stephen Frears's *Hero*, with Dustin Hoffman and Geena Davis. What a cast! What a director! What a concept! It was a bomb.

Garcia was also getting a reputation as a support system. He says of his colleague Michael Douglas, who starred in *Black Rain*, 'Every time I see him he says, "So when are you gonna carry a movie? Come *on*. You guys come in, work two scenes, steal the movie!"' Sure enough, Andy's co-stars were more famous than he, the real big boys of Hollywood: Douglas, Kurt Russell, Jeff Bridges, Kevin Costner, Sean Connery, Richard Gere, Al Pacino, Dustin Hoffman . . . But Garcia was holding his own corner, projecting the steely charisma of a star-regent.

Andy Garcia is also extremely selective when it comes to choosing scripts. 'There's a danger,' he says, 'in young actors being in total submission to the industry, in accepting the audition process as a do-or-die situation, where it can affect your emotional state. The only way to survive the process is by concentrating on your craft, on your passion for the work.'

Garcia is passionate about his work alright, although he can be spectacularly modest at the same time. 'I've survived,' he admits of his stubbornly burgeoning career. And yet if Garcia had refused to ever play a cop, that career would be non-existent. He's rather good at playing men on the right side of the law – 'I do *look* the part' – although his first showy role was as a cocaine dealer, and his most famous part that of the psychotic Mancini in *The Godfather Part III*.

Andres Arturo Garcia Menendez was born on 12 April 1956, in Havana, Cuba, the youngest of three children. His father, known as 'The Mayor', was a lawyer who owned considerable property, and his mother, Amelie, taught English. When the Americans invaded in the Bay of Pigs debacle, Amelie

and her children boarded a plane for Miami. At Miami Beach Senior High, Andres Garcia excelled at sport and admitted, 'If I could have made a living as a basketball player, I would have." However, following a bout of mononucleosis, he was knocked sideways and at a mere 5'11'' was too short for college basketball anyhow.

Instead, he turned to drama, left school in 1977 and faffed around in the Caribbean before moving to Los Angeles to take his craft seriously. In the tradition of all future stars he became a waiter, and started getting bit parts here and there. While performing with an improvisational group, he played a young gang leader in the TV pilot of *Hill Street Blues* and got small roles in the features *Blue Skies Again*, *A Night in Heaven* and *The Lonely Guy*.

If his professional life wasn't exactly going places ('I was rejected' he says with some bile), his personal life was. He met, courted and then married Maria Victoria (Marivi for short) back home in Miami. Ironically, that was where Phillip Borsos was filming *The Mean Season* with Kurt Russell and Mariel Hemingway, and the director signed Garcia to play Ray Martinez, a Hispanic homicide detective. This led to another sizeable role in Hal Ashby's *8 Million Ways To Die*, in which the actor played Angel Maldonado, an urbane, ponytailed cocaine lord.

As Vincent Mancini, nephew of Al Pacino's Michael Corleone, in Francis Coppola's *The Godfather Part III*

Garcia's villainous turn impressed Brian De Palma, who was then casting the role of Frank Nitti, the Mafia hitman in *The Untouchables*. In order to avoid typecasting, Garcia asked if he could play the good guy instead. De Palma agreed, and the actor found himself billed alongside Kevin Costner and *above* Sean Connery and Robert De Niro. Garcia was the Italian cop, George Stone – aka Giuseppe Pedri – and his opening scene was a classic. Connery and Costner are recruiting crack shots for their team of 'untouchables' to combat Al Capone. Connery, unimpressed with Stone's false moniker, calls him a 'wop'. Garcia whips out a gun, pushes it into Connery's Adam's apple and slowly, hesitantly murmurs, 'You stinking Irish . . . *pig.*' With a flippant, 'He'll do!,' Connery enlists him on the spot.

The film was a colossal hit for Paramount Pictures, and the studio took note of Garcia as a man worth grooming for stardom.

He won top-billing in the dire British-Australian political thriller *American Roulette*, and took a supporting role in the fact-based, hard-hitting *Stand and Deliver* – as a favour to its director, Ramon Menendez (no relation). He was top-billed again, and made an engaging leading man, in the cable movie *Clinton and Nadine*. Garcia was Clinton, a magnetic gun-smuggler; Ellen Barkin was Nadine, a classy prostitute. Jerry Schatzberg, who directed, offered, 'It's very difficult not to get along with Andy.'

Andy Garcia as *Internal Affairs* detective Raymond Avila in Mike Figgis's *Internal Affairs*

Garcia with Nancy Travis in *Internal Affairs*

he would be very interesting in this country environment.'

The actor then teamed up with Dustin Hoffman and Geena Davis in the satirical *Hero*, directed by Stephen Frears – the *sixth* English director he has worked with. Frears originally saw the part of John Bubber – a homeless Vietnam vet who falsely claims a hero's reward – as a vehicle for Kevin Costner. But Garcia's vision of Bubber as a man 'propelled into a role by destiny' impressed the director, and Garcia got the part. He'd also gone up for the Hoffman role – but that is another story. Although a critical success, the film was not embraced by the public, which was surprising. It was both funny and poignant, and raised a lot of important issues, not least the dichotomy of good and evil in all of us. It should have been the movie that turned Garcia's career around.

Next, he teamed up with Meg Ryan for Disney's romantic drama *When a Man Loves a Woman*.

Garcia with Geena Davis in Stephen Frears's very funny, thought-provoking *Hero*

Andy Garcia as the urban cop on the trail of a serial killer in rural California – in Bruce Robinson's atmospheric *Jennifer 8*

more serious contenders. Even Robert De Niro was after the part, but was dismissed as being too old. Garcia got it, and was paid his first million for the honour.

He was then brought in to replace Nick Nolte in George Miller's *Lorenzo's Oil*, as Augusto Odone, the father who struggles to find a cure for his dying six-year-old son. But Garcia's interpretation of the gentle Italian banker grated with Miller's vision of the character, who knew the real Augusto. According to the director, Garcia 'went off on a completely different track. It would have meant the story would have had to shift enormously.' As it happens, Nolte suddenly became available again, and Garcia dropped out of the project in the spring of 1991. Instead, he did a couple of cameos – in the ill-fated *A Show of Force*, with Amy Irving, and in the Kenneth Branagh hit *Dead Again* – and then turned down the lead in *The Mambo Kings* (the role went to Armand Assante). Next, he played *another* cop – in Bruce Robinson's atmospheric, intelligent thriller *Jennifer Eight*. This time he had a romance on the side – with a blind Uma Thurman – as an LA sergeant who moves to a small Northern Californian town to escape the rat race. There he stumbles onto a vicious serial killer who specializes in dicing up blind girls. Robinson cast Garcia, he says, because 'Andy has a very potent star quality – and I thought

FILMOGRAPHY

1981: *Hill Street Blues* (TV; pilot). 1983: *Blue Skies Again*; *A Night in Heaven*. 1984: *The Lonely Guy*. 1985: *The Mean Season*. 1986: *8 Million Ways To Die*. 1987: *The Untouchables*. 1988: *American Roulette*; *Stand and Deliver*; *Clinton and Nadine* (aka *Blood Money*). 1989: *Black Rain*. 1990: *A Show of Force*; *Internal Affairs*; *The Godfather Part III*. 1991: *Dead Again*. 1992: *Jennifer Eight*; *Hero* (UK: *Accidental Hero*). 1994: *When a Man Loves a Woman*.

Jami GERTZ

Jami Gertz is a talented actress who never got the breaks. More often than not she was better than the films she appeared in, and even if the film was good, it seemed to gain little attention. Born in Chicago on 28 October 1965, Gertz displays the hot-blooded Latin sex appeal of a latter-day Dolores Del Rio or Maria Montez. However, she is still young enough yet to capitalize on her intelligence, good looks and range as an actress.

Raised in Glenview, Illinois, Jami first aspired to a career as a figure skater, until playing Dorothy in a school production of *The Wizard of Oz* turned her head. For a while she studied at New York University and worked as a model, while taking small roles in the movies *On the Right Track*, *Endless Love* and *Sixteen Candles* – all filmed around her native Chicago. When she was offered the part of the insufferable Muffy Tepperman in CBS TV's offbeat sitcom

Paramount gave him second-billing to Michael Douglas in Ridley Scott's *Black Rain*, a big-budget, hard-hitting thriller set in Osaka, Japan. Garcia was another cop, Charlie Vincent, who is brutally beheaded by a gang of Yakuza thugs. The role of Sgt. Raymond Avila, a new recruit in LA's *Internal Affairs* department, was written specially for him. Richard Gere played the rogue cop Garcia has to tame, and it was a welcome switch in stereotypes to see the Hispanic cop on the side of the angels.

Paramount was also packaging Francis Ford Coppola's third instalment in *The Godfather* saga, and there was much speculation in the press as to who was going to play the young Vincent Mancini, heir to the bloody Corleone throne. Such names as Sylvester Stallone and John Travolta had been bandied about, while Alec Baldwin and Matt Dillon looked like

Square Pegs, she moved to Los Angeles and started her acting career in earnest. The series ran for over a year, and by the time the last episode was aired on 12 September 1983, Jami was an established face in the business.

She continued to work in television, taking guest spots in *Diff'rent Strokes* and *The Facts of Life*, and playing rock singer Martha Spino in the short-lived sitcom *Dreams* (1984). On film, she had a couple of decent roles in two tolerable movies before landing the female lead in Walter Hill's *Crossroads*, in which she played Frances, a runaway who falls in with and for Ralph Macchio, a self-assured guitarist escorting a legendary bluesman to Mississippi. Joe Seneca was simply mesmerizing as the latter, and Ry Cooder's music was dynamic, but the film failed to secure a theatrical release in Britain. Neither did the next two, which were brutally buffeted by the American press – *Quicksilver*, with Kevin Bacon, in which she played a streetwise bicycle messenger; and *Solarbabies*, in which she and Jason Patric found themselves imprisoned in a futuristic fortress.

On stage, she won glowing reviews for her theatrical debut, *Out of Gas on Lover's Leap*, a two-hander with Patric, and she went on to perform in a number of plays, most notably *Come Back, Little Sheba* with Tyne Daly.

On film, she was back in the arms of Patric in *The Lost Boys*, a stylish, entertaining vampire movie, with a demonic Kiefer Sutherland competing for her affections. In

Less Than Zero, based on the cult novel by Brett Easton Ellis, she played Blair Kennedy, the shallow, substance-sniffing model involved with crackhead Robert Downey Jr, but who still harboured thoughts for old boyfriend Andrew McCarthy. It was another stinker.

Listen To Me was no better, but Gertz was. She played Monica Tomanski, a brilliant scholarship student again trapped between the devotions of two men (Kirk Cameron, Tim Quill). This time the arena was 'college debating', a cerebral school sport little explored by the cinema. Gertz was impressively feisty and attractive as the blue-collar workaholic from Chicago, and the film was equally hard-working in its efforts to cram in such topics as abortion, AIDS, capital punishment, rape, divorce and more. Still, in spite of its obvious plot devices, *Listen To Me* was entertaining soap.

In *Renegades*, a decidedly routine cop thriller with Kiefer Sutherland and Lou Diamond Phillips, she was wasted as the mandatory gun moll, but then found the part she had been waiting for in *Silence Like Glass*. A powerful, superbly played drama set in a cancer clinic, the film starred Gertz as Eva Martin, a beautiful, privileged ballerina trapped in a room with an impossible patient, Claudia (Martha Plimpton). While Eva refused to face up to the inevitable, Claudia had accepted her lot and her bitter rejection of the world proved to be an unbearable attitude for Eva to live with. Both actresses

Jami Gertz in *Jersey Girl*

were nothing short of excellent, and the film, financed in West Germany, went straight for the jugular. To add salt to the wound, it was based on a true story.

Ms Gertz followed this with two daft comedies, both starring female graduates of the popular TV sitcom *Cheers*. Shelley Long played a meddlesome novelist in the entirely disagreeable *Don't Tell Her It's Me*, in which, again, Ms Gertz was courted by two men – Steve Guttenberg and Kyle MacLachlan. In *Sibling Rivalry*, a slyly plotted farce of mistaken identity, the actress played Kirstie Alley's

Jami with Jason Patric in Joel Schumacher's *The Lost Boys*

With Steve Guttenberg in *Don't Tell Her It's Me*

sister, the fickle, fun-loving Jeanine, who admits, 'I don't cook. I re-heat' and whose idea of a relationship is anything that lasts longer than 24 hours. It is Jeanine who pushes her sister into an extra-marital affair and ends up falling for the guy's brother (Ed O'Neill). Directed by Carl Reiner with a bullwhip, *Sibling Rivalry* was actually quite funny, in spite of an overdose of ham. Ms Gertz was delightful.

She returned to the small screen in the James L. Brooks-produced sitcom *Sibs*, as the manipulative Lily, the romantically dumped-on sister of Margaret Colin and Marsha Mason, who moves in with the latter just as Mason has quit her job to get some peace.

Gertz then starred in her most gratifying film to date. Commanding top-billing (for the second time, following *Silence Like Glass*), she took the title role in *Jersey Girl*, the story of a working-class *Pretty Woman* who dreams of dating a handsome millionaire. When she finds him (Dylan McDermott), she becomes a blooming nuisance, turns his head and then

With Dylan McDermott in David Burton
Morris's *Jersey Girl*

realizes that her dreams had nothing to do with reality. Although bordering on the irritating, Gertz delivered a passionate, funny performance as a dreamboat coming to terms with her roots. Taken on its own terms, *Jersey Girl* was an irresistible modern fairy tale.

FILMOGRAPHY

1981: *On the Right Track*; *Endless Love*. 1984: *Sixteen Candles*; *Alphabet City*. 1985: *Mischief*. 1986: *Crossroads*; *Quicksilver*; *Solarbabies*. 1987: *The Lost Boys*; *Less Than Zero*. 1989: *Listen to Me*; *Renegades*; *Silence Like Glass*. 1990: *Don't Tell Her It's Me*; *Sibling Rivalry*. 1992: *Jersey Girl*.

Steve GUTTENBERG

Steve Guttenberg has all the prerequisites for major stardom. He is handsome, boyish, athletic, muscular, amiable and, as has been frequently noted, 'extremely cute.' He has also starred in some very successful films, four of which – *Police Academy*, *Cocoon*, *Short Circuit* and *Three Men and a Baby* – were profitable enough to spawn sequels. Another, *Diner*, was a critical milestone and gave young actors a new cinematic standard to aim for. It also helped launch the careers of Mickey Rourke, Kevin Bacon, Daniel Stern, Ellen Barkin and director Barry Levinson.

And Steve Guttenberg was in demand. *Variety* listed him as the busiest screen actor in the business during the 1985–88 period, in which time he out-grafted such workaholics as Gene Hackman and Michael ('pass that screenplay') Caine. And yet in spite of all the work and exposure, Guttenberg failed to arouse the sort of media attention that his contemporaries were privy to. Or even to secure decent billing. In *Short Circuit*, he was second-billed to Ally Sheedy, in *High Spirits* was third-billed after Daryl Hannah and Peter O'Toole.

Perhaps one reason he never became a bigger name was that he seemed perfectly content to be upstaged by his co-stars. In *Police Academy*, an ensemble comedy, he was overshadowed by a 6'6'' florist wannabe and a cadet with the vocal range of Industrial Light & Magic. In *Cocoon*, his turn as a straight-arrow leading man was eclipsed by a cast of frisky geriatrics. In *Short Circuit* he was competing with a hyperactive robot, and in *Three Men and a Baby* was upstaged by a puking newborn. It was this ability to be a supportive star that made Guttenberg such a useful leading man, and, ultimately, confounded his efforts to carve a distinctive niche for himself.

The son of a New York policeman, Steve Guttenberg was born on 24 August 1958 in Brooklyn, and was raised in Massapequa, Long Island. He was 16 when he worked for a messenger service that delivered actors' résumés to advertising agencies and, on a whim, he slipped his own photograph in a delivery. It set his mind working. Putting his

Steve Guttenberg

aspirations to become a dentist on the back burner, Guttenberg spent his last two years' education at New York's High School for the Performing Arts, and appeared in an off-Broadway production of *The Lion in Winter*. At the Julliard workshop he studied acting with the venerable John Houseman, and also worked with Uta Hagen and Lee Strasberg at the Actors' Studio.

In the summer of 1976, Guttenberg moved to California to attend UCLA, popped up in such prime-time TV fodder as *Doc* and *Police Story*, and co-starred in the high-grade, true-life tearjerker *Something for Joey*, with Geraldine Page. The following year he landed the starring role in the ill-named *The Chicken Chronicles*, in which he played David Kessler, a wealthy, amorous student who worked in a fast-food joint (run by Phil Silvers). The film certainly had its moments, and Guttenberg was endearing in his first lead, but who would see a film with that title?

He was still at UCLA when he took a leave of absence to join Gregory Peck and Laurence Olivier in Portugal, where he played an ill-fated Jewish spy in *The Boys From Brazil*. Then, during his summer vacation, he had a supporting role in *Players*, a glossy romance with tennis elbow and Ali MacGraw.

He returned to TV to play the daydreaming *Billy* Fisher, in America's short-lived reincarnation of Britain's *Billy Liar*, and was equally unlucky to be a part of the disastrous musical *Can't Stop the Music*, a

Wish-fulfilment: Guttenberg with Tahnee Welch in *Cocoon*

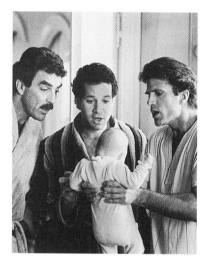

Steve Guttenberg (*centre*) with Tom Selleck and Ted Danson (and infant) in the box-office sensation *Three Men and a Baby*

bloated vehicle for the ephemeral gay pop group Village People. He also played the manager of the Hotel Pelican in the offbeat sitcom *No Soap, Radio*, a fleeting TV series seemingly inspired by *Monty Python's Flying Circus*.

There were two more TV movies before Guttenberg got his big break in *Diner*, Barry Levinson's perceptive look at Baltimore youth in the 1950s. Guttenberg top-billed as Eddie, the football fanatic who stipulated that his fiancee take an exam on the subject before he'd marry her. Guttenberg then had a supporting role in the controversial, critically applauded TV movie *The Day After*, an intelligent look at the aftermath of nuclear war, which was shown theatrically overseas.

Following the 3-D turkey *The Man Who Wasn't There*, Guttenberg was signed up to play Carey Mahoney, a rebellious parking lot attendant forced to join a *Police Academy* in favour of prison. The film's excessive sexism, poor taste and whacky cast of characters appealed to audiences everywhere, while Guttenberg put the success of his character down to the fact that, 'he's the kind of guy you can trust to take care of your wife, or go out with for a drink and chase women.'

The actor's gravy train continued chugging along nicely with the enormously popular

Police Academy 2: Their First Assignment, and the even bigger *Cocoon*, which out-grossed the original *Police Academy*. This was the fanciful tale of a troop of old age pensioners (Don Ameche, Hume Cronyn, Jessica Tandy et al) who are given renewed life when they encounter mysterious alien pods. Guttenberg provided sex appeal in the form of Jack Bonner, an amiable charter boat skipper who falls in love with an otherworldly Tahnee Welch. The scene in which he and Tahnee consummate their passion in a swimming pool was worth the price of admission alone.

Guttenberg's next brush with commercial success arrived in the form of *Short Circuit*, another wildly escapist yarn featuring a loveable robot (Number Five) who thinks he's alive. Again, Guttenberg lent enormous human appeal to a bizarre scenario, playing

an amiable techno whiz kid who falls for Number Five's defender and human friend, Ally Sheedy. Although *Short Circuit* was successful enough to prompt a sequel, it couldn't compete with the *Police Academy* comedies and, sure enough, Guttenberg returned to play Mahoney for a third time in *Police Academy 3: Back in Training*. This was the least successful entry yet and, indeed, Guttenberg seemed to have very little to do this time round.

He put his nice-guy image on hold in the romantic comedy *Surrender*, as the unlikely boyfriend of Sally Field, a smarmy Yuppie lawyer obsessed by money. Although brandishing an oily moustache, he still looked far too young to partner Field (he *is* 12 years her junior), but nevertheless displayed a keen flair for character acting. He took another U-turn in the superior film noir thriller *The Bedroom Window*, playing Terry Lambert, a man who covers for his mistress (Isabelle Huppert, as his boss's wife) when she witnesses an assault outside his bedroom window. As a witness without a cast-iron alibi, Lambert gets into no end of trouble with the police, his boss and even the killer he never saw. Martha Schumacher, the film's producer, cast Guttenberg because, she says, 'Steve has a screen presence which is extremely likeable and humorous. To play the role of Terry, it was important to have an actor whom the audience would readily believe could get himself into this complex situation – where he testifies in a murder trial and ends up becoming the suspect. Most important was to have an actor who conveyed a feeling of "Everyman," someone who could make you feel that this could all be happening to you.'

He was funny and likeable again in *Three Men and a Baby*, as one of three swinging bachelors (the cartoonist) who are saddled with an infant. Also starring Tom Selleck and Ted Danson, the film was a saccharine but frequently amusing re-make of the 1985 French comedy *Trois Hommes et un Couffin*, and went on to become the biggest hit of the 1987–88 period.

Next, he played an American tourist who falls in love with an Irish ghost (Daryl Hannah) in Neil Jordan's chaotic, painful comedy *High Spirits*, and reprised his role as Jack Bonner in *Cocoon: The Return*, a box-office disappointment.

Worse still was the preposterous romantic comedy *Don't Tell Her It's Me*, in which he played a cartoonist (again) recovering from Hodgkin's disease, who masquerades as a New Zealand biker in order to win the hand of Jami Gertz. It was then sequel time once

more (and his second cartoonist that year), with Guttenberg, Selleck and Danson travelling to England to attend the stately wedding of their baby's English mom. The kid, now a precocious five-year-old, prompted the new title *Three Men and a Little Lady*, and the film made the most of its new set-up: three worldly New York guys adrift in the English countryside. Thankfully, the comedy avoided treading old ground, boasted a decent plot, plenty of good jokes and enough genuine charm to keep the gagging at bay.

On 30 September 1988, at the urging of Tom Selleck and Ted Danson, Steve Guttenberg married the model Denise Bixler. Consequently, the actor has slowed his workaholism down to a walking pace and decided that a regular TV series – ABC's *Showroom*, with Paul Dooley – would keep him closer to home.

FILMOGRAPHY

1977: *The Last Chance* (walk-on); *Rollercoaster* (walk-on); *Something for Joey* (TV); *The Chicken Chronicles*. 1978: *The Boys from Brazil*. 1979: *Players*. 1980: *Can't Stop the Music*; *To Race the Wind* (TV). 1981: *Miracle On Ice* (TV). 1982: *Diner*. 1983: *The Day After* (TV); *The Man Who Wasn't There*. 1984: *Police Academy*. 1985: *Police Academy 2: Their First Assignment*; *Cocoon*; *Bad Medicine*. 1986: *Short Circuit*; *Police Academy 3: Back in Training*; *Amazon Women On the Moon*. 1987: *Surrender*; *The Bedroom Window*; *Police Academy 4: Citizens On Patrol*; *Three Men and a Baby*. 1988: *High Spirits*; *Cocoon: The Return*. 1990: *Don't Tell Her It's Me*; *Three Men and a Little Lady*. 1994: *What Do Women Want?* (also executive produced).

Antony Michael HALL

At first glance, Anthony Michael Hall was the most unlikely of stars. Geeky, gawky and not exactly handsome, he looked destined to be consigned to the butt of acne jokes, to play the younger brother, the whiz kid, the school nerd. But Anthony Michael was so good at what he did, that he cornered the dork market at a time when films about teenage angst were *the* thing at the box-office.

It also helped that he was a star member of the estimable *Hughes' Who*, that select circle of actors who got to play in the extremely perceptive and successful movies of filmmaker John Hughes. In fact, it was Hughes who wrote the screenplay of *National Lampoon's Vacation*, in which Hall played Chevy Chase's unbearable son Rusty Griswald, and who then wrote the role of 'Geek' in *Sixteen Candles* specially for him. Some even suggested that Hughes adopted Hall as his alter ego, but later the director denied this: 'People ask me, "Were you the geek?" No I wasn't. "So which one were you?" I don't get it. Who was Alfred Hitchcock in *his* movies?' Later, Hughes directed Hall in *The Breakfast Club* and *Weird Science*, by which he continued to provide hope for the underdog and gave dignity to the guy who happened *not* to look like Rob Lowe.

Anthony Michael Hall was born on 14 April 1968 in Boston, and, at eight, started acting in TV commercials. He was chosen by Steve Allen to play the comic as a boy in the latter's semiautobiographical play *The Wake*, and decided acting was for him. 'Working with someone of Steve's calibre really turned me on to performing,' Hall says. 'It was very gratifying, and it was something I felt I was good at.'

He was 'Doc', a young orphan adopted by stock car driver Kenny Rogers in Daniel Petrie's *Six Pack*, which marked the film debut of both Rogers and Hall. On the small screen, he played Huckleberry Finn in the routine TV movie *Rascals and Robbers*, and then co-starred in the excellent human drama *Running Out*, with Deborah Raffin.

Next came *National Lampoon's Vacation*,

Anthony with the Griswald family, Dana Barron, Beverly D'Angelo and Chevy Chase – in Harold Ramis's *National Lampoon's Vacation*

and Anthony Michael displayed a keen sense of comedy in a role that could have gone unnoticed. The film was a hit, and so was Hughes' *Sixteen Candles*, a knowing, funny look at puppy love, with Hall excellent as the hustling freshman who asks Molly Ringwald if he can borrow her knickers. He was even better in *The Breakfast Club*, as the class 'brain' condemned to Saturday detention with Ringwald, Emilio Estevez, Judd Nelson and Ally Sheedy. This time he went for the heart, as the bright, sensitive virgin who gradually gathers courage to stand up for himself.

He returned to comedy with *Weird Science*, his last film with Hughes, in which he played a horny, nerdy whiz kid who creates the perfect woman (Kelly LeBrock), but then doesn't know what to do with her. The film offered an appetizing smorgasbord of possibilities, but failed to capitalize on any of them.

He was recruited for the 1985-86 season of the cult TV revue *Saturday Night Live*

Biker with a heart: Steve Guttenberg shows off in *Don't Tell Her It's Me*

With Kelly LeBrock in *Weird Science*

As the geek in John Hughes's *The Breakfast Club,* flanked by Molly Ringwald and Judd Nelson

Daryl Hannah

(alongside Robert Downey Jr, Jon Lovitz and Joan Cusack), but his internship was short-lived. Then, back on the big screen, he starred in the thriller *Out of Bounds*, but was out of his depth as an Iowa farm boy chased by drug dealers and the police, and the film sank without trace. Even worse was the horrendous comedy *Johnny Be Good*, in which the actor was cruelly miscast as a sought-after high school jock.

He had a supporting role in Tim Burton's winsome fairy tale *Edward Scissorhands*, and was virtually unrecognizable as the beefy, bullying boyfriend of Winona Ryder. He then combined his new macho image with his old comic finesse to good effect in *Into the Sun*. In the latter he played an egocentric, posturing method actor who hitches up with real-life pilot Michael Pare to help him prepare for an action movie. It was Hall's best performance in years, which was a shame, as few got to see the movie.

FILMOGRAPHY

1982: *Six Pack; Rascals and Robbers: The Secret Adventures of Tom Sawyer and Huck Finn* (TV). **1983:** *Running Out* (TV); *National Lampoon's Vacation*. **1984:** *Sixteen Candles*. **1985:** *The Breakfast Club; Weird Science*. **1986:** *Out of Bounds*. **1988:** *Johnny Be Good*. **1990:** *Edward Scissorhands*. **1992:** *Into the Sun; Who Do I Gotta Kill?* **1993:** *Six Degrees of Separation*.

Daryl HANNAH

Daryl Hannah could not escape her looks. Although she herself says, 'When I look in the mirror now, I see a crooked nose, stringy hair and blotches,' journalists scrambled for their dictionaries to find superlatives to describe her beauty. Indeed, whether Daryl Hannah likes it or not, her career has been dictated by her appearance. At her best, she could be ravishing, ethereal, divinely desirable. In such films as *Splash* and *Roxanne*, she seduced the camera with a magic spell. But, equally, she could look a complete dork. She was offered the Julia Roberts role in *Steel Magnolias*, but turned it down to play the awkward, mousy, bespectacled beauty parlour assistant instead. And, come Oscar time, Julia Roberts walked away with an Oscar nomination.

At her best, Daryl Hannah was the perfect foil for her leading men – but she was no run-of-the-mill beauty spot. No way. Her off-beat perfection has lent itself to such roles as an android, a mermaid, a cavegirl, an Irish ghost and a mental patient! And she was no common-or-garden glamour queen, either. Although a favoured model of such celebrated photographers as Helmut Newton and Steven Meisel, she would shuffle down the street in torn jeans and a lowered baseball hat. A favourite pastime was to browse in second-hand shops. At interviews, she was notoriously nervous, projecting a flighty, childlike eccentricity. A former publicist called her, 'a space cadet from hell,' while screenwriter Mitch Markowitz (*Crazy People*) admitted she once broke into his apartment and decorated the eggs in his fridge.

And yet Daryl Hannah has her serious moments. When Diet Coke used her image in a TV commercial, she fought back. 'The thing is,' she complained, 'I've turned down *millions* of dollars in commercial offers – more than I've made in films.' She threatened to sue, but, 'Coke tried to put me off, as if this were a temporary female problem. But I didn't go away. I got an apology, I got $128,000 – which I gave to the Christic Institute – and I got to make *Steel Magnolias* [Coke owned Columbia Pictures at the time].'

Daryl Hannah with Tom Hanks in *Splash*

Daryl as the deadly replicant Pris in Ridley Scott's mind-blowing *Blade Runner*

Daryl Hannah, one of three children, was born on 3 December 1960 in Chicago into a middle-class family (her sister, Page, is also an actress). The performing arts beckoned early. 'I started dancing when I was four because of some flexibility problems I had,' she reveals. 'They told my mother that I should have leg braces, so she just thought that maybe if she put me into dance classes, it would help.' Her legs were certainly a speciality, even then. An unpopular child at school, she was nicknamed 'Toothpick' and 'Beanpole'. But under the tutorship of former New York City Ballet star Maria Tallchief Paschen, Daryl blossomed. 'She was *very* talented,' Tallchief divulged. 'She has the figure, you see: long legs, small head and she's beautiful.'

Daryl was seven when her parents divorced, and the shock brought about a state of 'semi-autism'. She cannot recall the years after her father left, until, 'the next thing I knew, we were living in a hotel and my mom was getting married.' It was 1973, and Sue Hannah became Sue Wexler, wife of Jerry Wexler, the excessively rich Chicago real-estate tycoon and chairman of Jupiter Industries (and brother of the double Oscar-winning cinematographer Haskell Wexler). Daryl found it hard to mentally adjust to wealth, and couldn't shake off her desire to help support her siblings. Work, for her, became her focus.

The acting bug bit when she saw a production of *West Side Story* and, aged 17, she moved to Los Angeles – ostensibly to study literature at the University of Southern California (her mother and stepfather strongly disapproved of her acting ambitions).

But her early experiences of Hollywood were ugly. She lived among wife-beaters and drug dealers, and when her apartment was broken into it was the last straw. 'They stole my teddy bear. Not my TV, not the stereo – but one of my *favourite* teddy bears. That was enough for me.'

She moved in with a family friend, the actress Susan Saint James, and later shared an apartment, 'on top of the freeway,' with another privileged, unknown actress, Rachel Ward. She made her film debut with a small role in Brian De Palma's *The Fury*, had a slightly better part in *Hard Country*, with an unknown Kim Basinger, and then joined her flatmate (Ward) in Andrew Davis's backwoods slasher *The Final Terror*. In the latter, Daryl got to play the second female lead, a vulnerable beauty called 'Windy', who ends up with her throat cut from ear lobe to ear lobe. She played Pris, the athletic, mute android in Ridley Scott's definitive sci-fi nightmare *Blade Runner*, and literally catapulted her way into the collective awareness of cinemagoers. Crowned with a mop of peroxide hair, she looked like a demonic doll, and then somersaulted herself into battle, wrapping her muscular thighs round Harrison Ford's neck. Seldom had the cinema produced such a sinister, sexy villainess.

She shed her clothes as the female lead in Randall Kleiser's featherweight beach romance *Summer Lovers*, and played a teenage model in Ed Zwick's unremarkable TV movie *Paper Dolls*, with Joan Collins. She was in James Foley's trashy, but enjoyable low-budget romance *Reckless*, with Aidan Quinn, and then made another huge impression – this time in the central role – in Ron Howard's *Splash*. She played Madison, a mermaid from Cape Cod who saves Tom Hanks from drowning and falls in love with him. Turning in her fins for a very respectable pair of legs, she pops up at the Statue of Liberty stark naked and goes in search of her human prince. The quintessential fish-out-of-water fantasy, *Splash* was funny, charming and enormously popular, and turned Daryl Hannah into a star.

She was largely wasted as Mickey Rourke's abused girlfriend in *The Pope of Greenwich Village*, and even though she was ideal in the central role in *The Clan of the Cave Bear*, the film was a stiff. Next, she played a performance artist opposite Robert Redford in the successful *Legal Eagles*, but felt cheated. 'They told me I could wear a punk wig,' she griped, 'so they let me wear it on the first day of shooting. And then they took it away on the second day. Day by day they took everything away from me, until I ended up just how they wanted me.'

Daryl in the title role of *Roxanne*, see here with Steve Martin

In *Roxanne*, arguably the brightest comedy of 1987, she had the title role, as a highbrow astronomer pursued by a nasally-advantaged Steve Martin. The latter also wrote the screenplay, an update of Edmond Rostand's 1898 romance, and the film was an enormous success.

Having watched Oliver Stone's *Salvador* four times, Daryl told the director she'd work with him on anything. So he cast her as Michael Douglas's mistress in *Wall Street*, but the experience was an unhappy one. She says, 'he made me feel alienated and uncomfortable.' She was also a fan of the Irish director Neil Jordan, and agreed to star in his ghostly farce *High Spirits*. It should've been a good career move – she was billed above Peter O'Toole and Steve Guttenberg – but she was miscast (as a 16th-century spectre) and the film was a mess.

Another prestigious filmmaker, Woody Allen, was looking for 'a Daryl Hannah type' to speak two lines in his movie *Crimes and Misdemeanors*. Coincidentally, he rang Daryl's agent when she was in the office. 'I'm a Daryl Hannah type,' she offered, and she got the role. After the Diet Coke debacle, she joined Julia Roberts, Sally Field, Dolly Parton, Shirley MacLaine and Olympia Dukakis in *Steel Magnolias*, a resounding hit, and then starred opposite Dudley Moore (after John Malkovich left the movie mid-shoot) in the sporadically amusing, but formulaic comedy

Daryl dressing herself down in Herbert Ross's *Steel Magnolias*, with Dolly Parton

Crazy People. She and Dudley played mental patients who fall in love and, again, she was irresistible.

When Laura Dern turned down the role of John Lithgow's rebellious wife in the epic, Amazon-set *At Play in the Fields of the Lord*, Daryl jumped at it. 'The fact is, I don't get offered these sorts of parts all the time,' she said. 'But if you want to work, you take the best of what you can get. I didn't even ask my agent how long I'd be there, what kind of money I would be making, what my billing would be, where I would be living . . . I just said: "When do I get on the plane?" And he said: "Four days." '

Sadly, Daryl was not up to the material, and the film was a colossal flop. She was better in John Carpenter's inventive, highly enjoyable comedy-thriller *Memoirs of an Invisible Man*, with Chevy Chase, but, inexplicably, the film failed to capture an audience. Then she joined such *Grumpy Old Men* as Jack Lemmon, Walter Matthau and Burgess Meredith. Next she starred in Christopher Guest's re-make of the dubious 1958 classic *Attack of the 50 Ft Woman*, 'the story of a girl who gets mad, gets big and gets even!' (per the poster).

If her films were no longer making a splash, Daryl Hannah herself was still making headlines. In September of 1992, she broke up with her long-standing boyfriend, the singer and composer Jackson Browne. According to newspaper reports, the parting was far from amicable, and the actress ended up with a black eye and two fingers in plaster. A month later the *National Enquirer* published photographs to confirm the rumours. Then, shortly afterwards, millions of American TV viewers were treated to a 16-minute amateur video (broadcast on the show *A Current Affair*), showing the actress in a revealing embrace with John F. Kennedy Jr. The star refused to talk about her relationship with the former president's son, while well-briefed friends vehemently denied the romance. But the video spoke volumes.

FILMOGRAPHY

1978: *The Fury*. 1981: *Hard Country*; *The Final Terror* (UK: *Campsite Massacre*). 1982: *Blade Runner*; *Summer Lovers*; *Paper Dolls* (TV). 1984: *Reckless*; *Splash*; *The Pope of Greenwich Village*. 1986: *The Clan of the Cave Bear*; *Legal Eagles*. 1987: *Roxanne*; *Wall Street*. 1988: *High Spirits*. 1989: *Crimes and Misdemeanors* (cameo); *Steel Magnolias*. 1990: *Crazy People*. 1991: *At Play in the Fields of the Lord*. 1992: *Memoirs of an Invisible Man*. 1993: *Grumpy Old Men*; *Attack of the 50-Foot Woman*. (TV).

Woody HARRELSON

Few actors have made the transition from TV to the large screen with much success, which makes Woody Harrelson's achievement all the more remarkable. He had only done one small film part when he landed a supporting role in NBC's *Cheers* during its fourth season. He was brought in to replace the regular character of 'Coach' (played by Nicholas Colassanto, who died in 1985), and had mixed feelings about doing TV. His dream was to appear on Broadway. Still, it was a part, and the show was a winner, so he took it. He was 23 when he first played Woody Boyd, the slow-witted barman who could turn a *non sequitur* into a jewel of wisdom – and then miss the point. And he was a stand-out. His naive charm proved to be the perfect antidote to the barbed asides of Rhea Perlman and the roguish scheming of Ted Danson, and in 1987 Harrelson won the American Comedy Award and in 1989 the Emmy as Outstanding Supporting Actor. Woody the Emmy-winner feels a strong allegiance for Woody the barman, which probably accounts for the character's lasting success. He may be dumb, but he's no instant mix caricature. 'Actually, I've always considered Woody naive, not dumb,' the actor argued. 'If anything, he's an idiot savant. He has an amazing knowledge of trivia and can beat anybody at chess.'

Woody, the actor, was a savant himself when he started courting Hollywood. He started with a well-placed cameo – as a crazy TV producer in Steve Martin's hip, hilarious *LA Story* – and followed it with a good character role in *Doc Hollywood*, as the

actor says, 'didn't seem to make much of a difference,' but when Harrelson Snr was imprisoned in 1982 for two life sentences (for the assassination of a federal court judge), Woody believed in his innocence. 'The truth will out,' he says simply.

As a child, his great loves were reading, writing poetry and picking fights. 'I wanted to be a minister,' he says, 'I was the head of the youth group and used to lead Bible studies. But I also fought a lot.' He then became interested in drama, did the requisite number of school plays and, on a Presbyterian scholarship, enrolled at Hanover College in Indiana, where he majored in Theatre Arts and English. It was around this time that he lost faith in organized religion, and dedicated himself to a career in the theatre. Moving to New York, he landed an understudy job in Neil Simon's *Biloxi Blues* and, in 1986, made his film debut in the comedy *Wildcats*. In the latter he was 13th-billed as Krushinski, and got to hoist football coach Goldie Hawn onto his shoulders. Interestingly, the film also marked the screen debut of Wesley Snipes, Woody's co-star in the far more successful sports comedy *White Men Can't Jump*.

Cheers followed *Wildcats*, and Woody embarked on his career as rabble-rouser and womanizer. Besides his 18 months with Carol Kane, the actor was romantically linked with

redneck companion of Bridget Fonda and rival to Michael J. Fox. Fox was already a friend from their days on the Paramount lot, where the latter was shooting NBC's *Family Ties*. Harrelson was rather good at making influential allies. When he dated the actress Carol Kane, ten years his senior, he felt at home in the company of her friends Jack Nicholson and Anjelica Huston, and, later, when he appeared opposite Glenn Close in the play *Brooklyn Laundry*, he became more than close to his co-star. Despite their 14-year age difference and Woody's reputation as a brawler and womanizer, the distinguished actress (and mother) accepted his proposal for marriage (however, the engagement was short-lived).

Harrelson was also careful when it came to the parts he played on screen. 'I have turned down roles – like a rapist, once – in which I would be too different from Woody. I've looked for parts that are an appropriate transition, like my character in *Doc Hollywood*. He had some of Woody's innocence, but he was *considerably* more in touch with his sexuality.' Indeed, the first starring film role the actor accepted was yet another variation on the dimwit. In the basketball comedy

Woody Harrelson

The Woodman as redneck, with Bridget Fonda in Michael Caton-Jones's endearing *Doc Hollywood*

White Men Can't Jump, the actor played Billy Hoyle, a sartorial disaster area in baggy shorts and sagging socks, who used his nerdish image to con black jocks into competing with him on the court. Hoyle is, of course, a phenomenal bounder in both senses of the word, and proves that at least one white man *can* jump. The film was an enormous success, grossing $19 million in its opening week in the US, and clocking up $70m in less than three months. Thanks to his astute planning, Woody Harrelson was a movie star.

The second of three boys, Woodrow T. Harrelson was born on 23 July 1961 in Midland, Texas, into a strict Presbyterian family. When he was seven, his father left home and his mother moved the family to Lebanon, Ohio, where Woody was looked after by his grandmother and great-grandmother. His father's departure, the

Brooke Shields, Moon Unit Zappa and Ally Sheedy. Earlier, when he was understudying *Biloxi Blues*, he had married the daughter of Neil Simon, Nancy, when they happened to be in Tijuana, Mexico. Later, the actor explained, 'the whole point was doing something just for the fun of it. I do a lot of

things on a whim that maybe wouldn't be kosher.' However, by 1993 it looked as if he had finally settled down when, on 26 February, his girlfriend Laura Louie gave birth to a seven pound baby girl, Deni Montana.

He also indulged his love of the theatre, writing the baseball-themed one-act play *2 on 2*, in which he starred in a double-bill with Edward Albee's *The Zoo Story*. He was also showing an interest in matters beyond showbusiness, sparked by a trip to Machu Picchu, the mountain city in Peru which has become something of a spiritual Mecca. He came back a changed man, took up vegetarianism and began exploring, for him, the more consequential things in life. For starters, he now puts his spirituality above his sexuality. 'That's a big step,' he concedes, 'because the only thing sacred about my physicality prior to this was the frequency of it.' He is now an outspoken critic of the American government, was an active campaigner against the Gulf War and, like Ted Danson, is contributing considerable effort on behalf of such environmental groups as the Earth Communications Office and the American Oceans Campaign.

Film-wise, his career was going from strength to strength, although not always without a hitch. He was signed to play the part of Benny in MGM-Pathe's *Benny and Joon*, opposite Johnny Depp and Mary Stuart Masterson, when he pulled out to take the role of Demi Moore's husband in Adrian Lyne's Paramount thriller *Indecent Proposal*. MGM head Alan Ladd Jr hit back with a lawsuit indicting Harrelson, Paramount, Lyne and the film's producer, Sherry Lansing. MGM claimed that Harrelson had signed a pay-or-play contract to star in their film, and that

Pimp or lover? Woody Harrelson as Demi Moore's deserted husband in Adrian Lyne's *Indecent Proposal*

the actor, Paramount, Lansing and Lyne, 'knowingly and wilfully entered into an agreement or agreements whereby they conspired to induce Harrelson to breach their contractual obligation to Pathe and/or deny the existence of such a contract.' Eventually, Aidan Quinn was signed up for the role Harrelson had vacated.

Next, the actor created another ruckus when he jumped at the chance to star in Oliver Stone's *Natural Born Killers*, from a white-hot script by Quentin Tarantino. Michael Madsen, who had appeared in Tarantino's *Reservoir Dogs*, thought he was a definite for the lead, and fired his manager and agent when Harrelson got the role. Then Harrelson was announced as the star of Universal's *The Cowboy Way*, a comedy about two rednecks who clash with city slickers when they try to save a friend's daughter from a vicious Cuban drug lord. After that, he was paid $5.5 million to re-team with Wesley Snipes in *The Money Train*.

When he is not acting, romancing or saving the planet, Harrelson performs and writes songs for his own band, Manly Moondog and the Three Kool Kats.

FILMOGRAPHY

1986: *Wildcats*. 1989: *Casualties of War* (bit); 1991: *LA Story* (cameo); *Doc Hollywood*; *Killer Instinct* (video); *Ted and Venus*. 1992: *White Men Can't Jump*. 1993: *Indecent Proposal*. 1994: *Natural Born Killers*; *The Cowboy Way*. 1995: *The Money Train*.

A conman with legs: Woody with Wesley Snipes in the surprise hit *White Men Can't Jump*

Ethan HAWKE

Ethan Hawke is not so much a star as a useful leading man. He is an accomplished actor, who displays the same range of sensitivity that River Phoenix used to – but without the quirks. He has made few films, but they are notable for their critical kudos. Even the teenage comedy *Mystery Date* is better than its title would suggest, being a dark, inspired exercise in mistaken identity.

Jeremy Irons, who played the actor's professor in the critically lauded *Waterland*, volunteered, 'Ethan is great. He's like all of the best actors. You can't tell when he starts and when he stops. And he's far too good-looking for his age!'

Ethan Hawke was an only child born in Austin, Texas, on November 6, 1970. His parents divorced when he was young, and his mother moved to Connecticut, Vermont, Georgia and Brooklyn, before settling in Princeton, New Jersey, with a new husband. There, she produced two more children, providing Ethan with a stepbrother and stepsister. He was eight years old when he saw a production of *Annie* and decided to become an actor, making his stage debut in *St Joan* and, at 14, landing the lead in Joe Dante's sci-fi fable *Explorers*, which also marked the theatrical film debut of River Phoenix.

'It was such an amazing experience to be 13 in California, the lead in a movie,' the young actor recalls now. But, 'when it got released, I went from being a big celebrity in my town to being the big fool in my town in a period of about two days.'

Although *Explorers* was exceptionally well acted by its young cast and was full of inventive twists and sly movie references, the film's increasing departure from reality (and overblown climax) sent it spinning to an early grave. At 14, Ethan Hawke retired from acting. 'I had a rough time after *Explorers*, so I wasn't really interested in the theatre, but this teacher got me back into it.'

Ethan continued his studies at the British Theatre Association in England and, fleetingly, at Carnegie-Mellon University in Pittsburgh, which he left after being thrown out of his very first class. He was 19 when he won the role of the shy, soft-spoken Todd Anderson in Peter Weir's *Dead Poets Society* – and the film changed his life. 'It allowed me to continue his life.' 'It allowed me to continue to work,' he says. 'Peter Weir had all this confidence in us, let us goof around and put it together so that it told a great story. Then I started to realize that if I didn't keep working, I wouldn't get better.'

Ethan got better, and in *Dad* was terribly

good as Ted Danson's independent, rebellious son Billy Tremont – in what threatened to be a Kleenex festival. Sure, *Dad* exuded its share of sentimentality, but it didn't drown in it, thanks largely to director Gary David Goldberg's insightful, heartfelt screenplay and to the high standard of acting (Hawke, Danson, Jack Lemmon, Olympia Dukakis). Next, Ethan speared the starring role in *White Fang*, a beautifully photographed but ponderous version of Jack London's classic love story of a boy and the half-wolf/half-dog he adopts.

In *Mystery Date* Ethan repeated his turn as a painfully shy youth, this time unable to summon up the courage to ask his beautiful neighbour (Teri Polo) out on a date. When he does get up the nerve (thanks to his older brother's suit, car and credit card), his dream liaison turns into a nightmare as he

Ethan Hawke with Jed in *White Fang*

Ethan as Sgt Will Knott in Keith Gordon's masterly *A Midnight Clear*

Ethan as Uruguayan survivor Nando Parrado in Frank Marshall's riveting *Alive*

finds himself mistaken for his brother who's in trouble with the police, the Chinese Mafia and a fuming flower delivery boy.

In *A Midnight Clear* Hawke was the callow, 19-year-old commander of a bedraggled squad of young soldiers up against the Nazis at war, drawing its power not from guns and bloodshed but from the quality of acting. 'That part, more than anything I've ever done, is just *me*, you know?' the actor explains. 'It was all very simple and very honest and very quiet, and that's ultimately why I think it works.'

He took a supporting role in *Rich in Love*, Bruce Beresford's starry tale of a dysfunctional Southern family, playing the confused outsider who falls for Kathryn Erbe (Albert Finney, Jill Clayburgh and Kyle MacLachlan were also in the cast) – but the film was not well received.

Waterland, however, was critically cherished. Like *A Midnight Clear* and *Rich in Love*, this was another adaptation of a literary work (Graham Swift's novel), in which Hawke played Mathew Price, a bright, outspoken Pittsburgh student who questions his history professor's teaching methods. Filmed partly in America and partly in England's Fen district, *Waterland* was directed by the American Stephen Gyllenhaal, who described Ethan as a 'fabulous young actor emerging as a major movie star.' Jeremy Irons top-billed as the teacher, and taught his young colleague how to draw on his own experiences.

'Working with Jeremy Irons gave me a lot more respect for the profession than I originally had,' Hawke acknowledges ' – with the amount of freedom and discipline that he approaches his work with. It makes it seem like a worthy thing to do with your life.'

Hawke then took his most demanding role to date, as Nando Parrado, a 22-year-old Uruguayan rugby player in Frank Marshall's harrowing true-life drama *Alive*, based on the best-selling account by Piers Paul Read. Parrado, and his college team mates, find themselves struggling for their lives when their plane crashes into the Andes, killing 18 passengers and crew. Rationed to one piece of chocolate and a sip of wine a day, the survivors find themselves abandoned, frozen and starving, and are forced to eat their dead to stay alive. Hawke, playing a character older than himself for the first time, lost over 20 pounds to look right for the part. Marshall, who had previously produced such films as *Raiders of the Lost Ark*, *Back To the Future* and *Dad*, offered, 'I didn't know this until I met him, but Ethan is very serious about his work. He's very sincere, and he studied very hard. I look at him as a young Harrison Ford. He has that silent strength and mystery.'

The actor is also keen to pursue a career as filmmaker and, in 1992, directed a 30-minute short starring his *Alive* co-star (and friend) Josh Hamilton as a Texas honeymooner.

FILMOGRAPHY

1985: *Explorers*. 1989: *Dead Poets Society*; *Dad*. 1991: *White Fang*; *Mystery Date*. 1992: *A Midnight Clear*; *Rich in Love*; *Waterland*; *Alive*. 1994: *Reality Bites*; *White Fang 2: Myth of the White Wolf* (cameo); *Floundering*; *Search and Destroy*; *Before Sunrise*.

C. Thomas HOWELL

Unlike his co-stars in *The Outsiders*, C. Thomas Howell had just come off the most successful picture ever made. And, from Steven Spielberg he had moved on to Francis Coppola – landing the starring role in a film that was to change the face of Hollywood stardom. And yet, unlike his co-stars in *The Outsiders*, Howell never found another hit. Well, not a *big* hit. Not like *Top Gun*. Or *The Karate Kid*. Or *Ghost*.

A boyish-faced actor with a tendency to sulk on screen, C. Thomas Howell coasted

C. Thomas Howell (*left*) with Ralph Macchio in Coppola's seminal *The Outsiders*

along in some atrocious movies on the strength of his youth and good looks. However, there was one year, 1986, which made a difference. He starred in a relatively visible hit, *Soul Man*, and gave a very good performance in *The Hitcher*. In the latter, in which he played the tormented victim of a psychotic Rutger Hauer, Howell revealed a credible sensitivity combined with a muscular aggression. It was the first role that showed he had the stuff for better things. Unfortunately, better things didn't happen.

Born in Van Nuys, California, on 7 December 1966, Tom (as he was then known) was the son of a professional rodeo performer. 'I grew up doing rodeo,' the actor reveals. 'I was kinda born into it. I could ride before I could walk. I didn't want to act at all. I didn't know anything about it.'

Tom was proficient at what he did, and between the years 1978 to 1980 was named All-Round Cowboy by the California Jr Rodeo Association and, in 1981, won the Kern Jr Rodeo Association title.

He did, however, make a smattering of commercials, appeared in an Afternoon Special on TV and had a (very small) bit in the TV movie *It Happened One Christmas*, starring Marlo Thomas and Orson Welles. Besides his rodeo riding, Tom's father also dabbled in stunt work for the cinema, and

introduced his son to the medium. 'I did some movie stunts with my father,' Tom continues. 'And that's what I had decided to do. I even had a commercial agent. One day a theatrical agent who worked at the company that represented me was sifting through some pictures and pulled my photo out. I was sent on the call for *E.T.* and I got the job.'

In *E.T. The Extra-Terrestrial* Tom played Robert MacNaughton's schoolfriend, Tyler, the sewer mouth who uttered such niceties as 'douche bag' and made puns on Uranus. Still, Tom got to cycle across that famous Amblin moon with fellow co-stars MacNaughton, Henry Thomas and Drew Barrymore – and a myth was born.

E.T. The Extra-Terrestrial went on to become the highest grossing movie of all time and everybody involved gleaned some of its gold. Tom Howell upgraded his name to 'C. Thomas' Howell and speared the central role of Ponyboy Curtis in Coppola's *The Outsiders*. The film, based on the cult novel by S(usan).E. Hinton, was a lyrical, poetic look at alienated youth, boosted by some extraordinary performances from an unknown cast. Ponyboy was the dreamy-eyed youth, the product of a broken home, who shared a tumbledown house with his older brothers Sodapop (Rob Lowe) and Darrel (Patrick Swayze). The film begins with a close-up of Howell lit in an auburn glow, staring moodily into space. He opens a composition book and on a page headed 'The Outsiders' he starts to write: 'When I

Black and tan: Howell blacked up for a scholarship in *Soul Man*

With Ann-Margret in *A Tiger's Tale*

stepped out into the bright sunlight from the darkness of the movie house . . .' The impassioned strains of Stevie Wonder's 'Stay Gold' begin, and so do the opening credits.

As narrator and onlooker, Ponyboy lends the film a dream-like, surreal quality, his passion for *Gone With the Wind* mirrored in the elaborate, sweeping style of Coppola's filmmaking. But, although it is Ponyboy himself who is on the run from the police, he is still very much a witness to the events around him. He doesn't get the girl (Diane Lane), he doesn't get to kill a Soc (a 'socially superior' youth) and he isn't made a martyr. The glory goes to Ralph Macchio, Matt Dillon and, to a lesser extent, Swayze. Still, Howell *did* get top-billing.

If the actor didn't win the calibre of role offered to his colleagues, he did get the fan following. This, at least, prompted a series of high-profile roles. In *Tank* he played the wrongfully imprisoned son of army sergeant James Garner; in *Grandview, USA* he was re-teamed with Swayze, competing for the affections of Jamie Lee Curtis; and was with Swayze again in John Milius's *Red Dawn*, as a teenage guerrilla fighting the Commies.

He got top-billing in *Secret Admirer*, a dainty romantic comedy about a misleading, unsigned love letter; and then came *Soul Man*. This was a stretch for Howell, who played a white boy masquerading as a black student in order to qualify for a minority scholarship. The film was likeable enough, with a few valid points to make, but Howell was hardly a convincing Afro-American in fright wig or no

fright wig. Rae Dawn Chong played his love interest, whom he later married in real life. Still, *Soul Man* grossed a comfortable $28 million in the States and spawned a popular soundtrack.

Next came *The Hitcher* which, Howell says, was 'the toughest thing I've ever done,' and then *A Tiger's Tale*, a heavy-going, obsolete comedy in which the actor bedded down Ann-Margret, 27 years his senior. Enough said.

And then things got steadily worse, with a mediocre TV movie, *Into the Homeland*, and Franco Zeffirelli's disastrous *Young Toscanini*. In the latter he was improbably cast as the celebrated Italian conductor, but he did get to top-bill Elizabeth Taylor. He was the adopted son of Athos (Oliver Reed) in Richard Lester's ill-fated *The Return of the Musketeers*, a misguided attempt to resurrect the Dumas classic; and he played himself in the even worse *Far Out Man*, a home movie directed by and starring Tommy Chong as a regurgitated 1960s dopehead. He was better served by *Breaking the Rules*, an engaging road movie with Jason Bateman and Jonathan Silverman on their way from Cleveland to California; and then it was back to routine teen fodder with *Side Out*, a dumb programmer about beach volleyball.

Never one to dodge injudicious casting decisions, Howell took on the title role in *Kid*, the odd story of a teenage Clint Eastwood who arrives at an Arizona

backwater to stir up trouble. Squinting menacingly, Howell played his role totally straight, prompting the audience to wonder how to take this corny romantic thriller. Actually, *Kid* was so bad that it transcended its genre and ended up being hugely enjoyable.

After that there were more TV movies (including *Curiosity Kills*, with Rae Dawn Chong); a modestly amusing comedy, *Nickel and Dime* (with Howell on good form as an absolute cad); and the moderately appealing romantic drama *That Night*, opposite Juliette Lewis. He also starred in *First Force*, with David Carradine, in *Kiss and Tell*, opposite Ally Sheedy, and in the cop thriller *To Protect and Serve*.

FILMOGRAPHY

1977: *It Happened One Christmas* (TV). 1982: *E.T. The Extra-Terrestrial*. 1983: *The Outsiders*; *Tank*. 1984: *Grandview, USA*. 1985: *Red Dawn*; *Secret Admirer*. 1986: *Soul Man*; *The Hitcher*. 1987: *A Tiger's Tale*; *Into the Homeland* (TV). 1988: *Young Toscanini*. 1989: *The Return of the Musketeers*; *The Eyes of the Panther* (TV). 1990: *Far Out Man*; *Breaking the Rules* (aka *Sketches*); *Side Out*; *Kid*; *Curiosity Kills* (TV). 1991: *Nickel and Dime*. 1992: *That Night*; *First Force*; *Kiss and Tell* (UK: *Tattle Tale*). 1993: *Streetwise*; *To Protect and Serve*; *Gettysburg*; *Jail Bate*. 1994: *Teresa's Tattoo*; *Power Play*; *Acting on Impulse*. (UK: *Secret Lies*); *Dark Reflection*; *Treacherous*.

Holly HUNTER

Holly Hunter could not be described as a versatile actress, but what she did she did very well indeed. She was hilarious in comedy, she could wrench your guts out in drama and she could skip between the two with the finesse of one of the most skilled actresses of her generation. Most famous for playing Southern firebrands on screen, Holly Hunter has done Ibsen on stage, played Henry Higgins's mother in a production of *Pygmalion*, and still aspires to Chekhov. However, she is best at playing variations of herself: spunky, sexy, feisty Southern women who speak their mind and can hold their own against any man (or woman).

Steven Spielberg, who directed the actress in *Always* and found himself romantically linked with her in the tabloids, says, 'She shatters all stereotypes. She has an enormous amount of firepower. This is someone no taller than my mom, but on the screen, she is overwhelming.'

Albert Brooks, Hunter's co-star in *Broadcast News*, added: 'With Holly, there's no bullshit. Period. You know where you stand. If you spend three minutes with her, you get to see who she is.'

Holly Hunter, 5'2'', was born on 20 March

Holly Hunter in the role that made her a star – as TV executive Jane Craig in James L. Brooks's *Broadcast News*

Holly as Carnelle with dreams of local celebrity in Thomas Schlamme's *Miss Firecracker*

1958 in Conyers, Georgia, the youngest of seven children (she has five brothers and one sister). Her father was a sporting goods sales rep, and raised his children on a 250-acre cattle-and-hay farmstead. 'My father did not approve of my learning to drive a tractor,' Holly reveals, 'which is probably why I'm so stubborn. He made the rules, and I broke them. But, like everyone who grows up on a farm, I got a working knowledge of life and death and what goes on in between.'

There were few theatrical influences in Holly's young life, and the local cinema had been transformed into a revivalist meeting house – although, as the actress relates, 'When they spoke in tongues and became possessed by the Lord, it was more fun than a movie.' Holly discovered acting aged 16, when she got a role in a high school production of *The Boyfriend*, and decided to go to drama school. Her grades weren't good enough to get her into a leading drama academy, but she knew if she could only get an audition she could get in anywhere else. She got an audition, and enrolled at the

Carnegie-Mellon University in Pittsburgh for four years, concentrating solely on acting.

She graduated in 1980 and moved to New York where, two weeks later, she landed her first film role, saying, 'Hey, Todd, over here!' in *The Burning*, a Z-grade slasher, notable only for Tom Savini's bloody special effects and a score by Rick Wakeman. Nevertheless, casting director Joy Todd was impressed. 'She read a couple of lines in this accent you could spread on a piece of bread. I just sat up and took notice. She was so good she could do whatever she wanted.'

One play Joy Todd sent Hunter up for was Beth Henley's *The Wake of Jamey Foster*. But on the way to the audition, the actress found herself trapped in an elevator – with Beth Henley. The two became inseparable, Holly won the role in *Jamey Foster* and on top of that was asked to replace Mary Beth Hurt in *Crimes of the Heart* on Broadway. 'She picks up a script of mine,' Henley offered, 'and it becomes alive. Holly and I share a Southern sensibility: that joyous-despairing view of life.'

Holly received rave reviews for *Jamey Foster* and two years later was given the lead in Henley's *The Miss Firecracker Contest*, another triumph, which was later filmed – with Holly repeating her stage role. But before the actress was big enough news to star in her own movie, she had a few turkeys to pluck.

For a while she shared an apartment in the Bronx with fellow actress Frances McDormand, who later became the girlfriend of filmmaker Joel Coen. Also, Hunter's boyfriend, the photographer John Raffo, shared office space with Joel and his producer-writer brother Ethan. In 1984, while Holly took a small role in the TV movie *With Intent to Kill*, saw her part in Jonathan Demme's *Swing Shift* trimmed to just a few scenes, and appeared in the awful *Animal Behaviour*, Frances McDormand got to star in the Coen's critical triumph *Blood Simple*. But Holly had made some useful friends. Says Joel Coen, 'Ethan and I got to know Holly well, and when *Blood Simple* was finished, we thought it would be fun to write something for her. *Raising Arizona* developed out of that.'

In *Raising Arizona* Holly Hunter played the highly emotional Edwina McDonnough, an infertile cop who marries a habitual criminal (Nicolas Cage), and then orders him to steal a baby. Combining a number of film genres, *Raising Arizona* was a miracle of style over content, a rollercoaster ride of belly laughs and imagery, a touching fable of contemporary America married with a Gothic, surreal nightmare vision. Above all it was an hilarious

Holly with Richard Dreyfuss in Steven Spielberg's magical romance, *Always*

original, which – paradoxically – grew funnier with repeated viewings. The film was chock full of memorable moments, but the scene in which a pissed-off Hunter confronts a grotesque, heavily-armed bounty hunter with the words, 'Gimme dat buy-bay, you warthog from hay-ell,' was a classic.

Sadly, *Raising Arizona* was *too* original to catch on with mainstream audiences, but became a cult phenomenon on its own terms. Meanwhile, Hunter had to make do with her burgeoning theatre career, a good role in Volker Schlondorff's excellent TV movie *A Gathering of Old Men*, and a secondary role (as a redneck's wife) in the capricious *End of the Line*, executive produced by actress Mary Steenburgen.

To James L. Brooks, who had won an Oscar for directing *Terms of Endearment*, Holly Hunter was still an unknown. He was currently casting the role of Jane Craig in *Broadcast News*, his sophisticated and satirical look at the world of TV news, and already had his male stars lined up – William Hurt as a slick, but intellectually lacking anchorman, Albert Brooks as a hard-working, hard-sweating correspondent, and Jack Nicholson, in a cameo, as a super-powerful news presenter. Jane Craig was the movie's central character, an intelligent, highly focused TV

executive caught off guard by the love of Hurt and Brooks, a part the director had written with Debra Winger in mind. When the latter became pregnant, Brooks considered Sigourney Weaver, Judy Davis, Elizabeth Perkins, Elizabeth McGovern, Christine Lahti and Mary Beth Hurt, but none of them seemed to fit the bill. He hadn't heard of Hunter and, frankly, didn't think a Southern actress adept at comedy sounded ideal but, with 48 hours left before the start of filming, he was willing to see anybody.

When Holly turned up for the audition, she wasn't in the least bit nervous, as she recalls, 'There was no way in hell I was going to get that role.' She arrived early, and when Brooks turned up, he looked straight through her. 'I missed her completely,' he admits, 'I thought she was a researcher or something.' But when the actress started bouncing her lines off Hurt, the latter remembers, 'Five lines into the reading I knew she was the one.' Afterwards, Hurt couldn't stop himself proclaiming, 'We've found her, we've found our Jane! And she's an actress – not a movie star!' Brooks himself added: 'She read her part like a dream. No, wait. I'm building legends here. She read *better* than a dream. She read like a gifted actress.'

The film was a hit, and an immensely intelligent, entertaining and well-acted one. For her role, Holly Hunter was voted best actress by the New York Film Critics, the Los Angeles Film Critics and the National Board

Holly Hunter as Ed, the cop with a maternal instinct – in the Coen brothers' *Raising Arizona*

of Review, and was nominated for an Oscar. She was a star.

Next came *Miss Firecracker*, the film version of Beth Henley's play about a small-town beauty contestant, and again the actress gave a performance of unlimited depth, cramming her small features with pain, humour and passion, and demanding the audience never to take their eyes off her (in spite of a cast that included Tim Robbins, Mary Steenburgen and Alfre Woodard).

Active with the National Abortion Rights League since the early 1980s, Hunter jumped at the chance to play Norma McCorvey in the TV movie *Roe vs. Wade*. McCorvey – who was fictionalized as Ellen Russell in the film – took on the Texas judicial system (in 1970) in order to have an abortion, hiding under the pseudonym of Jane Roe. An unmarried Texas mother desperately looking for work (at the film's outset she is the presenter of a travelling freak show), Hunter's Jane Roe was a woman with no pat answers, but with an overriding passion for what she knew was right (the right of a woman to choose whether or not she is fit to bear a

child). The film, which also starred Amy Madigan and Kathy Bates, astutely avoided soapbox lecturing, and revealed both sides of the abortion issue with articulate level headedness, while letting Hunter carry the story's human passion. For her performance, she won the Emmy for best TV actress of the year.

Steven Spielberg's desire to update the 1943 romantic fantasy *A Guy Named Joe* (which had starred Spencer Tracy and Irene Dunne), had suffered many false starts, but when Spielberg settled on Hunter to play the love-torn girlfriend of forest firefighter Pete Sandrich (Richard Dreyfuss), he kicked the film into high gear. The result was a whimsical, touching and magical love story, with Dreyfuss and Hunter making an irresistibly off-beat couple. They teamed up again to grand effect in Lasse Hallstrom's *Once Around*, a moving dramatic-comedy about an overbearing salesman (Dreyfuss) who creates waves when he romances an inhibited Hunter and then alienates her family.

Next, she starred in the TV movie *Crazy In Love*, directed by Martha Coolidge, in which she and Frances McDormand played sisters with unfaithful husbands. However, the movie was sabotaged by a cloying gentility, and Hunter was at her most strident. She then went to New Zealand to star in Jane Campion's *The Piano*, an 1850s love story about a woman who moves Down Under with her young daughter and a piano, with Sam Neill and Harvey Keitel. This time she was better served by her material and won the Best Actress Award at the Cannes Film Festival, while *The Piano* itself snatched the Palme d'or. Next she teamed up with Tom Cruise in the big-budget legal thriller *The Firm*, based on John Grisham's phenomenal best-seller. It was an amazing year. Not only was *The Firm* a resounding list, but Hunter won the Emmy for best actress in the fact-based and highly comical TV movie *The Positively True Adventures of an Alleged Texas Cheerleader Murdering Mom*, and won the Oscar for *The Piano*.

FILMOGRAPHY

1981: *The Burning*. **1983:** *An Uncommon Love* (TV); *Svengali* (TV). **1984:** *With Intent To Kill* (TV); *Swing Shift*; *Animal Behaviour* (released 1989). **1987:** *Raising Arizona*; *A Gathering of Old Men* (TV); *End of the Line*; *Broadcast News*. **1989:** *Miss Firecracker*; *Roe vs. Wade* (TV); *Always*. **1991:** *Once Around*. **1992:** *Crazy In Love* (TV). **1993:** *The Piano*; *The Firm*; *The Positively True Adventures of an Alleged Texas Cheerleader Murdering Mom* (TV).

Timothy HUTTON

A ferociously dedicated actor and a stickler for research, Timothy Hutton was a star by the time he was 20. Although his subsequent career never topped his early promise, his consistently high standard of performance kept him in the good books of the best directors. There were decidedly sticky patches, to be sure, but it was easy to see why Hutton made the choices he did. When he agreed to star in the romantic fantasy *Made in Heaven*, it was to work with the celebrated maverick filmmaker Alan Rudolph. Likewise, when he surprised his peers by playing a Russian aristocrat in the picture-postcard *Torrents of Spring*, it was under the guidance of the acclaimed Polish director Jerzy Skolimowski. And Hutton proved he was up to the challenge. To prepare for his role, the 6'1" star learned to ride, play the piano, dance Russian-style and worked hard on his accent. The resultant performance was only jarring for those who entered with preconceived notions of who the actor was. For Timothy Hutton, it was a courageous move to prove that he could do something different.

Hutton was born on 16 August 1960 in Malibu, California, the son of Maryline Adams and Jim Hutton. His father was a relatively successful, if lightweight actor, whose films numbered *Where the Boys Are*, *Bachelor in Paradise* and *The Horizontal Lieutenant*, and was best known on TV as the canny detective *Ellery Queen*. Timothy was two when his parents divorced, and moved with his mother and older sister, Heidi, to Cambridge, Massachusetts, and then to his mother's home town of Harwinton in Connecticut. He was 14 when the family moved to Berkeley, western California, and there Hutton enrolled at LA's Fairfax High School, moving in with his father two years later.

He was five when he made his film debut in the domestic comedy *Never Too Late*, starring his father and Connie Stevens, but he explained that, 'at five, acting wasn't my primary goal. It wasn't until I was 17 that I decided I wanted to act. My father was very supportive, but he told me that I would have to do it on my own. No nepotism.' Nevertheless, Hutton admits that, 'I left school to do a show with my dad [*Harvey*], and then I started to get television work.'

The 'television work' was a string of TV movies, starting with a small part in *Zuma Beach*, a corny surf-and-sand caper co-scripted by John Carpenter and featuring

Timothy Hutton in his Oscar-winning performance as Conrad Jarrett in Robert Redford's *Ordinary People*

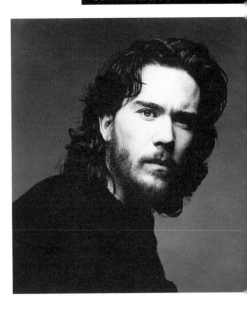

Hutton as Daniel Isaacson

As Jack in Gregory Nava's florid *A Time of Destiny*

sequestered in foster homes, and then he was signed up to play the lead in the military drama *Taps*, co-starring George C. Scott, Sean Penn and Tom Cruise. To prepare for his role as Brian Moreland, the senior cadet who leads his men on a rebellion to keep their academy open, Hutton spent two months in military school. The film was a box-office success, and the actor was nominated for a Golden Globe award for his performance.

After that, the commercial stature of his films was iffy, but his commitment to his roles was never less than admirable. In Sidney Lumet's *Daniel*, adapted by E.L. Doctorow from his own novel (*The Book of Daniel*), Hutton was electric as the anguished son of a man and woman (Mandy Patinkin, Lindsay Crouse), executed for leaking secrets to the Russians. For his role as a scientist in Fred Schepisi's underrated *Iceman*, he took courses in anthropology and an Inuit [Eskimo] language.

In August of 1983, Hutton was scheduled to star in MGM's contemporary western *Roadshow*, opposite Jack Nicholson. The terms of his 'pay or play' contract stipulated that he would receive $1.5 million whether the film was made or not. But when MGM cancelled the picture in the spring of 1983, they failed to inform Hutton, who had turned down other projects in the interim. Meanwhile, Nicholson was paid an undisclosed sum out of court, while Hutton was completely overlooked. However, the actor had the last laugh. Eventually a Los Angeles Superior Court jury found MGM guilty of breach of contract, and awarded Hutton $2.25 million in compensation and $7.5 million in punitive damages.

Meanwhile, his career chugged on undramatically. He was re-teamed with Sean Penn in John Schlesinger's mildly diverting, fact-based spy drama *The Falcon and the Snowman* (this time *he* was leaking to the Russians), and then attempted to change his solemn image with the goofy *Turk 182!*. This was an innocuous enough, fairly amusing fable about a graffiti artist who fights for his right to mess up the neighbourhood, becoming a mythical figure in a highly publicized war with the Mayor of New York (Robert Culp).

Earlier, Hutton had met the actress Debra Winger, five years his senior, at an intimate Los Angeles party. He remembers, 'We ended up talking to each other and it was as if no one else was there.' A year passed, and they met again, and again – at a Farm Aid concert. The tabloids had tried in vain to find a key to unlock Hutton's private life, and gaily

Suzanne Sommers, Michael Biehn, Rosanna Arquette, P.J. Soles and Tanya Roberts. His second TV film, the real-life based *Friendly Fire*, was altogether better, winning four Emmys, including an award for Outstanding Drama. Carol Burnett and Ned Beatty (both nominated for Emmys) starred, with Hutton as their frightened, bewildered son who watches the family fall apart after the death of his brother in Vietnam. It was this performance that prompted Robert Redford to sign up the young actor to play the central role of Conrad Jarrett in his directorial debut, *Ordinary People*. Again, Hutton was the son in a disintegrating family unit, again caused by the death of an older brother. This time Mary Tyler Moore and Donald Sutherland played his parents, but it was Hutton, who, at the tender age of 20, walked off with the Oscar, the Golden Globe and the Los Angeles Film Critics award. And yet there was a sadness to Hutton's glory. Four months before he began work on *Ordinary People*, his father died, aged 45, of cancer of the liver. Clutching his Oscar at the podium of the Dorothy Chandler Pavilion in Los Angeles, the actor concluded his thanksgiving speech with a simple, 'I'd like to thank my father. I wish he were here.'

There was another TV movie, the highly-acclaimed *A Long Way Home* in which he played a young a man searching for his brother and sister, both of whom had been

reported his dates with a chain of famous women: Rosanna Arquette, Elizabeth McGovern, Tatum O'Neal, Kristy McNichol, Patti Davis Reagan, Belinda Carlisle, Diane Lane ... But, in truth, they were all just friends, not girlfriends. Then, on New Year's Eve of 1985, he and Winger clicked. But it was their secret.

Ironically, the media was busily exposing the 'affair' Winger was having with Hutton's old mentor Robert Redford, on the set of *Legal Eagles* – but they were way off target. On New Year's Day, 1986, Hutton rang the

Timothy Hutton with Jessica Lange in
Everybody's All American

As Dimitri in *Torrents of Spring*

Lange. Quaid and Lange provided the acting, but Hutton was by far the most effective, as the 'serious' writer who narrates the story. The film spanned 25 years in the lives of these all-American folk, providing Hutton with an opportunity to age for the first time on screen. He was even older – and far from American – in Jerzy Skolimowski's lush adaptation of Ivan Turgenev's 1872 novel *Torrents of Spring*, as an old Russian man reflecting on his tempestuous romance with two women (Nastassja Kinski, Valeria Golino). After one got over the shock of seeing Hutton in top hat and sideburns (and speaking in a thick Russian accent), the film was an engrossing romance – and looked stunning.

In June of 1990, Hutton and Winger were divorced, and the star's career showed no signs of box-office improvement. But he was still a good actor, and was still attracting the attention of major filmmakers. In Sidney Lumet's gritty, commanding New York drama *Q & A*, he played a conscientious assistant DA pitted against Nick Nolte's malevolent, rogue cop, and then starred in Stephen King's *The Dark Half*, as a novelist who encounters the human manifestation of his nom de plume.

He then embarked on another 'commercial' venture, playing a young executive who suspects his temporary secretary (Lara Flynn Boyle) of murder – in Tom Holland's derivative thriller *The Temp*. Unfortunately, the actor looked out of place in this manipulative, tacky piece, and the film took a header at the box-office.

Timothy Hutton also acted frequently in the theatre, explaining, 'I like to split my time between screen and stage. It is as exciting for me to receive an enthusiastic round of applause on stage as it is to have my screen work acknowledged.' He is also a talented musician and an avid collector of art, having acquired works by Picasso, Warhol, Calder, Magritte, Dali and James Wyeth.

FILMOGRAPHY

1965: *Never Too Late.* 1978: *Zuma Beach* (TV). 1979: *Friendly Fire* (TV); *The Best Place To Be* (TV); *And Baby Makes Six* (TV); *An Innocent Love* (TV); *Young Love, First Love* (TV). 1980: *Father Figure* (TV); *Ordinary People.* 1981: *A Long Way Home* (TV); *Taps.* 1983: *Daniel; Iceman.* 1984: *The Falcon and the Snowman.* 1985: *Turk 182!* 1987: *Made in Heaven; A Time of Destiny.* 1988: *Everybody's All American* (UK: *When I Fall In Love*). 1989: *Torrents of Spring.* 1990: *Q & A.* 1992: *The Dark Half.* 1993: *The Temp; Katya; Zelda* (TV). 1994: *The Last Word.*

actress and just over ten weeks later they were married. On their wedding night, the actress got pregnant, but miscarried, and then got pregnant again shortly afterwards. They named their son Emmanuel Noah Hutton. 'I'd never met anyone like her,' the actor revealed, 'and I don't imagine I ever will again. She's an original. I loved spending time together in a way I hadn't experienced before.'

The following year he starred in the sickly-sweet romantic fantasy *Made in Heaven*, a surprising hiccough from the iconoclastic filmmaker Alan Rudolph, and, as an in-joke, Winger cropped up in an unbilled cameo as – wait for it – a male angel called Emmett! Hutton then starred in the well-made, soap operatic epic *A Time of Destiny*, as William Hurt's war-time buddy who, unknown to the latter, accidentally killed his father in a car accident. He took third-billing in the equally soapy *Everybody's All-American*, as the star-struck nephew of football icon Dennis Quaid, secretly in love with the latter's wife, Jessica

Nicole KIDMAN

Nicole Kidman was doing very well, thank you, receiving heaps of critical praise and accumulating a number of awards in her native Australia. But then everything went right. She met Tom Cruise, married him and became a household name. Suddenly, the critics were not so sure about her. They dipped their pens in vitriol to describe her performance in *Days of Thunder*, but then the film did provoke a good deal of mud slinging. Her next picture, *Billy Bathgate* (an even bigger box-office disappointment), at least landed her a Golden Globe nomination as best actress. But still the critics carped. Nicole's main problem was that she was Australian. Furthermore, she was an Australian playing Americans. *And* she had married the all-American, super-clean crown prince of Hollywood.

But you only have to re-wind to 1988 to see Kidman's performance in the Australian ocean thriller *Dead Calm* to know that the lady can act. Her flaming red hair blowing in the sea breeze, she immediately reminded one of Sigourney Weaver in *Aliens*, a strong, tall woman facing impossible odds – and coming out on top. Nicole was only 20 years old at the time, but she had already been voted Best Actress of the Year by the Australian public. And the following year she was to be nominated Best Supporting Actress by the Australian Film Institute for her role in *Emerald City*, on top of her two best actress awards for the mini-series *Bangkok Hilton* and *Vietnam*.

George Miller, the producer of *Dead Calm*, could sense something special. 'Nicole is not just someone who is acting for the short term,' he ventured. 'She's an absolutely serious actor. Some ten years ago I met Mel Gibson fresh out of drama school. I had this same gut feeling about him. He had this presence on film one couldn't stop watching. I feel that quality in Nicole.'

Robert Benton, director of *Kramer Vs Kramer* and *Billy Bathgate*, would seem to confirm this opinion. 'She was just astounding,' he said. 'She's an astonishingly gifted actress, even more so when you consider how young she is. There was not one person in the movie who did not adore her. She's truly one of the most amazing actors I've worked with.' And this from a man who directed both Meryl Streep and Sally Field in Oscar-winning performances.

The daughter of a biochemist and psychology lecturer (her father) and a nurse and teacher (her mother), Nicole Kidman was born in 1968 in Hawaii, a descendant of

the Australian cattle baron Sir Sidney Kidman. Hers was a tall family. Her father is 6'10", her mother and sister 5'10", and by the time Nicole was 13, she was also 5'10". She admits, 'I wanted to act from the moment I was born. No really, it was always a fantasy. But my growth took over everything. I hated my looks. What with my height *and* hair – weird, curly, messy – I was considered a bit odd.' Nevertheless, Nicole pursued her fantasy. 'I did street theatre and mime when I was seven. I did ballet when I was three – I did that for many years. When I was 12 I joined a local theatre group and worked with them and did plays and was a stagehand.'

Nicole in fact made her acting debut aged four, playing a sheep in a local nativity play. 'I wore car-seat covers, I bleated through the whole show, and I got my first laugh. I was this stupid kid trying to upstage baby Jesus. That was it. I thought, "Wow, this is fun!"'

At 10, she persuaded her parents to let her attend drama school, and at 14 made her film debut in *Bush Christmas*. In the popular *BMX Bandits* she played a super-market girl who teams up with a pair of young bikers, and then played a rock singer in love with Tom Burlinson in *Windrider*. In the Disney Channel mini-series *Five-Mile Creek*, she was, 'a little roughie who herded sheep.' Then she played a schoolgirl who becomes an anti-war protester in the mini-series *Vietnam* (1986), directed by Phillip Noyce. Noyce explained, 'We first became aware of Nicole from several Australian TV productions – what we call "domestic movies" – films hardly seen outside Australia. We felt she would be right for a key role in *Vietnam* that we [the Kennedy Miller organization]

Nicole (*right*) with Thandie Newton in John Duigan's superb evocation of adolescence, *Flirting*

Nicole Kidman as Rae Ingram in Phillip Noyce's dynamic thriller *Dead Calm*

Nicole with Loren Dean in Robert Benton's adaptation of E.L. Doctorow's *Billy Bathgate*

Kidman as the hot-blooded Shannon Christie in Ron Howard's epic romance, *Far and Away*

were developing. Little did we realize that in just three nights she would become a household name across the entire country.'

A slew of local awards followed, including a nod from the Sydney Theatre Critics who voted her Best Newcomer for her performance in *Steel Magnolias*. Next, she nabbed the lead in Noyce's breath-catching thriller *Dead Calm*, in which she played the wife of Sam Neill stranded on an 80-foot ketch with psycho Billy Zane for company. *Dead Calm* was the year's surprise treat, a stylish movie with fresh faces that sent the pulse on overdrive. Warner Brothers released the film in the States, and Hollywood jumped.

Meanwhile, Kidman won more local acclaim for her role as a heroin addict in the BBC-Australian mini-series *Bangkok Hilton*. For her, it was another breakthrough. 'It's a great role,' she said back then. 'I may look terrible, with my hair pulled back and sack-like dresses, but it's what acting is all about.' The late Denholm Elliott played her father, and volunteered, 'Nicole was a joy. She not only took the work seriously, but could always turn up the brilliance when she had to.'

Following her two AFI awards for *Vietnam* and *Bangkok Hilton*, Kidman was nominated for best supporting actress for her performance in *Emerald City*, as the live-in girlfriend of a ruthless writer (Chris Haywood). Based on the hit play by David Williamson, the film was a witty satire on the Australian film industry, but proved too insular for international tastes. She also had a delicious supporting role in John Duigan's *Flirting*, a magical, painfully accurate homage to boarding school life, a surprisingly superior

sequel to the director's 1987 *The Year My Voice Broke*. Kidman played Nicola Radcliffe, a 17-year-old head prefect. 'Blonde wig, loads of make-up, flirts like crazy and all the boys are in love with her,' the actress summarized her part succinctly. The film went on (deservedly) to sweep the Australian Film Critics' Circle Awards, winning statuettes for best film, best director, best actor (Noah Taylor) and best cinematography.

By now, *Dead Calm* had left its mark on the international market, and Nicole was duly signed up to play the romantic interest in the $55 million car racing actioner *Days of Thunder*. Directed by Tony Scott and starring Tom Cruise and Robert Duvall, the film was burdened with enormous expectations, which it duly failed to fulfil. In truth, it was a skillful, frequently wry piece of escapism with some fantastic racing sequences. OK, so Kidman looked out of her depth and her accent was enigmatic, but she did have her moments. And the film's worldwide gross of $230 million was no tragedy. Neither was Nicole's new liaison with her leading man. It was, she revealed, her first real romance. Earlier, she had confessed, 'Although it embarrasses me to admit it, I have not had a serious relationship. I wanted to establish my own independence first without having to depend on a man.'

The character of Drew Preston in E.L. Doctorow's celebrated novel *Billy Bathgate*, was described as, 'so blindingly beautiful under that cut gold hair, her eyes were so green and her skin was so white, it was like trying to look into the sun, you couldn't see her through the brilliance and it hurt to try for more than an instant.' Robert Benton's big-budget film version of the book was to star Dustin Hoffman, and Kidman was desperate to play Miss Drew. Three weeks before her audition, she spent four hours a day studying with a dialect coach to get the aristocratic New York accent just right. To be honest, nobody thought she could carry it off but, according to Benton, 'when she walked into my office, everyone was knocked out by her.'

The film was not a commercial success, but Nicole got her Golden Globe nomination. In Ron Howard's sweeping 1890s romantic epic *Far and Away*, the actress played a stiff Irish heiress opposite her new husband, who played a cocky, illiterate farmhand. Again, there were doubts about her handling the accent and, again, she came through with flying colours. The film was glossy, romantic tosh, but was executed with such technical verve, and if taken in the right spirit, was a good old-fashioned romantic wallow. And, with a domestic gross of $59 million, it was apparent that audiences adored it.

Next, the actress won the central role in Harold Becker's erotic legal drama *Malice*, with Alec Baldwin, a film which the actress hoped would reveal her in a new, more adult light. She had just completed the film when she rushed to Miami to collect the baby girl she and Cruise had put in for adoption. A nurse at the scene revealed, 'In 20 years of working with adoptions, I have never seen anyone so overjoyed as Nicole was when she first held her new daughter. There were tears of happiness in her eyes as she held the child close to her.'

She was then teamed opposite Michael Keaton in Bruce Joel Rubin's maudlin, sugary *My Life*.

FILMOGRAPHY

1982: *Bush Christmas*. 1983: *BMX Bandits*. 1986: *Windrider*. 1988: *Dead Calm; Emerald City*. 1990: *Flirting; Days of Thunder*. 1991: *Billy Bathgate*. 1992: *Far and Away*. 1993: *Malice; My Life*. 1994: *Portrait of a Lady; To Die For*.

Val KILMER

Val Kilmer was a stone's throw away from being a major star. But his films were never quite the successes they could've been. He had the lead in his very first movie, *Top Secret!*, from the same directorial team that reaped gold with the daffy comedy *Airplane!*. But *Top Secret!* failed to catch on, even though the team's *next* picture, *Ruthless People*, was another hit. Four years later he had the lead in Ron Howard and George Lucas's ambitious $30 million fantasy-adventure *Willow*. But, again, it failed to live up to expectations. And three years after that he won the coveted role of Jim Morrison in Oliver Stone's much-anticipated *The Doors*. Both critically and commercially, it was a disappointment. Val Kilmer was definitely out there. He just wasn't hitting any home runs.

Born on 31 December 1959 in Los Angeles, Kilmer, part Cherokee Indian, was raised in California's San Fernando Valley. There, he attended the Hollywood Professional School and later became the youngest student ever admitted (at the time) to the drama division at Julliard, in New York. A keen amateur poet, he also tried his luck as a dramatist, co-writing the play *How It All Began*, which Joseph Papp later presented at the Public Theatre, with Kilmer in the leading role. After graduation, he honed his skills on

Val Kilmer

Shakespeare, appearing in Joseph Papp productions of *Henry IV, Part I* and *As You Like It*, and on Broadway co-starred with fellow unknowns Kevin Bacon and Sean Penn in *Slab Boys*.

On screen, he made a dashing, straight-faced hero in Jim Abrahams, David Zucker and Jerry Zucker's barmy farce *Top Secret!*, playing an Elvis-like rock star who encounters Nazis while touring East Germany. A joint spoof of World War II melodramas and Elvis Presley musicals, the film's silliness was a bit too much at times, and the jokes pretty hit-or-miss. Still, Kilmer got a chance to display his singing talents, and did a good job with such classic numbers as 'Are You Lonesome Tonight?', 'Tutti Frutti' and 'How Silly Can You Get?'

He was given the lead in Martha Coolidge's *Real Genius*, playing a college whiz-kid exploited by a villainous William

Atherton, but the film's novel satirical angle was diluted by cliché and stereotypes. This led to a supporting role, but a flashy one, as the gum-chewing 'Iceman' in *Top Gun*, the biggest movie of 1986. Kilmer didn't have *that* much screen time, but his glacial posturing made him a memorable villain, and he won billing over Anthony Edwards and Tom Skerritt.

There was a decent TV movie, *Murders In the Rue Morgue*, with George C. Scott and Rebecca De Mornay, and then another lead, in *The Man Who Broke 1,000 Chains*, also for TV. The latter was only so-so, with Kilmer cast as real-life convict Robert Eliot Burns (first created by Paul Muni in the classic *I Am a Fugitive from a Chain Gang*). He was then given the biggest opportunity of his career yet: the starring role in *Willow*.

Willow was the dream child of George Lucas, who thought up the idea even before he had embarked on his ground-breaking *Star Wars* trilogy. But, back then, his vision of fairies, magic spells, two-headed monsters and general sword and sorcery could not be

Kilmer in his first film, the Elvis/WWII spoof *Top Secret!*, with Lucy Gutteridge

With the wife: Val and Joanne Whalley-Kilmer on the set of *Kill Me Again*

realized with the available technology. As it happens, *Willow* required more than 400 individual special effects, supplied courtesy of Lucas's own Industrial Light and Magic. Kilmer, his muscular chest bared and his hair flowing down his back, played Madmartigan, a roguish thief and rather good swordsman who reluctantly teams up with the goblin of the title (Warwick Davis) to combat an evil queen (Jean Marsh). The film proved to be a little frightening for children, and overly familiar for adults (it resembled *Star Wars* in enormous detail), but had enough verve and gusto to skate over the cliches. *Willow* grossed in the region of $54 million in the States, which was less than anticipated, but still nothing to cry over.

Also in the movie was the English actress Joanne Whalley, who played the witch's wilful but beautiful daughter Sorcha. To date, Ms Whalley was best known for her performance as Nurse Mills in the BBC's acclaimed musical series *The Singing Detective*, but had enjoyed enough exposure that Kilmer was already besotted by her before they met on the set of *Willow*. He admits that she took some persuading ('No, I can't, no,' he mimics her), but she eventually succumbed to his charms and the couple were married in March of 1988.

After a bout of domestic bliss, Kilmer starred in another TV movie, *Gore Vidal's Billy the Kid*, as the young outlaw, and then teamed up with his wife (now going under the professional name of Joanne Whalley-

Kilmer) in the film noir thriller *Kill Me Again*. This was an enjoyable, taut yarn that refused to stop for a tea break, and was distinguished by some unusual locations and a charismatic, laid-back turn from Kilmer (as a double-crossed private eye at the mercy of femme fatale Joanne Whalley-Kilmer).

Around this time, the actor had grown tired of the movie business and was concentrating on his poems (he had a book of verse published), the stage (he played *Hamlet* at the Colorado Shakespeare Festival) and writing screenplays (he knocked out several). He was also working on a documentary dealing with nuclear issues.

And then he heard Oliver Stone was casting the role of Jim Morrison in *The Doors*. The film had long been in gestation, and such names as John Travolta and Timothy Hutton had already been announced to play the rock legend. But Kilmer felt an affinity with the tragic star, and set about preparing for the role. After a meeting with Stone, the actor put together a rock video in which he sang Morrison's 'The End', 'LA Woman', 'Peace

His greatest role? Kilmer as Jim Morrison in Oliver Stone's *The Doors*

Frog' and 'Roadhouse Blues.' It won him the part.

Growing his hair to Morrison's length and squeezing his legs into tight leather trousers, Kilmer absorbed the persona of the singer and revealed an uncanny resemblance. The film, like Morrison's life, was not exactly easy to sit through, but Kilmer's performance was nothing short of admirable. It was, in acting terms, his magnum opus. And, yet, in spite of all the publicity, the merchandising, the books and the successful re-release of The Doors's hit single 'Light My Fire,' the film failed to make an impact at the box-office.

In *Thunderheart*, directed by Michael Apted and produced by Robert De Niro, Kilmer played a dedicated FBI agent from Washington DC who's dispatched to an Indian reservation to solve a murder. The film, based on an amalgam of events that occurred in the 1970s, looked great, but suffered from an overbearing self-importance. It was not a hit.

The actor then co-starred in Russell Mulcahy's off-beat romantic thriller *The Real McCoy*, playing a small-time thief who idolizes a master bank robber called Karen McCoy (Kim Basinger). He then joined Christian Slater, Gary Oldman and Dennis Hopper for Tony Scott's action-comedy *True Romance* (as the ghost of Elvis!), and and then played Doc Holliday superbly opposite Kurt Russell's Wyatt Earp in the $25 million western *Tombstone*.

FILMOGRAPHY

1984: *Top Secret!* 1985: *Real Genius.* 1986: *Top Gun*; *Murders In the Rue Morgue* (TV). 1987: *The Man Who Broke 1,000 Chains* (UK: *Unchained*) (TV). 1988: *Willow.* 1989: *Gore Vidal's Billy the Kid* (TV); *Kill Me Again.* 1991: *The Doors.* 1993: *Thunderheart.* *The Real McCoy*; *True Romance*; *Tombstone.* 1974: *Galatea*; *Wings of Courage.* 1995: *Batman Forever.*

Diane LANE

Diane Lane deserves a place in this book if only for being the sole female star of Francis Coppola's *The Outsiders*. Although she failed to share screen time with such co-stars as Tom Cruise, Emilio Estevez, Rob Lowe or Patrick Swayze, she did get to pour her Coke over Matt Dillon. She was also in the other seminal Brat Pack movie of that year, *RumbleFish*, likewise directed by Coppola, based on a novel by S.E. Hinton and featuring Matt Dillon. Again, she dumped Dillon.

Francis Coppola and the Brat movies gave her career a much-needed jump-start – after she had stormed on to the screen half a decade earlier in George Roy Hill's totally winning *A Little Romance*. In the latter she played a sweet, entirely edible 14-year-old falling in love in Paris. The daughter of a multi-wed, socialite mother, Lauren King is a sheltered, gifted and lonely child who is introduced to love through the wily machinations of her eccentric sidekick, Laurence Olivier.

Whereas Ms Lane's Romeo was a young *garçon* plucked from a Parisian playground (Thelonious Bernard), Ms Lane herself was a hardened showbiz professional. Born on 22 January 1963, in New York, she is the daughter of drama coach Burt Lane and Colleen, a former Playboy centrefold (Miss October 1957). From the age of six, guided by her father, Diane was appearing in such Greek tragedies as *Medea*, *Electra* and *The Trojan Women*.

'We did *Medea* in Greece, and we spoke it phonetically in the ancient Greek language,' the actress recalls. 'We didn't know what we were saying and neither did the Greeks. But they loved it.'

Later, she performed Shakespeare and then Chekhov at New York's Lincoln Center and, aged 13, was cast in the leading role of Elizabeth Swados's *Runaways* on Broadway. In the latter she was spotted by director George Roy Hill and signed up for the lead in *A Little Romance*. The film was a success, and Ms Lane's adolescent beauty beguiled the camera – and audiences worldwide. At 14, she made the cover of *Time* magazine.

In London to promote the film, she came across as an intriguing blend of old pro and naive starlet. But, whatever else she was, she was gorgeous. And unintentionally funny. 'I learned so much from Laurence Olivier,' she confided earnestly. But when asked what this education consisted of, she tenuously replied, 'I don't exactly remember *what* . . .'

After *A Little Romance*, Diane Lane was in demand, but her films got steadily worse. After turning down the leading roles in *Little Darlings* (which eventually starred Tatum O'Neal and Matt Dillon) and *The Blue Lagoon* (Brooke Shields), she teamed up with another legend, Burt Lancaster, in the likeable but commercially disastrous western *Cattle Annie and Little Britches*. She then played a victim of cerebral palsy in the sincere, often moving *Touched By Love*, another box-office dud.

TV movies followed, and the little-seen and, indeed, unpalatable *Ladies and Gentlemen: The Fabulous Stains*, with Lane as a punk rocker supported by members of The Clash and The Sex Pistols (not to mention Christine Lahti and Laura Dern). And then, after a mediocre vehicle for country singer Kenny Rogers – *Six Pack* – came *The Outsiders*.

Although she only appeared in two scenes in the latter, Diane's physical allure and fiery performance stuck in the memory. She was Cherry Valance, the preppy, privileged beauty who sympathizes with the rebel 'Greasers', but refuses to go out on a limb for them. She repels Matt Dillon, but strikes up a faltering rapport with the film's star, C. Thomas Howell.

In *RumbleFish* she played Patty, a similar part to Cherry Valance, a pretty schoolgirl

The Brat Packess: Diane Lane with C. Thomas Howell in *The Outsiders*

courted by a rough-and-ready Matt Dillon. This time she beds him – at least, they get down on the sofa – but eventually dumps him in favour of Nicolas Cage. Again, she had little to do, besides appearing in her underwear in Dillon's daydreams. The film, in spite of its critical standing, only played at two cinemas in the US before being shunted onto video.

The following year she appeared in her third Coppola picture in a row, *The Cotton Club*. This was a far better picture than either *The Outsiders* or *RumbleFish*, but due to a troubled production and a runaway budget ($47 million), it was a box-office catastrophe. Nevertheless, the film allowed Lane to play her first *femme fatale* – aged 18, no less – a platinum-blonde libertine in 1920s New York. This time, as Vera Cicero, she was a hardened temptress, property of gangster Dutch Schultz (James Remar) who enjoys a torrid, clandestine affair with a jazz musician (Richard Gere).

'I had this real insecurity complex about my age and I was genuinely worried I'd been miscast,' she reveals. 'I was honoured and flattered to have been given the part, but I had a very bad case of no-confidence inside.'

As she was then: a 14-year-old Diane Lane with Thelonious Bernard in George Roy Hill's enchanting *A Little Romance*

With Richard Gere in Francis Coppola's magnificent *The Cotton Club*

Diane with her husband Christopher Lambert in *Knight Moves*

During the shoot she broke up with her high school boyfriend of three years, guitarist-keyboardist Rick Kolster, and met the French star Christopher Lambert while promoting *The Cotton Club* in Paris. Appearing together on a TV chat show, they ended up doing the tango in front of the cameras. 'We laughed so much,' she remembers. 'We had a real [good] time.' They became (just good) friends.

Changing tack dramatically, the actress played a singer kidnapped by biker Willem Dafoe in the slick, energizing and stylish futuristic rock fantasy *Streets of Fire*, directed by Walter Hill. However, she was lost amongst the moody smoke, rain and neon, and her songs were dubbed.

She had greater impact in *The Big Town*, shedding her clothes as a 1950s stripper opposite Matt Dillon's big-time gambler. The irony that the film was set at the same time that her mother disrobed for *Playboy* was not lost on her. 'It took nerve to play that stripper,' she insists; adding 'excuse me for being well-endowed.' As for her mother, the actress says she now 'feels bad about doing *Playboy*, because she contributed to the demise of the female *whatever*.'

That same year Diane Lane flew to Rome to star opposite Christopher Lambert in the romantic fantasy *Priceless Beauty*. He played a pop star, she was a magic genie (promise). Pretty soon their friendship turned into something else. 'He was somebody who would not take no for an answer,' she

explains. 'The wall began to crumble and I relaxed and said, "Wow! I know who I am again, I know what I like again." '

The couple married in 1988 and also starred together in *Knight Moves*. This time the plot was rooted deeper in reality, but only slightly. Lambert was an international chess champion suspected of murder, and Lane was (miscast as) the psychologist assigned to suss him out. Romance inevitably followed and the body count climbed . . .

In between Lambert vehicles, Diane Lane returned to the stage (to play Olivia in *Twelfth Night*) and joined the all-star cast of the acclaimed TV mini-series *Lonesome Dove*, for which she was nominated for an Emmy. The trade paper *Variety* wrote, 'As Lorrie, Diane Lane is a delight. Her study of a resilient but vulnerable goodtime girl has a gentle persuasiveness to it.'

However, besides the role of Paulette Goddard in Richard Attenborough's *Chaplin*, the actress's films of late have been on the inconsequential side, although the quirky *My New Gun* did have its converts. An off-beat black comedy directed by first-timer Stacy Cochran, the film top-billed Ms Lane as a passive housewife whose life is turned upside down when her husband (Stephen Collins) gives her a gun. Those critics that managed to see the film agreed that in it the actress gave the best performance of her career.

She then joined the ensemble cast of Mike Binder's *Indian Summer*, with, among others, Alan Arkin, Elizabeth Perkins and Vincent Spano; and played the female lead in the Japanese-Chinese epic *The Setting Sun*, also starring Masaya Kato and Donald Sutherland.

FILMOGRAPHY

1979: *A Little Romance.* **1980:** *Cattle Annie and Little Britches; Touched By Love.* **1981:** *Child Bride of Short Creek* (TV); *Ladies and Gentlemen: The Fabulous Stains.* **1982:** *Miss All-American Beauty* (TV); *Six Pack; National Lampoon Goes To the Movies/National Lampoon's Movie Madness.* **1983:** *The Outsiders; RumbleFish.* **1984:** *The Cotton Club; Streets of Fire.* **1987:** *The Big Town; Priceless Beauty; Lady Beware.* **1989:** *Vital Signs.* **1990:** *Descending Angel* (TV). **1991:** *Knight Moves; My New Gun; Chaplin.* **1993:** *Indian Summer; The Setting Sun; Oldest Living Confederate Widow Tells All* (TV). **1994:** *Judge Dredd.*

Jennifer Jason LEIGH

Small (5'3"), delicate, almost sparrow-like in appearance, Jennifer Jason Leigh can transform herself before your eyes. She is accomplished at playing tough, and has bared her emotional armour on a myriad of occasions. But she's also the mouse, the pathetic, stepped-on rodent, reluctant to part from her gutter. It is this chameleonic quality that made the actress ideal casting as the dowdy, pitiable roommate of Bridget Fonda in Barbet Schroeder's thriller *Single White Female*. Soft, gentle, a little awkward, Leigh's Hedra Carlson was a sympathetic if slightly unappetizing creation, who, after layer and layer of narrative had been stripped away, was revealed as a ruthless, psychologically tormented monster – who would go to any lengths to satisfy her warped sense of justice. Had it not been for Leigh's performance, *Single White Female* would have ended up a very hollow thriller.

But then Jennifer Jason Leigh has lent distinction to a vast number of dubious projects. Constantly seeking the underside of the characters she plays, she explains her predilection thus: 'It's a fantastic feeling, because you go in new territories that most people really try and stay away from. You get to explore these extremes without losing yourself. It's exhilarating. Everyone is fascinated with the dark side. I mean, I know a few people who don't look when they pass an accident, or who won't read the most sordid, horrific newspaper story, but not many.' She then suggests, 'Maybe I'm drawn to strange characters because my life is so boring.'

Barbet Schroeder, who has directed both Glenn Close and Faye Dunaway, puts Leigh in the same class. 'She has the same intelligence and mad, creative temperament,' he offered. 'It's a combination of being totally possessed and lucid at the same time.'

The writer Hubert Selby Jr, on whose novel *Last Exit to Brooklyn* was based, was reduced to tears when he watched Leigh recreate his tragic heroine – the prostitute Tralala – at the film's epic gang-rape finale. 'What Jennifer gets you to experience is Tralala and her suffering,' he said. 'The fact that she brings such humanity to such a degrading situation is an indication of her magnificence as an actress.'

Maybe it is her all-consuming obsession for changing herself from role to role that kept Leigh out of the public eye for so long.

The Whore: Ms Leigh as Tralala in the melodramatic *Last Exit to Brooklyn*

The Victim: Jennifer Jason Leigh at the hands of rapist Steve Buscemi in *Heart of Midnight*

She considers it a compliment not to be recognized from the films she's appeared in, and is fiercely protective of her secrecy. After *People* magazine did a cosy photo-report on her and the actor David Dukes (she was 19, he was 35), Leigh avowed, 'reading that *People* article made me want to throw up.' For a while she was romantically involved with Eric Stoltz, whom she met while filming the Gothic thriller *Sister, Sister*, so when she played opposite Stoltz's then-current girlfriend Bridget Fonda in *Single White Female*, the tabloids moved in. Leigh says the reports of friction between her and her co-star were totally unfounded. 'I told Bridget the press would have a field day. But it wasn't an issue at all. We loved working together.'

The actress's relative anonymity has enabled her to research roles that otherwise might have been closed to her. She talked to abused children for *Heart of Midnight*, and attended crisis clinics. To play a performance artist in *The Big Picture*, she became a regular on the Los Angeles performance circuit. For Hedra Carlson she interviewed inmates of mental institutions and quizzed their psychiatrists. And for Robert Altman's *Short Cuts*, she hung out at a bustling phone-sex office, to get just the right feel for her character (a mother and part-time tele-seductress).

The Cop: As Kirsten Yates in the hardboiled *Rush*

She does, however, admit that the intensity of her research intimidates some people. 'I know, for instance, it frightened [director] Lili Zanuck on *Rush* – at first. The prep I do isn't for anyone else but me. I gives me a place of truth to draw upon. I often discover something that could inspire a scene.' She also acknowledges that, 'things have upset me – but I always assume that that's a good thing.'

Jennifer Lee Morrow was born on 5 February 1962 in Los Angeles, the second of three girls. Her mother, Barbara Turner, a TV actress-turned-scriptwriter, and father, the actor Vic Morrow (TV's *Combat*), divorced when she was two. She was never close to her father, and when he lost his life in 1982 on the set of *Twilight Zone – The Movie* (he was decapitated by a helicopter), he only left her $78.18 in his will (he left $600,000 to his oldest daughter, Carrie Ann).

A few years after their divorce, the ex-Mrs Morrow married the TV director Reza Badiyis, who cast Jennifer in a non-speaking role in his movie *Death of a Stranger*. 'I wanted to take acting lessons right away,' his stepdaughter recalled, 'but my mother said I had to wait until I was 14 – because she didn't want me to develop bad habits.'

However, at the Pacific Palisades High School Leigh acted in and directed numerous plays, and true enough, aged 14, she won a part in *The Young Runaway*, a Disney TV movie. Two years later she became a member of the Screen Actors Guild and changed her name to Jennifer Jason Leigh, to avoid any association with her father. She took her middle name from Jason Robards, a family friend.

She was then approached to play Tracy – a deaf, dumb and blind girl stalked by a psycho – in the feature *Eyes of a Stranger*, and learned Braille. 'When I was offered the film, I left high school promising my mother that I would take the equivalency exam – which, of course, I never did.'

When Jodie Foster was considered too fat to play an anorexic in the TV movie *The Best Little Girl in the World*, Leigh won the role and dieted down to 86 pounds. There were more TV movies – the commendable *Angel City* and *The Killing of Randy Webster*, the latter featuring Sean Penn in his film debut – and then she was offered the starring role of Stacy Hamilton, a virgin who seeks love and finds sex, in the comedy *Fast Times at Ridgemont High*. The film, which top-billed Penn and co-starred Phoebe Cates (now a bosom friend), was a hit and Jennifer Jason Leigh was on her way.

She had supporting roles in *Wrong Is Right*, with Sean Connery, and in the Rodney Dangerfield hit *Easy Money*, and was top-billed as a white slave transported to Japan in *Girls of the White Orchid*, for TV. She was a gum-chewing bimbo in *Grandview, USA*, with Patrick Swayze, and then starred opposite Rutger Hauer in Paul Verhoeven's sword-and-sex epic *Flesh + Blood*, as a princess violated by thugs. While developing her role, she employed a historical researcher but, as it turned out, this was not preparation enough. 'We all thought we were going to die,' she recalls. 'It was colder that year than it was in Russia. During the rape scene, which took five nights to shoot in zero-degree weather, they wouldn't even let me wear underwear to cover myself while I was lying on the ground.'

She was back with Hauer in the contemporary thriller *The Hitcher*, as a sexy, small-town waitress who ends up being torn apart by a tractor-trailer, and in *The Men's Club* she played a foul-talking whore who models herself on Jean Harlow. She was a copper's narc in *Under Cover*, directed by the actor

The Psycho: The deranged Hedra Carlson in the flashy hit *Single White Female*

John Stockwell; was a disturbed young woman manacled and sexually ravaged in *Heart of Midnight*; and was an eccentric performance artist – who befriends Kevin Bacon – in Christopher Guest's hilarious satire on Hollywood, *The Big Picture*. Guest, a malleable actor himself, commented, 'She looks different every time I see her in person.'

She then played Tralala, the tough prostitute in *Last Exit to Brooklyn*, and another hooker in the Jonathan Demme-produced *Miami Blues*, who dreams of becoming a housewife – but ends up being used and abused by ex-con Alec Baldwin. For her two performances, she won the New York Film Critics' Circle award as best supporting actress.

If Jennifer Jason Leigh seemed to be concentrating on movies slightly off the beaten track, it wasn't because she was an unknown quantity in Hollywood – or that she was avoiding the big names. She did go up for the lead in *Basic Instinct*, but lost the role because director Paul Verhoeven 'thought I was way too young for it, and though Sharon Stone isn't much older, she looks like a woman.' She talked herself out of *Pretty Woman* (she referred to the film as 'a recruiting movie, the *Top Gun* of prostitution'), refused to read for *A League Of Their Own* and turned down *sex, lies and videotape* to do *Miami Blues*.

After Alec Baldwin came Billy Baldwin, with whom she made love on top of a fire engine in Ron Howard's big-budget *Backdraft*, and then she had to compete against some major actresses for the role of Kristen Cates in *Rush*. This was the gruelling film version of Kim Wozencraft's semi-autobiographical novel about an undercover cop who

becomes a heroin addict in the course of duty. The film was far too bleak to become a box-office property, but Leigh was sensational in probably the best performance of her career.

However, *Single White Female* was a huge hit, and brought the actress the spotlight she so rightly deserved. Her co-star, Bridget Fonda, was originally ear-marked for the female lead – opposite Tim Robbins and Paul Newman – in Joel and Ethan Coen's 1950s' fantasy *The Hudsucker Proxy*, but the part fell to Ms Leigh and, at least on paper, it was the most prestigious of her career.

FILMOGRAPHY

1967: *Death of a Stranger* (bit). 1977: *The Young Runaway* (TV). 1980: *Eyes of a Stranger*; *Angel City* (TV). 1981: *The Best Little Girl In the World* (TV); *The Killing of Randy Webster* (TV). 1982: *Fast Times at Ridgemont High* (UK: *Fast Times*); *Wrong Is Right* (UK: *The Man With the Deadly Lens*). 1983: *Easy Money*; *Girls of the White Orchid* (later *Death Ride to Osaka*) (TV). 1984: *Grandview, USA*. 1985: *Flesh + Blood*. 1986: *The Hitcher*; *The Men's Club*. 1987: *Sister, Sister*; *Under Cover*. 1988: *Heart of Midnight*; *The Big Picture*. 1989: *Last Exit to Brooklyn*; *Miami Blues*. 1990: *Fire Princess*; *Buried Alive* (TV). 1991: *Backdraft*; *Crooked Hearts*; *Rush*. 1992: *Single White Female*. 1993: *Short Cuts*; *The Prom*; *The Hudsucker Proxy*. 1994: *Mrs Parker & the Vicious Circle*; *Dolores Claiborne*.

Juliette LEWIS

Barely old enough to say 'I do', Juliette Lewis was launched into the headlines thanks to three men: Robert De Niro, Woody Allen and Brad Pitt. An undeniable beauty who knew how to act, Ms Lewis hit pay dirt when she won a key role in Martin Scorsese's *Cape Fear*. The film was a hit (Scorsese's biggest), and starred De Niro, Nick Nolte, Jessica Lange, Robert Mitchum and Gregory Peck. Come Oscar time, De Niro received his customary vote of confidence and Juliette Lewis was nominated best supporting actress. The rest of the cast was ignored.

A breakneck thriller top-billing De Niro as a convict exacting a terrible revenge on the lawyer who put him behind bars (Nolte), *Cape Fear* gave its quietest and most sympathetic moments to Lewis. As Danielle Bowden, Nolte's 15-year-old daughter

Juliette Lewis, with Jessica Lange, terrorized by Robert De Niro, in Martin Scorsese's *Cape Fear*

tormented by De Niro, Lewis was an innocent, faltering and credible heroine, a blossom not yet in flower – waiting to be crushed by the force of evil.

De Niro, who had casting approval on the movie, suggested Lewis to Scorsese after their first meeting. 'I met her at the Beverly Hills Hotel for a preliminary chat,' he revealed. 'And I had an interesting feeling about her. She had a natural thing. You have to have a certain kind of awareness of yourself to be an actor, and I was impressed with how she handled the highly emotional stuff in *Cape Fear*. It's not easy to pull that out of yourself, to know where to get it. Some people don't even know how to begin to do it.'

A year after she shot *Cape Fear* Juliette Lewis was chosen by Woody Allen to replace Emily Lloyd in *Husbands and Wives*, his 22nd picture as writer-director. She was cast as 'Rain', a 21-year-old student who falls under the spell of an English professor, played by Woody himself. The irony of this was that Juliette was 18 at the time, the same age (journalists noted) as Soon-Yi Previn, Woody's lover and the adopted daughter of Mia Farrow. The actor-filmmaker maintained

Soon-Yi was nearer 21, but his stand made little difference in the face of the public furore that surrounded his separation from Ms Farrow. Opening bang in the wake of the court case (Woody fighting for child custody), *Husbands and Wives* captured its share of the media spotlight, further establishing Juliette Lewis as a household name.

Cape Fear and *Husbands and Wives* aside, the actress was accumulating more print mileage thanks to her romantic liaison with Brad Pitt, the coolest new male star of 1992. Six months before *Cape Fear* opened to ecstatic reviews in the States, Pitt appeared in *Thelma & Louise*, a film of equal critical clout. When the couple started turning up at premières together, their separate morsels of fame fed off one another. Soon, the tabloids were hailing them as the hottest new couple since Johnny Depp and Winona Ryder.

Brad and Juliette first met under less than romantic circumstances. She was starring in the true-life TV movie *Too Young To Die?* as Amanda Sue Bradley, a 14-year-old girl raped by her stepfather, discarded by her mother and abandoned by her 18-year-old husband. Enter Brad Pitt who, by comparison, seemed

something of a saviour. But sooner than you could say 'hard luck story,' he's bashing her in the face, pumping her full of drugs and selling her on the streets. It was love at first sight.

Thankfully, the romance lasted longer than the movie, the latter being a brutal, artless and totally pointless piece of audience manipulation. Still, Juliette Lewis held the attention – if not our sympathies – revealing the potential of a very fine actress. But then she'd had a head start.

Born at home on 21 June 1973, in Southern California, Juliette Lewis is the daughter of Geoffrey Lewis, veteran character actor of such movies as *Heaven's Gate*, *Every Which Way But Loose* and *The Lawnmower Man*. He and Juliette's mother, Glenis Batley, a graphic designer, divorced when she was two, and she moved to Los Angeles with her father – along with her older brother, Brian, and younger sister, Brandy. Between the ages of six and nine she lived with her mother in Florida, although she frequently visited her father on movie sets. On one such occasion, aged seven, she even made a brief appearance in Clint Eastwood's *Any Which Way You Can* and was instantly branded 'a natural.'

A self-confessed troublemaker at school, she made her official acting debut aged 12, in the two-part TV movie *Home Fires*. Although an uninspired look at the trials of an American family, the film won Lewis an Emmy nomination as best supporting actress.

Juliette with Woody Allen in the latter's controversial *Husbands and Wives*

She then co-starred in the ABC sitcom *I Married Nora* – as Nora's stepdaughter.

At 14, she sought legal emancipation and moved to Hollywood, where she stayed briefly with the actress Karen Black, a family friend. She had a recurring role in the comedy-drama series *The Wonder Years*, and made her feature film debut – as 'Lexie' – in *My Stepmother is an Alien*, after which she was launched onto the cinemagoing public.

In 1989 she had a small part in *The Runnin' Kind*, played Cindy Hollowhead in *Meet the Hollowheads* and was Audrey Griswold, Chevy Chase's daughter, in *National Lampoon's Christmas Vacation*, a hit. In the NBC sitcom *A Family For Joe*, she was Robert Mitchum's adopted daughter, Holly, and then won the role that accelerated her career – the lead in *Too Young To Die?* After that there was a small part in the domestic drama *Crooked Hearts*, and then came *Cape Fear*.

In *That Night* she had another starring role, as an animated teenager impregnated by local undesirable C. Thomas Howell. However, there was little animation between the two stars. Of his colleague, Howell volunteered, 'The biggest problem was just getting around her. I mean, she sometimes wouldn't show up for rehearsals. She's very talented, but she doesn't really know where it comes from – or why. If you don't know what you're doing and that makes you feel uncomfortable, it makes everybody else feel uncomfortable.'

Meanwhile, the film's first-time director, Craig Bolotin, added: 'She's very opinionated about how to do things, and there was a clash.' But, 'out of that clash came a really terrific performance.'

There was a better rapport between her and her leading man on the set of *Kalifornia*, the tale of a 'white trash couple' seriously into serial killing. Her leading man was Brad Pitt, who confessed, 'It was a fun shoot, because it was so easy and I got to hang out with my love.' Adding that, 'a lot of it is really sweet, believe it or not.' Ms Lewis played the killer's moll, a part Pitt describes as 'a little bird with a clipped wing.'

She auditioned to play the wildly flirtatious Lucy Westenra in *Bram Stoker's Dracula*, but lost the part to British unknown Sadie Frost. However, she did get to act opposite Gary Oldman in his next film, the black comedy *Romeo is Bleeding*. After that she played the central role in Susan Seidelman's *Yesterday*, with Dianne Wiest (Brad Pitt's favourite actress), and skewered the female lead in Lasse Hallstrom's unequivocally bizarre *What's Eating Gilbert Grape*, alongside Johnny Depp. She then starred opposite Woody Harrelson in the Oliver Stone-produced *Natural Born Killers*, from a screenplay by Quentin Tarantino.

FILMOGRAPHY

1980: *Any Which Way You Can* (bit). 1987: *Home Fires* (TV). 1988: *My Stepmother is an Alien*. 1989: *The Runnin' Kind*; *Meet the Hollowheads*; *National Lampoon's Christmas Vacation* (UK: *National Lampoon's Winter Holiday*). 1990: *Too Young To Die?* (TV). 1991: *Crooked Hearts*; *Cape Fear*. 1992: *That Night* (aka *One Hot Summer*); *Husbands and Wives*. 1993: *Kalifornia*; *Romeo Is Bleeding*; *Yesterday*; *What's Eating Gilbert Grape*. 1994: *Natural Born Killers*; *Strange Days*.

Ray LIOTTA

Considering the wattage of the critical spotlight trained on Ray Liotta, the actor has exhibited a remarkably low profile in Hollywood. His career has consisted of a series of dramatic breakthroughs, but has failed to transform him into a household name. He avoids the glitzy parties of LA, the media-saturated premières, the famous girlfriends. And he is refreshingly open about his belated intimacy with the movies – and acting.

'Becoming an actor wasn't a big, burning passion for me,' he revealed. 'I just did the whole jock thing in high school. Acting was sort of just something to do, but I liked it.' In fact, Liotta preferred playing baseball to anything else. He occasionally went to the cinema, but gleaned little from it. 'I was never really into movies enough when I was growing up to understand who Robert De

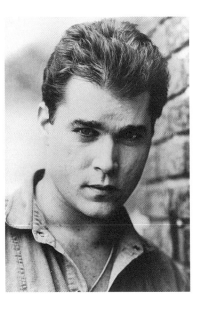

Ray Liotta

really sure?'" Only after meeting Liotta, did Winkler change his mind. 'We started chatting, and I realised that Marty was absolutely right. Ray was warm and gracious and had a lot of the qualities that Marty wanted for his character.'

Something Wild was another Liotta vehicle that promised instant stardom. And it was another role that the actor had had to declare war for. Eventually, he went direct to the film's star, Melanie Griffith, and begged her to let the film's director, Jonathan Demme, see him. A meeting was arranged and Liotta got the role (even though the part had been earmarked as 'a star vehicle').

As Ray Sinclair, Griffith's psychotic, redneck husband, Liotta again walked off with the acting honours. He won the Boston Critics' award for best supporting actor and was nominated for a Golden Globe to boot.

'I like to play people who feel deeply about something,' the star explained, 'and that's pretty much what Ray Sinclair was about. And I was angry, waiting around for five years to be in a movie. I was primed. I worked my ass off.'

Born on 13 December 1955, in Union, New Jersey, Ray Liotta was the adopted child of an auto-parts shop owner. He was raised in a quiet middle-class suburb and dismisses his upbringing as, 'fine. It was a nice life. I grew up nice.'

He enrolled at the University of Miami to study drama because, he says, that's where his good friend Vinny was and because the weather was nice. At least, it was better than

working in his father's store or tending cemetery grounds in New Jersey. Moving up to New York to become an actor, Liotta was out of work for two days before landing a K-Tel record commercial. This was going to be easy. Next, he won a regular spot on the daytime soap *Another World*, playing Joey Perrini, 'the nicest guy in the world,' he says. 'I couldn't have been any sweeter. It was sickening.' For three years, no less, he was the nicest guy.

He had a starring role in the TV movie *Crazy Times*, alongside Michael Pare and David Caruso, a nostalgic and mediocre look at three teenage friends growing up in 1955. And then the work stopped.

Liotta moved to Los Angeles, befriended two other unemployed actors – Andy Garcia and Kevin Costner – and played a lot of paddle tennis. He also got a girlfriend, former stuntwoman Heidi Von Beltz, who was paralysed from the neck down (she had doubled for Farrah Fawcett in *The Cannonball Run*). By all accounts, Liotta was devoted to the beautiful blonde, an intimate of Melanie Griffith's. At the time, Liotta saw a lot of Griffith, too, who was married to another good friend, actor Steven Bauer (Al Pacino's sidekick in *Scarface*), from their days together at Miami University.

And so, after a miserly bit in the awful *The Lonely Lady* (as the assailant who strangles Pia Zadora in the shower), the script of *Something Wild* fell into Liotta's hands. The film was a hit, and Liotta was a hit in it. The screwball tale of a Yuppie Jeff Daniels

Niro or Martin Scorsese were. I wasn't in awe. I just thought they were filmmakers who worked hard. And I don't think that's being arrogant, it's just because I never really wanted to do this, even when I was taking acting in college. I didn't know anything about them.'

It is ironic, then, that it was De Niro who suggested Liotta for the part of gangster-wannabe Henry Hill in Scorsese's *GoodFellas*, the film that turned Liotta into a major contender for Hollywood stardom.

Exuding a sexual charimas that could stop a gangster's moll at twenty paces, Liotta acted De Niro off the screen. Dangerous, edgy, psychotic, Liotta's amoral womanizer was a character actors would have killed for. OK, so Tom Cruise turned the part down, but reportedly the likes of Alec Baldwin, Nicolas Cage and Val Kilmer were fighting for the role. Yet Liotta almost didn't get it – because he was perceived as *too* dangerous, too manic. And still he managed to make Henry Hill likeable, which was no small feat.

The film's producer, Irwin Winkler, admitted, 'frankly, I didn't want him in the movie. I felt that the character needed a lot of sympathy. I had just seen Ray in *Something Wild*, so I kept saying to Marty, "Jeez, are you

Liotta (*centre*), surrounded by *GoodFellas* Robert De Niro and Paul Sorvino in Martin Scorsese's masterpiece

Liotta as the LA cop from hell in Johathan Kaplan's relentless thriller *Unlawful Entry*

ensnared by wildcat Griffith, the film changed track dramatically half-way through when Liotta gate-crashed their dream. An ex-con from hell, Liotta trashes the couple's romance and makes Jeff Daniels confront his own manhood. So convincing was Liotta in the part, that journalists at the film's press junket gave him a wide berth. It was the start of some serious typecasting.

Determined to make the most of his new standing, Liotta turned down every psycho in Hollywood (and the large salaries that went with them). Finally, he opted for the role of Tom Hulce's caring brother, Gino, in Robert M. Young's brave little story of fraternal commitment, *Dominick and Eugene*.

Again, he nearly didn't get the part. The producer, actor Mike Farrell, caught a screening of *Something Wild* and blanched. Farrell recalls: 'I called my partner and said, "Wait a minute! This murdering, outrageous, satanic, bastard guy scares the shit out of me!" So we took Ray out to lunch, and he was so sweet that he instantly erased all my fears.'

Dominick and Eugene was not a success, and any good reviews the film got concentrated on Hulce's part as the retarded Nicky. However, as the medical student struggling to find the balance between his own life and his brother's, Liotta was also very good.

Next, he was announced as the star – opposite Linda Fiorentino – of *The War at Home*, but the film never materialized, and then came a supporting role in *Field of Dreams*. Liotta played the ghost of baseball legend 'Shoeless' Joe Jackson, and his old friend Kevin Costner was the farmer who heard voices in the cornfields ('If you build it, He will come'). The film was a hit, but nobody seemed to notice Liotta.

GoodFellas changed all that. Martin Scorsese's picture was voted best film by the Los Angeles, New York and US National Society of Film Critics and by BAFTA, and that was just for starters. Joe Pesci, who played fellow gangster Tommy DeVito, won the Oscar, and the film proved to be a milestone for all concerned – including Scorsese.

For once, Liotta was able to pick and choose his scripts, and in another bid to beat typecasting he played the heroic Dr Leonard Sturgess in *Article 99*, a black comedy-drama set in a Veterans' Administration hospital. This time he was top-billed (above Kiefer Sutherland, Forest Whitaker, Lea Thompson, Kathy Baker and Eli Wallach), but the public were not yet ready to see their favourite psycho as a good boy. However, the movie did have its champions. The trade paper *Variety* thought it 'a timely and provocative' piece and said that 'Liotta shows inexhaustible spirit and convincing leadership qualities as the crusading doctor . . .'

On TV, he played a concerned husband in the three-part *Women & Men 2: In Love There Are No Rules*, in the episode labelled 'Domestic Dilemma'. Andie MacDowell played his alcoholic wife, but the segment was the weakest of the three (Matt Dillon and Scott Glenn starred in the other two). If Liotta was to grab people's attention, he had to stride down the psycho path again.

This he did with a vengeance in Jonathan Kaplan's chilling *Unlawful Entry*, the story of a Yuppie couple who call the police when an intruder breaks into their dream house. Kurt Russell and Madeleine Stowe were the couple, and they wished they'd never dialled 999. Liotta played Pete Davis, a handsome, highly-decorated police officer who sets up the couple's security system and then turns nasty. At first shy, aloof and sexually dangerous, Liotta's maniac cop never *acts* crazy, which makes him all the more of a lethal opponent. Only in the film's final passage does Liotta allow his psycho to snarl. Released during the aftermath of the Rodney King furore in Los Angeles, *Unlawful Entry* was a hot potato and made audiences particularly uneasy in the scene in which Liotta lays

into a black man with a baton. Ray Liotta found himself in another hit.

FILMOGRAPHY

1980: *Hardhat and Legs* (TV). 1981: *Crazy Times* (TV). 1983: *The Lonely Lady*. 1986: *Something Wild*. 1988: *Dominick and Eugene* (UK: *Nicky and Gino*). 1989: *Field of Dreams*. 1990: *GoodFellas*. 1991: *Women & Men 2: In Love There Are No Rules* (TV). 1992: *Article 99*; *Unlawful Entry*. 1994: *No Escape*; *Corrina, Corrina*.

Rob LOWE

Whether he warranted it or not, Rob Lowe was the star representative of the Brat Pack. He went to school with Emilio Estevez, Charlie Sheen and Sean Penn. He made his film debut in *The Outsiders*, alongside Estevez, Tom Cruise and Matt Dillon. He surfaced in the requisite amount of teen fodder alongside such distaff regulars as Jodie Foster, Ally Sheedy, Demi Moore, Winona Ryder and Meg Tilly. He was seen at parties and premieres with a steady stream of famous girlfriends: Princess Stephanie of Monaco, Nastassja Kinski, Marlee Matlin, Fawn Hall, Chynna Phillips, Brigitte Nielsen, and his on-off love of six years, Melissa Gilbert. And he was a bad boy. He once claimed, 'If I haven't been with 'em, I know 'em, or I've been engaged to 'em. I looked at my calendar and said, "Shit, it's a few weeks into the new year, and I haven't been engaged to anyone yet. I'd better get to work."'

But appearances can be deceptive. Underneath the pretty face, the moulded jaw line and those penetrating blue eyes, Rob Lowe was just a regular guy who wanted to be loved. He claimed, 'It's really weird, but I am the most shy when it comes to girls. *Really* shy.' He also wanted to prove that he was more than just a cute facade, and worked hard to find challenging roles. In fact, he was only 19-years-old when he was nominated for a Golden Globe award for his role as a boy undergoing a heart transplant in the TV movie *Thursday's Child*. Three years later, he was nominated a second time, for playing a retarded 21-year-old Texan in the movie *Square Dance*. And he had his champions. The celebrated New York critic Andrew Sarris wrote, 'I don't think Lowe gets enough credit. He has a real talent. He could be like Alain Delon, playing high-quality villains – interesting, complex people. I could see him playing Ted Bundy.' And Lowe was the first person not to take himself seriously. At the 1989 Oscar ceremony he poked fun at himself singing 'Proud Mary' with Snow

Rob Lowe in 1983

White, but the prank backfired when Disney sued the Academy for breach of copyright.

And there was that Atlanta thing. The night that turned Rob Lowe into the laughing stock of the world, the personal catastrophe that all but hammered the last nail into the actor's faltering career. The media smirked when the star was reduced to accepting a supporting role in a Feydeau stage farce in New York. But Lowe was savvy enough to face the problem head on, and dared to play a sleazy hustler who covertly videos a couple having sex – in the movie *Bad Influence*. And, to add pepper to the stew, the guy having sex was James Spader, fresh from *sex, lies and videotape*. Then, when even that failed to save him, Lowe did something that he was strongly cautioned against: he took a supporting role in a film starring two unknowns based on a TV sketch. The film was *Wayne's World* and, grossing $132 million on its first US release, became the most successful movie of Rob Lowe's career. Once again, the Romeo of Malibu was back where he belonged: on the cover of countless magazines.

Robert Hepler Lowe, the eldest of three

children, was born on 17 March 1964 in Charlottesville, Virginia. The son of a lawyer, he grew up in Dayton, Ohio, until his parents divorced, and his mother remarried. But he already knew he wanted to be an actor, inspired by a local production of the musical *Oliver!* He was nine when he made his first stage appearance in summer stock, following it up with commercials and bits on local television. When he was 12, his mother married a third time, and the family moved to Malibu. Behind him, Lowe left his two best friends, both brothers: one dead, killed in a car chase with the police; the other a young dad at 17 who'd been in and out of jail. Lowe realizes that, had he stayed, 'I don't know what I would have become.'

In Malibu he went to school with Emilio and Charlie, and they, together with Rob's younger brother Chad (also an actor), became obsessed with making home videos. Rob continued his career in real showbusiness, but found the LA competition tough. He got a Coke commercial, and then, in 1979, landed a regular spot on the domestic TV sitcom *A New Kind of Family*, playing Tony Flanagan, the son of a widowed Eileen Brennan. A year later he was the lead in The Afternoon TV Special *Schoolboy Father*, and also appeared in the Emmy-winning *A Matter of Time*.

Lowe's big-screen debut arrived with *The Outsiders*, in which he played gas attendant

Sodapop Curtis, brother of C. Thomas Howell and Patrick Swayze. He had little to do, but he was naturalistic and pretty, and the scene in which he arm-wrestled Tom Cruise got him noticed. Next came the TV movie *Thursday's Child*, and its attendant critical attention, and then top-billing in the romantic teen comedy *Class*. This was no small feat, as the movie was essentially about the romance between Lowe's roommate, Andrew McCarthy, and his mother, played by Jacqueline Bisset. In *Hotel New Hampshire*, based on the John Irving novel, he romanced Nastassja Kinski and Jodie Foster, the latter playing his sister (!), and went to England to play an amorous jock in *Oxford Blues*. He was good in *St Elmo's Fire*, as a sax-playing philanderer who neglects his wife and child, and learned to smoke for the role. In *Youngblood* he was re-teamed with Patrick Swayze, in which they played ice hockey players, and then wooed Demi Moore in 'About Last Night ...', a trashy film version of David Mamet's serious play *Sexual Perversity in Chicago*. As his male co-star in the latter, Jim Belushi, told his character, 'You know what your problem is? Your face. Come on, wise up, man. You're too good-looking.'

Lowe tried to remedy this by making a brave career move, taking a pay-cut and accepting fourth-billing in the low-budget drama *Square Dance* (starring Jason Robards, Jane Alexander and Winona Ryder). He even

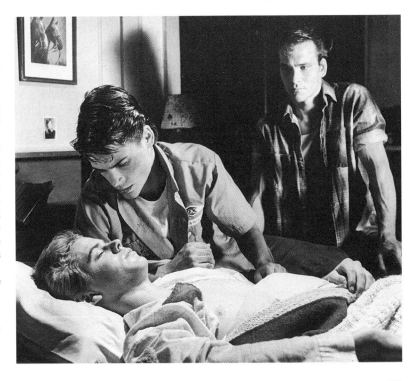

Rob Lowe (*centre*) as Sodapop Curtis in *The Outsiders*, with C. Thomas Howell (in bed) and Patrick Swayze

had to audition for the part. 'I hadn't read for a role in a long time,' the actor admitted. 'It was scary. They were not sure someone perceived as a leading man could do a role such as this without damaging the project.' Unfortunately, in spite of all Lowe's efforts, it was hard to separate the star from the stammering, drawling retarded youth he played. Still, he was nominated for a Golden Globe award, which was more than he got for his next film, the courtroom farce *Illegally Yours*, in which he attempted broad comedy to disastrous effect. He was much, much better in Bob Swaim's *Masquerade*, a yuppie *Body Heat*, in which he played a 'two dollar gigolo' preying on rich women. At the time, he admitted, 'The character's a real stretch for me. He is the kind of man people might never imagine I'd play. He's a sponge, a chameleon. He doesn't feel guilt and he doesn't see any reason to.' Swaim was impressed. 'Rob's underestimated by a lot of people,' the director offered. 'They ought to give him a break. He's a very bright kid, a director's dream.'

The year was 1988 and it was an emotionally bruising time for the actor. He had been dating the actress Melissa Gilbert (TV's *Little House On the Prairie*) on and off

Lowe in his Golden Globe-nominated performance as the retarded Rory, in Daniel Petrie's *Square Dance*

for six years when she suddenly married actor-producer-director Bo Brinkman. Obviously stung by the break-up, Lowe revealed, 'Melissa chose to let me hear about it by calling up a radio station and broadcasting it to the public. I had never met the guy and have no idea who he is.'

But the year wasn't over yet. On 17 July 1988, Lowe was in Atlanta for the Democratic National Convention. After attending a party thrown by the media tycoon Ted Turner (now Jane Fonda's husband), he ventured on to the Club Rio. There, he was asked to prove his age at the door – so, naturally it never occurred to him that anybody else would be underage. He had several drinks, talked to a lot of girls and noticed that one in particular was making a play for him. By the time he left the club, he was accompanied by the latter, Lena Jan Parsons, and her friend Tara Siebert, and they all went back to his hotel room. What followed became household news. And because of it a civil suit was filed against the actor, claiming that Lowe, 'used his celebrity status as an inducement to females to engage in sexual intercourse, sodomy, and multiple-party sexual activity for his immediate sexual gratification, and for the purpose of making pornographic films of these activities.'

Jan Parsons, 16, was recovering from the collapse of her parents' marriage, and was a confirmed truant. Tara Siebert, 22, was, according to court documents, a known lesbian. Following their sexual marathon in Lowe's hotel room, they slipped off while he was in the bathroom, taking with them $100 from his wallet and the mini-cassette from his video camera. The following day they couldn't contain themselves, and told friends of their experience. A month later, Jan's mother, Lena, found the video and all hell broke loose. In January of 1989 Lena's lawyer contacted Lowe and court proceedings commenced. Lowe's attorney suggested a $35,000 'take it or leave it' offer, but it was rejected. It was too late, anyhow. Copies of the video had mysteriously started to circulate and before the whole ugly thing was over, Lowe had been threatened with 20 years in prison and a fine of $100,000. Meanwhile, parts of his home movie had been broadcast on network TV (on *A Current Affair*) and the X-rated cable show *Midnight Blue*. As it happens, no charges were brought in the end, but Lowe was a changed man. He also enrolled in a 12-step AA programme and, according to newspaper reports, entered a clinic to stem his voracious sexual appetite.

Later, he told *Rolling Stone* magazine, 'It

Lowe as the smarmy TV executive Benjamin Oliver in the smash-hit comedy *Wayne's World*

was one of those quirky, sort of naughty, sort of wild, sort of, you know, drunken things that people will do from time to time. I had people come up to me on the street afterward and say, "Hey, you know, I do it all the time. The difference is you got caught."'

Career-wise, Rob Lowe couldn't top his home movie. *Bad Influence*, *If the Shoe Fits*, *The Dark Backward* (in which he had a jokey cameo as a broken-nosed Hollywood hustler) and *The Finest Hour*, were all box-office duds. But then Lowe had the last laugh.

In 1991 he secretly married make-up artist Cheryl Berkoff (former girlfriend of Emilio Estevez), whom he first met in 1983 and became reacquainted with on the set of *Bad Influence*. And then he played the villain in *Wayne's World*.

FILMOGRAPHY

1983: *The Outsiders*; *Thursday's Child* (TV); *Class*. 1984: *The Hotel New Hampshire*; *Oxford Blues*. 1985: *St Elmo's Fire*. 1986: *Youngblood*; *'About Last Night . . .'*; *Square Dance*. 1987: *Illegally Yours*. 1988: *Masquerade*. 1990: *Bad Influence*; *If the Shoe Fits*. 1991: *The Dark Backward* (UK: *The Man With Three Arms*) (cameo). 1992: *The Finest Hour*; *Wayne's World*. 1994: *The Stand* (TV); *Frank and Jesse*.

Ralph MACCHIO

If Bambi were Italian he would look like Ralph Macchio. And that was Macchio's problem. Even as a married man heading into his thirties, he looked the eternal teenager. With his big brown eyes, teenage-crooked teeth and sweet, self-conscious smile, he was a Peter Pan for the Italian-American market.

He insisted, 'there's an adult somewhere under here,' but he kept on playing chaps younger than himself. In *My Cousin Vinny*, aged 31, he played a 21-year-old student, but his moustache looked so undernourished he seemed even younger. It was hard to believe that another Italian-American, Nicolas Cage, was in fact two years Macchio's junior.

Ralph Macchio was actually born on 4 November 1961 in Long Island, New York, the son of the owner of a chemical waste company. At an early age he sang and danced in local musical productions, when he was spotted by a talent scout and signed up to do commercials. He was 16. In 1980, he beat out 2,000 candidates for the part of Betty Buckley's troubled nephew, Jeremy, in ABC TV's successful comedy-drama series *Eight Is Enough*, and then landed a big role (Chooch) in Robert Downey's primitive comedy *Up the Academy*, set in a boy's military college. The film's star, Ron Leibman, thought it so bad that he had his named removed from the credits.

Next, Macchio appeared in *Dangerous Company*, with Beau Bridges as a violent, real-life law-breaker, and then won the catalyst role of Johnny Cade in Francis Coppola's *The Outsiders*. Cade is the Bambi-faced underdog who, while defending himself and Ponyboy Curtis (C. Thomas Howell) against 'socially superior' attackers, knifes a guy to death. And so Johnny and Ponyboy are forced to leave town and, in an ironic twist of fate, the former becomes a hero and martyr.

The look of *The Outsiders* was the thing. The conflagrant sunsets, the reflection of rain on faces, silhouettes transfixed on a horizon. And so Ralph Macchio's defiant, cherubic features were ideal to mirror the injustice of his persecution. And while he may have been cast for his face, the actor gave Johnny a naturalistic edge that snatched him from the gulf of sentimentality. The film, which featured Matt Dillon, Patrick Swayze, Rob Lowe, Tom Cruise and Emilio Estevez in smaller parts, went on to become a classic of its kind.

The following year Macchio played a juvenile delinquent in *Teachers*, with Nick Nolte, and then landed the lead in *The Karate Kid*, a formulaic little movie aimed at audiences too young to appreciate the

subtleties of *Rocky*. Inspired by a news report about a wimp who whipped his elders and biggers into shape after a crash-course in karate, the film was directed by John G. Avildsen himself, he who brought the first *Rocky* to life. But karate was different from boxing and cinematically, at least, had mostly been confined to cheap films from Hong Kong. But the scenarist Robert Mark Kamen was eager to reveal the martial art in a kinder light.

Macchio played Daniel, a victim of school bullies, who befriends an eccentric Japanese gardener called Miyagi (Noriyuki 'Pat' Morita). Miyagi, as it happens, is not only great at training bonsai trees, but can catch a fly with a pair of chopsticks. He is also an authority in the martial arts and reluctantly takes Daniel on as a pupil, stressing that, 'fighting always last answer to problem. To fight enemy without fighting is the highest skill.' Well, surprise surprise, Daniel becomes a deft hand (and foot) at karate and gets to kick the living daylights out of his oppressors. In a year when *Ghostbusters*, *Indiana Jones and the Temple of Doom* and *Beverly Hills Cop* were changing the face of box-office history, *The Karate Kid* broke a few records of its own, and Macchio became an overnight pin-up.

In the well-received TV movie *The Three Wishes of Billy Grier* he was re-teamed with

Ralph Macchio (*right*) with C. Thomas Howell in *The Outsiders*

Macchio with Elisabeth Shue in *The Karate Kid*

Macchio with Noriyuki 'Pat' Morita in *The Karate Kid Part III*

Betty Buckley, playing a teenager stricken with an ageing disease, and was then a cocky guitarist who befriends a blues legend (Joe Seneca) in Walter Hill's *Crossroads*.

He was back as Daniel in *The Karate Kid Part II*, a sequel that managed to be more original than its predecessor. This time he accompanied his mentor to Japan, where he finds an Oriental girlfriend and helps Miyagi battle an old enemy. In between the sickening crunches, the film revealed a winning tenderness and was an engrossing look at Japanese culture. It also made a mint, far out-grossing the original, and becoming the second biggest hit in America that year (after *Top Gun*). In 1986, Macchio was voted more popular than Harrison Ford, Meryl Streep and Michael Douglas. That year he also made his Broadway stage debut in *Cuba and His Teddy Bear*, and the play's seven-week run – at New York's Public Theatre – was completely sold-out three hours after it's announcement. Macchio played the troubled son of a Hispanic drug peddler (Robert De Niro, his idol), and received the best reviews of his career.

In April of 1987 he married a cardiac-care nurse, Phyllis, and played John Lithgow's abandoned son in the Canadian-produced *Distant Thunder*, an earnest, but overly sentimental drama that flopped at the box-office. A year later he was due to star in

Young Men With Unlimited Capital, as a young rock promoter who teams up with Emilio Estevez to finance the 1969 Woodstock music festival. However, insiders revealed that the actors quibbled over billing, and the venture was abandoned. Still, there was always *The Karate Kid Part III*, although Macchio grumbled, 'I'm not that excited about doing the picture, except for the opportunity to entertain little kids.' As it happens, *Part III* was a box-office disappointment, making about a third of the first sequel.

He was in Robert Downey's ludicrous, insulting farce *Too Much Sun*, dumped in a sub-lot with Robert Downey Jr, and then starred opposite Martin Sheen in the little-seen drama *Garwood: Prisoner-Of-War*. Off-Broadway, he appeared in the play *Only Kidding*, and was all but forgotten when he re-emerged as Bill Gambini in *My Cousin Vinny*. The latter was a small-budget comedy in which the actor played an UCLA student waylaid in Alabama accused of a murder he didn't commit. In desperation, the lad contacts his cousin Vinny La Guardia Gambini (Joe Pesci), a Brooklyn lawyer who knows as much about court procedure as he does about women (which is zilch). Thanks to tight direction, a witty script and some superb ensemble playing, *My Cousin Vinny* was one of the year's funniest comedies and went on to gross an entirely unexpected $52 million in the States alone.

In 1993, Macchio joined the all-star cast of the Martin Scorsese-produced *Naked In New York*, with Eric Stoltz, Mary-Louise Parker, Kathleen Turner, Timothy Dalton, Tony Curtis and Whoopi Goldberg.

FILMOGRAPHY

1980: *Up the Academy.* **1982:** *Dangerous Company* (TV). **1983:** *The Outsiders.* **1984:** *Teachers; The Karate Kid; The Three Wishes of Billy Grier* (TV). **1986:** *Crossroads; The Karate Kid Part II.* **1988:** *Distant Thunder.* **1989:** *The Karate Kid Part III.* **1991:** *Too Much Sun; Garwood: Prisoner-of-War* (video). **1992:** *My Cousin Vinny.* **1993:** *Naked In New York.*

Andie MacDOWELL

Andie MacDowell had three problems. She was beautiful, she was making good money and she had an accent as thick as molasses. Hollywood has never taken kindly to models who think they can act, and when MacDowell's voice was dubbed by Glenn Close in her first film – *Greystoke, The Legend of Tarzan, Lord of the Apes* – Tinseltown laughed. Andie MacDowell had a nervous breakdown, took a small part in a Brat Pack

Andie MacDowell

movie and then disappeared.

Four years later she played a brittle, sexually repressed Southern wife in a small, low-budget feature made by a first-time director. 'My thought was that I would at least get something on tape that I could show to casting directors,' she explained. But then the unexpected happened. The film, blessed with the intriguing title of *sex, lies, and videotape* (in lower case letters), won the Palme d'Or at Cannes and gained a huge critical following. 'Its success only sank in properly,' she says, 'when I began to be offered films without being asked to audition.' Better still, the Los Angeles Film Critics' Circle voted her best actress of the year (in a tie with Michelle Pfeiffer), and she was nominated for a Golden Globe award. Soon, MacDowell was starring in some very classy pictures opposite some very classy actors, not least John Malkovich, Gerard Depardieu and Ray Liotta. There was one hiccough, the $55 million box-office turkey *Hudson Hawk*, but this time most of the blame was shovelled onto her co-star Bruce Willis.

She was born Rosalie Anderson MacDowell on 21 April 1958, in Gaffney, a small town in South Carolina. When the director James Cameron shot *The Abyss* at a disused nuclear power plant there, he told *Rolling Stone*, 'Filming in Gaffney is like filming in Tibet, but at least Tibet would be interesting.' MacDowell, who was known as

appeared on the covers of countless magazines. She returned to New York 'a star' and landed a lucrative contract with L'Oreal Cosmetics, who paid her $500,000 for 12 days' work a year for modelling their make-up. She also posed for The Gap, where she met former model Paul Qualley and three months later married him. Subsequently, he became a successful singer (reaching Italy's top-ten – as PJ Qualley) and she became the mother of their son, Justin.

She was Jane in Hugh Hudson's visually sumptuous *Greystoke*, dressed – not in a chamois leather – but in Victorian lace and frills, and was romanced by a gentrified Tarzan (Christopher Lambert). The film was a success, but when MacDowell's Southern vowels were dubbed over by Glenn Close, she revealed, 'I was furious. I had a nervous breakdown about it. It was the worst thing I could imagine. I called my manager. I called everyone.' A year later she was ninth-billed in *St Elmo's Fire*, playing the heart's desire of Emilio Estevez, but felt ostracized from the rest of the cast (Rob Lowe, Andrew McCarthy, Demi Moore, Ally Sheedy). Although the film was a success, few remember that she was in it.

She joined Ben Kingsley in the little-seen Italian mini-series *The Sahara Secret* and

Andie in her greatest role, as the suppressed housewife Ann Millaney in Steven Soderbergh's brilliant *sex, lies and videotape*

Andie with Gerard Depardieu in Peter Weir's winning romantic comedy *Green Card*

'Rosie' as a child, was the youngest of four girls. Her father worked in the lumber trade and her mother was a music teacher. They divorced when Rosie was six. After her father remarried, the ex-Mrs MacDowell began drinking heavily, lost teaching jobs and was reduced to working in fast-food joints (she died in 1982). Meanwhile, Rosie and her sisters modelled at local shops, and Rosie began a secret portfolio. She left Gaffney to attend college in Winthorpe, South Carolina, but dropped out to pursue her modelling career in New York. There, she was signed up by the Elite modelling agency almost immediately and had her name changed to 'Andie'. She tired of the work after a month ('I'd done all this stuff already, when I was 15'), so the agency sent her to Paris, where she became an enormous success and continued modelling. In a series of Calvin Klein ads on TV, she appeared as herself and wrote her own script – in which she addressed the camera with intriguing tales of the South. It was the first time people were genuinely aware of her accent.

She then read Steven Soderbergh's screenplay for *sex, lies, and videotape*. 'I was so touched by the role [of Ann Millaney],' she recalls. 'I wanted to live her, I wanted to be her so badly. And then I learned later that I almost didn't get to go up for it, because Steven, judging by my history, wasn't that enthusiastic about me.' Soderbergh admits, 'There were some people who weren't willing to consider her. But at the audition, she completely blew me out. I went to my producers and said, "I think Andie's it", and they exchanged looks like, "Uh, oh." I knew people would be caught off guard by her work, which means now I get to look like a smart guy.'

Shot on a budget of $1.2 million, the film was a ferociously honest look at sex and the stagnation of marriage, and MacDowell (who was then pregnant with her second child) was perfect as the emotionally constipated wife of Peter Gallagher, who is cheating on her with her sister (Laura San Giacomo). Soderbergh, who may have been aware of the irony, begins the film with a voice-over

Andie MacDowell and Bruce Willis in the Flop That Won't Go Away: Tri-Star's disastrous *Hudson Hawk*

from MacDowell, who is talking to her therapist. 'Garbage,' she drawls, 'all I've been thinking about all week is garbage.'

She wasn't even asked to audition for the role of Tina in the British black comedy *The Object of Beauty*, in which she played a skittish American tourist trapped in a London hotel with John Malkovich. 'At first, I wasn't really sure if I liked the script or not, because Tina is weak – or can seem weak,' she mused. 'Then I looked beyond that weakness and I saw that Tina is very colourful and fun.' The film was a delightful comedy of manners, and MacDowell exposed a new playful side to her persona. She was repressed again in Peter Weir's utterly charming and touching romantic comedy *Green Card*, in which she was an aristocratic New Yorker who marries a French lump (Gerard Depardieu) in order to qualify for the apartment of her dreams. The outcome was predictable enough, but it was a sheer joy to follow the film to its five-Kleenex conclusion. *Green Card* was a success, and MacDowell won another Golden Globe nomination.

When the Dutch actress Maruschka Detmers had to withdraw from *Hudson Hawk* because of back troubles, the *National Enquirer* claimed she was removed from the film at Demi Moore's insistence. 'Bullshit,' scoffed Bruce Willis, the film's star and Demi's husband. Anyway, Andie MacDowell was hastily flown in to replace Detmers. For MacDowell, her role as 'a hip nun in Ray-Bans' was, 'a whole new departure for me, to be in a real broad, screwball comedy.'

Unfortunately, few were amused, and the $55 million movie was christened *Hudson the Duck* by the media and became the year's biggest bomb.

Her next role, in the omnibus TV feature *Women & Men 2: In Love There Are No Rules*, was a brave one. In the segment entitled 'A Domestic Dilemma', co-starring Ray Liotta as her concerned husband, MacDowell faced the spectre of her mother's alcoholism by playing a woman who succumbs to the bottle. The only shame was that she didn't have more time to develop her character in the half hour allotted her.

Next, she played herself in Robert Altman's acclaimed *The Player*, and then won top-billing in the romantic mystery *Ruby Cairo*, as a woman searching for her husband across LA, Mexico, Egypt and Germany – assisted by Liam Neeson. In Harold Ramis's successful, high-concept comedy *Groundhog Day*, she was delightful as a smart, fun-loving TV producer tenaciously courted by a cynical weatherman (Bill Murray), and then joined the all-star cast of Robert Altman's blue-collar satire *Short Cuts*. In Mike Newell's enchanting, hilarious *Four Weddings & a Funeral* she was romanced by Hugh Grant's serial monogamist, and the film went on to become the first British feature to reach No. 1 in the States since *A Fish Called Wanda* six years earlier. Ironically, it was knocked off its post after one week by *Bad Girls*, in which MacDowell played a whore on the run and which the critics hated. Nevertheless, Andie MacDowell was all over the place.

FILMOGRAPHY

1984: *Greystoke, The Legend of Tarzan, Lord of the Apes*. 1985: *St Elmo's Fire*. 1987: *The Sahara Secret* (TV). 1989: *sex, lies, and videotape*. 1990: *The Object of Beauty*; *Green Card*. 1991: *Hudson Hawk*; *Women & Men: In Love There Are No Rules* (TV). 1992: *The Player* (bit). 1993: *Ruby Cairo*; *Groundhog Day*; *Short Cuts*. 1994: *Four Weddings and a Funeral*; *Bad Girls*; *Unstrung Heroes*.

Kyle MACLACHLAN

John Ford had John Wayne, Akira Kurosawa had Toshiro Mifune, Martin Scorsese had Robert De Niro, Woody Allen had himself and David Lynch had Kyle MacLachlan. Variously described as a visionary filmmaker and as Hollywood's resident weirdo, Lynch made the most bizarre, unsettling pictures, and yet never appeared less than normal himself. MacLachlan, too, with his short black hair, straight features and conventional, boy-next-door good looks, was your basic Mr

Kyle MacLachlan (*right*) in David Lynch's
sci-fi epic *Dune*, his film debut, with
Francesca Annis

Kyle MacLachlan with Isabella Rossellini in
Lynch's weird and wonderful *Blue Velvet*

Average. Of course, this was the perfect
veneer for Lynch's weird reprogramming of
the everyday, and when MacLachlan wasn't
working for Lynch he went off and played an
alien.

Born in Yakima, Washington, on 22
February 1959, the oldest of three sons,
MacLachlan graduated *cum laude* from the
University of Washington, Seattle, in 1982.
He immediately joined the Oregon
Shakespeare Festival and, over a period of
seven months, played Romeo in *Romeo and
Juliet*, Octavius in *Julius Caesar* and The Boy in
Henry V. The same year he returned to
Seattle to play Damis in *Tartuffe*, was spotted
by a talent scout and asked to audition for a
new film. The film was *Dune*, a $50 million
epic screen version of Frank Herbert's classic
sci-fi novel, with David Lynch (*Eraserhead*, *The
Elephant Man*) to direct. Lynch had already
conducted a nationwide hunt for an actor to

play the starring role of Paul Atreides, the
heroic prince, and had amassed a supporting
cast that included Jose Ferrer, Virginia
Madsen, Silvana Mangano, Jurgen Prochnow,
Sting, Dean Stockwell, Max Von Sydow and
Sean Young. MacLachlan got the part – and
spent the next year working on the movie.

Part of his contract stipulated that he
could take no other film part until the release
of *Dune* which, when it bombed, spelled
career-death. 'I stepped out of nowhere into
the spotlight,' the actor remembers. 'You hear
stuff like, "You're gonna be a star, this
character is going to change your life." So

when the film was poorly received, I kind of
went into a tailspin. No one was interested in
hiring me.'

True. Disillusioned and dejected,
MacLachlan – the boy with the
unpronounceable name from the film
nobody saw – returned to Seattle and
resumed his stage career. Later, Lynch sent
him the screenplay for *Blue Velvet*, the story
of corruption in a sleepy North Carolina
town, and MacLachlan turned it down. Lynch
continued holding auditions for the lead role
– a naive college boy who turns private
detective – but held the part open in the
hope that MacLachlan would change his
mind. The actor did, and was perfect as the
ingenuous Jeffrey Beaumont, beaten by
Dennis Hopper, loved by Laura Dern and
seduced by Isabella Rossellini – at knife point.
Two years after *Dune*, the film opened to
critical praise, moral condemnation and
became an instant cult phenomenon.
MacLachlan also hit it off with his leading lady,
the leggy, gawky and gorgeous Ms Dern, with
whom he co-starred in *Palace of Amateurs*
off-Broadway.

Now Hollywood was willing to throw
scripts at MacLachlan, although, in spite of his
clean-cut appearance, he continued to
appear in off-the-wall pictures. Next, he
landed the lead in a novel, witty sci-fi opus,
The Hidden, playing a clean-cut alien agent on
the trail of a garden slug which variously
disguises itself as a middle-aged accountant, a
stripper and a dog. OK, so *The Hidden* wasn't
exactly *Alien*, but it had all the potential to be
a midnight classic. There was another dud,
Don't Tell Her It's Me, a goofy romantic
comedy with MacLachlan fourth-billed as the
smarmy boyfriend ('Trout') of Jami Gertz, and
then David Lynch came to the rescue. Again.
This time Lynch proposed a TV series with a
difference. 'We all went in with the idea that
this would revolutionize the medium,'
MacLachlan explained at the time. 'We went
in like warriors. What we were doing was
trying to hit against the walls and force them
out and see what happened.'

Well, *Twin Peaks* caused a furore. A cross
between *Blue Velvet* and *Peyton Place*, the
series bent the rules of television, spat in the
face of soap opera and anchored an
enormous devoted following. People who
only used TV to support a vase, rushed
home early from office dinners to find out
who killed Laura Palmer. Except that David
Lynch never let on – not, that is, until the
second series. *Twin Peaks* was to the yuppie
class what *Coronation Street* and *Dallas* were
to normal people.

The show's pioneers, Lynch and Mark

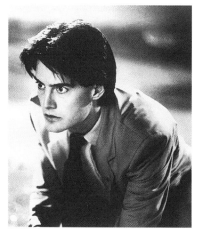

MacLachlan as mysterious FBI agent Lloyd Gallagher in Jack Sholder's effective sci-fi thriller *The Hidden*

Kyle MacLachlan as Josef K in *The Trial*

MacLachlan began dating the Canadian supermodel Linda Evangelista, who had just broken up with her husband of five years, Gerald Marie, head of the modelling empire Elite.

FILMOGRAPHY

1984: *Dune.* **1986:** *Blue Velvet.* **1987:** *The Hidden.* **1990:** *Don't Tell Her It's Me* (aka *The Boyfriend School*). **1991:** *The Doors; Tales From the Crypt* (TV). **1992:** *Twin Peaks Fire Walk With Me; Where the Day Takes You; Rich in Love; The Trial.* **1994:** *The Flintstones; Against the Wall* (TV); *Roswell.*

MADONNA

By the early 1990s, what the world didn't know about Madonna wasn't worth knowing. Not only was she the pop phenomenon of her time, but also an actress, songwriter, dancer, businesswoman, sex symbol, fashion queen and, above all, self-publicist. Spike Lee, who knows about such things, proclaimed, 'Marketing is something I'm very proud of. The only artist that does it better than me is Madonna. She's the champ.'

Indeed, she was *the* commodity of the sex-starved 1990s, a golden-throated siren who understood the currency of lust. She also recognized the dangers of over-exposure, and consequently spread her celebrity over increasingly diverse domains. In 1992, a year which saw the release of her eighth album, *Erotica*, and her appearance in two films, she brought out a book succinctly titled *Sex*. A compilation of erotic photographs celebrating the joys of bisexuality and sadomasochism, the tome displayed Madonna in various degrees of undress, accompanied by her arbitrary thoughts on anything and everything erotic. Bound in aluminium and accompanied by a CD, *Sex* cost a cool £25 in Britain and sold out instantly. In Germany they were flogging it for the equivalent of $65, and it sold out there, too. In short, it was the publishing sensation of the year.

In another attempt to flex her versatility, the star took to the New York stage in David Mamet's critically celebrated play *Speed-the-Plow*. Although she was not happy with the way her part turned out ('it ended up being a plot manipulation,' she complained), her director, Gregory Mosher, was impressed. 'It is not Madonna's habit to lie,' he revealed. 'Her habit is to be truthful. And that is the essence of being an actor – to tell the truth in imaginary circumstances. She tells the truth in her life. In her dancing. In her lyrics. I love her straightforwardness.'

Frost, had created a serial specifically aimed to confuse, infuriate and mesmerise audiences bored with the size of Joan Collins's shoulder pads. They also created the role of clairvoyant FBI agent Dale Cooper especially for Kyle MacLachlan, whose catchphrase, 'Damn fine cup of coffee – and hot!' inspired a lucrative TV commercial for Walker's Crisps.

'Those commercials,' MacLachlan revealed, 'have given me the financial flexibility to be able to choose the parts that I want and don't want to do.' However, the show's initial strangeness grew tiresome after a while, and

even the weirdest devotees wandered back to their wine bars. The serial was abandoned in February of 1991. Even the subsequent film – *Twin Peaks: Fire Walk With Me* – starring MacLachlan and boasting cameos from Chris Isaak, David Bowie and Kiefer Sutherland, flopped badly.

However, *Twin Peaks* did introduce MacLachlan to his live-in girlfriend, the leggy, gawky and gorgeous Lara Flynn Boyle, who played Donna Hayward, Laura Palmer's best friend. And it had made Kyle MacLachlan a household name.

Before the *Twin Peaks* movie, MacLachlan played Ray Manzarek, keyboardist and co-founder of *The Doors* – for Oliver Stone – and afterwards took another supporting role, as a drug dealer, in the ensemble homeless drama *Where the Day Takes You*, also featuring Lara Flynn Boyle. He played the wry but caring son-in-law in a dysfunctional Southern family in Bruce Beresford's *Rich in Love*, and then landed the most prestigious role of his career: Josef K in *The Trial*. Scripted by Harold Pinter from the Kafka novel, the film featured an impressive supporting cast, not least Anthony Hopkins, Jason Robards and Juliet Stevenson. However, the picture's dry, sterile tone kept audiences at bay.

Shortly after Thanksgiving of 1992,

Kyle as keyboard star Ray Manzarek in Oliver Stone's *The Doors*

'I said, "OK, I don't need *anybody*," and I hated my father for a long, long time,' she revealed. 'And I made a promise to myself that no one was going to hurt me again. I was going to be somebody, I was going to rise above it.'

At school she dreamed of becoming a nun, but her desire for boys eventually clouded her more pious aspirations. The day after she ditched her vision of sisterhood she landed her first kiss – in a convent, naturally. It was, she recalls, 'incredible'.

She was a bad girl, stealing kisses from boyfriends of girlfriends, setting up shoplifting contests and going to church naked under her coat. After school, she trained as a dancer in Detroit, and in 1978 moved to New York where she worked on choreog-

Madonna as Susan in Susan Seidelman's *Desperately Seeking Susan*

Madonna as Nikki Finn in Warner Bros's monumental flop *Who's That Girl*

If any far-flung corner of the Madonna machine revealed a weak link, it was her movie career. After a promising film 'debut' in *Desperately Seeking Susan*, in which she proved she could be as comfortable in front of a camera as a microphone, the singer embarked on a series of cinematic flops that grew in magnitude as her fame increased. *Shanghai Surprise* was a vehicle for her and her husband, Sean Penn, and both of them were embarrassing in it. *Who's That Girl* was a farce so moronic that it defied belief, while *Bloodhounds of Broadway* was so bad it didn't even get a British release. However, when Madonna replaced Sean Penn with Warren Beatty in her life, she was given the female lead – as Breathless Mahoney – in the latter's *Dick Tracy*. Although the seventh highest grossing movie of 1990, *Dick Tracy* was considered a box-office disappointment by Buena Vista, its distributor. Of all Madonna's films, only *A League of Their Own*, in which she had a supporting role, could be considered an out-and-out home run.

The star was born Madonna Louise Veronica Ciccone in Detroit, Michigan, on 16 August 1959, the daughter of a Chrysler engineer. The third child of eight, she was immediately immersed into the strict authoritarian rule of her strict Italian Catholic family. When she was six her mother died of cancer, which transformed her into a hypochondriac and daddy's girl. When her father later remarried it almost destroyed her.

As the sexy chanteuse Breathless Mahoney in Warren Beatty's *Dick Tracy*

raphy in Alvin Ailey's dance troupe. It was around this time that she made her 'unofficial' film debut in the underground movie *A Certain Sacrifice*, later dismissed as 'a sex-slave romp'. For her part, she was paid $100 and played a teenage drifter out to revenge the men who gang-raped her. Later, when the film was released directly on video, Madonna sued the distributors, but to no avail.

She followed this with an excursion to Paris with the Patrick Hernandez Revue, and then returned to the States to cut a series of demo tapes. Sire Records signed her on, and soon she was pumping out singles, racking up such number one hits as 'Like a Virgin', 'Material Girl', 'Crazy For You', 'Into the Groove', 'Open Your Heart', 'Papa Don't Preach', 'True Blue', 'La Isla Bonita', 'Who's That Girl', 'Like a Prayer', 'Lovesong' (with Prince), 'Vogue' and 'Justify My Love'. With that lot she became the hottest female singer of the 1980s, with her records reportedly selling an average one million copies a week worldwide. To provide an indication of her popularity, when her 1987 Wembley concert in London was announced all 144,000 tickets sold within the space 18 hours and nine minutes. Between the years 1986 and 1990 it was estimated that she earned a phenomenal $90 million and, in 1992, cut a deal with Time Warner that was to net her a further

$60m. Madonna not only made records, she broke them.

In 1985, with two albums under her belt (*Madonna*, *Like a Virgin*), she appeared briefly in *VisionQuest* singing 'Crazy For You', and then landed a central role in Susan Seidelman's *Desperately Seeking Susan*, as Susan. Playing a zany, man-devouring slut, Madonna could not have found the part too much of a stretch, but she did it extremely well and helped the low-budget comedy become a huge cult.

A year later, she played a 1930s missionary in the British-American *Shanghai Surprise*, an adventure yarn inspired by *The African Queen* and *Casablanca*, produced by George Harrison and co-starring her new husband, Sean Penn. The press declared war on the film and the public stayed away, and all for perfectly good reasons: the movie was a stiff, with Madonna delivering the worst performance of the year.

Who's That Girl was equally dumped on by the critics, but at least it generated three hit singles to help pump up its box-office. A cliche-ridden farce about a zany jailbird (Madonna) reluctantly escorted by a hapless Griffin Dunne, the film was cluttered by obvious stereotypes and tired plot devices. Its director, James Foley, had previously directed Penn in *At Close Range* (featuring Madonna on the soundtrack), and obviously felt a rapport with the Penns. However, even he pleaded, 'please let's not talk about it. OK, so it was one big fat flop. But that is beside the point. For me, after the darkness of *At Close Range*, it seemed like a rather extravagant and exciting opportunity to do something totally crazy. Now, I'm trying very hard not to think of it in commercial terms.' And, almost in apology: 'You know, there's more than one way of looking at a movie.'

Any which way you looked at *Bloodhounds of Broadway*, it was a flop. Devoid of wit or charm, the film was an amalgamation of four Damon Runyan stories, with Madonna a nightclub singer in love with gambler Randy Quaid. At least Madonna seemed to have a grip on her material, which is more than can be said of the rest of the cast, which included Matt Dillon, Rutger Hauer and Jennifer Grey. For some extraordinary reason, the media greedily exploited the rumour that Madonna was having an affair with Ms Grey, no doubt prompted by Madonna's teasing appearance on TV's *Late Night With David Letterman*

As mischievous Mae Mordabito in the huge 1992 hit *A League of Their Own*

show. She and her good friend Sandra Bernhard decided to 'have some fun' and owned up to a lesbian affair – which the media took at face value and milked to the full.

Snubbing her critics, Madonna embarked on a whirlwind romance with the ultra-straight Warren Beatty, following an equally tempestuous divorce from Sean Penn. Neither actor-director relished the attention of the press, so it was odd that they both chose to court such a public figure. Still, Beatty found her irresistible. He said, 'Madonna is simultaneously touching and more fun than a barrel of monkeys. She's funny, and she's gifted in so many areas and has the kind of energy as a performer that can't help but make you engaged.'

Beatty's last picture, *Ishtar*, had been a box-office bomb, due – according to popular theory – to the star's reluctance to publicize it. So no doubt it helped that Beatty cast Madonna in his next, which he not only starred in but directed and produced. Beatty took the title role, *Dick Tracy*, and Madonna played Breathless Mahoney, a sultry nightclub singer who, in the film's most famous line, purred to her leading man, 'I know how you feel: you don't know if you want to hit me or kiss me. I get a lot of that.' In spite of a starry cast that included Al Pacino, Dustin Hoffman and James Caan, it was Madonna who stole the show – along with the film's amazing make-up effects.

Dick Tracy, backed up by an enormous publicity and marketing campaign, was a resounding hit, and won Oscars for best make-up, art direction and the song 'Sooner

or Later', the latter composed by Stephen Sondheim and delivered by Madonna.

The following year she found herself in another success, *Truth or Dare*, an eye-opening documentary chronicling the singer's 'Blond Ambition' world tour. Packed with provocative, show-stopping Madonna hits, the film also revealed the star in private – backstage with Beatty, flirting with her male dancers and making fun of Kevin Costner. She also disclosed her inexhaustible obsession with sex and told how she handled the pressures of stardom. Some accused the film of being a set-up job, but it was nonetheless as entertaining a rockumentary as you could find.

In 1992 she took a cameo in Woody Allen's *Shadows and Fog*, as a trapeze artist who conducts an affair with John Malkovich's clown. She then took a supporting role in the baseball hit *A League of Their Own*, directed by Penny Marshall. In the latter she played the streetwise, knicker-flashing 'All the way' Mae, and gleefully announced, 'Mae. That's not a name, that's an attitude.' Although Geena Davis and Tom Hanks had the bigger roles, Madonna added some much-needed grit in the sentimental stew and the film stormed off with $105 million at the US box-office.

Next, she starred in the erotic thriller *Body of Evidence*, with Willem Dafoe and Joe Mantegna, in which, in the words of director Uli Edel, 'she plays a woman accused of murdering her lover. . . with sex.' However, critics dismissed the film as a bargain-basement rip-off of *Basic Instinct*, and at a private screening in New York the audience greeted it with jeers and laughter. Worse still, her acting was called into question. Although a Hollywood executive vouchsafed, 'they are going to edit a good performance out of her,' Madonna's acting coach on the movie offered, 'This girl will never be an actress. She is too vulgar and she thinks she knows it all.'

Next, the singer was announced as the star of the low-budget *Dangerous Game*, a drama set in the world of moviemaking, and created by Madonna's own production company, the Maverick Picture Co. As part of her lucrative deal with Time Warner, the film co-starred Harvey Keitel and was directed by Abel Ferrara (who had directed the latter in the highly controversial *Bad Lieutenant*).

Also, there was the role of a Brooklyn girl in *Angie* (written especially to show off her range as an actress), but when pre-production conflicted with the shoot of *Dangerous Game*, Geena Davis was brought in to replace her. Madonna reportedly faxed Joe Roth, the film's producer, saying, 'I can

Body influential: Madonna's physique is on trial in Uli Edel's ludicrous *Body of Evidence*

understand why you had reservations about my ability. I can see why you would think Geena Davis is the better actress for the part. After all, she's Italian and has an edge.' Roth, ignoring this sarcasm, simply explained, 'She was offered the role but chose to do *Dangerous Game* instead.'

Madonna was also announced to play the title role in the long-awaited film version of the stage hit *Evita*, beating Meryl Streep to the part. Before she knew the role was hers, the singer announced, 'I've decided that if anybody's going to do it, I'm going to do it – I'll kill Meryl Streep.' As it happens, Walt Disney Productions couldn't come to terms with the production's enormous budget and *Evita* was put on hold. But then many Madonna projects met similar fates. At various points in her career she was due to do a remake of Dietrich's *The Blue Angel*; *Blessings in Disguise* (a love story to be produced by Warren Beatty); and *Leda and Swan*, with Demi Moore. She was also famous for deserting films at the eleventh hour, having been inked to appear in such projects as *Soapdish*, *Three of Hearts*, *The Bodyguard*, *Boxing Helena* and *Even Cowgirls Get the Blues*. But then everybody wanted Madonna. They still do.

FILMOGRAPHY

1983: *A Certain Sacrifice* (filmed 1978-81). 1985: *VisionQuest*; *Desperately Seeking Susan*. 1986: *Shanghai Surprise*. 1987: *Who's That Girl*. 1988: *Bloodhounds of Broadway*. 1990: *Dick Tracy*. 1991: *Truth or Dare: On the Road, Behind the Scenes & In Bed With Madonna* (UK: *In Bed With Madonna*). 1992: *Shadows and Fog*; *A League of Their Own*. 1993: *Body of Evidence*; *Dangerous Game*.

Virginia MADSEN

Virginia Madsen radiates the kind of smouldering sex appeal that would have made her a major star if only she had stumbled on to a hit movie. Nevertheless, she has turned in enough head-turning performances (in some notable films) to secure herself a stable place in the filofaxes of casting directors. Even the titles of her lesser pictures (*Fire With Fire*, *Hot to Trot*, *Third Degree Burn*) and two of her better ones (*Electric Dreams*, *The Hot Spot*) reflected the incendiary nature of her allure.

Variously proclaimed as the successor to Lana Turner, Marilyn Monroe, Kim Novak and Faye Dunaway, Ms Madsen commandeered her own place in Hollywood history when, in September of 1989, she married Danny Huston, the director son of the legendary filmmaker John Huston and brother of the Oscar-winning actress Anjelica.

Born in 1963 (her birthday remains characteristically secret) on Chicago's South Side, Virginia Madsen was the youngest of three children. Her mother, Eileen, turned down a well-paying PR job to pursue a career in screenwriting, while Virginia's father, Cal, was a legend in his own right as one of Chicago's foremost firefighters. To hear Virginia tell it, it was her father who stoked her interest in acting. 'Not only was he a fireman, but the all-time great story teller,' she reveals.

As a teenager, Virginia divulges, 'I never had a boyfriend in high school. I was the kid who brought her dog to school, who never wore shoes and was the class loudmouth.' On graduation, she taught ballet to toddlers, which helped finance her acting lessons with the celebrated teacher Ted Liss.

For a while, Virginia's older sister, Cheri, was also an actress (but switched careers to motherhood), and her brother, Michael, is the successful film actor who made notable impressions in *Thelma & Louise* and *Reservoir Dogs*. In her native Chicago Virginia landed a small part as Alan Arkin's daughter in the American Playhouse TV production of *A*

Virginia Madsen with Lenny Von Dohlen in the delightful romantic comedy *Electric Dreams*

Virginia Madsen as the ethereal seductress in Lloyd Fonvielle's *Gotham*

Matter of Principle and, a year later, played Lisa in the Brat Pack-laden *Class*. Turning 21, she followed her brother to Hollywood and was immediately snapped up by David Lynch to play the evil, icy Princess Irulan in his stellar, over-budgeted flop *Dune*.

Immediately afterwards came the actresses's first female lead – in Steve Baron's outstanding *Electric Dreams*. She was Madeline, the beautiful cellist who has to juggle the mixed attentions of the Joe Blow upstairs (Lenny Von Dohlen), a sleazy Maxwell Caulfield and an amorous computer called Edgar. Borrowing its concept from *Cyrano de Bergerac*, the film had Von Dohlen passing off his computer's love songs as his own, unaware that his machine was zoning in on Madeline as well. Directed with all the pizzazz of an award-winning music video, the film artfully integrated old-fashioned romance, humour and state-of-the-art technology with an exhilarating music score. The film had 'hit' written all over it, but thanks to a fatally misjudged marketing campaign sank without trace.

Madsen's subsequent films were no more successful. Indeed, the actress looks fondest on her TV work, particularly her role as Clarette Petacci, Il Duce's mistress in *Mussolini: The Untold Story*, with George C. Scott; the role of screen siren Marion Davies, William Randolph Hearst's mistress, in *The Hearst and Davies Affair*, opposite Robert Mitchum; and her role as Dixie Lee Box, a small-town beauty queen in the baseball comedy *Long Gone*.

The director of the last-named, Martin Davidson, was proud of his star. 'Someday Virginia's going to get the right part, the right director, the right situation,' he volunteered. 'Then people will see how much she has going for her. She's alive – touch her, and you sense something happening.'

Meanwhile, the actress was working herself to the bone, appearing in film after mediocre film. Today, she says, 'I've learned to take more joy in my work. There used to be a sort of desperation that I should work, work, work. I had no private life and I lived the character 24 hours a day.'

What little private life she had became all-too public as she dated a variety of semi-famous men. Before she met her husband on *Mr North*, she enjoyed a long romance with Bill Campbell (*The Rocketeer*) and had a brief fling with the media-conscious Dweezil Zappa. But work came first, and soon the 'girl-next-door' roles were to vanish.

She barely had three scenes in Wayne Wang's *Slamdance*, but the poster – strategically displayed above Sunset Boulevard – revealed her in a slinky black evening dress slashed to her navel. It was a mouth-watering vision, and even though the film turned out to be another flop, the image had burnt itself into the collective mind of the Hollywood industry.

Besides, she says, a *femme fatale* is far more interesting to play. Nevertheless, she was uncomfortable with the number of nude scenes she was now forced to undergo, reaching a climax in Dennis Hopper's torrid sex-and-blackmail film noir drama *The Hot Spot*. Madsen disrobed with gay regularity as the town slut, seducing drifter Don Johnson while two-timing her husband. But who can forget the line she fired at Johnson when he first ambles into her dead-zone town? 'There are only two things to do around here. You got a TV? No? Well, now you're down to one.' Her cupola-lidded eyes hid a pandora's box of sin.

Two years earlier, in *Mr North*, Danny Huston's amiable adaptation of Thornton Wilder's novel *Theophilus North*, Ms Madsen was on very different form. She played Sally Boffin, the sprightly Irish maid who was all innocence and sugar, and skipped away with the lion's share of the reviews – in spite of a cast that included Robert Mitchum, Lauren Bacall and Anjelica Huston.

During the shoot Ms Madsen admits that she fell head-over-heels for her director, but the couple didn't start dating until the film's completion. Since then, Huston Jr has directed his wife in *Becoming Colette*, in which the actress played Polaire, the lesbian lover of

Mary STUART MASTERSON

It is a symptom of our times that Mary Stuart Masterson is not a bigger star than she is. She has the looks, the talent and even the connections, but there was no place for her brand of wholesome, spunky spirit in the special-effects-laden, designer-sex movies Hollywood doled out in the late 1980s and early 1990s. In order to see Mary Stuart Masterson you had to seek her out, scour the video shelves, study the movie magazines.

Had she been around in the 1930s or 1940s, they would have built entire movies around her, exploiting her elfin good looks and steely charm. She would have knocked Deanna Durbin into a cocked hat. Later, she would have been the star of countless pillow frolics and beach movies, pairing Rock Hudson or even Elvis Presley. Sandra Dee would've been history.

Mary Stuart Masterson's cherubic allure and feisty temperament was not the make-up for dreamy-eyed schoolboys who clipped pictures of Michelle Pfeiffer and Julia Roberts to their headboards. Perhaps she appealed more to older men (who never went to the cinema), as the pretty daughter who would've stood up to them.

The perfect role for the New York-born actress was the tomboy in Some Kind of Wonderful, a deftly engineered teen romance that didn't even get a theatrical release in Britain. Written and produced by John Hughes, the film starred Eric Stoltz as a shy, likeable student who courts the preppie, sophisticated Lea Thompson. Masterson, who loves Stoltz herself, conspires with him to land the girl of his dreams. An endearing blend of masculine posturing and feminine strategy, Masterson anchored the film's fairy tale predictability in emotional reality.

The 1988 Motion Picture Annual was impressed. It wrote: '. . . far and away, this is Masterson's film. An amazingly mature young actress, Masterson skillfully brings subtlety, depth, and nuance to her character that most assuredly do not exist in Hughes's tired screenplay. Her scenes with Stoltz are some of the most refreshingly honest and emotionally complex interactions to hit the screen in quite some time. She is simply the most vibrant, interesting, and natural teenager to be found in John Hughes's entire ouvre.'

'She can get a little intense, though,' the

Madsen as femme fatale Dolly Harshaw in Dennis Hopper's sweltering The Hot Spot

Bee-sieged: Candyman (Tony Todd) holds Virginia in his evil clutches

the film certain credibility, while enduring some gruelling scenes, not least a sequence in which she is seduced slap bang in the middle of a swarm of bees.

The actress found the experience fortifying. 'Candyman was more challenging than anything I'd done before,' she disclosed. 'It changed me completely as an actress. Helen was a very strong and substantial female character, a role model; not just a victim or someone's girlfriend.' Absolutely not.

In 1992 she divorced her husband, following three years of marriage. 'Danny's a wonderful man,' Virginia Madsen insisted, 'but we just could not stay married because it would have become awful. Now it's over and at least we're friends.'

FILMOGRAPHY

1982: A Matter of Principal (TV). 1983: Class. 1984: Dune; Electric Dreams. 1985: Creator; Mussolini: The Untold Story (TV); The Hearst and Davies Affair (TV). 1986: Fire With Fire; Modern Girls. 1987: Slamdance; Long Gone (TV); Zombie High. 1988: Hot to Trot; Mr North; Gotham (TV) (UK theatrical release: The Dead Can't Lie). 1989: Third Degree Burn (TV); Heart of Dixie. 1990: The Hot Spot. 1991: Highlander II: The Quickening; Becoming

the French novelist (portrayed by Mathilda May).

She's also been playing some impressive leads. In Ironclads, a TV movie (made for cable) set during the American Civil War, she was a Southern spy for the Union troops. In another TV film, Love Kills, she portrayed an heiress who had a one-night stand with a serial killer (Lenny Von Dohlen, again). And then she landed the lead in Bernard Rose's box-office hit Candyman, a superior horror film in which she played Helen Lyle, a mature student researching a thesis on 'Graffiti Art and Urban Despair'. Sticking her nose into a local legend about a gruesome killer, Helen becomes an agent for the demon, who frames her for his murders. As the intelligent victim of a horrific apparition, Madsen lent

Mary Stuart Masterson with Andrew McCarthy in Michael Dinner's *Heaven Help Us*

Mary Stuart Masterson and Sean Penn cower from the brutality of Christopher Walken in James Foley's hard-hitting *At Close Range*

director James Foley confided. 'We were filming a dramatic sequence for *At Close Range* and I could see that she was getting gridlocked in her own emotions. So I started shouting to the crew that we had to pack up and leave because we didn't have the correct permit to film there. So after I had yelled at everybody, we did her scene with Sean [Penn] in one take. She was brilliant.'

Born on 28 June 1966 in New York City, Mary Stuart Masterson grew up in a showbusiness milieu. Her father is the actor-director Peter Masterson, her mother the actress Carlin Glynn. Aged seven, she made her film debut playing her father's daughter in Bryan Forbes's *The Stepford Wives*. But, besides understudying Kate Burton in a Broadway production of *Alice in Wonderland*, she concentrated on her education, modern dance and an obsession for basketball.

Following two consecutive summers at Robert Redford's Sundance Institute Film Workshop in Utah, she was signed up by her mother's agent. Shortly afterwards, she won the female lead in *Heaven Help Us*, a wry, comedic look at life in a 1960s' Brooklyn Catholic School, playing Andrew McCarthy's girlfriend.

At New York University she studied anthropology and film for one semester, when she abruptly resumed her film career

with *At Close Range*, playing Sean Penn's girlfriend. In an oppressively violent film based on a true story, Masterson's performance was a breath of fresh air, a role, she says, that 'seemed so alive and powerful to me.'

She had a supporting role in the dire 'disease-of-the-week' TV movie *Love Lives On*, starring Christine Lahti and Sam Waterston,

and then won the title role in the Merchant/Ivory-produced *My Little Girl*. This was an intelligent, sensitive portrait of a 16-year-old girl who turns her back on her affluent, upwardly mobile family to work with unwanted children – and Masterson was nothing short of superb. Unfortunately, very few people saw the film and the actress was resigned to playing another girlfriend – D.B. Sweeney's – in Francis Coppola's *Gardens of Stone*.

She made a good impression in *Some Kind of Wonderful*, had secondary roles in *Mr North* (as a shy debutante) and *Chances Are* (as Robert Downey Jr's girlfriend), and then landed her favourite part – at that time – in Jonathan Kaplan's *Immediate Family*. The story of a middle-aged, professional couple (Glenn Close, James Woods) who hire a pregnant teenager (Masterson) to give them a child, the film packed a powerful emotional wallop as it disclosed both sides of a painful dilemma.

Again, in a film loaded with talent, it was Masterson who gave the most intelligent, subtle, heart-rending performance, creating a sympathetic, all too-real character out of a potential cliche. Kaplan: 'It was important to get someone who could play on the same field with Glenn and Jimmy and not get blown away. She has real chops.' If anything, Mary Stuart blew Glenn and Jimmy away. For her performance, she was voted best

Mary Stuart Masterson with Stan Shaw in Jon Avnet's *Fried Green Tomatoes*

Masterson as the mentally unstable, unpredictable Juniper Pearl in Jeremiah Chechik's delightfully whimsical *Benny & Joon*

supporting actress by America's National Board of Review.

Like *Some Kind of Wonderful*, *Immediate Family* didn't get a British theatrical release, a symptom of the film's box-office failure in America. British cinemas were also denied a chance of showing *Funny About Love* and *Married To It*, both bombs, when *Fried Green Tomatoes at the Whistlestop Café* reversed the trend.

Although fourth-billed (after Kathy Bates, Jessica Tandy and Mary-Louise Parker), Masterson commanded centre stage as Idgie Threadgoode, a hard-drinkin', good-livin', life-seekin' small-town cafe owner who stands up for her and her friends' rights. Based on the Pulitzer Prize-nominated novel by Fannie Flagg, and coated with a glow of Southern nostalgia, the film was hamstrung by an awkward flashback technique, but whenever Masterson was on screen she quickly made the story her own. She also astonished crew members when she refused a stunt double for a scene in which she pulls a honeycomb out of a live beehive.

Considering the film's female cast and small-town, period subject matter, it seemed unlikely that *Fried Green Tomatoes* would do any better than the actress's last few films. However, thanks to some ecstatic reviews and positive word-of-mouth, it went on to gross over $81 million in the US alone. At last, Mary Stuart Masterson found herself at the centre of a resounding hit.

She says, filmwise, she'll 'consider anything – so long as it's not The Girlfriend.' Next, she starred in Martin Donovan's *Mad at the Moon*, playing a repressed 25-year-old virgin who marries a werewolf; and was outstanding as the mentally ill Juniper Pearl in *Benny and Joon*, who finds real life when she falls for an eccentric Johnny Depp. After that, she was hoping to direct her first screenplay.

On a private note, she was briefly married to a businessman, a friend from childhood summers spent on the Texas coast.

FILMOGRAPHY

1974: *The Stepford Wives*. 1985: *Heaven Help Us* (UK: *Catholic Boys*); *At Close Range*; *Love Lives On* (TV). 1986: *My Little Girl*. 1987: *Gardens of Stone*; *Some Kind of Wonderful*; *Amazing Stories* (episode: *Go To the Head of the Class*) (TV; UK: theatrical). 1988: *Mr North*. 1989: *Chances Are*; *Immediate Family*. 1990: *Funny About Love*. 1991: *Married To It*; *Fried Green Tomatoes* (UK: *Fried Green Tomatoes at the Whistlestop Café*). 1992: *Vanished*; *Mad at the Moon*. 1993: *Benny & Joon*. 1994: *Bad Girls*, *Radioland Murders*.

Mary Elizabeth MASTRANTONIO

Besides her obvious Mediterranean beauty, Mary Elizabeth Mastrantonio displays an intelligence and strength lacking in most actresses of her generation. The British director Michael Apted, who cast her as a corporate lawyer in *Class Action*, enthused, 'Mary Elizabeth is one of the few actresses around who can put over intellectual power.'

James Cameron, who signed her up to play the hard-boiled engineer Lindsey Brigman in his underwater epic *The Abyss*, was equally impressed: 'She's spectacular,' he raved. 'And I think she's only going to get better. She's very chameleonic. You meet her, and she has this very feminine, delicate quality, which was diametrically opposed to my conception of her part. But once she read the part, I couldn't imagine anyone else playing it.'

Mary Elizabeth Mastrantonio, the fifth of six daughters, came from a middle-class Catholic family (her father, Frank, was an Italian immigrant who worked as a foundryman in Chicago), and was born on 17 November 1958 in the Chicago suburb of Oak Park. A voice major at the University of Illinois, she spent summers singing Country & Western at Nashville's Opryland theme park, and dabbled in musical theatre back in Chicago. It was there that she auditioned for *Evita*, and so impressed the casting director that he hired her to understudy the part of Maria in the 1980 Broadway revival of *West Side Story*. Once in New York, the actress embarked on a career in musical theatre, but quickly found herself typecast.

'In New York, even if you have 19 awards for musicals, you're still not really considered an actor,' she laments. She was in *Amadeus* with Frank Langella, and a year later won a small role in Martin Scorsese's film *The King*

Mary Elizabeth Mastrantonio with Tom Cruise in Martin Scorsese's *The Color of Money*

of Comedy. Although her part landed up on the cutting room floor, she so impressed Scorsese that he made a mental note to use her in the future.

From Scorsese she bounced to Brian De Palma, playing Al Pacino's hot-blooded sister Gina in *Scarface*. It was a big film, and she had a big role, and a big scene – the one in which she sexually taunts her brother just before shooting him. De Palma explained, 'I needed somebody who could play a virginal younger sister and transform herself into a wild sexpot. There was nobody else who could do it.'

Mastrantonio with leading man Kevin Kline in the enjoyably daft *The January Man*

Mastrantonio as the iron-willed Lindsey Brigman, with Ed Harris, in James Cameron's thrilling underwater epic *The Abyss*

More theatre followed, including the original off-Broadway production of Stephen Sondheim's *Sunday in the Park With George*, and *Henry V* with Kevin Kline. On TV, she played Il Duce's daughter Edda in the mini-series *Mussolini: The Untold Story*, with George C. Scott, and then won the female lead in Scorsese's *The Color of Money*. As the feisty, no-bull girlfriend of Tom Cruise, Mastrantonio more than held her own in the formidable company of Cruise, Paul Newman and John Turturro. Only her second screen role, it won her an Oscar nomination for best supporting actress.

In Wayne Wang's self-consciously stylish murder mystery *Slamdance*, she played the cuckolded wife of Tom Hulce, and with very little material created an enormously substantial character. But, as ever, her first love was the theatre and she continued to make her presence felt in such plays as *Figaro*, *Measure For Measure* and *The Knife*.

She teamed up with Kevin Kline, her co-star from *Henry V*, in the sly thriller *The January Man*, in a starry ensemble that included Susan Sarandon, Harvey Keitel, Danny Aiello and Alan Rickman. Rod Steiger played her father, the Mayor of New York, and is not pleased when she takes up with

Kline. *The January Man* was a foxy, quirky and engaging thriller, but failed to excite an enormous following. It did, however, introduce Mastrantonio to her future husband, the film's Irish director, Pat O'Connor.

In 1989, Mastrantonio spent eight weeks in a nowhere town in South Carolina immersed in seven million gallons of water. The occasion was the filming of James Cameron's *The Abyss*, an experience that nobody – legend has it – enjoyed. Mastrantonio admits that the shoot was 'physically and emotionally draining,' but the ordeal paid off. *The Abyss* turned out to be a unique cinematic experience, a breath-catching rollercoaster ride 25,000 feet beneath sea level. A submerged *Close Encounters of the Third Kind*, the film was a breakthrough in special effects, but never let those effects dwarf its exciting story or the sterling acting from a first-rate cast (Mastrantonio, Ed Harris, Michael Biehn). Mastrantonio played Lindsey Brigman, designer of 'Deepcore' (a manned submersible drilling rig) and, in the words of one character, 'the bitch of the universe.' Mastrantonio made a steely heroine, swapping testosterone with the boys and still secretly nursing her love for her estranged husband (Harris). *The Abyss* cost a wallet-numbing $50 million and, so, when it only generated $54 million at the US box-office, was dismissed as a water-logged *Heaven's Gate*.

In need of a break from the demands of state-of-the-art filmmaking, Mastrantonio returned to her favourite man: Shakespeare. 'I love Shakespeare,' she glows, 'because all of your reason, all of your rationale, is on your tongue. If you're thinking it, he has you say it.' In *Twelfth Night* at New York's Public Theatre, she played Viola opposite no less than Jeff Goldblum, Gregory Hines and Michelle Pfeiffer. When the play opened, she personally received rave reviews, but Ms Pfeiffer was not so lucky. And although the great theatrical New York guru Joseph Papp exclaimed, 'Mary Elizabeth is a great Shakespearean actress. She was absolutely stunning in *Twelfth Night*. She has come a long, long way', Mastrantonio volunteered: 'if one gets good reviews and others bad, if you see a friend of yours suffering, it sort of takes the wind out of your sails.'

Now sharing a home with her husband in Dublin and London's Notting Hill, Mastrantonio starred in O'Connor's handsome but soapy Irish saga *Fools of Fortune*, from the acclaimed William Trevor novel. Mastrantonio, top-billed above Julie Christie, made a surprisingly convincing

made the scene hers (which was more than can be said for Kevin Kline). Indeed, hers was the only credible character in the film.

FILMOGRAPHY

1983: *The King of Comedy* (visible in crowd scene); *Scarface*. 1986: *The Color of Money*. 1987: *Slamdance*. 1989: *The January Man*; *The Abyss*. 1990: *Fools of Fortune*. 1991: *Class Action*; *Robin Hood: Prince of Thieves*. 1992: *White Sands*; *Consenting Adults*. 1994: *Two Bits*.

Mastrantonio with Kevin Kline, again, in Alan J. Pakula's disappointing thriller *Consenting Adults*

Samantha Mathis (*right*) – with Lala – as Nora, the bright, plucky high school student in Allan Moyle's hip, electric *Pump Up the Volume*

Samantha MATHIS

The first important thing to know about Samantha Mathis is that she is not Winona Ryder. 'I have dark hair and I was in a movie with Christian Slater,' she says – 'so they compare me to Winona.' But, 'I really have blond hair.' Besides, 'Winona was once told she was a Molly Ringwald type. Now there's the Winona Ryder type, and there will be others.'

The pigeon-holing began when Samantha Mathis starred opposite Christian Slater in *Pump Up the Volume*, the hippest, coolest high school movie since *Heathers*, which, incidentally, starred Christian Slater and Winona Ryder.

While *Heathers* achieved cult status, *Pump Up the Volume* was actually the better film

young English woman, and was the best thing in a film bogged down by incident.

Again, she was excellent as a San Francisco attorney at loggerheads with her father (Gene Hackman) in Michael Apted's *Class Action*, an intelligent court room drama in which a civil liberties lawyer and his daughter fight opposing ends of a seemingly open-and-shut case.

She returned to England to play Yelena in a BBC production of *Uncle Vanya*, prompting veteran co-star Ian Holm to volunteer: 'Yelena is a difficult part – a femme fatale who wanders round the household – but Mary brought more to the part than I've ever seen.'

When Robin Wright, on becoming pregnant, backed out of the role of Maid Marian in *Robin Hood: Prince of Thieves*, Mastrantonio stepped in. But the film, the most popular in Britain that year (1991), squarely belonged to the boys. And even they – Kevin Costner, Morgan Freeman and Christian Slater – were upstaged by Alan Rickman's hammy Sheriff of Nottingham. 'I'd originally thought that Maid Marian would be "one of the guys",' explains Mastrantonio. But, 'she comes across more timid than I'd anticipated.'

Mastrantonio also had little to do in the dreary *White Sands*, a thriller in which Willem Dafoe and Mickey Rourke hogged the action. Still, whenever the actress was on screen (playing a tantalizing adventuress who joins Dafoe in the shower), things picked up. In Alan J. Pakula's slick Yuppie thriller *Consenting Adults*, she joined Kevin Kline for the third time, playing his cuckolded wife. Again, she was given little to chew on, but whenever she *was* called on to speak her mind, she

and made more money. In the latter, Slater starred as the anti-hero Happy Harry Hard-On, an anarchic amateur DJ who, after dark, anonymously broadcast anti-establishment material, hard-nosed rock and erotic poetry. However, during the day he was nothing more charismatic than your average school nerd, hiding behind his books and spectacles. It is Samantha's spirited Nora Diniro (and Happy Harry's dream date) who turns private detective to uncover the identity of her mysterious idol of the airwaves. Needless to say she unmasks him, befriends him and beds him (in a very short time span) – and then takes up his cause for free speech.

Pump Up the Volume was the brightest, most pertinent teen movie of 1990, and both Slater and Mathis were superb in it. Slater gave the performance of his life, while Samantha's blend of breezy sexuality and iron-willed rebellion was nothing short of irresistible.

The film's director, Allan Moyle, took up the cause: 'Samantha has an inner beauty and when the camera is rolling she really turns it on. I know it sounds like a cliché, but she's going to be a big star. She has great instincts and I didn't turn down one of her suggestions.'

The actress's other big career-making role was as the 16-year-old daughter who becomes the butt of her mother's jokes in Nora Ephron's *This Is My Life*. Although 21 at the time, Mathis convinced the director that she was young enough to play the part, a plain, bespectacled girl who chews her lank hair while contemplating the prospect of her burgeoning sexuality.

Ephron was suitably impressed: 'We wanted someone who was funny and someone would could show the pain. Samantha was one of the few who could do both. She's also someone who can convince you that she could be going through a stage – that it's possible for someone as beautiful as she is to be alienated and angry and friendless.'

Indeed, following her sexy, vivacious performance in *Pump Up the Volume* (complete with topless love scene) a year earlier, the actress was unrecognisable as the miserable, hurt, complicated Erica Ingels in *This is My Life*. Ironically, in the latter she does bear some resemblance to Winona Ryder, and even plays a character who cites J.D. Salinger, Winona's pet prophet. And (this is a compliment) Samantha Mathis is one of a very, very select group of young actresses who can hold her own against the Lone Ryder.

Born in New York in 1971, Samantha Mathis is the daughter of actress Bibi Besch (*The Lonely Lady*, *Star Trek II: The Wrath of Khan*, *Betsy's Wedding*) and granddaughter of Gusti Huber, the first lady of Australian theatre. Her early days pretty much reflected the life of Erica Ingels ('it's kind of amazing how close it [the film] is to the truth,' she says). Her parents separated when she was two and divorced a year later. She stayed on with her mother, they moved to Los Angeles, and for months at a time her mother would be away filming. But the acting bug was already eating away inside.

'I toyed with the idea of acting when I was little,' Samantha says, 'but I also wanted to be a forward for the New York Knicks, or a firewoman. It wasn't until I was 12 that I did a play, and when I got up on that stage I had a cathartic experience.'

The 'play' was *Fiddler On the Roof*, the part Hodel and it was, she says, 'the most fun I'd had.' She announced her ambition to become a professional actress to unenthusi-

astic maternal ears, and almost immediately started taking classes. At 15 she was attending workshops with her mother. She then went out and got her own agent, and two months after that landed a pilot for a TV series, *Aaron's Way*, playing an Amish girl. She was 16.

Mathis made her film debut in *The Bulldance* in Yugoslavia (a nightmare she refers to as 'a great experience'), turned 18, and headed for Toronto to do an unsuccessful TV crime series with David Hasselhoff called *Knightwatch*. Now critics were comparing her to Martha Plimpton.

She had a small part in the TV movie *Cold Sassy Tree*, with Faye Dunaway and Richard Widmark, had a major role in the emotional true-life drama *To My Daughter*, with Rue McClanahan, and then won the central role in CBS's true-life drama *83 Hours 'Til Down*, winning excellent reviews as a wealthy businessman's daughter buried alive by Peter Strauss. Next came *Pump Up the Volume*.

She had a decent part in *Extreme Close-Up*, an OK TV drama from the *thirtysome-thing* production team (including director Peter Horton), and then won the central role in *This is My Life* on the strength of an audition that convinced the director that she was both young and plain enough for the role. When she later turned up as herself, Nora Ephron was astounded by the transformation. Indeed, Samantha Mathis is an uncanny character actress.

She joined Christian Slater again, voicing the heroine (Crysta) in the eco-cartoon *Ferngully The Last Rainforest*, and took a supporting role in the off-beat intellectual frolic *The Music of Chance*, with James Spader. Next, she captured the female lead, 'a princess from another dimension,' in the much-touted *Super Mario Bros.*, based on the Nintendo game, and teamed up with Juliette Lewis and Dianne Wiest in Susan Seidelman's *Yesterday*, in Paris. After that she played a musician opposite River Phoenix in Peter Bogdanovich's musical romance *The Thing Called Love*. She and Phoenix became an item, but the affair was to be short-lived when Phoenix died from a drug overdose on 31 October 1993.

FILMOGRAPHY

1988: *The Bulldance.* **1989:** *Cold Sassy Tree* (TV). **1990:** *To My Daughter* (TV); *83 Hours 'Til Dawn* (TV); *Pump Up the Volume*; *Extreme Close-Up* (TV). **1991:** *This is My Life.* **1992:** *Ferngully The Last Rainforest* (voice only); *The Music of Chance*; *Super Mario Bros.* **1993:** *Yesterday.* **1994:** *The Thing Called Love*; *Jack and Sarah*; *Little Women.*

In a dramatic change of pace, Samantha Mathis plays the vulnerable, introverted 16-year-old Erica Ingels in Nora Ephron's bitter-sweet *This is My Life*

Andrew McCARTHY

Andrew McCarthy was handsome without causing a disturbance. He had a boyish charm and a likeable, throwaway sense of humour. And, above all, he was a useful leading man. He was best as the slightly quirky, wise-ass characters he played in *St Elmo's Fire* and *Weekend at Bernie's*, and least effective as the sensitive, hard-staring types he essayed in *Less Than Zero* and *Fresh Horses*. Worse still, he made a thoroughly unconvincing political reporter (steamed up by Sharon Stone) in the implausible *Year of the Gun*.

Andrew McCarthy had talent, but his range was limited. He attempted to expand his horizons in the low-budget, Paris-set *Waiting for the Moon*, the story of Gertrude Stein and Alice B. Toklas, but the film turned out to be spectacularly boring. He returned to Europe to take a cameo (as a Berlin assassin) in Claude Chabrol's dreadful *Dr M*, and then starred in the latter's *Quiet Days in Clichy* which, according to *Variety*, reached 'new depths of trashiness', being a 'softcore, soft-brained period film . . . inspired by Henry Miller's autobiographical novel.' And, in another attempt to reveal his more serious side, McCarthy took a supporting role (as a wealthy Cambridge undergraduate) in *Common Pursuit*, a BBC production of Simon Gray's 1986 play. Unfortunately, his co-stars — most notably Tim Roth and Stephen Fry — walked away with all the good reviews. In

spite of Andrew McCarthy's commendable attempts at the unusual, he was at his best in amiable, undemanding romantic comedies.

Born in Westfield, New Jersey, on 29 November 1962, McCarthy was the third son (of four) of a financier father and an advertising executive mother. He was raised in the affluent suburb of Bernardsville, New Jersey, and enjoyed reading and sports (particularly tennis) as a child. At New York University he majored in drama, when a fellow student noticed a newspaper advertisement announcing auditions for a new film. At his friend's insistence, McCarthy went up for the leading role of a virginal schoolboy in *Class* and won the part. It was

Andrew McCarthy

Andrew McCarthy slams the door on Rob Lowe in the romantic comedy *Class*

Andrew McCarthy in 1983

an auspicious start. Rob Lowe played his roommate, whose mother – Jacqueline Bisset – has a torrid affair with McCarthy. The film was a mild success, helped, no doubt, by the scene in which McCarthy makes love to Ms Bisset in a glass lift.

He rejoined Lowe for the all-star *St Elmo's*

Fire, and won favourable reviews for his offbeat performance as Kevin, a vulnerable, devil-may-care writer. In a cast that included Emilio Estevez, Demi Moore and Andie MacDowell, McCarthy offered by far the most interesting character, deftly handling dialogue that may well have died in anybody else's mouth. Responding to a routine question like, 'How are you?', his laid-back answer was classic: 'Me? You know. It ain't easy being me.'

After the success of *St Elmo's Fire*, he won top-billing in the much-admired teen comedy, *Heaven Help Us*, playing a Catholic schoolboy smitten by outsider Mary Stuart Masterson. Again, he gave a performance of subtle sensitivity, in marked contrast to the outlandish pranks played at the expense of the presiding monks (Donald Sutherland and John Heard among them).

McCarthy then landed his biggest hit yet, playing the handsome, wealthy suitor of poor girl Molly Ringwald in Howard Deutch's hilarious *Pretty in Pink*, a teen comedy distinguished by an exceptionally perceptive script by John Hughes. However, it was the superb comedy playing of co-stars Jon Cryer and Annie Potts that walked off with the acting honours. The film also featured James Spader in a mesmerizing turn as McCarthy's snotty friend, and the two became firm friends. The latter volunteered, 'Andrew has mastered a sort of supreme discomfort. He tells great stories even if it's about something horrible. He finds a great deal of humour in anxiety. And he's funny.'

McCarthy was funny – to a degree – in another hit, *Mannequin*, playing a stockroom

clerk who falls in love with the dummy of the title (Kim Cattrall), which just happens to be the reincarnation of an Egyptian princess. However, James Spader, as an unctuous vice president, was far funnier in what was essentially a lightweight farce short on laughs. Nevertheless, the film's blend of fantasy and romance appealed to enough cinemagoers to prompt an equally feeble sequel four years later.

McCarthy was now in trouble and suffered four flops in a row, two of which re-teamed him with old friends: *Less Than Zero*, with Spader and *Fresh Horses*, with Molly Ringwald. The latter came to the rescue of her co-star: 'Andrew is fascinating. He's a terrific actor, or I wouldn't have worked with him again. He gives a lot and really keeps you on your toes.' The terrific actor was given a brief reprieve with the amiably daft *Weekend at Bernie's*, in which he and Jonathan Silverman conspired to keep the death of their boss secret. It was basically a reworking of Hitchcock's 1955 *The Trouble With Harry*, but was performed with such energy and pizzazz that it was far more likeable than it should've been. This, too, produced a sequel, imaginatively titled *Weekend at Bernie's II* (which, if anorexic for ideas, was competent).

After that, McCarthy's career went into a tailspin. In 1992, so little confidence was

bestowed in the romantic comedy *Only You* (with McCarthy romantically caught between Kelly Preston and Helen Hunt), that its theatrical release was abandoned entirely.

FILMOGRAPHY

1983: *Class.* **1985:** *St Elmo's Fire*; *Heaven Help Us* (UK: *Catholic Boys*). **1986:** *Pretty in Pink*. **1987:** *Mannequin*; *Waiting for the Moon*; *Less Than Zero*. **1988:** *Kansas*; *Fresh Horses*. **1989:** *Weekend at Bernie's*; *Dr M* (US: *Club Extinction*). **1990:** *Quiet Days in Clichy*. **1991:** *Year of the Gun*; *Tales From the Crypt* (TV). **1992:** *Only You*; *Common Pursuit* (TV). **1993:** *Weekend at Bernie's II*; *The Joy Luck Club*; *Student Body*; *Mrs Parker and the Vicious Circle*; *Night of the Running Man*; *Dead Funny*.

Kelly McGILLIS

A beautiful, tall (5'10"), versatile and dedicated actress, Kelly McGillis shot to stardom on the back of three distinguished features. Her third film made for the cinema, *Top Gun*, saw her name above the title, and it became the biggest grossing movie that year (1986). She was a household name, a role model, an icon – but then her personal demons took over. Her old lack of self-confidence returned, she took to drinking too much, she was losing the battle of her weight problem, and she was alone. Seldom had a star come up from nowhere so fast, and then stumbled so quickly out of the limelight. However, it took one film, *The Accused*, for McGillis to finally face and partly exorcise a traumatic rape; and one man, yacht broker Fred Tillman, to give her the self-esteem and baby that would anchor her life.

A doctor's daughter, Kelly McGillis was born on 9 July 1957 in Newport Beach, California, the eldest of three girls. She was an overweight adolescent (at 200 pounds she 'couldn't get a date to the prom to save myself') and showed little interest in anything but acting. At 15, she won an award in her high school's production of *The Serpent* and, with stars in her eyes, dropped out of school, drove north and enrolled at the Pacific Conservatory of Performing Arts in Santa Maria, California. She stayed there for almost three years and then, in 1980, auditioned – successfully – for Juilliard in New York, where she studied for a further four years. At 21, while working as a waitress to make ends meet, she got married because, 'I thought that's what I should do. It lasted about two years.'

She was also brutally raped in her own apartment, where two men, one 15, the

As leading man: Andrew McCarthy (with Sharon Stone) battles political forces beyond his control – in John Frankenheimer's *Year of the Gun*

Kelly McGillis

Kelly McGillis in her first film, *Reuben, Reuben,* with Tom Conti

other 20, forced their way in and, 'took turns with me. They did vile and horrible things . . .' A month after the assault, the 15-year-old pleaded guilty to rape, sodomy and robbery, and served three years in prison. The older man got off scot-free. Initially, Kelly kept the trauma to herself. 'For a great many years, I felt as if I had done something wrong,' she disclosed, 'which will probably take me the rest of my life to deal with. I mean, I know intellectually that I didn't do it, but there will always be a part of me that says I did something to cause that – I must have been a bad girl – whatever.'

Very shortly afterwards, she auditioned for the role of Geneva Spofford in *Reuben, Reuben,* the film of Peter De Vries's novel. In the words of De Vries, Geneva had, 'hips that swayed like a bell when she walked, and big round eyes the colour of butterscotch. Her golden hair fell to her shoulders . . .' A tall order to fill. The producer, Walter Shenson, despaired that of the 'two or three hundred' Californian actresses he had auditioned, 'they all looked like beach girls.' In desperation, he moved east to view actresses there, and happened on McGillis. 'She was perfect,' he says, 'a lovely, intelligent, preppy New England girl. I said, "Tell me about yourself." She said, "I'm from California." I said, "Don't tell me that!"'

The role was hers, but Kelly politely explained that she couldn't do it after all. She was sorry, but she was in the middle of doing a student play, and couldn't let the team down. Shenson wasn't going to let his

Geneva escape so easily, and so re-arranged the film's shooting schedule to accommodate its unknown star. During the week Kelly performed at Juilliard, in the weekends she flew 500 miles south to make her first film.

Reuben, Reuben was a beautiful, witty and intelligent comedy, and won Tom Conti an Oscar nomination for his role as a lecherous Scottish poet. Kelly herself gave one of the most incandescent debuts in recent memory. Shenson glowed, 'No one was prepared for how Kelly would look on screen. As soon as I saw her I said, "There's a movie star." You could hear people saying, "Movie star. Movie star."'

Nevertheless, the actress was not inundated with further offers of work. She was forced to return to waitressing before winning the female lead in *Bachelor Party*, opposite Tom Hanks. But even then the gods were against her. 'We'd been shooting a week,' she explains, 'when the producers came and told me I wasn't pretty, I wasn't sexy enough. That's exactly how they put it.'

Kelly McGillis as the hard-edged Assistant District Attorney Kathryn Murphy – in *The Accused*

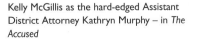

As the spirited mountain woman Collie Wright – in Ted Kotcheff's *Winter People*

The first thing I did was get drunk. I had taken the part in *Bachelor Party* – a really trashy movie – thinking, "Well, I can learn by doing." And then to be fired! In the long run, it probably saved my career.'

Meanwhile, Peter Weir had been hunting for a suitable actress to play the Amish widow Rachel Lapp opposite Harrison Ford in *Witness*. The director had given up auditioning American starlets and was now 'flying in planeloads of European actresses.'

He had been tipped to watch Ewa Froling in Ingmar Bergman's *Fanny and Alexander*, but when he found the film sold out, he saw *Reuben, Reuben* instead. Paramount insisted on a big star to partner Ford, but Weir was so impressed by Ms McGillis that he fought for her. And she did him proud. Shedding her image as the dream girl with the tumbling honey tresses, she pulled her hair back, hid her seductive curves under billowing skirts, and transformed herself into a woman of strict moral codes. In preparation for the role, Kelly moved to Pennsylvania, stayed with a real Amish family and completely cut herself off from the comforts of the twentieth century. She learned to sow corn, to milk a cow, and recorded the local dialect on her walkman. When everybody else turned up to make the movie, Kelly McGillis was unrecognizable.

Witness was a considerable hit, and won an Oscar nomination as best film of 1984. But again, on screen McGillis found herself romantically paired with a much older man. She was 25 when she was wooed by a 42-year-old Tom Conti. And in *Witness*, Ford was 17 years her senior.

After two mediocre TV movies – *Sweet Revenge*, with Alec Baldwin, and *Private Sessions*, as a nymphomaniac – she was signed up to star opposite Jack Nicholson (who was then 49) in the *Chinatown* sequel, *Two Jakes*. She spent almost two years preparing for the part – as Faye Dunaway's daughter – when the whole production folded. She was bitterly disappointed. 'After *Two Jakes* I desperately wanted to work,' she cried. 'I'm terrified if I don't have something

to do. After *Witness* I wanted to play a modern woman, and to work with actors my age.'

Actually, Tom Cruise was five years *younger* than she, but what's half a decade between friends? Anyway, she returned to the big screen to play the glamorous astrophysicist Charlotte Blackwood in *Top Gun*. This time Paramount gave her billing above the title – placing her name right next to Cruise's. And Ms McGillis took the honour to heart. To prepare for her part, she spent a considerable amount of time with Christine Fox, her character's role model, and read up extensively on G forces and inverted flight dives. Generating both a self-assurance and vulnerability, an intelligence and sexuality, the actress looked fit to eat Cruise for breakfast – as the instructor who bawls him out in front of class and then balls him back at her condo. In real-life she was seeing Barry Tubb, the little-known actor who played Wolfman, Cruise's nemesis in *Top Gun*. She was, however, quick to point out, 'that, for the moment, my work comes first. I've always told anybody I was ever involved with that that's the way it is.' Nevertheless, the fame that came with *Top Gun* was a disturbing prospect. 'In the midst of all this hype, I was suddenly a movie star, which I never set out to be,' she revealed. 'It scared me. I tried to hide from it by not taking care of myself, by denying the physical part of me, the part people wanted to look at.' She also took some unwise career decisions.

She starred in an Israeli drama, *Once We Were Dreamers*, with John Shea, which barely saw the light of day; she played an angel in love with earthling Timothy Hutton in the cloying *Made in Heaven*; and was a politically-motivated picture editor who stumbles onto an espionage plot, in *The House on Carroll Street*. The last named was a good star vehicle for the actress, but was too plodding to be a commercial success. But triumph was just around the corner.

This arrived in the form of Jonathan Kaplan's *The Accused*, a story inspired by a true event in which a multiple-rape victim charged her onlookers with criminal solicitation. McGillis was offered the role of the victim, but felt too vulnerable to re-live her ordeal of 1982. She did, however, want the film to be made and, more importantly, the issues brought to the public's attention. So

With Peter Weller in Abel Ferrara's political thriller *Cat Chaser*

she took the role of the cold-blooded prosecuting attorney instead, a professional who shows little initial compassion for her client. It was a courageous move to do the movie, and an even harder professional one not to take the showier part. Jodie Foster was cast as her client, and stormed off with an Oscar for the privilege. Still, *The Accused* made its point, and was one of the most-talked about movies of 1988.

Next, McGillis was in an engrossing period drama, *Winter People*, playing Collie Wright, a 1934 backwoods woman who falls for a stranger (Kurt Russell) and has to suffer the consequences. The role was not unlike Rachel Lapp in *Witness*, but McGillis countered, 'I think Collie knows how to have fun. Rachel knew what fun was, but never had it.'

In 1988, while shooting the film noir melodrama *Cat Chaser*, with Peter Weller, the actress decided to give up drinking. 'I just decided: no more,' she divulges. 'Maybe I was at a point where I didn't feel so scared and overwhelmed by everything.' A short while later, on New Year's Eve, she married her second husband, whom she had met in her native Newport while shopping for a yacht. 'When I met Fred,' she says, 'I had kind of resigned myself to not being with anybody for the rest of my life.' Life, indeed, was looking up. At least, personally.

Cat Chaser, in which she shed her clothes with surprising abandon, was a dud, and so was her next one, *Grand Isle*, in which she likewise disrobed. She also produced, and starred as an 1899 married woman who rebels against the stuffy society that cocoons her. McGillis wasn't particularly sympathetic in the part, but as producer did round up a sterling cast to back her: Adrian Pasdar, Ellen Burstyn, Glenne Headly and Julian Sands. Next, she played Claire Ruth, wife of the baseball legend in Arthur Hiller's *The Babe*, an expensive flop with John Goodman, and then won glowing reviews for her role as a woman who falls for a simple-minded man (Treat Williams) in the TV movie *Bonds of Love*, based on a true incident.

If her more recent films failed to live up to the success of her earlier ventures, there is one production Kelly McGillis is inordinately proud of: Kelsey Lauren, born in May 1990. In 1991, she glowed, 'I'm very happy. My child and husband are my universe.' In April of 1993 the Tillmans produced a second baby girl, Sonora, but five days later the event was louded due to the arrest of Fred Tillman by the Florida vice-squad for offering $30 to an undercover police officer for sexual services.

FILMOGRAPHY

1982: *Reuben, Reuben*. 1984: *Witness*; *Sweet Revenge* (TV). 1985: *Private Sessions* (TV). 1986: *Top Gun*. 1987: *Once We Were Dreamers*; *Made in Heaven*. 1988: *The House On Carroll Street*; *The Accused*. 1989: *Winter People*; *Cat Chaser*. 1991: *Grand Isle*. 1992: *The Babe*; *Bonds of Love* (TV). 1994: *Bitter Blood* (TV); *North* (cameo).

Elizabeth McGOVERN

There is a fresh, well-bred sweetness about Elizabeth McGovern that had her neatly pigeon-holed in a number of pictures. Although she started out sultry – as the calculating Evelyn Nesbitt in *Ragtime* – she was best known as a nice girl with a cultural leaning. And she did it superbly. Sporting big blue eyes and spectacular chipmunk cheeks, she was always delightful to watch and invariably good value. In her very first film, *Ordinary People*, she registered a strength and humanity that made her irresistible. But even if her roles were for the most part similar, her leading men have ranged from the sublime to the ridiculous – Timothy Hutton, Dudley Moore, Robert De Niro, Sean Penn and Michael Caine. However, she played off them well, regardless of who they were.

Elizabeth McGovern in 1983

She was born on 18 July 1961 in Evanston, Illinois, the daughter of a law professor (her father) and a high school teacher (her mother). Her family moved to California when she was ten and she went to school in North Hollywood. There, she appeared in a production of Thornton Wilder's *The Skin of Our Teeth*, and impressed an agent (Joan Scott) enough to offer her representation. Thus encouraged, McGovern spent a summer at the American Conservatory Theatre and later, in order to pay for her tuition at the Juilliard School in New York, she attended a 'cattle call' audition for Robert Redford's *Ordinary People*. Redford was so impressed with her potential that he ended up casting her as Timothy Hutton's girlfriend, Jeannine. The film was both a critical and box-office success, and McGovern found herself in the spotlight alongside a new breed of actress. Subsequently, *Newsweek* magazine published a cover story on up-and-coming actors and McGovern was one of them.

'I was very grateful for that article,' she said at the time, 'because it brought to light a group of us who were serious about our craft in the same way that a writer or a painter is. We do exist, and I think it's important that people realize it.'

The sudden attention forced her to abandon Juilliard prematurely. 'I've always felt as if I had to educate myself since I didn't

Elizabeth McGovern with Dudley Moore in *Lovesick*

Elizabeth McGovern with Robert De Niro in Sergio Leone's magnificent *Once Upon a Time in America*

Mickey Rourke and Elizabeth McGovern in *Johnny Handsome*

finish school,' she says. 'As a result, I'm an avid reader and an extremely inquisitive person.'

Next, she was cast as Evelyn Nesbitt in Milos Forman's *Ragtime*, in a starry cast headed by James Cagney. For her role as the mistress of the celebrated architect Stanford White (Norman Mailer) and wife of the millionaire Harry K. Thaw (Robert Joy), she was nominated for a best supporting actress Oscar.

She was elevated to billing above the title in the sweet, but only sporadically amusing *Lovesick*, as psychiatrist Dudley Moore's romantic obsession (she was divine), and then won the romantic female lead in Sergio Leone's gargantuan masterpiece *Once Upon a Time in America*. Spanning 46 years in the lives of two gangsters, the film featured McGovern as the childhood romantic fixation of one of them, Robert De Niro, who, in a memorable sequence, hires an elegant restaurant in which to dine and woo her. An orchestra plays in the background, a battalion

of waiters serve them food, wine, whatever. Afterwards, by the sea, De Niro begs her to marry him. She refuses, explaining she's leaving for Hollywood. The scene is one of enormous poetry and sensitivity, of broken dreams and tenuous hopes. Later, on the way home in his chauffeur-driven car, De Niro tears off her clothes and rapes her. Mixing dignity, strength and sadness, McGovern was heart-breaking. Only in her later scenes, muffled in old-age make-up, is she less effective.

In the war-time romance *Racing With the Moon* she played the delicate Caddie Winger, the rich girl who eventually falls for local poor boy Sean Penn. In real life, the couple became an item until Penn was blind-sided by Madonna.

Since then, McGovern's more notable roles have included the waitress in the Hitchcock-style thriller *The Bedroom Window*, in which she teamed up with Steve Guttenberg to unmask a killer; the streetwise girlfriend of deformed crook Mickey Rourke in *Johnny Handsome*; and a junior executive in the sly black comedy *A Shock to the System*, as an unwitting accomplice to a homicidal Michael Caine.

She was about the only good thing in the Harold Pinter-scripted film of Margaret Atwood's novel *The Handmaid's Tale*, cast against type and making the most of it as a rebellious lesbian in a futuristic dystopia. In

Victim or hunter?: Elizabeth McGovern (with Brad Greenquist hovering) in Curtis Hanson's effective thriller *The Bedroom Window*

the thick of an impressive cast that included Natasha Richardson, Faye Dunaway and Robert Duvall, she abducted the acting honours and revealed a startling new depth as an actress.

More recently, she was noteworthy as the bitter sister of Patricia Wettig in the feuding sibling drama *Me and Veronica*, and then joined Jeroen Krabbe, Spalding Gray and Karen Allen in Steven Soderberg's adaptation of the A.E. Hotchner novel *King of the Hill*.

FILMOGRAPHY

1980: *Ordinary People*. 1981: *Ragtime*. 1983: *Lovesick*. 1984: *Once Upon a Time in America*. 1984: *Racing With the Moon*. 1986: *Native Son*. 1987: *The Bedroom Window*. 1988: *She's Having a Baby*. 1989: *Johnny Handsome*. 1990: *A Shock to the System*; *The Handmaid's Tale*; *Tune in Tomorrow* (UK: *Aunt Julia and the Scriptwriter*); *Women & Men: Stories of Seduction* (TV). 1991: *The Favor*. 1992: *Me and Veronica*; *Tales From Hollywood* (TV). 1993: *King of the Hill*. 1994: *The Changeling* (TV); *Wings of Courage*.

Matthew MODINE

Matthew Modine was doing something right. With filmmakers like Robert Altman, Jonathan Demme, Stanley Kubrick, Alan J. Pakula, Alan Parker, Tony Richardson, Alan Rudolph and John Schlesinger queueing up for his services, he had to be pretty damn good.

Modine had very little to do in his first film, *Baby, It's You*, but his naturalness caught the attention of director Harold Becker, who had previously made stars of Tom Cruise and Sean Penn in the 1981 *Taps*. 'Matthew's a natural,' Becker noted. 'And I've always used that term for him from the first time I saw him. You never felt you were watching somebody who wasn't already completely accomplished. There were no rough edges on him.'

Alan Parker, who directed Modine in the title role of *Birdy* – William Wharton's story of a boy obsessed with becoming a bird – added, 'He is a wonderfully natural actor with a built-in phony-detector, which makes it difficult for him to make a dishonest move. Birdy's obsession had to be strange but believable – I still wanted audiences to keep in touch with him, to care for him, to like him.'

In John Schlesinger's romantic thriller *Pacific Heights*, the actor played Drake Goodman, a young man head-over-heels in love (with Melanie Griffith), who is forced to re-evaluate his human priorities when a psychopathic conman (Michael Keaton) takes over their new home. Schlesinger explained, 'Drake is the type of person who is always trying to organize things, but sometimes flies off the handle too soon. For that, I needed someone with a certain character and youthfulness, but still able to cope with the violence that occurs. Matthew was my choice. He is a man, yet he still has a boyish charm, a certain naivete about his personality. And he's a *very* good actor.'

The youngest of seven children, Matthew Modine was born on 22 March 1959 in Loma Linda, California, but grew up in Utah, where his father was the manager of a drive-in theatre. 'I saw so many movies,' he recalled, 'that I'm sure it influenced my desire to be an actor.' Matthew's father was also a Mormon, which conflicted with his professional calling. 'The church leased the land, but they said they'd take back the lease if my dad showed restricted films. There wasn't much else to show. They didn't want *Rosemary's Baby* shown, and now it's on TV! I think my parents recognized the tremendous amount of prejudice the Mormons have against *everything*,' Modine noted, and, indeed, when he was 12, they left the church.

He was 18 when he headed for New York to study acting with the legendary drama coach Stella Adler. He then appeared in the obligatory commercials and performed

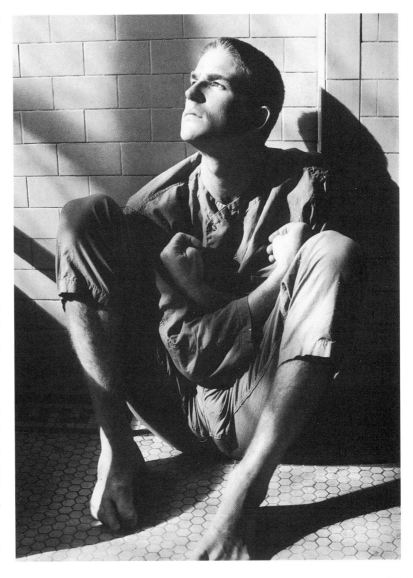

Matthew Modine as the unusual hero of Alan Parker's extraordinary film, *Birdy*

As Private Joker in Stanley Kubrick's gut-kicking *Full Metal Jacket*

In lighter mood, Matthew Modine plays FBI agent Mike Downey in Jonathan Demme's *Married To the Mob*

in such stage productions as *Our Town*, *Tea and Sympathy* and *The Brick and the Rose*. On TV, he had a role in *Texas*, a daytime soap modelled on *Dallas*, and in 1981 appeared in the ABC Afternoon Special *Amy and the Angel*.

It was around this time that he bumped into a woman on the street, helped carry her packages, took her to a movie and married her. She understood his vocation to be an actor and soon he was able to support her in the manner to which she was about to become accustomed. He made his film debut in John Sayles's *Baby, It's You*, and in his first scene on celluloid he had the pleasure of Rosanna Arquette throwing up over him. He was a star. Well, not quite.

Harold Becker, fresh off *Taps*, earmarked him for *VisionQuest*, but first Modine had the humiliation of appearing in the limp sex comedy *Private School*, starring Phoebe Cates. At the time he was still in acting school in New York, and explained, 'I had a chance to go to Hollywood.' His big break arrived with the central role of Billy, the sexually ambivalent soldier in Robert Altman's screen version of David Rabe's anti-war play *Streamers*. The entire cast were jointly awarded the best actor prize at the 1983 Venice Film Festival. In *The Hotel New Hampshire*, Tony Richardson's breezy film of John Irving's best-seller, Modine had *two*

roles, as Chip Dove, the idol and rapist of Jodie Foster, and as Ernst, her radical German seducer. Few realized it was the same actor playing both roles.

Next came *VisionQuest* – the story of a 'mystical' high school wrestler who sets his sights on the state championship – a film Modine is not proud of ('we all have to work'), and then Gillian Armstrong's downbeat *Mrs Soffel*, based on real events that occurred in 1901. In the latter he played Mel Gibson's younger brother, Jack Biddle, who is sentenced to hang as an accessory to murder, but is then sprung from jail by the warden's wife (Diane Keaton).

And then came Alan Parker, who was casting *Birdy*. Parker, who prepares his films with the care and foresight of a Utopian interior minister, explained, 'I met with every possible young actor who could play the part, and my video tapes were starting to take up more room than my luggage. In Philadelphia, we saw over 2,000 in one day, each one reading a couple of pages of the script, smiling for the Polaroid and being shown the back door. Winnowing through the video tapes, we gradually zeroed in on Matthew Modine for Birdy. Originally I read the part of Al with him [which eventually went to Nicolas Cage], but Matthew's gentle, introverted and honest qualities seemed to say "Birdy". He never could understand how

I had cast him without reading a single word of the Birdy part, but I had worn out the rewind button on my tape machine.' For Modine, *Birdy* was a very special experience. 'I love Alan Parker,' the actor volunteered, 'because he's, like, an inventor. They're ready to close the patent office and he comes along with something new and they have to open it again.'

The film was a real original, a magical, funny and supremely well-crafted evocation of lost innocence that swept through the 1985 Cannes Film Festival with the force of a tornado. That year, *Birdy* won the Special Grand Jury Prize for, 'its originality and spirit of research.'

From the brilliance of Parker, Modine found himself in the clutches of an even greater cinematic legend – Stanley Kubrick. Kubrick propelled the actor into the middle of his searing Vietnam war epic *Full Metal Jacket*, a brutal, numbing accomplishment that managed to meld cinematic mastery with emotional impact. Modine played Private Joker, the story's narrator, and it was the star's most rewarding experience yet. 'Stanley doesn't pay people much,' Modine explained, 'but I don't know any actor who doesn't want to work with him. It's a great apprenticeship.'

In *Orphans*, Alan J. Pakula's efficient film version of the play by Lyle Kessler, Modine played Treat, an urban outcast who kidnaps a genteel mobster (Albert Finney), prompting *Esquire* magazine to observe, 'Modine goes head-to-head with Albert Finney and takes your breath away.' He turned to comedy for Jonathan Demme's offbeat, eminently enjoyable *Married To the Mob*, as an FBI agent and master of disguise who falls in love with the gorgeous, edgy widow of a Mafia gangster. Modine was surprisingly engaging as the incompetent G-man who will go to any lengths to prove the innocence of his ward (who, as she was played by Michelle Pfeiffer, was hardly surprising).

He was less successful as a trainee doctor in the dramatic-comedy *Gross Anatomy*, set in medical school, which *Variety* thought was, 'about as exciting as a pop quiz', but had another hit (at least in Britain) with *Memphis Belle*. Produced by David Puttnam, this was the polished, gung-ho story of ten young Americans who crew the B-17 of the title, a 'Flying Fortress' that flew 25 bombing missions over Nazi Germany. Modine was Captain Dennis Dearborne, but had little opportunity to shine in the face of the World War II hardware and a cast of young actors all trying to top each other.

He had more screen time in *Pacific*

Back to the thrills dept: Modine, with Melanie Griffith, confronts con man Michael Keaton in John Schlesinger's *Pacific Heights*

Heights, an effective, if unlikely thriller that was surprisingly inspired by real events. The film was a modest hit, and Modine was very good as a hapless first-time house buyer – but it was Michael Keaton's menacing tenant that cinemagoers remembered. He was an unexpected ingredient in the banal Italian costume melodrama *La Partita*, and although he contributed much enthusiasm as a young cad, he was badly miscast (while Faye Dunaway, camping it up as a scheming noblewoman, seemed far more at home).

For Alan Rudolph, the acclaimed, maverick director of *Choose Me* and *The Moderns*, Modine starred in *Equinox* as identical twin brothers. Separated at birth, the doubles Henry and Freddy are as different as chalk from cheddar in character, one being a timid nerd, the other a strutting thug. As in all Rudolph's films, the blessings were mixed, but there was enough charm and innovation to keep punters of the unusual happy, while Modine himself was at the top of his form.

In *Wind*, he had little to act on, as an introspective sailor who loses the America's Cup *and* his girlfriend (Jennifer Grey) – forcing him to re-think his values. This was familiar territory, and banal at that, while by all accounts the film was a pain to work on. He then joined the all-star cast of Robert Altman's ensemble picture *Short Cuts*, a series of loosely related tales based on the short stories of Raymond Carver.

FILMOGRAPHY

1983: *Baby, It's You*. 1983: *Private School*; *Streamers*. 1984: *The Hotel New Hampshire*; *VisionQuest*; *Mrs Soffel*; *Birdy*. 1987: *Full Metal Jacket*; *Orphans*. 1988: *Married To the Mob*. 1989: *Gross Anatomy* (UK: *A Cut Above*). 1990: *Memphis Belle*; *Pacific Heights*. 1991: *La Partita* (aka *The Gamble/The Match*). 1992: *Wind*; *Equinox*. 1993: *Short Cuts*; *And the Band Played On*. 1994: *The Browning Version*; *Fluke*; *Jacob* (TV); *Bye Bye Love*.

Demi MOORE

Demi Moore just couldn't keep her name out of the papers.

It all began when she became engaged to Emilio Estevez and cancelled the wedding after the invitations had already been sent out. She explained that 'there were things I needed, like security, that Emilio wasn't in a position to offer me.' She then married Bruce Willis on a whim, after a whirlwind, four-month courtship. Following a Las Vegas boxing match, the couple rang for a priest at 11.15pm and were exchanging vows by midnight.

Then there was the story that surfaced about her former marriage. On a TV chat show she informed viewers that Willis was her first husband, and that her wedding licence backed up the fact. But then her real first husband, rock musician Freddy Moore, exposed the sham. 'She's probably very embarrassed that she made a mistake,' he revealed to the press. 'It's so interesting that she lied – perhaps she never told Bruce about me.' The musician claims she also lied about her age when she married him, saying she was 21 when, in fact, she was only 16. Three years after the wedding she walked out on him, and became engaged to Emilio while she was still married.

Then there was the furore over her posing naked for the cover of *Vanity Fair* – while seven months pregnant. Numerous newsstands in Britain and America refused to display – or even sell – the magazine, deeming the cover pornographic. However, Demi stuck to her guns, saying, 'to me, being pregnant is the sexiest thing in the world. I feel proud and my intention of doing those photos was to convey that pride.' The issue became the most talked-about edition in the magazine's history and was a sell-out.

Then there were the well-publicized threatening phone calls and one ominous note, fashioned out of newsprint, that warned Mr and Mrs Willis: 'watch out for your darling daughter.' This was apparently

Demi Moore back in 1986 – as she appeared in Ed Zwick's *'About Last Night . . .'*

provoked by an injudicious comment Willis made, blaming the unions for the high cost of filmmaking in Hollywood. Which was good coming from a man who was reportedly charging Twentieth Century Fox $16 million to star in *Die Hard 3*. To back up the threats, an anonymous car forced Willis onto the curb of an LA street.

Then more outraged newsprint was devoted to Mrs Willis declaring that she was going to give birth to her second child in front of her husband, brother, sister-and-law *and* her three-year-old daughter, Rumer Glenn. The actress countered by saying, 'I wanted Rumer there to share the joy of her sister's birth.'

And, just in case Joe Public had failed to read about her for a month or two, Demi appeared on the cover of *Vanity Fair* again, this time naked save for a prudently placed thong and a layer of body paint patterned after a man's suit and tie. Much publicity followed and the magazine was another best-seller.

Demi Moore was famous, alright, and the press had a heyday reporting her *prima donna* behaviour, going on about her ubiquitous entourage and revealing her insistence that she be chauffeured in limousines and private jets.

But she has her defenders. Ezra Litwak,

who co-scripted *The Butcher's Wife*, volunteered: 'Demi is very much a movie star. Everything revolves around that fact. She knows what she wants and how to get it. She's a very focused woman.'

But Demi Moore's world has not always been big news and big cars. Starting life as Demi Gene Guynes on 11 November 1962, in Roswell, New Mexico, she had an unhappy childhood. Born to teenage parents, she was carted around America by her stepfather, newspaper adman Duane Guynes, who had married her mother, Virginia, when the latter was pregnant. In the space of 13 years, Demi was uprooted 48 times ('at a wild guess, I went to 30 schools,' she says). When she was 15, her mother left Guynes, who committed suicide two years later – a month before Demi's 18th birthday. At 16, Demi quit school and left home to pursue a modelling career, appearing nude in *Oui*. After landing two words on the TV series *W.E.B.*, she got her big break when she replaced Genie Francis on the daytime soap *General Hospital*, playing cub reporter Jackie Templeton. She also got married.

On the big screen, she made her film debut in *Choices*, a small-scale drama about a deaf teenager, had a cameo in the comedy *Young Doctors in Love* and then battled a giant slug in a 3-D *Alien* rip-off called *Parasite*. Then she was signed up to play Michael Caine's daughter in the vacation comedy *Blame It On Rio*, and spent four months in Brazil. When she returned to Los Angeles she had outgrown her marriage.

In the role Meg Ryan junked: Demi as the country clairvoyant come to New York, in Terry Hughes's delightful *The Butcher's Wife*

She had the female lead in *No Small Affair* (replacing Sally Field), playing a struggling rock singer worshipped by Jon Cryer, and made an impression. Craig Baumgarten, who cast her in the film, marvelled, 'I knew from the very, very beginning Demi was going to be a movie star. I knew it when I saw dailies on *No Small Affair*. She can rip your heart out, make you care. That's a rare quality and part of what makes a star. When she was in pain, you just wanted to make her feel better.'

Demi *was* in pain, struggling against a ruinous alcohol and drug addiction. 'When I was in school, doing Quaaludes and smoking pot and drinking was what a majority of the kids did,' she disclosed. But it had got out of hand.

She was in the thick of it when, at Universal Studios, she was spotted by the director Joel Schumacher, who was casting *St Elmo's Fire*. 'I just saw this beautiful girl with long dark hair flashing by my office,' he recalls. 'She was running around a corner. I said to my assistant, "Get that girl!" He chased her down in the parking lot.'

She was signed up to play Jules, a young banker addicted to cocaine. But when Schumacher caught wind of her real addiction, he threatened to fire her. Demi immediately started attending rehab, turned herself around and delivered the most attention-grabbing performance of her career to date: playing a beautiful, tough-on-the-outside, vulnerable-on-the-inside beauty careening out of control in the fast lane.

Demi in her biggest hit – *Ghost* – with Patrick Swayze

Demi as Lt. Cdr. JoAnne Galloway – in Rob Reiner's $200 million-plus earner, *A Few Good Men*

Demi as Diana Murphy, the woman who thought she couldn't be bought – in Adrian Lyne's *Indecent Proposal*

Emilio Estevez was also in the film, and the couple started dating.

More pictures followed – *One Crazy Summer*, a comedy with John Cusack; *'About Last Night . . . '*, a romantic drama with Rob Lowe; and *Wisdom*, with Emilio co-starring, scripting and directing. The last-named was a formidable flop, and marked the end of Demi and Emilio's relationship. In the meantime, she married Bruce and was carrying his daughter when she starred in *The Seventh Sign*, a flashy apocalyptic thriller. Demi played a pregnant mother haunted by a very disturbing Jurgen Prochnow, and endured many violent scenes (causing some concern for her real-life, unborn child). She even did a nude scene, setting the pattern for events to come. The role was a showy one, and the actress disported herself well. If Steven Spielberg had directed *The Omen* it may well have looked like *The Seventh Sign*.

She was in good company – with Robert De Niro and Sean Penn – in the dramatically unfunny comedy *We're No Angels*, and was then cast in the starring role of *Ghost*. While Patrick Swayze and Whoopi Goldberg had to fight to get in the movie, Demi was first choice in what turned out to be the biggest grossing film of 1990. As the loving wife of Swayze (who is killed by a mugger, but returns to express his love), Demi, with her hair cropped short, had never looked more beautiful and delivered a star-making performance.

At this point Bruce Willis was also doing well, top-billed in *Die Hard 2*, the most successful action movie of the year. Mr and Mrs Willis were ordained 'the hottest couple in Hollywood.'

But the good fortune was short-lived. While Bruce found himself in three monumental flops – *Bonfire of the Vanities*, *Hudson Hawk* and *Billy Bathgate* – Demi turned producer with *Mortal Thoughts* (co-starring Willis), another fiasco, and then teamed up with Chevy Chase, Dan Aykroyd and John Candy in *Nothing But Trouble*, which lived up to its name. She replaced Meg Ryan in *The Butcher's Wife*, a delightful, magical romantic comedy, but was miscast as a naive clairvoyant, and the film died at the box-office.

But then her career took a turn for the better. In Rob Reiner's box-office hit *A Few Good Men* she played a fastidious, passionate trial lawyer, teamed with Tom Cruise to defend two Marines accused of murder. The film, budgeted at a colossal $41m, was one of the most prestigious of the year (1992), and boasted a supporting cast that included Jack Nicholson, Kevin Bacon and Kiefer Sutherland. As Cruise's senior officer determined to stick to the rule book, Demi made a feisty, formidable operator, but never lost sight of her vulnerability. After that she skewered the female lead in Adrian Lyne's controversial *Indecent Proposal*, playing a married beauty bought by millionaire Robert Redford for one night of nookie. The film grossed over $250 million worldwide.

In February of 1993, the *National Enquirer* claimed that the actress secretly visited a divorce lawyer to end her five-year marriage to Bruce Willis. There were also reports of rows in public places, while one insider revealed: 'They've already moved into separate quarters in their New York condo. She's living on one floor with the children, and he's living on the other.' Moore retaliated with a passionate defence in *Hello* magazine, saying: 'We have never taken any of this Hollywood gossip stuff seriously. But these latest stories have hit too close to home. We started getting calls from friends, asking us if

everything was all right. We have to let the truth be known. Bruce and I both make a great effort to compromise and our marriage continues to grow stronger and stronger.'

FILMOGRAPHY

1981: *Choices*. **1982:** *Young Doctors in Love*; *Parasite*. **1983:** *Blame It On Rio*. **1984:** *No Small Affair*. **1985:** *St Elmo's Fire*. **1986:** *One Crazy Summer*; 'About Last Night . . .'; *Wisdom*. **1988:** *The Seventh Sign*. **1989:** *We're No Angels*. **1990:** *Ghost*. **1991:** *Mortal Thoughts* (also co-produced); *Nothing But Trouble*. **1991:** *The Butcher's Wife*. **1992:** *Tales From the Crypt Volume 3* (UK: video); *A Few Good Men*. **1993:** *Indecent Proposal*. **1994:** *Disclosure*; *The Scarlet Letter*.

Dermot MULRONEY

Should Dermot Mulroney appear in a film that makes a lot of money, or gathers a cult reputation, or just wins a few Oscars, the actor should find himself hurtling towards professional prosperity and longevity. It hasn't happened yet. Nevertheless, Mulroney continues to be given starring roles in fine TV movies and small-budget curios that never quite make it. Those cinemagoers and videoviewers who *have* discovered him seem to want to know more, and usually find themselves scampering down to the nearest Blockbuster to see if he's on the shelf.

Dermot, older brother of actor Kieran

Mulroney (born 1966), is not only good-looking in an inoffensive way (hunky without the smarm), but has a naturalness that makes him the sort of guy-next-door with charm to spare. But he can also summon up an edge that would make him a prime candidate to play, say, the serial killer Jeffrey Dahmer. To be honest, he is no box-office star, but his burgeoning workload would suggest that he is one of the most in-demand actors of his generation.

Born in Alexandria, Virginia, on 31 October 1963, Dermot Mulroney was an award-winning cellist before setting his sights on acting. Graduating from Northwestern University, he made his professional debut in the TV movie *Sin of Innocence*, as a teenager who falls in love with his stepsister (Megan Follows). He then played a high school drug addict in the Afternoon Special *Toma – the Drug Knot*, and made his theatrical film debut in *Survival Quest*, starring Lance Henriksen, as a juvenile delinquent sent to wilderness school to shape up, and does so to heroic effect.

For his next role, as a hotshot Southern baseball player in the entertaining HBO comedy *Long Shot*, he was nominated for an ACE award as best supporting actor. Next,

Dermot Mulroney (*centre*) with screen brothers Sean Astin and Tim Quill in Lee Grant's affectionate *Staying Together*

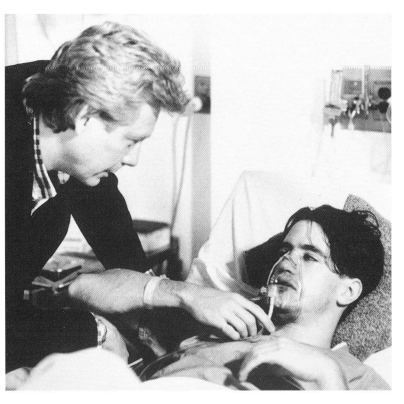

performance of his career as a naive 18-year-old who hitches up with the worldly Lili Taylor. The supporting cast, too, was impressive, and included Sam Shepard, Valerie Perrine, Bill Pullman and Burt Young.

Career-wise, the actor took a step down in writer-producer John Hughes's threadbare romantic comedy *Career Opportunities*, in which he and his brother Kieran played 'bumbling crooks with hearts of gold,' who break into a cut-price department store only to come up against an enterprising nightwatchman (Frank Whaley) and a sexy shoplifter (Jennifer Connelly). Actually, the

Mulroney (*right*) with Bruce Davison in Norman Rene's acclaimed AIDS drama *Longtime Companion*

Dermot Mulroney in the 1993 TV movie *Family Pictures*

he had the lead in the disturbing TV movie *Daddy*, in which he played a happy-go-lucky student who is forced to face the responsibilities of fatherhood when one of his girlfriends (Patricia Arquette) gets pregnant. On the big screen he had a nice turn as a Hollywood drunk in Blake Edwards's otherwise excruciating comedy-murder mystery *Sunset*, and then took an unexpected career move, joining Emilio, Kiefer etc. in *Young Guns*, as the unsavoury, tobacco-chewing Dirty Steve. 'In the first seven roles I played,' Mulroney explains, 'I kissed the girl in every one. I was playing the starry-eyed romantic quite a lot. I knew it was time to branch out and try something a little different. Dirty Steve certainly got me away from the boy-next-door look.'

The film was a hit, and the young actor followed it by starring in the TV movie *Unconquered*, as a loser who surmounts his physical disabilities to become a celebrated hurdler and football luminary. Then, in Lee Grant's *Staying Together*, he joined Sean Astin and Tim Quill as the brothers McDermott, three sparring siblings who attempt to save the family chicken business from developers. 'This was the first time anyone had ever offered me a role without my auditioning for it,' the actor noted. 'I walked into the

meeting, and they said, "here". It was amazing.' And Mulroney didn't let his producers down, giving a keenly etched portrait of a small-town lad coming to grips with love, family and the whole damn thing. Unfortunately, the film drowned in its own glucose, but did boast some sterling performances.

He was in even better company (Bruce Davison, Mary-Louise Parker, Campbell Scott, etc.) in the ensemble AIDS drama *Longtime Companion*, as John, the first of the cast to be diagnosed with the virus. Although dealing with a potentially more mawkish subject than *Staying Alive*, Norman Rene's intelligent, challenging film avoided sentimentality like the plague and, at times, seemed almost distant in its study of death and friendship. The actor was also in good hands in *Bright Angel*, a commendably fresh re-invention of the road movie, with Mulroney possibly giving the best

Mulroney Bros were not bad, but they had little to work with.

He was the boy-next-door again in the uneven comedy *Samantha*, caught between a feisty Martha Plimpton and a bitchy Ione Skye, but seemed out of his depth. He was top-billed in the ensemble drama *Where the Day Takes You*, and was very good indeed as the magnetic leader of a gang of street urchins. However, the film's treatment of a serious subject was too glossy to be taken seriously, while the starry supporting cast (Lara Flynn Boyle, Sean Astin, Kyle MacLachlan, Laura San Giacomo, Christian Slater) helped detract from the reality.

In the well-written TV movie *Heart of Justice*, Mulroney played a psychotic rich boy with unhealthy yearnings for his sister (Jennifer Connelly), and was then wasted (along with Richard Harris and River Phoenix) in Sam Shepard's extraordinary mystic western *Silent Tongue*, as the son of Irish charlatan Alan Bates. Next, he joined Bridget Fonda in *Point of No Return*, John Badham's re-make of the stylish French thriller *Nikita*, and was very good, too. In the TV movie *Family Pictures* he played the son of Anjelica Huston and was required to age from 17 to 37. He then teamed up with River Phoenix and Samantha Mathis as one of a trio of musicians looking for the big time in Nashville – in Peter Bogdanovich's *The Thing Called Love*. He supplied the love interest in *Bad Girls*, with Drew Barrymore, Mary Stuart Masterson and Andie MacDowell – as the boyfriend of homicidal prostitute Madeleine Stowe.

He is married to the actress Catherine Keener, who won excellent reviews for her performance opposite Brad Pitt in *Johnny Suede*.

FILMOGRAPHY

1986: *Sin of Innocence* (TV). **1987:** *Survival Quest; Long Gone* (TV); *Daddy* (TV). **1988:** *Sunset; Young Guns.* **1989:** *Unconquered* (TV); *Staying Together.* **1990:** *Longtime Companion.* **1991:** *Bright Angel; Career Opportunities* (UK video: *One Wild Night*); *Samantha.* **1992:** *Where the Day Takes You; Heart of Justice* (TV). **1993:** *Silent Tongue; Point of No Return* (UK: *The Assassin*); *Family Pictures* (TV); *The Thing Called Love; The Last Outlaw.* **1994:** *Bad Girls.*

Eddie MURPHY

In the early 1980s Eddie Murphy rose like an unstoppable warhead. And, like all meteoric phenomenons, he found that both his image and his personal life suffered soundly for it. He has been bashed by the critics, attacked by the black community and hit by more lawsuits than featured in an entire series of *LA Law*. He has been sued for sexual harassment, at least three women have claimed to have had his baby and, most famously, the humorist Art Buchwald (and his partner Alain Bernheim) sued Murphy and Paramount for $6.2 million for reputedly stealing Buchwald's storyline to *Coming to America*.

Murphy estimates that he has paid out several million dollars settling 'spurious lawsuits,' but reserves his greatest contempt for the media.

'The press builds you up and tears you down,' he told *Playboy* in 1990. 'I'm in the tear-down stage right now ... Most of the people who want to talk to me, I feel, want to get me.'

But things got worse. When he was filming

Eddie Murphy in his film debut, as Reggie Hammond in *48 HRS*

Boomerang in 1992, the trade paper *Variety* reported that on one occasion the star never showed up for a re-shoot in Atlanta – which cost Paramount Pictures $300,000. Another time he arrived at the location so late that the crew had started filming another scene. Furious, he walked off again. On yet another instance Murphy decided to see *Cape Fear* on the way to the set, and kept the crew waiting and guessing as to whether or not they'd ever see their star again. Sources estimated that overall *Boomerang* lost almost 100 working hours due to Murphy's tardiness. The producer, Brian Grazer, acknowledged that *Boomerang* actually went '$2 million to $3 million over budget.'

The most popular black screen idol of all time, Murphy has been criticized – particularly by the filmmaker Spike Lee – for not

helping the black cause more. Indeed, racism has never been a big issue for Murphy.

'I grew up in a black neighbourhood and did not stray from the block,' he says. 'Consequently, I did not encounter any racism until I was 18. Everybody is preoccupied with the system and injustice and shit like that. But I am very nonchalant about everything. There's a lot wrong, but it's getting better.'

'Eddie doesn't want to be viewed as The Black Messiah,' added the star's personal assistant, Mark Corry. 'He'll do as much as he can to open doors for minorities, but he thinks the best way to do that is [through] good "colourless" TV and films.'

However, while shooting *Boomerang*, Murphy did persuade Paramount to fund ten paid positions for the Black Filmmaker Foundation Observer Program. According to the film's co-producer Warrington Hudlin, 'this is the first time in 25 years, by my count, where a major studio has financed a learning experience for people of colour.'

With a star as big as Eddie Murphy it's hard to evaluate the true picture. Constantly surrounded by five bodyguards and at one point employing as many as 52 people, Murphy is not so much a recluse as an enigma blurred by contradictory media reports. Today, he is wary of talking to the press and certainly doesn't need the publicity. Reputed to be impossible to work with, his *Boomerang* co-star Halle Berry acknowledged that she was terrified at her screen test. 'I was a wreck,' she confided. 'I had read all those horror stories. But when I walked in, he just looked like a little boy with a big smile on his face, and all those fears went away.'

Another co-star, David Alan Grier, volunteered, 'what freaks you out is that his talent is so deep. He can mimic, he can mime, he can do physical comedy, he can do verbal comedy, and then he'll sit down at the piano and play just beautifully. Not rock 'n' roll, but serious piano. This guy is really, really heavy.'

Eddie Murphy was born on 3 April 1961, in Bushwick, Brooklyn. The son of a New York cop, he lived with his mother, a switchboard operator, and his stepfather, a worker in an ice-cream factory. He was a poor student and his mother despaired of her son's future. 'Don't worry, Ma,' he comforted her, 'I'm going to be famous.'

At 15 he was fat and bespectacled and performed impromptu comedy routines in the school playground to gain favour. It was then that he first stepped on to a stage – at the Roosevelt Youth Center on Long Island. He continued his stand-up comedy routine at local bars and joined New York's Comic Strip following graduation. He would do mime, tell dirty jokes, impersonate the likes of Elvis Presley, Michael Jackson and Richard Pryor, grab his crotch and pepper his humour with a roll call of profanity. And then he would laugh that big, self-possessed open laugh, inviting the audience to laugh along with him – *at* him.

At 19 he joined the 1980-1981 season of TV's cult *Saturday Night Live*. Previously a springboard for such comic talent as Chevy Chase, John Belushi, Dan Aykroyd and Bill Murray, the revue was undergoing a rocky patch. At first Murphy was just a 'featured player' and could not stem the show's downward spiral of disfavour with the public. However, when he was brought on board as a regular, he won three Emmy nominations in four years and turned the revue around. He was a star.

Cashing in on his TV popularity, Paramount paid Murphy $200,000 to appear

Murphy as Axel Foley in the mega-hit *Beverly Hills Cop*

opposite Nick Nolte (who was paid $2 million) in *48 HRS*, Walter Hill's hard-hitting comedy about a tough cop (Nolte) and a wily crook (Murphy) who spend two days insulting each other. The public loved the sinewy mix of broad comedy and violence, and *48 HRS* went on to gross over $30 million in the States alone. Worldwide, it amassed almost $100 million.

A year later Paramount paid Murphy $300,000 to replace Richard Pryor in *Trading Places*, John Landis' high-concept comedy about a pampered financier (Dan Aykroyd) and a street-smart bum (Murphy) who change places for a bet. Again, the public lapped up Murphy's high-octane display of comedy and the film gobbled up over $40 million in the US.

With two smash-hits to his name, Eddie Murphy could do no wrong and accepted $1 million to support Dudley Moore in the catastrophic *Best Defense*. 'They started offering me all this money,' he explained later. 'I was 21 years old. I said to hell with it and went for it. I knew the script for *Best Defense* was horrible, but I got talked into the movie by Paramount.'

He was offered considerably more – $4.5 million, plus a percentage of the profits – to play unorthodox cop Axel Foley in *Beverly Hills Cop*, a film he was very happy with. Originally intended as a vehicle for Sylvester Stallone, the film had a muscular storyline alleviated by some high comedy playing from Murphy. It was a winning combination.

'I think I could play Foley forever,' he says. 'I really enjoy him and I'm grateful audiences seem to feel the same way.' Indeed, *Beverly Hills Cop* grossed a phenomenal $350 million worldwide and some say Murphy hasn't stopped playing Foley since.

Still, it's a formula that works – the rule-breaking smart-ass with the Grand Canyon laugh – and Murphy has mined it like gold. Paramount paid him $6.5 million to star in *The Golden Child*, another palpable hit, but this time one lambasted by the critics. He got $8.5 million for *Beverly Hills Cop II*, another critical bomb and the highest-grossing movie of 1987. Paramount paid him the same again for *Coming to America* (in which he played four different characters and wrote the story), and once more critics and public disagreed.

At a time when the Hollywood star system was supposedly dead, Eddie Murphy was breaking the rules. While other icons were counting their flops and licking their wounds, Eddie triggered box-office queues for whatever he starred in. And he was now critic-proof.

Besides starring in his record-breaking movies, Eddie was spreading his talent elsewhere. He produced two comedy albums, the Grammy-nominated *Eddie Murphy* and Grammy-winning *Eddie Murphy: Comedian*; started a singing and songwriting career (his LPs consist of *How Could It Be*, *So Happy* and *Love's Alright*); taped a concert, *Delirious*, for HBO (now a best-selling video); and executive-produced the film of his one-man show, *Eddie Murphy Raw*, which became the most successful filmed concert in history.

Although now one of the richest stars in Hollywood, Eddie Murphy was still unhappy with his Paramount contract. He renegotiated his $15 million, five-picture deal with the studio *twice*, and told *Playboy* 'I have a *horrible* deal at Paramount. Whoever's gonna give me the most lucrative deal, that's where I'm going' (later, he received $12 million, plus 15 per-cent of the gross, for *Boomerang*). Reputedly, he was furious that Tom Cruise, Arnold Schwarzenegger and Jack Nicholson were getting paid more than he was.

Then came the fall. Eager not to lose face with his Afro-American peers (Spike Lee, Keenen Ivory Wayans, Robert Townsend), Murphy decided to direct and produce his next picture, the period gangster comedy *Harlem Nights*. Based on his own screenplay, and co-starring his idols Richard Pryor and Redd Foxx, the film was dumped on *hard* by the critics and is an unpleasant memory for the star.

'*Harlem Nights* was the first time I did a

movie that flopped,' Murphy acknowledges. 'It didn't flop on a monetary level, but it was, like, "Ugh, did you see that piece of shit?" And I had never gone through that before.'

Eddie Murphy had slumped to No. 22 in the box-office polls, even though his reunion with Nick Nolte in *Another 48 HRS* (trashed by the critics) grossed a resounding $89 million in the US. But even Eddie was now aware of his professional slump, in spite of a new deal with Paramount that promised a much ballyhooed $50 million.

'I walked through *Another 48 HRS*. I was depressed. I was fat. I was, like, 185 pounds.' By now, he also knew he'd been ego-tripping. However, he rationalized, 'There's no such thing in this business as someone who is successful *and* humble.'

Ensconced in Bubble Hill, New Jersey, his four-acre, $3.5 million answer to Elvis Presley's Graceland, Murphy worked out in his private gym, played with his little daughter Bria (by Murphy's live-in girlfriend, model Nicole Mitchell), worked on his third album and occasionally showed up on the set of *Boomerang*. Loaned a new lease of life by Nicole, Bria and his music, Murphy shed 15 pounds.

Boomerang, the story of a self-centred, womanizing marketing executive who meets

As Prince Akeem in John Landis's entertaining (but litigation-plagued) *Coming To America*

Eddie Murphy as 'Quick' in the disastrous comedy *Harlem Nights,* which he wrote and directed himself

Murphy with Robin Givens in Reginald Hudlin's *Boomerang*

his match when he's employed by the gorgeous, ruthless Robin Givens, was admired by two critics in Washington and earned $13.7 million in its first weekend on release. One insider grumbled, 'It's too bad the movie's so good, because Murphy behaved so awfully and there'll be no reason for him to shape up. He's magic on screen.' *Boomerang* grossed an agreeable $67 million in the US, but his next comedy, Disney's *The Distinguished Gentleman*, a broad satire on Washington politics and chicanery, only attracted $46m. This fact, coupled with Murphy's salary of $12m, was bad news to everybody. However, the star was perfect as the slick con man who tricks his way into Congress, although the supporting cast of Caucasian character actors were encouraged to mug shamefully.

After that, he was lined up for *Beverly Hills Cop III*, but the movie's escalating budget stalled the start of production. He was also contemplating a revisionist version of *The Magnificent Seven*, based on his own story and co-starring Denzel Washington, Morgan Freeman, Wesley Snipes, Keenen Ivory and Damon Wayans, and Halle Berry.

On 18 March 1993, Eddie Murphy married his long-time girl friend Nicole Mitchell. Among the 500 guests at the lavish ceremony were Quincy Jones, Bill Murray, Stevie Wonder, Bruce Willis and the bride and groom's children, Bria, 3, and Myles, four months.

FILMOGRAPHY

1982: *48 HRS*. 1983: *Trading Places*. 1984: *Best Defense*; *Beverly Hills Cop*. 1986: *The Golden Child*. 1987: *Beverly Hills Cop II*. 1988: *Eddie Murphy Raw*; *Coming to America*. 1989: *Harlem Nights*. 1990: *Another 48 HRS*. 1992: *Boomerang*; *The Distinguished Gentleman*. 1994: *Beverly Hills Cop III*; *Vampire in Brooklyn*.

Would you trust this man? Eddie Murphy cons his way into Congress in Jonathan Lynn's *The Distinguished Gentleman*

Mary-Louise PARKER

Thanks to a handful of astutely realized performances in some very good pictures, Mary-Louise Parker was suddenly a force to reckon with. It was hard to miss her in Norman Rene's critically acclaimed *Longtime Companion*, as she was virtually the only woman in it. In Lawrence Kasdan's intelligent, contemplative *Grand Canyon*, she was equally hard to overlook, as she was the only 'non-star' alongside the likes of Danny Glover, Kevin Kline and Steve Martin. While, in *Fried Green Tomatoes*, she was one of four women who held the story strands together.

In the space of two years Mary-Louise Parker appeared in five films, and found herself upgraded from respected stage actress to respected film actress – although, in 1991 she revealed: 'I've never had much of a fascination for film. I respect it, but people in Hollywood can have cash registers where their hearts are.'

Born in Fort Jackson, on South Carolina, 2 August 1964, Mary-Louise gave up thoughts of medicine to pursue acting and enrolled at the North Carolina School of Arts.

Outside of New York, she appeared in such plays as *The Importance of Being Earnest*, *Hay Fever*, *Night of the Iguana* and, in Texas, *The Little Foxes*. On TV, she appeared with Ricky Schroder in the so-so war movie *Too Young the Hero*, based on a true story, and had a recurring role in the daytime soap *Ryan's Hope*. In 1989, she made her film debut in the warmly received 'American Playhouse' drama *Signs of Life*, in which she played Charlotte, the waitress girlfriend of Kevin J. O'Connor (who punches him on the head when he announces his plan to leave her for Miami). In a cast that included Arthur Kennedy, Beau Bridges and Kathy Bates, Parker was sensational – particularly in view of her underwritten role.

But she was most comfortable on stage, explaining, 'Theatre is ephemeral, and that, to me, is romantic – those moments between people that come and then disappear.'

She was nominated for a Tony for originating the part of Rita Boyle in Craig Lucas's *Prelude to a Kiss*, opposite Alec Baldwin, and became involved with Timothy Hutton when the latter took over the male lead. Later, she and Hutton appeared together again in the play *Babylon Gardens*, at New York's Circle Rep.

Mary-Louise Parker (*left*) and Mary Stuart Masterson enjoy each other's company in Jon Avnet's winning *Fried Green Tomatoes*

Mary-Louise as Dee in Lawrence Kasdan's thoughtful, intelligent drama *Grand Canyon*

It was Norman Rene, who had directed her in *Prelude*, who cast her as Lisa in *Longtime Companion*, Craig Lucas's beautifully written and perceptive look at a group of gay men coming to terms with AIDS. Of her performance, Peter Travers wrote in *Rolling Stone*, 'Parker, in the only major woman's role, is a radiant actress of rare spirit and sensitivity.'

In *Fried Green Tomatoes* she played Ruth, the demure, God-fearing innocent who is befriended by Mary Stuart Masterson's hard-drinking, hard-talking Idgie Threadgoode. Set in the 1940s, the story is related in flashback by a garrulous 82-year-old Jessica Tandy, who embroils a spellbound Kathy Bates in her tale of rural Alabama in the good ol', bad ol' days. Considered a risk by Hollywood investors, the comedy-drama – superbly played by its female cast – went on to gross over $81 million in the States, something of a small miracle.

In a total turnabout, the actress played Dee, secretary and part-time lover of Kevin Kline, in Lawrence Kasdan's biting adult drama *Grand Canyon*. Single, desirable and confused, Dee is a woman of intelligence and vulnerability, driven to distraction by her affair with Kline (who is married to Mary McDonnell). The actress explained, 'Dee is feeling very lonely and alienated, and I think *Grand Canyon* is about how people's problems are so relative to themselves. I loved the fact that the movie cannot be easily pigeon-holed. In some ways it seems as though nothing really happens, yet a million things happen. And there is such wonderful humour. But it's not fabricated and it's not elitist. It's "human humour."'

Next, Parker joined Matt Dillon and William Hurt (as the former's girlfriend) in the bittersweet romantic comedy *Mr Wonderful*, an exploration of the ironies and complexities of human relationships, directed by the British writer Anthony Minghella (*Truly, Madly, Deeply*). After that, she starred in the Martin Scorsese-produced *Naked in New York*, as Joanne, a young Bostonian whose ambition to become a photographer divided her loyalties between her boyfriend (Eric Stoltz) and a prosperous gallery owner (Timothy Dalton).

FILMOGRAPHY

1988: *Too Young the Hero* (TV). 1989: *Signs of Life*. 1990: *Longtime Companion*. 1991: *Fried Green Tomatoes* (UK: *Fried Green Tomatoes at the Whistlestop Café*); *Grand Canyon*. 1993: *Mr Wonderful*; *Naked in New York*. 1994: *The Client*; *Bullets Over Broadway*; *A Place for Annie* (TV); *Boys on the Side*.

Sarah Jessica PARKER

When Sarah Jessica Parker gave Steve Martin a run for his money in *LA Story*, she was inundated with the sort of enthusiastic press usually reserved for bright young newcomers. Indeed, she was a sensation as the exuberant, sexy SanDeE* (*sic*) whose breasts are so real that Martin thinks there's something wrong with them. Martin himself offered that Parker's acting, 'combines a completely natural style with impeccable comic timing.' She then landed the female lead opposite Nicolas Cage in the engagingly daffy comedy *Honeymoon in Vegas* which raked in over $10 million in its first week of release. After that the scripts started piling up at her door, and she was lined up to star opposite Bette Midler in *Hocus Pocus* and then landed a leading role in *Anything But Love*, with Sally Field and Tom Selleck.

But the truth is that Sarah Jessica Parker has been around for a long time. In the 1983 movie *Somewhere Tomorrow*, a touching, unusual drama, she had the starring role as a teenage amnesiac who befriends a ghost. She also won glowing reviews for three TV series although, she notes, 'every TV show I do gets great ratings, wins Emmys and is cancelled.' And then there was all the tabloid ballyhoo over her romance with John F. Kennedy Jr, following on from her seven-year relationship with Robert Downey Jr. When, in 1992, she started dating Matthew Broderick, she learned to keep her affairs to herself. Earlier, she had publicly praised Kennedy for his 'perfectly distributed' chest hair and lived to regret it.

She was born in Nelsonville, Ohio, on 25 March 1965, one of nine children, and was raised in Cincinnati. She was eight when she appeared in her first TV special, *The Little Match Girl*, and then studied with the Cincinnati Ballet and American Ballet Theatre companies. When her father began a business venture in New York, the family moved with him, where Sarah Jessica broadened her creative interests to include acting. She appeared off-Broadway in the play *By Strouse* which, in turn, led to the title role in a two-year Broadway run of *Annie*.

In 1979 she had a brief appearance in the Robert Altman-produced *Rich Kids*, and by 1982 was starring in the hit TV sitcom *Square Pegs*. In the latter she was Patty Greene, a bespectacled, gawky student at Weemawee High, and the critics cheered. When the show ended in the autumn of 1983, she was already the star of *Somewhere Tomorrow*.

She then contemplated a career hiatus so that she could attend university. 'I wish I had

gone to college,' she says now. 'I wanted to go to Smith, but I got a part in *Footloose*, so I didn't apply. Then I got another movie, and my life went a different way.' She had a supporting role in *Firstborn* and was then top-billed again, in the affable teen comedy *Girls Just Want To Have Fun*, as a young thing who just wants to dance – and very good she was, too. She had less to do in Disney's routine sci-fi fantasy *Flight of the Navigator*, and then returned to the small screen to play Kay Gardner, the daughter-in-law of Richard Kiley in the domestic drama series *A Year In the Life*. This, too, received much critical admiration, but was dropped after eight months. She also appeared in the TV movies *The Room Upstairs*, with Stockard Channing, the real-life drug drama *Dadah is Death*, starring Julie Christie, and another 'based-on-fact' heart-wrencher, *The Ryan White Story*, about a haemophiliac boy (Lukas Haas) with AIDS.

She was reticent to appear in another TV series ('I was afraid of having it taken away again'), but couldn't resist the part of novice prosecutor Jo Ann Harris in *Equal Justice*. This time the show was a hit with the critics *and* the public, and Parker was relieved to be playing, 'a professional who is challenged every day – they're allowing me to be a grown-up.'

In between shows she did another TV movie, the ludicrous *Twist of Fate*, with Ben Cross, and then took on the role of Steve

Sarah Jessica Parker as Janey Glenn in the 1985 *Girls Just Want To Have Fun*

Sarah Jessica as Betsy Nolan in Andrew Bergman's *Honeymoon in Vegas*.

Sarah Jessica with Nicolas Cage also in *Honeymoon in Vegas*

New York school teacher who badgers her boyfriend (Nicolas Cage) to marry her – until he loses her to smarmy hustler James Caan in a poker game. The deal is that Caan entertains her for the weekend, but the latter has less virtuous thoughts on his mind. Meanwhile, Cage is forced to track Betsy down in Hawaii, where Caan's employees do everything in their power to waylay him. 'It's a very grand tale,' the actress explained, 'very "1940s". You know, people running around doing crazy, big things for love.' Again, the critics adored her. She then teamed up with Bruce Willis for the action-thriller *Striking Distance*, and played a reincarnated witch in the Touchstone comedy *Hocus Pocus*. After that, she starred in *Anything But Love*.

FILMOGRAPHY

1979: *Rich Kids*. 1982: *My Body, My Child* (TV). 1983: *Somewhere Tomorrow*. 1984: *Footloose*; *Firstborn*. 1985: *Girls Just Want To Have Fun*. 1986: *Flight of the Navigator*. 1987: *The Room Upstairs* (TV). 1988: *Dadah is Death* (TV). 1989: *The Ryan White Story* (TV); *Twist of Fate* (TV). 1991: *L.A. Story*. 1992: *In the Best Interest of the Children* (TV); *Honeymoon in Vegas*. 1993: *Striking Distance*; *Hocus Pocus*; *Anything But Love*. 1994: *Ed Wood*; *Miami*.

Jason Patric in Joel Schumacher's MTV treatment of the vampire genre, *The Lost Boys*

Jason PATRIC

Nobody could accuse Jason Patric of being prolific. And yet, in a remarkably short time, he became a household name. Not, mind you, because of his meagre handful of films, but because of an all-too brief fling with the highest paid actress in Hollywood. And there was irony to spare. When Patric made his first celluloid breakthrough – in Joel Schumacher's slick MTV vampire comedy, *The Lost Boys* – he played a handsome hunk who steals the girl from Kiefer Sutherland. In real life, in June of 1991, when Julia Roberts cancelled her wedding to Sutherland, Patric escorted her on an impromptu holiday to Ireland. A month later, in a blaze of media coverage, she moved in with him, finished work on Steven Spielberg's *Hook*, and they went on another holiday. By November, rumours of the stars' engagement was plastered over the tabloids, followed by talk of pregnancy. All this was nothing but the product of the fertile imagination of story editors, and a year later Julia was dating a 'scruffy' (tabloid quote), unknown actor called Russell Blake. However, in private, she and Patric were still holding hands. At least, for a while.

This explosion of unwanted publicity could not have happened to a shyer man. Although blessed with the kind of looks models die for (note those perfectly formed lips, those Mel Gibson-blue eyes), Patric didn't even like to be photographed. In interviews he is at pains

Martin's flaky mistress in *L.A. Story*. She invested the latter part – 'a fully unrepressed sexual LA thing' – with so much pizzazz that she almost stole the movie from her co-star. In 1991 she told *US* magazine that she was desperate for a baby, relaying, 'I was so excited when my character got pregnant on *A Year in the Life*. I thought I could get pregnant at the same time – but they cancelled the show.' Instead, she played a mother of five in the outstanding TV movie *In the Best Interest of the Children*. Based on a true story, the film featured Parker as Callie Cain, a promiscuous manic-depressive whose offspring plead for adoption. Parker was nothing short of brilliant, and won some of the best reviews of her career.

More kudos followed with *Honeymoon in Vegas*, in which she played Betsy Nolan, a

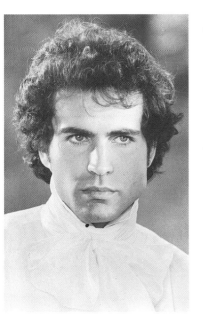

Jason as Lord Byron in *Roger Corman's Frankenstein Unbound*

Jason Patric as Jim Raynor, the cop addicted to duty – and ultimately drugs – in Lili Fini Zanuck's *Rush*

kid who was very sports orientated. He was there to learn and he learned. But he did not leave the movie with any desire to be an actor that I could see.'

Patric inspired no more confidence when he landed the young male lead in the awful sci-fi nonsense *Solarbabies*, opposite Jami Gertz. The latter was not impressed: 'Jason would mumble and wouldn't look me in the face when he talked,' she revealed. 'Finally I told him I wasn't going to talk to him anymore unless he looked at me. I couldn't believe he was so shy.'

Nevertheless, Ms Gertz later teamed up with him in the two-handed play *Outta Gas on Lover's Leap* – at the Coast Playhouse in Los Angeles – and played his romantic interest in *The Lost Boys*. The latter presented Patric with his breakthrough cheesecake role in a film with a decidedly high profile. As Michael Emerson, a recent arrival in California's Santa Carla, the murder capital of the world, Patric is seduced into the dangerous company of a gang of supernatural bikers (led by Kiefer Sutherland). Gertz is the attraction, but to win her love Michael must first become a 'creature of the night' – at great personal cost. *The Lost Boys* proved to be hugely entertaining hokum, which thankfully never took itself seriously and boasted a cast of fine young actors at the peak of their performance.

Less could be said for *Denial*, a really confusing mess about a woman (Robin Wright) still obsessed by her old brooding swain (Patric). Filmed under the eye-catching title of *Loon*, the film went straight to video three years later. In more serious mode, Patric played the brave, compassionate driver of a Russian tank, nicknamed *The Beast*. The

to point out, 'I'd rather not talk about my personal life, if that's OK,' and that was *before* the Kiefer kerfuffle. Patric won't even thank you for mentioning his formidable lineage. But, for the record, it has to be said that he is the grandson of comedy legend Jackie Gleason and son of the playwright and actor Jason Miller.

Jason Patric was born in New York City on 17 June 1966, and was raised in the neighbourhood of Queens. At 16, he moved to Los Angeles, where he performed in a number of stage productions at Santa Monica High, before spending a summer with Vermont's Champlain Shakespeare Festival. There, he stretched himself in such classics as *The Tempest* and *Love's Labours Lost* before making his film debut in the TV movie *Toughlove*, playing Bruce Dern's son.

Earlier, Patric had come across Dern when he acted as a trainee on the film *That Championship Season*, the film version of his father's Pulitzer Prize-winning play. According to Dern, 'Jason was a 16-year-old high school

As the disenchanted ex-boxer Kevin 'Kid' Collins in James Foley's brooding *After Dark, My Sweet*

film, although a tad predictable, was an intelligent look at the strife in Afghanistan and a welcome antidote to the jingoistic excesses of *Rambo III*. He took a supporting role – as a brooding Lord Byron – in *Roger Corman's Frankenstein Unbound*, a schlocky time-travelling slant on Mary Shelley's novel. Still, Patric looked stunning in tight trousers and lace.

Next, he was offered the leading role in *Flatliners* by Joel Schumacher, who had discovered him in *The Lost Boys*. But Patric thought he was now beyond such things, and his old friend Kiefer Sutherland took the part. Instead, he accepted the lead in *After Dark, My Sweet* – for a seventh of the price.

'With everything I do,' he explained, 'I have to move forward. I'm not willing to put myself in things that are not worthy of the emotional investment and the time commitment.' Of course, this would not explain his obligation to *Frankenstein Unbound*, but *After Dark* did provide him with his best role yet. Based on the novel by Jim Thompson, the film starred Patric as a scruffy, dislocated ex-boxer who stumbles into bed with Rachel Ward and ends up in the middle of a kidnapping scam engineered by her friend 'Uncle Bud', played by Bruce Dern. For all its knowing close-ups and stifling atmosphere, *After Dark* – directed by James Foley – was very dull film noir superbly acted by Dern and Patric.

This time, Bruce Dern was more impressed with his co-star. 'In all my career, I had never seen anybody as prepared to play a role,' he vouchsafed. 'When I saw the movie, I said to myself, "This kid has a chance to be the acting movie star of his generation." I actually thought that I watched a star being born.'

After Dark was not exactly the most visible film of 1990, and in fact producer Richard Zanuck and his wife Lili Fini were intending to see another movie when they found it was sold out. 'Somebody was coming out of another cinema,' Mr Zanuck relayed, 'and said, "You ought to see this picture *After Dark, My Sweet* – there's an incredible actor in it."'

The Zanucks were currently casting *Rush*, the movie adaptation of the semi-autobiographical best-seller by Kim Wozencraft. The story of an undercover narcotics cop who becomes a drug addict in the line of duty, the film was earmarked for Tom Cruise, but the latter became unavailable. Jason Patric was duly signed.

Like *After Dark*, the film was a raw, unrelenting look at the underbelly of American life, and Patric turned in another mesmerizing performance as a man at war with his inner demons. Again, *Rush* was an atmospheric, if depressing tale, redeemed by outstanding performances from its two leads – Patric and Jennifer Jason Leigh (the latter playing his committed partner).

FILMOGRAPHY

1985: *Toughlove* (TV). 1986: *Solarbabies*. 1987: *The Lost Boys*. 1988: *The Beast*. 1990: *Roger Corman's Frankenstein Unbound*; *After Dark, My Sweet*; *Teach 109*. 1991: *Denial* (aka *Loon*; filmed in 1988); *Rush*. 1993: *Geronimo: An American Legend*.

Sean PENN

Sean Penn was the genuine angry young man. Pugnacious in appearance, he became better known for punching out photographers than for his films. Blisteringly outspoken in his views on the press, he was an intensely serious actor who, ironically, became a star in a comedy. He then married a rock singer more famous than himself which, according to many, caused more bitterness, ending in a Waterloo of press coverage. Finally, Penn ended up behind bars, serving 32 days in Los Angeles County Jail for assaulting a photographer and violating probation. For his critics, it was just deserts.

But not according to Sean's friend and colleague, Dennis Hopper. 'I tell you,' Hopper declared, 'if that incident had happened to anybody but Sean Penn – *anybody* but Sean Penn – he would never have gone to jail. I mean, if somebody says, "Don't step on my blue suede shoes," and somebody comes over and steps on his blue suede shoes, what does that guy think is gonna happen to him?'

Gary Oldman, who starred opposite Penn in *State of Grace*, joined the fray: 'We were shooting in Times Square and all these newspaper photographers showed up, and they wouldn't stop. They took flash photographs while we were doing takes. I said, "I don't mind you taking photographs, but don't do it while I'm working! 'Cause it ruins the film." And they just wouldn't stop. There was this one particular guy, and I said to Sean, "I'm gonna go whack this guy out!" And Sean was just . . . he waved it all aside. What a life!'

And yet Sean Penn was an unlikely candidate for screen celebrity. He wasn't pretty like Tom Cruise or Rob Lowe. He wasn't funny like Matthew Broderick. And he didn't emerge from a hit TV series like Michael J. Fox. He got to the top through sheer good acting and devotion to his craft. And, when the exposure became too much for him, he became a filmmaker of some accomplishment.

According to James Foley, who directed the actor in *At Close Range*, 'Sean is one of the greats. And it's a shame he's become a director, because there are already too many directors out there, but not enough actors of his calibre.'

Hopper: 'Sean is a much more disciplined actor than I was at his age. I'm not gonna say he's more talented than I was, but my fight was a different fight. I wasn't punching out photographers – I was punching out directors.'

While the director Rick Rosenthal offers: 'The only reason that people compare Sean to Robert De Niro is that Sean is the only actor of his generation who can really become a different person for each acting job.'

Sean Penn was born on Robert De Niro's birthday, 17 August 1960, in Burbank, California, the second of three sons. His father was the TV and film director Leo Penn, his mother the actress Eileen Ryan,

who retired when he was born. His younger brother Christopher has become an actor of some repute (*Reservoir Dogs*, *Pale Rider*), while his older sibling, Michael, is a successful singer/songwriter (*No Myth*).

For the first ten years of his life, Sean lived in different parts of LA's San Fernando Valley, from North Hollywood to Woodland Hills. When he was 10, the family moved to Malibu, where Sean became obsessed with surfing. His friends included neighbourhood boys Emilio Estevez, Charlie Sheen and Rob Lowe, and they would often dabble in a bit of Super-8 filmmaking, although this was nothing more than a hobby. The surf was still Sean's first love.

After graduating from Santa Monica High School, he skipped college and spent two years with the Los Angeles Group Repertory Theatre, where he worked backstage and directed a one-act play, *Terrible Jim Fitch*. He then studied with the legendary drama coach Peggy Feury and, at 19, made his professional acting debut with one line in an episode of TV's *Barnaby Jones*. He had a supporting role in the acclaimed TV movie *The Killing of Randy Webster*, with Hal Holbrook, and appeared in *Hellinger's Law*, an unsuccessful pilot for a TV series starring Telly Savalas.

Dissatisfied with TV, he bought a one-way ticket to New York and tried his luck on stage. His first audition was for the Broadway play *Heartland*, and it went badly. 'He was nervous, tight and nearly inaudible,' the director Art Wolff remembers. Nevertheless, a second reading won him the role and decent reviews which, in turn, led to his first film, *Taps*.

Set in a military academy, the movie starred Timothy Hutton as a rebellious cadet

Sean Penn as the goofy Mick O'Brien in Amy Heckerling's influential teen comedy *Fast Times*

with newcomers Penn and Tom Cruise as his partners-in-defiance. Penn simply acted his co-stars off the screen and was immediately the talk of Hollywood as the Next Big Thing. He landed top-billing in the riotous high school comedy *Fast Times at Ridgemont High* playing the spaced-out surfer Jeff Spicoli who famously orders pizza in the middle of class. Penn was very, very funny, the film was a hit and a whole school of new stars graduated with honours.

Penn turned to drama with Rick Rosenthal's hard-hitting *Bad Boys*, the story of a 16-year-old Chicago kid (Penn) who accidentally kills the younger brother of a drug dealer. Incarcerated in a juvenile correction facility, Penn finds himself face-to-face with his victim's brother – leading, inevitably, to some pretty violent confrontations. Again, Penn was sensational in a part he studied for rigorously, accompanying Chicago's police gang-crimes unit on duty and reportedly applying real tattoos to his arms. Generally, the film was extremely well acted by a cast of young unknowns, but Penn towered over them all, displaying the steely bile of a latter-day James Cagney.

In *Crackers* he returned to comedy, third-billed behind Donald Sutherland and Jack Warden as a dopey misfit forced into crime. Surprisingly, this limp comedy was directed by none other than Louis Malle, which is presumably why Penn took it. He had the lead in Richard Benjamin's war-time romance *Racing With the Moon*, a turgid, period-bound piece that failed to arouse any sympathies for its protagonists. As a romantic leading man, Penn was lacking in charisma, but did display a raw, touching ingenuousness that might have worked under more auspicious circumstances. He played Henry 'Hopper' Nash, the son of a graver-digger who falls for the local Gatsby girl, Elizabeth McGovern. Rumours of an off-set romance were reported, but worse, word got out that Penn persuaded McGovern not to publicize the picture.

'Totally bogus,' the actor scoffed. 'I was busy in Mexico shooting another movie. There wasn't time to allow me to participate in the publicity for the film. But the people involved in that movie didn't respect my answer when I said no, and then they did something I don't believe has been done any other time: They spoke in public against the actor who was in their movie! They also

Sean Penn with his missus, Madonna, in the catastrophic *Shanghai Surprise*

insinuated that I had influenced the other actors.'

So, 'I wouldn't play the game. I'd had no problems at all with the press up to that time. I was doing what I wanted to do – I was acting. I was trying to do the best job that I could.'

Penn as the quick-tempered LA cop Danny 'Pacman' McGavin in Dennis Hopper's hard-hitting *Colors*

The 'Mexican' film was John Schlesinger's *The Falcon and the Snowman*, the true story of two young men (Penn, Timothy Hutton) who decide to sell government secrets to the Russians. Again, Penn stole the notices as the unpredictable, out-of-his-mind drug pusher Daulton Lee. Schlesinger admitted that he found Penn 'quite difficult,' but did volunteer that he, 'really gets into the skin of the character he's playing. And as Daulton Lee resists all authority, so Sean naturally hated me. I must say that the feeling was reciprocated, although I thought he was marvellous in the film.'

The actor had a better time on his next movie, *At Close Range*, another true-life drama, about a teenage boy (Penn) who comes to blows with his criminal father (Christopher Walken). James Foley directed, and the filmmaker and actor worked well together. However, there was one incident (much admired in the media) in which Penn reportedly slugged a crew member for flirting with co-star Mary Stuart Masterson. Penn denies it.

It was at this time that the actor entered into a whirlwind romance with – and married – the singer/songwriter Madonna Louise Ciccone, whose song 'Live To Tell' was featured on the soundtrack of *At Close Range*. If the paparazzi was finding Penn a pain, they unleashed a monster when they zoned in on his wife. Unlike her husband, Madonna was not adverse to publicity, but even she found the mounting battery of flash-bulbs an unwelcome intrusion.

Penn with Robin Wright, the mother of his two children, in Phil Joanou's gritty drama *State of Grace*

Penn directing Dennis Hopper in a scene from his atmospheric drama, *The Indian Runner*

Penn, back from retirement, threatens Al Pacino in *Carlito's Way*

'You have to understand,' Penn explains, 'when Madonna and I got together, she was an up-and-coming star. She was not a superstar; she was not an icon. Soon she became public property, and her husband-to-be was treated likewise.'

The couple's wedding turned into the ultimate media circus, with press helicopters hovering above the outdoor ceremony. The groom became so incensed by the intrusion that he reputedly started firing a gun into the air. And Penn doesn't deny it.

Career-wise, he and Madonna teamed up for the abysmal *Shanghai Surprise*, a movie he did for the money and, no doubt, to be with his wife. Ironically, it was the only film he made during his marriage. After the divorce and tabloid stories of Penn beating Madonna with a baseball bat, the actor simply conceded, 'I can just say it ended. It just didn't work out.' It is charitable of Mr Penn not to put more blame on the media.

He returned to the cinema with something of a splash, playing a rookie LA cop who believes the only way to fight violence is with more violence. The film was *Colors*, and Penn took the screenplay to Orion Pictures himself, suggesting that Dennis Hopper direct. Orion agreed, and Hopper had the script re-written to accommodate Penn and co-star Robert Duvall (the original story centred on a black cop and a white cop in Chicago). *Colors* was a movie both timely and ahead of its time, examining the escalating gang warfare in Los Angeles and the limited police resources to combat it. When the movie opened in April of 1988, it caused such an uproar that many cinemas refused to show it. In New York, protests were staged

in an attempt to deter cinemagoers, while two days later, in LA, a teenager was shot dead while queueing to see it. Arguably, *Colors* is Sean Penn's best film, and a frightening piece of contemporary *cinema verité*.

He had a small part, but was very good, in his father's *Judgement in Berlin*, playing a German defector (with a convincing accent), and portrayed the brutish Sergeant Meserve in Brian De Palma's *Casualties of War*. Based on a true incident, the latter was a rather obvious drama in which the bad guys – American soldiers who rape a Vietnamese girl – were really, really bad, and the good guy (Michael J. Fox) too squeaky clean to be true.

Worse still was the misguided comedy *We're No Angels*, a re-make of the 1955 Humphrey Bogart caper which wasn't very good to start with. Robert De Niro and Sean Penn played a couple of goofy escaped convicts disguised as priests, and De Niro mugged shamefully. Penn was not much better. His next film, the gritty, violent *State of Grace*, was about a gang of Irish-American criminals in New York, and the acting honours went to Ed Harris, Gary Oldman and Robin Wright.

Still, the movie introduced Penn to Robin Wright, who later bore the actor's child, Dylan Frances. Of his new girlfriend, Penn said, 'She's the first young actress of her generation to come along, I think, who has intelligence and elegance. She's been extremely choosy in everything she's done. She's got a really big career ahead of her.'

Sean Penn's acting career, however, was about to stop in its tracks. 'I hooked into acting real strong,' he illuminated, 'and it grew

into an obsession. It got to be such an obsession that I didn't realize how much I *wasn't* enjoying it. I got to the place where if I wasn't doing it, it was like withdrawing from an addiction, so that I'd start barfing on the floor or something like that.' In short, 'I realized acting was no longer making me happy.'

Instead, he turned to directing and writing, and made the thought-provoking drama *The Indian Runner*, about two brothers, one a heroic cop (David Morse), the other a self-destructive ex-con (Viggo Mortensen). Beautifully crafted and well acted, the film verged on the self-indulgent at times, but was nonetheless a powerful directing debut evincing much promise.

For three years after announcing his retirement from appearing in front of the camera, Penn kept to his word, turning down all offers – including a proposition from Mickey Rourke, an actor he much admires. However, he said that if the price was right, he would act again. This he did, when he accepted a co-starring role in Brian De Palma's *Carlito's Way*, playing a lawyer and mercurial friend to Al Pacino's former gangster. After that he embarked on his second film as director, *The Crossing Guard*, starring Jack Nicholson, Anjelica Huston and Robin Wright.

FILMOGRAPHY

1980: *The Killing of Randy Webster* (TV). 1981: *Hellinger's Law* (TV); *Taps*. 1982: *Fast Times at Ridgemont High* (UK: *Fast Times*); *Bad Boys*. 1983: *Crackers*. 1984: *Racing With the Moon*. 1985: *The Falcon and the Snowman*; *At Close Range*. 1986: *Shanghai Surprise*. 1988: *Dear America* (voice only); *Colors*; *Judgement in Berlin*. 1989: *Casualties of War*; *We're No Angels*. 1990: *State of Grace*. 1991: *The Indian Runner* (dir. only). 1993: *Carlito's Way*. 1994: *The Crossing Guard* (dir. only).

Elizabeth PERKINS

Elizabeth Perkins is a rebel. As a girl she hung out with motorcycle gangs and smooched in graveyards. When she became engaged to a local boy, her parents sent her off to boarding school. There, she smoked marijuana in the loo, but was suspended for stealing muffins. Later, she was expelled for telling the dean that he stank. She enjoys regaling journalists with the practices of serial killers ('Ed Gein skinned people alive and his furniture was made from human skin . . .') and is obsessed by the perverse photography of Diane Arbus ('she's a master of dichotomy'). After accepting a role in David Mamet's prestigious production of *Speed-the-Plow* on

Broadway, she bowed out, complaining, 'I'm not a raving fan of David Mamet. He doesn't write roles for women' – and was replaced by Madonna. In fact, after making a name for herself in the hit comedy *Big*, she turned down a lot of major Hollywood films. She says, 'I could have taken some serious blockbuster movies. It's not like the offers weren't there. But nothing came along that I wanted to do or that I thought was going to do anything for me as an actress. I'm not attracted to anything that's not off the beaten path. I get very bored playing comfortable people, people that just kind of come in and out of the room. I'd much prefer to stumble over the ottoman.'

Indeed, she was stealing the best notices in her very first film appearance – as Demi Moore's catty roommate in *'About Last Night . . .'* Penny Marshall, who directed the actress in *Big*, believes, 'Her work is never boring. When we were shaping the film, my editor and I kept saying, "'Let's cut to Elizabeth.'"' Alan Rudolph, who was behind the camera on *Love at Large*, reckons, 'She can steal a scene or she can be invisible, but if you watch Elizabeth when she's part of a large group of people, you'll see that she's always doing something.' Adding: 'She's sexy in unspectacular ways, but ways that last. To me, she's like a good standard song. Elizabeth is the actor's equivalent of "Star Dust."'

Elizabeth Pisperikos was born on 18 November 1960, in Forest Hills, New York, the youngest daughter (of three) of a writer-businessman and first-generation Greek immigrant. After her parents divorced when she was still little, she grew up with her mother on her stepfather's secluded 600-acre farm in Vermont, broken by occasional stays with her father in New York City. When the latter moved to Chicago, she followed him there, completed high school and contemplated becoming a veterinarian. 'But,' she recalls, 'all I was thinking about during biology class was getting back to the community theatre because we were doing a production of *Guys and Dolls*.' She had started acting in

Elizabeth Perkins as she appeared in Penny Marshall's *Big* in 1988

Perkins with Susan Sarandon in the ensemble comedy-drama *Sweet Hearts Dance*

school, and had already honed her interest in off-beat roles when, in seventh grade, she appeared in a production of *Hansel and Gretel* – as Hansel. At Chicago's Goodman School of Drama she studied for three years and, in 1984, moved back to New York and, within two weeks, won the role of Nora in a touring production of Neil Simon's *Brighton Beach Memoirs*. Six months later she was playing the character on Broadway.

In 1985 she married the actor-director Terry Kinney, co-founder of Chicago's Steppenwolf Theater Company, and was given the chance to audition for Debbie, the lead part in the Chicago-set movie *'About Last Night ...'* She declined the offer (the part went to Demi Moore), and won the far meatier supporting role of Joan, Debbie's sassy, wise-cracking sidekick. 'There are so many times that I read scripts and I love the supporting character more than I love the lead,' she says, 'because usually they're the ones that have a dark side, something that is not quite right.' The critics jumped on the picture with knives bared, but spared praise for Perkins who, with James Belushi, hijacked the film from Moore and Rob Lowe. Lowe, who is still a friend, noted, 'She reminds me of what Katharine Hepburn must have been like at 27 – strong, stubborn, and sexy. But she's very vulnerable.' In spite of the film's mixed reception, Perkins was suddenly in demand, and was a close contender for the Holly Hunter part in *Broadcast News*, opposite William Hurt. But everybody was offering her comic roles. 'You do one movie like *"About Last Night ..."* and that's all anyone in this industry thinks you *can* do,' she complained.

She did do another comedy, the legal farce *From the Hip* and, as Judd Nelson's down-to-earth girlfriend, was about the only credible character in the film. However, most of her contribution ended up on the cutting room floor. Meanwhile, Penny Marshall was casting the female lead in *Big*, the part of the toy executive Susan Lawrence. Marshall had envisaged Debra Winger in the role, but as the latter was pregnant, she sought her advice instead. 'I asked Debra, "Who's closest to you as an actress?", and she mentioned Elizabeth. Physically they're very different, but they have a similar appeal. There's always something going on behind their eyes.' Perkins was simply a knockout as the assertive but vulnerable Lawrence, who realises that her new boyfriend (Tom Hanks) is actually a 12-year-old trapped in the body of a 35-year-old man. *Big* was a colossal hit, and Perkins was suddenly in a position to turn down every film offered her.

Elizabeth Perkins as the quirky private detective Stella Wynkowski in Alan Rudolph's *Love at Large*

Perkins as the cancer victim June, with William Hurt as *The Doctor*

She took a supporting role in the silly, terminally saccharine *Sweet Hearts Dance*, as a plucky Vermont school teacher who falls in love with her principal (Jeff Daniels), and managed to make the dialogue sound witty. In a cast that included Daniels, Don Johnson and Susan Sarandon, Perkins was the only character worth spending time with, a mischievous spirit refusing to conform to small-town cliché. If there was any reason to see the film, it was to see her.

In Alan Rudolph's quirky, intermittently amusing *Love at Large*, she played a private detective, Stella Wynkowski, who falls in love with a private detective (Tom Berenger) she is asked to tail. In real life, following her divorce from Terry Kinney in 1990, she fell in love with the British writer-director Maurice Phillips, who steered her through the bizarre antics of the jet-black farce *Enid is Sleeping*. Enid was Perkins's sister, whom Perkins accidentally kills when she is caught in bed with her sister's husband, who happened to be a policeman (Judge Reinhold). Much to-ing and fro-ing followed, as Perkins attempted to dispose of the body, exhuming memories of similar corpse-dumping comedies as Hitchcock's *The Trouble With Harry*, *Weekend at Bernie's*, *Out Cold* and *Cold Dog Soup*. Sadly, the film was a stiff, and a waste of Perkins's comedic talents, who was reduced to a bleating dumb blonde. Still, some critics thought Perkins had never been better.

She turned to drama, and very successfully, in Barry Levinson's superb evocation of the life of an immigrant family in Baltimore, playing a character based on Barry Levinson's own mother. She lifted weights to prepare for her role, because, she says, 'a mother has strength in her arms and strength in her hips.' Then it was back to screwball romantic comedy with *He Said, She Said*, co-starring Kevin Bacon. The film, made by real-life couple Ken Kwapis and Marisa Silver, showed the same tempestuous relationship from two viewpoints, the male objective directed by

Kwapis, the female by Silver. Again, Perkins was the best thing in an uneven project, while the film was dismissed by critics for being gimmicky.

She was forced to drop out of the British comedy *The Object of Beauty* due to illness (and was replaced by Lolita Davidovich), but got her chance to act opposite William Hurt in Randa Haines's harrowing, funny and moving *The Doctor*. Discarding make-up and hair, she played a patient dying of cancer and gave both Hurt and Christine Lahti, as his wife, a run for their money. During production, she discovered she was pregnant. 'To deal with the issue of death for three months is very draining,' she revealed. 'And yet, knowing you've got life growing inside you made it twice as poignant. Yes, my character was dying, but she was so filled with life, experiencing so much for the last time, that my baby served as an impetus.'

For the next two years she devoted her life to motherhood ('I think the baby is enough of a production'), and then joined the ensemble cast of *Indian Summer*, co-starring alongside Alan Arkin, Diane Lane and Vincent Spano.

FILMOGRAPHY

1986: *'About Last Night . . .'*. 1987: *From the Hip*. 1988: *Big*; *Sweet Hearts Dance*. 1990: *Love at Large*; *Enid is Sleeping* (UK: *Over Her Dead Body*); *Avalon*; *Teach 109*. 1991: *He Said, She Said*; *The Doctor*. 1993: *Indian Summer*; *For Their Own Good* (TV). 1994: *The Flintstones*; *Miracle On 34th Street*.

Luke PERRY

He's not that duly charismatic. He has a slim build, is even wiry, stands at 5'10", and his voice is of the light, raspy variety. On a bad day, he resembles an undernourished, watered-down Bruce Willis. And yet Luke Perry was *the* small screen phenomenon of the early 1990s.

His fame rests squarely on the shoulders of the cult TV series *Beverly Hills 90210*. An ensemble teen drama following the ups and downs of a hip group of students at LA's West Beverly Hills High, the show suffered a wobbly start in the ratings and then built on word-of-mouth. Soon the stars of the series – Perry, Jason Priestley, Shannen Doherty, Tori Spelling, Ian Ziering et al – were the icons of American youth. *90210* became the bible of urban cool, attracting a colossal 69 per cent of the female teenage market. Merchandising, fan hysteria and the magazine covers followed.

Of all the show's stars, Luke Perry

Luke Perry

attracted the lion's share of the adulation. He played Dylan McKay, the super-rich ($100 million-rich), super-cool rebel with the permanently corrugated brow, lop-sided grin and defiant sideburns.

'The sideburns sort of took on a life of their own,' the star admits. 'They get their own fan mail. They have their own publicists.' Although Perry puts his acting above his facial hair, he does concede that, 'once you've been to Graceland, you have a whole new respect for what sideburns are about. I feel naked without mine.'

Consequently, when he shaved them off *on screen* in *Buffy The Vampire Slayer*, the scene took on a legendary air. But, in spite of all the meteoric glory, Perry remains serious about his craft.

'He has a sweet sexuality,' offers Howard Rosenman, producer of *Buffy*. 'I haven't seen anything like Luke since Tom Cruise. Luke and Tom have the same effect: they are deferential, they are polite, they are well mannered. They are *pros*. They are very similar in certain ways.'

Born Coy Luther Perry III on 11 October 1964, in a small Ohio town, the actor was

the second of three children (he has an older brother and younger sister). Their father was an itinerant, violent type and was divorced by their mother when Perry was six. Six years later she remarried, this time to the owner of a construction company, with whom Perry is still friendly (his father has since died). By all accounts, Luke was not a good student (although he *was* credited Biggest Flirt at high school), and graduated from Fredericktown, Ohio, with no aspirations for college.

Leaving for California at 17, he moved to New York after Los Angeles failed to provide work. For a while he shared an apartment in Harlem with actor Rocky Carroll (TV's *Roc*) and got his first break as a regular on the daytime soap *Loving* (as Ned Bates). He followed this with a second daylight serial, *Another World*. In between acting jobs, he studied his craft at workshops and paid his way as a construction labourer. Back in LA, he laid asphalt for a living and auditioned madly. He auditioned twice for *The Godfather Part III* and tried out for the role of the 'hip queer' Georgette in *Last Exit to Brooklyn*. The part went to Alexis Arquette instead, now a close friend of Perry's. The duo *did* work together in the forgettable teen drama *Terminal Bliss* (Perry's film debut, in which he played an alienated rich boy), filmed in South Carolina, and Perry stayed in the South

Luke Perry as the rebel Pike involved in supernatural shenanigans in *Buffy the Vampire Slayer*

(Louisiana) to play a young buck (Ray Ray) in the perfectly awful *Scorchers*.

Then he won the role of Dylan McKay in *Beverly Hills 90210*. Since becoming the next James Dean, Luke Perry has been inundated with offers to star in movies, but opted for a supporting role in *Buffy the Vampire Slayer* instead. A chic, comic slant on the vampire genre crossed with *Heathers*, the film was not a success, but did have its moments. It also boasted a splendid cast, with Kristy Swanson as Buffy, Donald Sutherland as her mentor, and with Rutger Hauer and Paul Reubens (Pee-wee Herman to you) sporting the fangs. Perry played the love interest, Pike.

'I chose to play Pike because he was 180 degrees away from Dylan,' the star explains. 'He is so sweet; he just doesn't expect a lot from anybody or anything. He's the damsel in distress. I'm serious about my work, but after nine months of making Dylan as dangerous and problematic as I can, it's so much fun to fall on your ass and make everybody laugh.'

As the film's writer, Joss Whedon, would have it, 'I'm sure many people advised Luke not to take it, because it's not his movie. But he didn't want to do *If Looks Could Fail at the Box Office*. He loves Corman and *Near Dark* and the B aesthetic.' It also allowed the actor to test the waters of stardom without having to shoulder the brunt of the picture.

He did, however, get top-billing in his next picture, *8 Seconds*, the true-life drama of a champion bull rider who was killed in a rodeo accident aged 23.

But before then he hit his female admirers where it hurt. In September of 1992 he announced his engagement to former model Minnie Rachel Sharp, with whom he had been living secretly for a year. He reportedly told a close source, 'I never knew what love was until I met Minnie. She's what's been missing in my life.' Adding, 'I've never been happier.'

FILMOGRAPHY

1991: *Terminal Bliss*; *Scorchers*. **1992:** *Buffy the Vampire Slayer*. **1993:** *8 Seconds*; *The Webbers* (cameo). **1994:** *Texas Rangers*.

Michelle PFEIFFER

She says, 'I think I look like a duck. I mean, my face is completely crooked. And my lips are lopsided. The less I have to think or talk about my looks, the better.' In spite of these words, Michelle Pfeiffer has become a synonym for beauty in an industry stuffed to the gills with cosmetic perfection. And yet Ms Pfeiffer has something more. She possesses that rare component that ignites the flame of beauty and turns it into a roaring furnace. She radiates sex appeal and intelligence, has simmered seductively in such pictures as *Grease 2* and *Tequila Sunrise*, but has never lost sight of her function as a human being. In *The Fabulous Baker Boys*, she asks Jeff Bridges, 'Listen, you're not going soft on me are you? I mean, you're not going to start dreaming about me, waking up all sweaty and looking at me like I'm some kind of princess when I burp?'

Michelle Pfeiffer could also be very funny, thrilling to the chase in Jonathan Demme's wonderful *Married To the Mob* and sending herself up rotten as Catwoman in *Batman Returns*, in which, with a simple 'Miaow', she brought the house down.

Women admired her down-to-earth honesty and self-deprecation, and men – well, they just adored her. There were reports of an affair with Alec Baldwin during the making of *Married To the Mob*. Michael Keaton fell for her years before he was menacingly cat-licked by her in *Batman Returns*. 'The truth of the matter,' Keaton reveals, 'is that we just dated for a while. It

Michelle Pfeiffer as Stepnanie Zinone, with Maxwell Caulfield, in *Grease 2*

probably enriched things [in the movie]. I think it was just enough history to help us and not enough of a history to get in our way. She's good to work with. I'm such a fan. In a way, I think she has more range than anybody.'

And then there was the furore over her fling with John Malkovich, on the set of *Dangerous Liaisons* – an affair which terminally damaged the actor's marriage to Glenne Headley. For three years she was involved with the character actor Fisher Stevens, seven years her junior, but she broke off the relationship when she caught him in the arms of a 17-year-old stand-in. At the time, she told friends, 'It's over. I deserve better than that.' Then, at the end of 1992, she was linked with the legendary guitarist Eric Clapton, and shortly after that was romantically involved with the producer-writer David Kelley. For years she had told journalists that she wanted children, and when Kelley supported her dream to adopt, he seemed a likely candidate for longevity. In November of 1993, Michelle and David were married.

And then there were the critics. For her role as the sexy, hard-edged chanteuse in *The Fabulous Baker Boys*, she won the Golden

Globe award and was voted best actress by the Los Angeles Film Critics' Circle, the New York Film Critics' Circle, the National Board of Review and the US National Society of Film Critics. The Oscar that year went to Jessica Tandy for *Driving Miss Daisy*, but then the Oscars aren't chosen by critics. Still, she won a nomination and, furthermore, was a front-runner for her roles in *Dangerous Liaisons* and *Love Field*. She was also a star player in innumerable lists of 'the ten most beautiful women in the world.'

Michelle Pfeiffer was born on 29 April 1957 in Santa Ana, California, the second of four children of a heating and air-conditioning contractor, and grew up in Orange County. At school she attended drama classes, but a teacher remembers her as, 'this sunshine surfer beach girl, more out of the class than in.' After school, she worked as a check-out girl in a local supermarket and, in 1977, won the Miss Orange County beauty title. This led to an agent, and small roles in TV. On *Fantasy Island* she got to say, 'Who is he, Naomi?', and was then levered into hot pants and a padded bra in the sitcom *Delta House*, a small-screen rip-off of *National Lampoon's Animal House*. This led to a regular role on the car chase series *B.A.D. Cats*, as Officer Samantha Jensen, but the show was dropped after five episodes. She also appeared in the TV movie *The Solitary Man*, about the break-up of a marriage, made her theatrical film debut as a car hop in *The Hollywood Knights*, a weak imitation of *American Graffiti*, and played Susannah York in the flashback sequences in *Falling In Love Again*.

At 22, she married the actor Peter Horton, who later became a star as Gary Shepherd in TV's *thirtysomething*, and the marriage lasted seven years. 'I had a great marriage with a great man,' she says in retrospect, 'but as we grew older our views changed and we went in different directions.'

There were three more TV movies and *Charlie Chan and the Curse of the Dragon Queen*, a dire attempt to resurrect the Oriental detective with Peter Ustinov, in which Pfeiffer played a wealthy airhead called Cordelia Farrington III. Then, following a nationwide search, she won the role of Stephanie Zinone, the sizzling leader of 'the Pink Ladies' in *Grease 2*. Although the musical died at the box-office, some critics thought it superior to the original, and Pfeiffer was a stand-out as the most beautiful catch at Rydell High (and probably all of California).

A year later she starred opposite Al Pacino in Brian De Palma's adrenaline-pumping *Scarface*, as Elvira, the cocaine-snorting gangster's moll with ice running

Michelle as the mysterious Diana in John Landis's supremely enjoyable *Into the Night*

Bewitching: Michelle Pfeiffer under the spell of Jack Nicholson's charismatic Satan in George Miller's *The Witches of Eastwick*

through her veins. She was even better in John Landis's terrific, offbeat comedy-thriller *Into the Night*, as the dream girl who leads Jeff Goldblum into no end of trouble, and did her only nude scene (which lasted for – what? – two seconds). She was miscast in Richard Donner's lush period fantasy *Ladyhawke*, as a beauty transformed into a hawk by day, but successfully competed with the beauty of the Italian scenery. She then had two roles in Alan Alda's likeable satire on the movie business, *Sweet Liberty*, playing a no-nonsense movie actress, and the virginal maiden she plays (in a costume drama set during the American War of Independence).

With George Miller's jet-black comedy *The Witches of Eastwick* she had her first major hit, as Sukie Ridgemont, a small-town reporter and recently widowed mother of six little girls who falls for the devil (Jack Nicholson). Ironically, she says, 'the first time I saw it, I hated it. It was so different than the way I had envisioned it. The original script was more of a dark comedy, as opposed to . . . there were no special effects; there wasn't all that flying in the air.'

Nevertheless, the film upped Pfeiffer's ante in Hollywood, and besides a cameo in the slipshod *Amazon Women On the Moon*, she headed for greater things. She was hilarious in Jonathan Demme's *Married To the Mob*, as the dizzy, red-headed Italian-American widow of a gangster (Alec Baldwin) who tries to escape the clutches of the Mafia by moving into a grotty apartment on Manhattan's Lower East Side. It was Pfeiffer's first instance of top-billing, and the film was a hit. She was second-billed to Mel Gibson, but billed above Kurt Russell, in the slick, moody romantic crime thriller *Tequila Sunrise*, but couldn't generate any sexual chemistry with Gibson, in spite of a steamy sequence in a hot tub. With Gibson and Pfeiffer stripping down for a bit of slap-and-tickle, the film should've been a monster hit, but wasn't.

Dangerous Liaisons was even less successful at the box-office (in America, at least), but was far sexier, and enjoyed an avalanche of rave reviews. Pfeiffer was the virtuous, convent-bred Madame de Tourvel who is ruthlessly courted by the unscrupulous womanizer Vicomte de Valmont (John Malkovich, on chilling form). Based on the well-written play by Christopher Hampton, and set in pre-Revolution France, the film was a mesmerizing look at the politics of debauchery, and gathered a handful of Oscar nominations, including ones for best film, best actress (Glenn Close) and best supporting actress (Pfeiffer).

Hot on the heels of her first Academy

As the hot-blood Mafia princess Angela DeMarco in Jonathan Demme's *Married To the Mob*

Michelle Pfeiffer (*right*) with Glenn Close and John Malkovich in Stephen Frears's *Dangerous Liaisons*

Award nomination, Pfeiffer was flooded with laurels for her portrayal of Susie Diamond, the earthy nightclub singer in *The Fabulous Baker Boys*. The actress trained hard to perfect her voice for the role, and who could forget her turn in a red dress, atop Jeff Bridges's piano, crooning 'Making Whoopee'? It was the sensation of the season.

She won more good reviews for her part as a Russian book editor involved with Sean Connery in *The Russia House*, from John Le Carré's novel, and then played a bored beautician from Dallas whose eyes are opened when she has an affair with a black man-in *Love Field*. Her swain was originally to have been played by Denzel Washington, but when he walked (Washington complained, 'it was Michelle's film, I was just a guy who helped the story move along'), he was replaced by an unknown Dennis Haysbert. The word on the film was outstanding, but then its distributor, Orion, ran into financial difficulties and the picture was jammed in pre-distribution hell.

Next, she was announced to play the shy, frumpy and love-starved waitress in Garry Marshall's adaptation of the off-Broadway play *Frankie and Johnny in the Clair de Lune*, a part originated by Kathy Bates. Linda Winer, the theatre critic for *Newsday*, was astounded. 'Either this is the funniest casting since Dustin Hoffman was Sean Connery's

Michelle in her award-laden performance as Susie Diamond in *The Fabulous Baker Boys*

son in *Family Business*, or director Garry Marshall has re-thought the concept.' Bates herself 'laughed hysterically' when she heard Pfeiffer was playing the role. As it happens, Pfeiffer *was* miscast, but she gave such an outstanding performance of emotional insecurity that at times you believed in her pathetic life. Al Pacino played Johnny, and he, too, looked misplaced.

She was the first choice for the role of Clarice Sterling, the FBI trainee on the trail of a serial killer, in Jonathan Demme's *The Silence of the Lambs*, but declined on the grounds that she found the subject, 'too chilling.' Jodie Foster replaced her and won an Oscar. Pfeiffer was also mentioned for the role of Catwoman in *Batman Returns*, competing alongside Julia Roberts and her friend Cher. However, Michael Keaton decided on Annette Bening, and only after the latter had to back out due to pregnancy (courtesy of Warren Beatty), was Pfeiffer handed the role (for a reported sum of $3 million). And thank God, for – frankly – she was the best thing in it. Strapped in skin-tight black leather, she oozed sexual menace and jumped into the spirit of the occasion, saying it was 'the most sophisticated and inspirational movie I have ever done.' It was certainly her most successful.

She then started research for her role in *Lorenzo's Oil*, as Michaela Odone, the mother of a boy stricken with a rare and supposedly fatal disease. Andy Garcia had already dropped out of the part of her husband (and

Purr-fect: Michelle as everybody's ideal Catwoman in *Batman Returns*

was replaced by Nick Nolte), when Pfeiffer got cold feet. The film's director, George Miller, who had previously worked with the actress on *The Witches of Eastwick*, explained, 'Michelle met Michaela and sort of got this sense that she wasn't up to the role. It's this terrible inferiority she's got about being uneducated. You know, she said, "I'm from Orange County, and I worked as a check-out girl." And I kept on saying, "*And* you're extremely intelligent."'

Susan Sarandon, who was also in *The Witches of Eastwick*, took over the role, and was duly nominated for an Oscar. But this time so was Pfeiffer, for *Love Field*, which was hurriedly dusted off to qualify for the 1992 Academy Awards.

Meanwhile, the actress landed the female lead in Martin Scorsese's 1870s romantic drama *The Age of Innocence* (based on the novel by Edith Wharton), as a bohemian countess courted by Daniel Day-Lewis. The advance word was sensational. She was then re-teamed with Jack Nicholson in the Gothic *Wolf*, under Mike Nichols's direction.

In March of 1993, Michelle Pfeiffer caused a storm of media controversy when – through a lawyer – she privately adopted a baby girl, Claudia Rose, making her an instant unmarried mother. Exactly a year later she was pregnant for real.

FILMOGRAPHY

1979: *The Solitary Man* (TV). 1980: *The Hollywood Knights*; *Falling In Love Again*. 1981: *Charlie Chan and the Curse of the Dragon Queen*; *Splendor In the Grass* (TV); *The Children Nobody Wanted* (TV); *Callie & Son* (TV). 1982: *Grease 2*. 1983: *Scarface*. 1985: *Into the Night*; *Ladyhawke*. 1986: *Sweet Liberty*. 1987: *The Witches of Eastwick*; *Amazon Women On the Moon*. 1988: *Married To the Mob*; *Tequila Sunrise*; *Dangerous Liaisons*. 1989: *The Fabulous Baker Boys*. 1990: *The Russia House*. 1991: *Love Field*; *Frankie and Johnny*. 1992: *Batman Returns*. 1993: *The Age of Innocence*. 1994: *Wolf*; *My Posse Don't Do Homework*.

Lou Diamond PHILLIPS

Let's get one thing straight, Lou Diamond Phillips is not an Indian. In his own words, he is 'mainly Filipino on my mother's side, but there are also strains of Hawaiian, Japanese, and Spanish, and on my father's side I'm Scotch-Irish and an eighth Cherokee Indian.' It's the 'eighth' part that got the actor cast as the knife-juggling Navajo half-breed in *Young Guns* and *Young Guns II*, as a Lakota Sioux in *Renegades* and as the Navajo cop in *The Dark Wind*. But then redskin movie stars are hard to find.

In real life, Lou Diamond has managed to sidestep the more unpleasant aspects of racism – he describes himself as, 'a middle-class kid from Texas' – and has taken full advantage of his ethnic looks while eschewing stereotyping. And he counts his blessings.

'Give me a brown race,' he says, 'and I can play it.'

The son of a Navy aircraft mechanic, the star was born on 17 February 1962 in the Philippines and named after the World War II hero Leland 'Lou' Diamond. As a child, he lived with his family in about a dozen states in America, before settling down in Corpus Christi in Texas. He became interested in acting in sixth grade and studied drama and film technique at the University of Texas, in Arlington. It was there that he worked as an assistant director and instructor at the Film Actor's Lab during the years 1983-86, and was soon clocking up performances in a series of local low-budget films. He co-scripted his first, *Trespasses*, on which he met his future wife, Julie Cypher, an assistant director. Later, she was to work behind the scenes on his films *La Bamba*, *Stand and Deliver*, *Dakota* and *Young Guns*.

He also served time in TV, appearing in *Dallas*, the NBC movie *Time Bomb*, with Morgan Fairchild and Billy Dee Williams, and *Miami Vice*. He was teaching acting technique in Dallas when he was called on to read for the part of Ritchie Valens's half-brother in *La Bamba*. 'When my agent sent me up to audition, they said it was for the Frankie Valli story,' the actor recalls. 'I thought I'd be too tall, but I'd give it a shot anyway.' His aim was true. In fact, the producers were so impressed with his audition that – out of the

Lou Diamond Phillips in the role that made him a star – Ritchie Valens in *La Bamba*

Lou Diamond as the knife-wielding Mexican-Indian Chavez Y Chavez in the Brat Pack western *Young Guns*

Lou Diamond as the Navajo tribal cop Jim Chee in the Robert Redford-produced *The Dark Wind*

500 candidates they saw – they signed him up to play the lead, even though he couldn't sing or play the guitar. To prepare for his role, Phillips spent hours practising on catgut until, 'my fingers bled and I lost five layers of skin.' He also put on an extra 15 pounds in weight to look the part. But the effort was worth it. *La Bamba* may have been a little film by studio standards, but it was being distributed by a major Hollywood company (Columbia) and Lou Diamond did have the lead. And he made the film his own.

On 17 July 1987 *La Bamba* opened at 1,251 cinemas across America and was soundly beaten at the box-office by four other movies: *RoboCop*, *Snow White and the Seven Dwarfs*, *Summer School* and *Superman IV*. A week later, at even fewer cinemas, *La Bamba* was making more money than any of the aforementioned. Meanwhile, the title song had rocketed to number one in the music charts, which was 48 places higher than Valens's original. By 1 November the film itself had amassed $53,668,276 at the US box-office, making it the fourth highest-grossing movie in LA that year (topping such established hits as *The Untouchables*, *Lethal Weapon*, *RoboCop* and *Three Men and a Baby*). Lou Diamond Phillips was a star.

Before *La Bamba* opened, the actor portrayed a mental patient in the TV movie *The Three Kings* and took a supporting role in *Stand and Deliver*, starring and co-produced by Edward James Olmos. In the latter he

played Angel, a troubled Hispanic gang member who is redeemed by Olmos's tough, caring teacher. He won the role over hundreds of young hopefuls, although his cards were stacked – he'd previously worked with Olmos on an episode of *Miami Vice*. 'We did a scene together,' he remembers, 'and Olmos turned around and said, "What are you doing in March?" I knew Ritchie was going to be a very identifiable role. And I wanted to do something 180 degrees away from it, so I took this very small film. And it turned out to be not such a small film.'

In a second attempt to circumvent the giddy demands of celebrity, Lou Diamond returned to his roots in Texas to make a local picture, *Dakota*, an old-fashioned romantic drama set on a ranch. He not only starred in it, but served as associate producer and got married mid-shoot. The picture's assistant director happened to double as a Justice of the Peace and conducted the ceremony on the set which, the actor recalls, 'was a very sweet, very romantic sort of thing.'

He was now a big enough name to join such tabloid-stirrers as Emilio Estevez, Kiefer Sutherland and Charlie Sheen, and travelled to New Mexico to co-star in the big-budget western *Young Guns*, a revisionist look at Billy the Kid (Estevez) and his gang of callow 'Regulators'. Phillips played the Mexican-Indian Chavez Y Chavez, whom he described as, 'a killer, a savage and at the same time very mystical, the quiet one.' The film was a hit, but for inexplicable reasons the actor was

then stranded in another ensemble picture, the silly chase comedy *Disorganized Crime*, as the youngest member of a gang of bank robbers (alongside Corbin Bernsen and Ed O'Neill). Next he teamed up with Kiefer Sutherland a second time, and played another Indian, in the fast-paced thriller *Renegades* (but looked entirely bored by the experience). In the limp horror outing *The First Power*, he was a cop tracking a supernatural serial killer, and then played a heavy – a drug lord – in the disappointing political drama *A Show of Force*, starring Amy Irving. He returned to the saddle for *Young Guns II – Blaze of Glory*, a superior sequel, which turned out to be his last commercial success.

He was another heavy in *Ambition*, a title which reflected the star's own sense of enterprise, as he wrote the screenplay for himself. As it happens, the film was a sluggish, underdeveloped thriller which did no service to Phillips the actor. He was no better in *The Dark Wind*, a self-consciously arty, sleep-inducing adaptation of Tony Hillerman's popular novel, about a rookie Indian cop up to his neck in corruption, witchcraft and murder. Robert Redford executive-produced, and intended it as the first in a series. But due to the film's sluggish performance at the box-office this now seems unlikely.

Lou Diamond then played an Inuit Eskimo hunter in *Shadow of the Wolf*, reportedly the most expensive Canadian film ever made, based on the celebrated novel *Agaguk* by Yves Theriault. He was announced as the star of the thriller *Touch* for director Tony Richardson, with Natasha Richardson, Mick Jagger and Sherilyn Fenn in support – but the film never materialized. He was then top-billed in *Extreme Justice* co-starring Scott Glenn and Chelsea Field, and made his directing debut on *Dangerous Touch*, in which he played an ex-con who embroils a radio psychologist (Kate Vernon) in a murder spree.

He also tours with his own band, The Pipe Fitters, and in 1993 was romantically linked with Jennifer Tilly, his co-star from *Shadow of the Wolf*.

FILMOGRAPHY

1983: *Trespasses* (also co-scripted) (released 1987). 1984: *Angel Alley*; *Time Bomb* (TV); *Interface*. 1986: *Harley*. 1987: *The Three Kings* (TV); *La Bamba*; *Stand and Deliver* (aka *Walking On Water*); *Dakota*. 1988: *Young Guns*; *Disorganized Crime* (aka *The Bank Job*). 1989: *Renegades* (aka *Lakota*). 1990: *The First Power* (aka *Pentagram*); *A Show of Force*; *Young Guns II – Blaze of Glory*. 1991: *Ambition* (aka *Mind Game*). 1992: *The Dark Wind*;

Shadow of the Wolf (aka *Agaguk*). 1993: *Extreme Justice* (aka *SIS*); *Dangerous Touch* (also dir). 1994: *Teresa's Tattoo*; *Sioux City* (also dir.); *Boulevard*.

River PHOENIX

River Jude Phoenix became a star in spite of himself. Avoiding the glitzy roundabout of Hollywood parties and premieres, the actor preferred to live with his parents in Gainesville, north-central Florida – i.e., the middle of nowhere. Exposure in the media had always repelled him. He insisted that, 'I've kept my ego and my happiness completely separate from my work. In fact, if I see my face on the cover of a magazine I go into remission. I shut myself out and freak.'

On top of his public shyness, the reluctant star lived a life unlike any of his contemporaries. He was a Vegan, an ardent environmentalist, eschewed material luxuries and was happiest making music – singing with his own band, Aleka's Attic. Even his name was unconventional. His parents chose the Phoenix bit for themselves, while he selected his forename from the River of Life in Hermann Hesse's *Siddhartha*. And if that sounded weird, his four younger siblings sounded weirder. They are: Rainbow Joan of Arc, Leaf Joaquim, Liberty Mariposa and Summer Joy.

Above all, River was a living antithesis of the hard-living, drug-taking Hollywood as represented by the likes of Rob Lowe, Charlie Sheen and Christian Slater. Indeed, he was vocally anti-drugs, denouncing them for being antisocial. Once, he admitted, 'I don't see any point or any good in drugs that are as disruptive as cocaine. I never tried heroin. I tried alcohol and most of the others when I was 15 and got it out of the way – finished with the stuff.'

So, when the spokesman for clean living died of a drug overdose at the age of 23, the news rocked Hollywood and beyond. In the early hours of Halloween, on 31 October 1993, Phoenix was in the company of his brother Leaf, his sister Rain and his girlfriend, the wonderfully talented actress Samantha Mathis. They were leaving The Viper Room club on Sunset Boulevard (part-owned by Johnny Depp) and Phoenix collapsed outside on the pavement. Later an autopsy revealed that a lethal combination of Valium, marijuana, ephedrine, cocaine and heroin was present in his system. Enough to kill a horse, let alone a clean-living soul like River Phoenix.

As River Phoenix's life had been nonconformist, so his upbringing was even more unorthodox. He was born on 24 August,

River Phoenix

1970, in a log cabin in Madras, Oregon. His parents, John and Arlyn, were 1960s hippies who believed in God and LSD, and picked fruit for a living in the American North-West. When River was just two, they moved to Venezuela to serve a denomination called The Children of God. There they toiled religiously, with John Phoenix serving as the sect's archbishop – until disillusionment set in in 1977. Poverty followed (for a while they dossed down in a rat-infested shed on the beach), and River and Rainbow sang religious songs on the street to scrape together a living. Still, River could now speak fluent Spanish (his first language), play the guitar and already understood the concept of humility.

Without money, River, Rainbow, Leaf, Liberty, John and a pregnant Arlyn stowed away on an old freighter and headed back for the US. In Florida, River and Rainbow began winning a series of local talent contests, which encouraged the family to up stumps again and head for Hollywood. The idea was that John and Arlyn would manage their children's respective careers in showbusiness

River, aged 14, with Corey Feldman in Rob
Reiner's *Stand By Me*

As the love-sturck Devo in Lawrence
Kasdan's ensemble black comedy *I Love You
To Death*

and, indeed, all five children went on to act.
River and Rainbow, sounding like a flower-
power double act, entertained audiences in
the warm-up to the TV show *Real Kids*
which, in turn, allowed River to twang his
guitar and sing on the TV game show
Fantasy. He then landed the part of Guthrie
in 22 episodes of CBS TV's *Seven Brides For
Seven Bothers*. By this time he was 12-years-
old.

TV commercials followed, but River felt
uncomfortable doing them ('I couldn't smile
on cue') and felt it a reprehensible occupation. Instead, he turned to the movies.

He had a small but effective role in a
highly-aclaimed TV film, *Surviving*, with Ellen
Burstyn and Molly Ringwald, and then played
the nerdy whiz kid Wolfgang Muller in Joe
Dante's teenage sci-fi fantasy *Explorers*. The
latter was no small feat for the actor, who
won the role over 4,000 young hopefuls.

He was then in another ensemble piece,
and a much better one, *Stand By Me*. Based
on a Stephen King novella called *The Body*,
the film focused on four adolescent boys
from Castle Rock, Oregon, who set off on a
two-day hike to find 'a body.' Although
essentially a naturalistic look at adolescent
youth, *Stand By Me* still retained an
enormous charm, thanks largely to Rob
Reiner's adroit direction. The film became a

sleeper success, Reiner adopted the name
Castle Rock for his production company and
Ben E. King's title song became a number
one hit (it had previously reached No. 4 in
the US charts, in 1961). Phoenix played Chris
Chambers, the brightest and toughest kid, an
abused child from a working-class home. For
an actor with so little experience, his was a
performance of extraordinary maturity.

He played Harrison Ford's son in *The
Mosquito Coast*, a film set in the Caribbean
jungle, about a man who forsakes American
consumerism for a life of Nature. Directed
by Peter Weir, it was only a sporadically
successful adaptation of Paul Theroux's novel,
but was remarkable how it mirrored River's
own upbringing. It also introduced the young
star to Martha Plimpton, the 15-year-old
actress daughter of Keith Carradine, who
later became his constant companion.

River landed his first solo starring role in *A
Night In the Life of Jimmy Reardon* – as a
pubescent Lothario. It was a brave, if unwise
choice, and was too much of a stretch for
Phoenix who, in real life, couldn't've been
further removed from his character. Besides,
the film was lousy.

Little Nikita fared no better, and was
unreleased in Britain (theatrically), in which
the actor played an all-American kid who
discovers that his parents are Soviet spies.
Sidney Poitier co-starred (and top-billed) as
the FBI agent who befriends Phoenix while
investigating his parents.

However, success did arrive in the shape
of Sidney Lumet's powerful, articulate and
intelligent *Running On Empty*, a drama that
shared some similiarites with *Nikita*. Again,
Phoenix played the son of parents at odds
with the American government, this time
1960s radicals who accidentally blinded a
janitor while bombing a napalm laboratory.
Judd Hirsch and Christine Lahti played his
parents, with Martha Plimpton the girl who
couldn't fathom his secret. River gave the
best performance of his career to date, as
Danny Pope, a 17-year-old trying to compre-
hend his family's cause while wishing for a
normal life. At the time, it was hard to
imgaine any other actor River's age (18),
who could've played a part of such
complexity and pent-up emotion with so
much honesty.

From critical acclaim he went on to
commercial success, playing the teenage Indy
in *Indiana Jones and the Last Crusade*, the
second highest grossing film of 1989 (after
Batman). However, the series had by now
succumbed to a touch of the infantile, but
the opening sequence was terrific – in which
we find Indy (Phoenix) and discover the
reason for his fear of snakes (and you
couldn't blame him). For River, it was a small
part, but it was the best one in the movie
and it gave him his biggest international
exposure to date.

Meanwhile, he was nominated for a best
supporting actor Oscar for *Running On
Empty*, but lost the actual award to Kevin
Kline (for *A Fish Called Wanda*). Ironically,
Kline was the star of Phoenix's next film, *I
Love You To Death*, an intermittently hilarious
comedy based on a true story about an
adulterous pizzeria owner. Phoenix was the
introspective and smitten friend of the wife
(Tracey Ullman), who helps arrange for her
husband's demise (at the hands of inept
hitmen William Hurt and Keanu Reeves).

He played a Marine in Nancy Savoca's
Dogfight, the charming story of a group of
soldiers who place bets to see which of

River Phoenix as Mike Waters, the narcoleptic gay prostitute in Gus Van Sant's *My Own Private Idaho*

them can bring the ugliest date ('a dog') to a party. He then teamed up with Keanu Reeves in *My Own Private Idaho*.

Taking its title from the B-52's song and its plot from Shakespeare's *Henry IV*, the film was a tedious mix of pretentious allusion and surrealism. It was, however, an enormous leap for the actor, who played a gay narcoleptic street hustler. Phoenix was quick to point out that his character's homosexuality was purely incidental ('the film actually focuses on this boy's quest for survival and finding home, getting back to his roots'). That's as may be, but the picture's strongest scenes are the tender revelations of 'friendship' between the two male stars. Critics were divided, although Phoenix did win the National Society of Film Critics' award for his performance, beating out such heavy contenders as Nick Nolte and Warren Beatty.

He turned down the lead in *A Kiss Before Dying* ('they came back eight times to try and get me to do it, and they went up, up, up with the money') – a wise decision, as it turned out (Matt Dillon took the part). Instead, he opted for a supporting role in *Sneakers*, a slick, high-tech caper with Robert Redford, Dan Aykroyd, Ben Kingsley, Mary McDonnell and former co-star Sidney Poitier. Phoenix played another variation of his screen persona, a quirky, introspective whiz kid, who could for all intents and purposes have been Wolfgang from *Explorers* seven

years on. Still, the film was undiluted escapism and sneaked off with $50 million at the US box-office.

After that, he took another supporting role, in Sam Shepard's very weird western *Silent Tongue*, as the unhinged son of Richard Harris who is plagued by the ghost of his dead wife. Next, he utilized his musical talents by playing a musician trying to make it in Nashville, but who is waylaid by romance – in Peter Bogdanovich's *The Thing Called Love*, co-starring Dermot Mulroney and his imminent girlfriend Samantha Mathis. He was then announced as the star of *Broken Dreams*, 'a love story in a futuristic, post-holocaust atomic world,' to be directed by John Boorman from a script by Neil Jordan. But first he began production on *Dark Blood*, with Judy Davis and Jonathan Pryce, and was announced to star opposite Tom Cruise in *Interview with the Vampire*. Then, with three weeks left to shoot on the first film, Phoenix was dead and production was scrapped.

FILMOGRAPHY

1985: *Surviving* (TV); *Explorers*. 1986: *Stand By Me*; *The Mosquito Coast*; *Circle of Violence: A Family Drama* (TV). 1987: *A Night In the Life of Jimmy Reardon* (UK: *Jimmy Reardon*). 1988: *Little Nikita*; *Running On Empty*. 1989: *Indiana Jones and the Last Crusade*. 1990: *I Love You To Death*. 1991: *Dogfight*; *My Own Private Idaho*. 1992: *Sneakers*. 1993: *Silent Tongue*; *The Thing Called Love*.

Brad PITT

As a sex symbol, Brad Pitt is unbearably cute. Puckish, boyish, athletic and as cool as a chilled glass of Evian, he has also proved himself to be a versatile actor. Whether playing the braindead, sexually naive *Johnny Suede*, or the wily, carnally confident JD in *Thelma & Louise*, he was totally the part – and had women swooning every which way.

Brad Pitt snatched his 15 minutes of fame in *Thelma & Louise* and kept on running. The part of JD, the hitchhiker who gives Geena Davis her first orgasm and takes her last penny, was pencilled in for William Baldwin, but the latter bowed out when he won the lead in *Backdraft*. Auditions were called, and nearly 400 hopefuls showed up. Casting director Lou Di Giaimo jumped on Brad Pitt. 'There are stars that aren't great actors,' Di Giaimo reckons, 'but when I met Brad, I

thought, "He's going to be a star *and* he can act. His career is going to be a capital B-I-G."'

Thelma & Louise was a hit, and Pitt's brief but telling contribution rocked the movie community in its seats. And yet the actor was already coming up fast on the outside – before *Thelma & Louise* had even opened. He had been having discussions with Robert Redford about starring in *A River Runs Through It*, had landed the title role in *Johnny Suede*, and movie publicists were falling over themselves to represent him. He was already a star of the gossip columns in 1989, thanks to a liaison with Robin Givens, and tabloid queen Liz Smith agitated things further when she reported that Pitt and Geena Davis were rumoured to be having an affair on the set of *Thelma & Louise*. The gunpowder was there; *Thelma & Louise* just lit the fuse.

Born William Bradley Pitt on 18 December 1965, in Oklahoma, Brad was raised in Springfield, Missouri. His father, Bill Pitt, owned a trucking company in the city, where his son was educated. After taking small parts in school musicals, Brad enrolled at the University of Missouri and majored in journalism – with an eye for the advertising industry. However, he continued acting in fraternity 'Spring Fling' shows.

In 1986 he left for Los Angeles to attend art school, when he decided he wanted to be in movies instead. While studying to act, he took on a variety of jobs, including a stint as a giant chicken plugging a fast-food chain and also chauffeured Strip-O-Gram artistes in a limousine. He got an agent and shortly

Pitt as Detective Frank Harris, a cop caught in cartoon land in Ralph Bakshi's awful *Cool World*

afterwards secured a part on *Dallas* as 'an idiot boyfriend who gets caught in the hay.' He had another regular turn on the daytime soap *Another World*, popped up in the family sitcom *Growing Pains*, and snatched a small role in the critically acclaimed TV movie *A Stoning in Fulham County*, starring Ken Olin and Jill Eikenberry.

He moved on to the big screen in the romantic comedy *Happy Together* and then landing a starring role in the slasher spoof *Cutting Class*. A dire attempt to lampoon such horror entries as *Friday the 13th* and *Prom Night*, *Cutting Class* featured Pitt as a high school sadist and bully who romances Jill Schoelen (of *The Stepfather* fame) while tormenting his old friend Donovan Leitch, the latter released from a mental home for supposedly murdering his father.

Pitt played another low-life, Billy King, in the mercilessly manipulative TV movie *Too Young To Die?*. The story of a 14-year-old girl (Juliette Lewis) dumped on by society, the film featured Pitt as a hirsute dope addict who pushes Lewis into prostitution and, eventually, murder. Neither Pitt nor Lewis thought much of the movie, although it was the beginning of a long-term romance.

'Yeah, it was quite romantic,' Pitt jokes, 'shooting her full of drugs and stuff.' He had another recurring role – as Walker Lovejoy, a college dropout – in the Fox series *Glory Days*, but the show was cancelled after six episodes; and then took a small bit in the so-so TV movie *The Image*, starring Albert Finney.

He was the competitive athletic brother of Rick Schroder in *Across the Tracks*, a tenable teen drama that failed to find its audience, and then played JD in Ridley Scott's *Thelma & Louise*. His next big breakthrough was the title role in Tom DiCillo's delightfully idiosyncratic *Johnny Suede*, the story of a dumb jock obsessed by his hair and Ricky Nelson. 'At the time I cast the movie,' explains DiCillo, 'Brad was a complete unknown. He read for the part, and there was no doubt that he was the one for the role. He was the only one to get that Johnny was this guy who has no idea what he's doing. And there was a beautiful transparency to his work – whatever's going on inside Brad, you can see it.' *Johnny Suede* was a real departure for Pitt, who played DiCillo's off-beat comedy completely straight – which, believe it or not, was no small feat. Although a decidedly low-budget independent feature (price tag: $1 million), the film attracted a respectable following in urban circles.

After that he was in *Cool World*, Ralph Bakshi's witless adult take on *Who Framed Roger Rabbit*, in which he played a young detective trapped in a bizarre cartoon universe. And then there was Robert Redford's meticulous recreation of Norman Maclean's celebrated autobiographical novel *A River Runs Through It*. Pitt played Maclean's troubled younger brother Paul and, with his sandy hair blowing in the Montana wind, looked uncannily like a young Redford. The film was beautifully composed and acted, but was so tastefully done that it nudged the boredom factor once too often.

In *Kalifornia*, the actor was back in trailer park territory with Juliette Lewis, the couple playing a pair of wildly attractive homicidal low-lifes. Then he joined the starry company of Christian Slater, Gary Oldman, Val Kilmer, Patricia Arquette and Dennis Hopper for Tony Scott's action-packed romantic comedy *True Romance*. And, as a true indication of his new standing in the industry, he turned down Disney's offer of the starring role in *The Three Musketeers* (replaced by Chris O'Donnell). He then starred opposite Tom Cruise in Neil Jordan's *Interview With the Vampire*.

FILMOGRAPHY

1988: *A Stoning in Fulham County* (TV). **1989:** *Happy Together*; *Cutting Class*. **1990:** *Too Young To Die?* (TV); *The Image* (TV). **1991:** *Across the Tracks* (aka *Nowhere To Run*); *Thelma & Louise*; *Dark Side of the Sun*; *The Favor*; *Johnny Suede*. **1992:** *Cool World*; *A River Runs Through It*. **1993:** *Kalifornia*; *True Romance*. **1994:** *Legends of the Fall*; *Interview with the Vampire*.

Brad Pitt as Paul Maclean in Robert Redford's excessively tasteful *A River Runs Through It*

Brad Pitt as the quintessential dumb jock in Tom DiCillo's *Johnny Suede*

Aidan QUINN

The trouble with Aidan Quinn is that he says what he means. Even when he was promoting his very first film, *Reckless*, when asked what he thought of it, he replied, 'not much.' He explains that he 'cannot lie' and is consequently very choosy when it comes to picking scripts. Sometimes *too* choosy. He rejected the leads in *My Left Foot* and *Sleeping With the Enemy*, the first a critical triumph, the second a box-office smash. 'I just have very strong principals,' he says. Caleb Deschanel, who directed Quinn as *Crusoe*, believes, 'he won't do something unless he really believes in it. I can't say there weren't times we disagreed, but any really terrific actor is difficult in one way or another.' Susan Seidelman agrees. 'I won't say we had an easy working relationship [on *Desperately Seeking Susan*], but what I got on film is worth it. He's a thinker; and it shows.' James Foley, the director responsible for exposing Quinn on screen in the first place, reckons, 'Aidan has the same strength that all great actors have – that is the ability to bring the character to him and then to find where he and the character cross over. Rather than assuming the characteristics of the part, Aidan accentuates the aspects of *his* self to match the character's. He also imbues his characters with a certain sweetness and innocent charm that is extremely endearing.'

So, in a nutshell, Aidan Quinn is worth the angst. Female viewers certainly think so. His sweet-natured smile and bottomless blue eyes are famous . And although he has failed to become a box-office property as such, he is grateful for the fact. As he says, 'I think it's too bad when you become divorced from everyday people through fame, since it is everyday people that an actor must portray.' Except, everyday people are not as charismatic as Quinn.

The second of five children (four boys and a girl), Aidan Quinn was born on 8 March 1959 in Chicago, where his father taught literature at a community college. Both his parents had emigrated from Birr in Ireland a few years previously, and returned there when Aidan was still a baby – and again when he was 13. For the most part, he grew up in Rockford, Illinois, where he excelled at competitive sports, but failed to fit in socially. Eventually his parents returned to Ireland for good and, after graduating from high school, Aidan followed them with ambitions to become a writer. In Dublin, 'I lived in a cold-water flat and read Joyce and Dostoyevsky – the fun stuff,' he laughs, but when he frequented a lunchtime theatre for the free sandwiches and soup, he found himself enjoying the plays more than the food. He returned to Chicago in 1978 and for seven months worked as a hot-tar roofer when he decided to turn to acting. He started taking classes and, at 19, landed his first play, Alan Gross's *The Man in 605*, which was a success. Local productions of Brecht, Chekhov and Faulkner followed when, for the grand sum of $20,000, he landed the lead in James Foley's *Reckless*, co-starring Daryl Hannah. Besides some explicit sex scenes the film was an unremarkable slice-of-life romance, and Quinn told the press as much, alienating the big-shots in Hollywood.

Disillusioned, he returned to Ireland once more, and then, back in Chicago, found himself waiting on tables. Theatre work – particularly a celebrated production of *Hamlet* (which won Chicago's 1985 Best Theatre Award) – restored his professional standing, and he landed the part of Dez, the projectionist who befriends Rosanna Arquette, in *Desperately Seeking Susan*. The film was a hit, and Quinn received favourable reviews, which led to the lead in the controversial TV movie *An Early Frost*, in which he played a homosexual lawyer with AIDS. This time he received even better press, was nominated for an Emmy, and revealed, 'It was my most fulfilling role.'

Aidan Quinn in *Desperately Seeking Susan*

As the psychotic Richard 'Stick' Montgomery in John Badham's exciting *Stakeout*

He was due for more controversy when he agreed to play Jesus in Martin Scorsese's adaptation of the Nikos Kazantzakis novel *The Last Temptation of Christ*, but the project folded a month before filming, only to be resurrected three years later (with Willem Dafoe). Instead, he took a supporting role in Roland Joffe's admirable *The Mission*, as Robert De Niro's ill-fated, younger brother, and was positively unnerving as the ruthless cop-killer in *Stakeout*, a huge hit. He then had the title role in a distinguished version of Daniel Defoe's *Crusoe*, 'a story of a very unremarkable man who's a racist slave trader, who comes back to America a changed man.'

When Quinn returned to America (*Crusoe* was filmed off the coast of Africa), he changed *his* spots and married the actress Elizabeth Bracco. He and she had first met two years earlier in a restaurant, when

Bracco was still a secretary. He joined her for dinner, and then made a habit of it. Quinn admits that he used to be, 'sort of – quite a bit – a ladies' man,' but in September of 1987 he settled down to domestic bliss and later became a father. Since then, Bracco has followed in the footsteps of her husband and sister Lorraine, and made a sizeable impression as the talkative stranger in Jim Jarmusch's weird and wonderful *Mystery Train*.

In 1988, Quinn played Stanley Kowalski in a Broadway revival of *A Streetcar Named Desire*, with Blythe Danner, and then landed the title role in the cable movie *Perfect Witness*, as the traumatized witness of a gangland killing. He had a supporting part – opposite Diane Keaton and Carol Kane – in Joyce Chopra's *The Lemon Sisters*, a sentimental farce which could well have done with a shot of citric acid. Still, it allowed him a rare stab at comedy, and he was simply wonderful. It was Carol Kane who strong-armed him into the film, contending, 'unlike many who have his "leading man" good looks (which, incidentally, he is completely unaware of), Aidan is interested in characters and challenges.' He then played the chauffeur who carries on an affair with his master's mistress (Natasha Richardson) in a lamentable screen adaptation of Margaret Atwood's novel *The Handmaid's Tale*.

To be honest, Quinn's film career was not looking good. But then he was handed one of the leads in one of the best American

Aidan Quinn as the reclusive chauffeur in Volker Schlondorff's *The Handmaid's Tale*

Quinn with Mary Stuart Masterson in *Benny & Joon*

films of 1990 – by one of Hollywood's most talented filmmakers. The movie was *Avalon*, Barry Levinson's moving, masterful portrait of three generations of Baltimore Jews. Quinn played Jules Kaye, formerly Jules Krichinsky, son of an eastern European immigrant (Armin Mueller-Stahl), who jumps onto the American bandwagon by selling neighbours their very first TV sets. Levinson, who steered Dustin Hoffman to an Oscar for *Rain Man*, wrote the role with Quinn in mind.

He was a passionate Christian missionary in the lumbering eco-melodrama *At Play in the Fields of the Lords*, and courted dysentery in the Brazilian rainforest. As it happens, it was the first time he was away from his daughter for an extended period, which wasn't helped by playing a character mourning the death of his son. But, Quinn says, 'I had read the book [Peter Matthiessen's novel] and loved it because it concerned everything I deeply care about – the environment and spirituality. I've been a member of Greenpeace since high school and live on a wildlife preserve in upstate New York.' He was better in the TV movie *Lies of the Twins*, as a psychiatrist and his sadistic twin brother (both involved with Isabella Rossellini), and was better still in the beguiling Irish drama *The Playboys*, for which he took a substantial cut in salary. As an itinerant actor courting a local, wilful beauty (Robin Wright), he was able to show off his Irish accent for the first time and contributed much rakish charm to a role originally earmarked for Liam Neeson. 'In Ireland, there are so many fucking actors,' he says. 'Irish actors don't have any training. It's a gift. The natural gift of the gab. I *had* to do it.'

Next, he played Sissy Spacek's husband in Joan Micklin Silver's touching, discerning TV movie *A Private Matter*, the story of a couple coming to terms with a Thalidomide pregnancy, and then took over from Woody Harrelson in *Benny and Joon* – after the latter reneged on his contract to join Demi Moore and Robert Redford in *Indecent Proposal*. In the latter, Quinn played an auto mechanic who puts his life on hold to care for his mentally unstable sister, Mary Stuart Masterson.

FILMOGRAPHY

1984: *Reckless*. 1985: *Desperately Seeking Susan*; *An Early Frost* (TV). 1986: *The Mission*. 1987: *Stakeout*. 1988: *Crusoe*. 1989: *Perfect Witness* (TV); *The Lemon Sisters*; *The Handmaid's Tale*. 1990: *Avalon*. 1991: *At Play in the Fields of the Lord*; *Lies of the Twins* (TV). 1992: *The Playboys*; *A Private Matter* (TV); *Benny and Joon*. 1994: *Blink*; *Legends of the Fall*; *Mary Shelley's Frankenstein*; *The Stars Fell on Henrietta*.

Keanu REEVES

Although Keanu Reeves has made a career playing gormless young men (braindead or otherwise) he has also, uncharacteristically, appeared in his share of costume dramas. He is, however, perhaps best known as Theodore Logan, the time-travelling high school moron in *Bill & Ted's Excellent Adventure* and *Bill & Ted's Bogus Journey*. These were a pair of wildly popular adolescent comedies that overcame the spectre of their self-conscious trendiness through an

(Keanu is Hawaiian for 'a cool breeze over the mountains'). And yet he has been commandeered for a number of serious period pieces in direct contrast to his personality. But whether he's playing a straight-F student or a far-from-straight street hustler, he invariably conveys a sense of upstanding propriety. Recently, he has been seen on the stage as Trinculo in *The Tempest*, played the righteous, profoundly Victorian Jonathan Harker in *Bram Stoker's Dracula*, played the lead in Bernardo Bertolucci's Himalayan epic *Little Buddha* and was Don

John in Kenneth Branagh's *Much Ado About Nothing*. Even Scott Favor, the male prostitute in *My Own Private Idaho*, had his genesis in Shakespeare – or, as Keanu eloquently put it: 'Yeh, Scottie's based on . . . Hal? Prince Hal? From, um, Shakespeare.'

Like his syntax, Keanu Reeves is from all

Keanu Reeves (*right*), with Alex Winter, in the totally bodacious *Bill & Ted's Excellent Adventure*

Reeves as the idealistic Martin Loader in Jon Amiel's *Tune in Tomorrow*

irresistible energy and enthusiasm. They even spawned a Saturday morning cartoon series. Keanu, who, previously, was best known as the sullen Matt in *River's Edge*, was a revelation as Ted, the bone-headed student who couldn't keep still for a moment. Whether playing air-guitar with co-star Alex Winter (as Bill) or romancing some 'medieval babes' from Olde England, his frenzied, infantile bonhomie was infectious.

In fact, Ted Logan was far more in keeping with the real Keanu, whose concentration and syntax are all over the place. He positively exudes a boyish excitement and speaks in a street lingo as fresh as his name

over the place. Born in Beirut, Lebanon, on 2 September 1964, to a Hawaiian-Chinese father and English mother, he lived for a while in Australia and New York and was raised in Canada. Confessing to 'a safe and sheltered upbringing', he dropped out of high school at 15 to study acting. A year later he made his professional debut in the Canadian TV series *Hanging In* and earned himself a handsome income from a Coca-Cola commercial. He then attended Toronto's High School for the Performing Arts. 'It was a fun year,' he says, 'but I got kicked out and failed. I was rude and stuff – talking too much.'

He then spent a summer at the Hedgerow Theatre in Pennsylvania and studied with Jaspar Deeter. His favourite role at that time was Mercutio – in, um, *Romeo and Juliet*. On TV, he played a psychotic assassin in the HBO movie *Act of Vengeance*, with Charles Bronson, and had a good part in the highly acclaimed TV movie *Under the Influence*, with Andy Griffith.

He made his theatrical film debut in *Youngblood*, an ice hockey melodrama with Rob Lowe and Patrick Swayze, in which he drew on his reputation as Most Valuable Player on his school's hockey team. He then had the lead in the slick TV movie *The Brotherhood of Justice*, as Derick, a hunky, privileged kid who not only drives a flash red sports car but is captain of the school football team. Derick is also nominated captain of a vigilante gang that gets out of control. Kiefer Sutherland played the good guy.

Next, Keanu joined Drew Barrymore for an overlong TV version of the Victor Herbert operetta *Babes in Toyland*, with a new score by Leslie Bricusse, and was in the CBS Disney 'Family Movie' *I Wish I Were Eighteen Again*. Then came *River's Edge*.

Both a critical success and something of a cult, *River's Edge* was a disturbing, honest drama inspired by a true murder case in 1981. Not since Francis Coppola's *The Outsiders* had a cast of unknowns exhibited such an ensemble force. Reeves was simply superb as Matt, the story's conscientious anchor, who reluctantly comes to terms with his moral duty. Although both Crispin Glover and Dennis Hopper enjoyed showier roles, it was Keanu who had the toughest part to play.

Marisa Silver's *Permanent Record* covered parallel ground, but failed to find an audience, and a similar fate befell the teen comedy *The Night Before*, in which Keanu played a high school nerd suffering from alcohol-induced amnesia. He had a supporting role in

Dangerous Liaisons, cast against type as the French nobleman Chevalier Danceny, and then landed the part of a rebellious teenager in *The Prince of Pennsylvania*, a genuine oddity. Still, it allowed Keanu to have a rare crack at comedy, although with lines like, 'I don't want to be a tadpole, I want to be a dolphin,' it was hard to distinguish between what was *meant* to be funny and what wasn't. The director, Ron Nyswaner, certainly took a risk with his casting.

'I loved Keanu in *River's Edge*,' Nyswaner ventured, 'but it was a very serious drama, and I had no idea whether or not he could be funny. So I had him up to the hotel in LA to talk about the part, and he made us laugh for a solid 45 minutes. After that, I knew he had to be ideal.' Although the film was not a hit, it mustered a small following and even prompted a dance called the Keanu Stomp, enthusiastically enacted by Toronto punks.

Keanu Reeves had found his own feet and, leaving teen angst behind him, started on a new career in comedy. First there was the phenomenally successful *Bill & Ted's Excellent Adventure* and then the even bigger hit, *Parenthood*, with Steve Martin. In the latter, Keanu played Martha Plimpton's compassionate boyfriend and a prospective parent, and delivered the film's most poignant line: 'You have to have a licence to have a dog, even to catch a fish, but you don't need a licence to be a father.'

He had another supporting role in the starry, sporadically hilarious *I Love You To Death* (as a reluctant hit man, partnered with William Hurt), and then played the idealistic young writer, Martin Loader, in *Tune in*

Tomorrow (based on the novel *Aunt Julia and the Scriptwriter* by Mario Vargas Llosa). The director was the London-born Jon Amiel.

'When I first met Keanu, his hair was shaved bald on one side and long on the other,' the filmmaker remembers. 'The hair had time to grow before rehearsals, but on the first day he turned up swathed in bandages and was limping after yet another tumble off his motorbike.' Reeves is a self-confessed speed freak, and doted on his various sets of wheels – his rented Harley, his 850 Norton Commando, his Moto Guzzi . . . And, as a confirmation of his first love, he has a prominent scar running from his navel to his chest and another on his calf. Cheerfully, he admits, 'My body's a wreck, man.'

He indulged in more dangerous sport when he took on the role of tough rookie cop Johnny Utah in *Point Break*, a part originally earmarked for Matthew Broderick. The part demanded that he not only learn to surf and fire a gun, but also jump out of an aeroplane. Till now, Keanu had steered clear of the action genre, but made an imposing, fast-talking cop in what turned out to be a popular, muscular get-up-and-go thriller. Patrick Swayze co-starred (as the villain), and Kathryn Bigelow signed on to direct.

'I've been an enormous fan of Keanu since *River's Edge*,' the director explained. 'When this film came up, I thought Keanu's innate physicality, intelligence and charm would make him perfect to play Utah. He holds the screen, and he's got a magical ability to put the audience in his back pocket. In addition, the role was a departure from the work he'd done in the past. We all felt it would be a fresh approach for the picture.'

He returned to familiar ground with *Bill & Ted's Bogus Journey*, and then starred opposite River Phoenix in Gus Van Sant Jr's dark, pretentious *My Own Private Idaho*. While the gimmick of mingling Shakespearian text with contemporary slang was a fatal mistake, the film did have its moments, not least the affectionate fireside confession between the two stars. Next, he was all but swallowed by the grisly special effects in *Bram Stoker's Dracula* (but who could refuse a Coppola movie?), and then did a cameo in *Hideous Mutant Freaks*, which his friend Alex Winter co-wrote and co-directed. Next came *Much Ado About Nothing*, alongside Branagh, Michael Keaton and Denzel Washington, and then he returned to the quirky world of Gus

Keanu in action mode in Kathryn Bigelow's adrenaline-pumping *Point Break*

Keanu (*left*) with Gary Oldman in Francis Coppola's awesome *Bram Stoker's Dracula*

Van Sant Jr for the latter's *Even Cowgirls Get the Blues*, based on the cult novel by Tom Robbins. The actor's subsequent performance in Bertolucci's *Little Buddha* promised to be the biggest move in his career. It wasn't.

And if Keanu Reeves's stream of movies weren't enough to keep boredom at bay, the actor started up his own rock band, Dog Star, which his manager Jay Davis describes as 'Nirvana mixed with The Sex Pistols'. He also appeared in a Paula Abdul video and acted in a couple of student movies.

In his spare moments he confesses to an insatiable appetite for reading, and favours Dostoyevsky, Philip K. Dick, T.S. Eliot and Greek mythology. Such workaholism and devotion to post-college education, not to mention his dedication to researching his roles, has left little time for Hollywood parties and the inevitable inclusion in the gossip pages. But, he insists, 'I dig going out, but I don't get many invitations. It's just kind of whatever happens. I'll go see art, buy a drink, dance, play. Have *fun*. I dig the blues, man.' And then, with a mischievous twinkle, he brushes off his apparent lack of famous girlfriends with, 'No, I'm not gay – but you never know.' However, just to set the record straight, in 1993 he was dating Sofia Coppola, actress daughter of the Brat Pack guru.

FILMOGRAPHY

1984: *Act of Vengeance* (TV). 1986: *Under the Influence* (TV); *Youngblood*; *The Brotherhood of Justice* (TV); *Babes in Toyland* (TV). 1987: *I Wish I Were Eighteen Again* (TV); *River's Edge*. 1988: *Permanent Record*; *The Night Before*; *Dangerous Liaisons*; *The Prince of Pennsylvania*. 1989: *Bill & Ted's Excellent Adventure*; *Parenthood*. 1990: *I Love You To Death*; *Tune in Tomorrow* (UK: *Aunt Julia and the Scriptwriter*). 1991: *Point Break*; *Bill & Ted's Bogus Journey*; *My Own Private Idaho*. 1992: *Bram Stoker's Dracula*; *Hideous Mutant Freaks*. 1993: *Much Ado About Nothing*; *Even Cowgirls Get the Blues*; *Little Buddha*. 1994: *Texas Rangers*; *Speed*; *Johnny Mnemonic*; *A Walk in the Clouds*.

Molly RINGWALD

Pauline Kael praised her 'charismatic normality,' Warren Beatty plagued her with phone calls, John Hughes wrote *Sixteen Candles* with her photograph pinned above his word processor. At the height of the Brat Pack phenomenon, the media labelled her 'Princess of the Brat Pack' and 'The Teen Queen.' In 1986 *Time* magazine put her on their cover, describing her as 'our model modern teen.' Molly wannabes ('Ringlets') materialized in their droves, emulating her thrift shop fashion sense while dying their hair orange.

Teen princess Molly Ringwald

At the age of three, Molly Ringwald was performing at the California State Fair, at six she recorded her first album ('Molly Sings'), and at 11 was a regular in the TV sitcom *The Facts of Life*. Her film debut at 14 prompted Beatty's interest (a subsequent romance was reported) and her three back-to-back films for John Hughes were all hits ('the Molly trilogy'). Hughes, who was largely responsible for the engineering of the Brat Pack, marvelled, 'Molly is in a class of her own.'

And then the actress grew up. Her career descended as fast as it had risen. Later Molly Ringwald explained that, 'I'm always looking for different things to do in my work' – but her fans were no longer behind her. She grew up, she says, when she opted to play Cordelia in Jean-Luc Godard's bizarre screen version of *King Lear* (also starring Woody Allen and Norman Mailer), but it was an ill-advised career move.

In an attempt to revive her popularity she teamed up with her *Pretty in Pink* co-star Andrew McCarthy for *Fresh Horses*, but it turned out to be a grim, unconvincing drama. Nevertheless, she stretched herself as an actress (playing a frumpish, abused wife) and won the admiration of her director, David Anspaugh. 'Once we began shooting I found

As she was then: Molly, aged 14, in Paul Mazursky's *Tempest*

Molly at the height of her fame in the John Hughes scripted/produced *Pretty in Pink*

myself mesmerized,' he allowed. 'It was fascinating to watch Molly work. She could do take after take and each would be different, yet each was as honest as the last. She was wonderful to work with and is one of the most talented performers of her generation.'

The producer of the abortive *Betsy's Wedding*, was equally impressed. 'She's a fine actress. There's a sense of joy about her. She's a contemporary young woman with a lot of energy and a mature quality.'

It was after that that her production company, Kelbeth Productions (named after her older brother and sister, Kelly and Beth), folded. At least now she could lead a less stressful life. Philosophically, she mused, 'I'd like people to see my movies, obviously. But I never wanted to get to the point of being some crazy superstar. I just don't think I could deal with it.'

Molly Ringwald was the most unlikely of 'crazy superstars.' She was pretty, to be sure, but not in the drop-dead good-looking sense of such contemporaries as Demi Moore or Diane Lane. She was blessed with the most generous set of lips, soulful doe eyes and a shock of astounding red hair (which she dyed constantly, hiding her natural dark reddish-brown). She was, unquestionably, photogenic, and unequivocally distinctive. But was this side enough of normal for her legion of

young female fans to identify with her. Her problems on screen were those of every Ringlet present, whether it be parental, academic, romantic or physical. She was not so much the Princess that the tabloids painted her, as the perfect everyteen.

Born on 18 February, 1968, in Roseville, California, Molly was the youngest daughter of the blind jazz pianist Bob Ringwald. At the age of four she was singing in her father's Great Pacific Jazz Band and, at five, played the Dormouse in a production of *Alice in Wonderland*. At eight, she landed a guest appearance on TV's *The New Mickey Mouse Club*, and, aged nine, played Kate in a 15-month tour of *Annie*. This, in turn, led to her recurring role as Molly Parker on NBC's *The Facts of Life*, set in an exclusive girls' boarding academy. She was axed from the show after a year, and for a further twelve months was out of work.

In 1982, following an unorthodox audition with the director Paul Mazursky, Molly won her film debut in the latter's *Tempest*. Loosely based on Shakespeare's play, the film starred John Cassavetes as a New York architect (Prospero) who escapes to a Greek island with his daughter Miranda (Ringwald). It was not a box-office success, but enough of the right people saw it (Beatty, Hughes) for Molly to find herself in demand.

After two inconsequential movies and a

mediocre TV film, she speared the starring role in Hughes's *Sixteen Candles*. Hughes explained, 'I was sent this picture of Molly in which she looked like a female version of Huck Finn. She was kind of boyish and interesting – not a beauty – but she had a real honest, innocent look. I stuck her picture up in my office and as I was writing I couldn't stop staring at her.' In *Sixteen Candles*, she played Samantha, a teenager gauchely in search of Mr Right. She was both charming and natural, and the film went on to capture a huge following in the States (although, strangely, it was never shown in British cinemas).

The Hughes-Ringwald success was repeated with *The Breakfast Club*, an ensemble comedy-drama that also starred Emilio Estevez, Anthony Michael Hall, Judd Nelson and Molly's future friend Ally Sheedy. At a time when *Porky's* and *Friday the 13th* offered the only opportunity for teenage actors to air their acting skills, *The Breakfast Club* was a godsend. Hughes, then aged 36, had an uncanny knack for capturing the content and cadence of teenage dialogue, while eliciting performances of adult complexity from his young cast. And, as simple as the film's dramatic structure was (five kids on detention in a classroom), the film made even more money than *Sixteen Candles*.

Molly won further good notices as a potential suicide in the superior TV movie *Surviving*, and then segued into her last film for Hughes, *Pretty in Pink*. This time the filmmaker handed the directing chores to Howard Deutch, but his sparkling script, comic invention and adolescent know-how was all over the screen. This time Molly played the poor girl romanced by a wealthy, good-looking Andrew McCarthy, whose proposition (well, an invitation to the prom) sends her into a tizzy. Again, the acting was of the highest order (Molly was enchanting, but almost had the movie stolen from her by co-stars Jon Cryer and Annie Potts), and the film was another formidable hit.

Not so *The Pick-Up Artist*, a romantic comedy developed by Warren Beatty and then disposed of when he took his name off the credits. This one had Molly top-billed, but she was secondary in spirit to the wild and wonderful Robert Downey Jr in the title role. In fact, whenever the former teen queen appeared on screen the movie stopped dead in its tracks. After that it was *King Lear* and then the enormously engaging *For Keeps*, which should have been a hit. The story of two teenage lovers (Ringwald, Randall Batinkoff) who have a baby, the film managed

met with equal applause. The difference here, though, was that the picture was written and directed by him, and he also starred, wrote the music and sang the songs. That same month, in May, the renaissance actor became a proud parent, fathering Susan Sarandon's second son, Miles Guthrie.

Six-foot-five, loose-limbed and baby-faced, Tim Robbins's physical appearance belies his fierce intellectual beliefs and his standing as a theatrical guru. Acclaimed as both director and playwright, the actor frequently ploughed his movie salary into a theatre collective, The Actor's Gang, which he set up with friends from his university days.

As a movie star, Robbins has shied away from making mainstream Hollywood pictures and has fought to work with directors of calibre. And although a deft performer, he has always put the film before his performance.

In *The New York Times* Pauline Kael wrote 'he has the gift of looking just right for each of his roles, and has a puckish, commanding presence ... He makes you feel that behind his sneaky, demon eyes he's thinking thoughts no character in a movie ever thought before.'

Mary Steenburgen, who played Robbins's sister in *Miss Firecracker*, called him 'the ultimate brother. He is amazingly mature and insightful one minute and a 9-year-old brat the next. The second we met, his odd sense of humour made me laugh – and that carried into our scenes together.'

Tim Robbins was born on 16 October, 1958, in New York City, the son of a magazine distributor (his mother) and Gil

to make us care about its protagonists while retaining its sense of humour. Unfortunately, the sight of Hollywood's favourite virgin coping with motherhood was too much for audiences and it was downhill from there.

Fresh Horses was a flop, *Strike it Rich* was worse (in which she replaced Emily Lloyd), and then there was a supporting role in Alan Alda's bland nuptial comedy *Betsy's Wedding* (she was Betsy), with Ally Sheedy playing her sister. Two TV roles followed (she was an unconvincing flapper in Ken Russell's *Dusk Before Fireworks*, and a real-life AIDS victim in *Something To Live For*) and then *Face the Music* in Paris, a romantic comedy in which she and Patrick Dempsey played a songwriting team who hate each other's guts.

Molly as Betsy Hopper with Alan Alda in the latter's *Betsy's Wedding*

Tim ROBBINS

Tim Robbins came into his own in 1992. Not only did he star in Robert Altman's critically worshipped *The Player*, but he walked away with the best actor prize at that year's Cannes Film Festival. If that was not enough to keep one ego buzzing, Robbins had another film at the festival, *Bob Roberts*, which

Tim Robbins bonding with real-life love Susan Sarandon in Ron Shelton's *Bull Durham*

FILMOGRAPHY

1982: *Tempest*; *P.K. and the Kid*. 1983: *Packin' It In* (TV); *Spacehunter: Adventures in the Forbidden Zone*. 1984: *Sixteen Candles*. 1985: *The Breakfast Club*; *Surviving* (TV). 1986: *Pretty in Pink*. 1987: *The Pick-Up Artist*; *King Lear*; *For Keeps* (UK: *Maybe Baby*). 1988: *Fresh Horses*. 1989: *Strike It Rich*. 1990: *Betsy's Wedding*; *Women & Men: Stories of Seduction* (episode: *Dusk Before Fireworks*) (TV). 1992: *Something To Live For: The Alison Gertz Story* (UK: *Fatal Love*) (TV); *Face the Music*. 1994: *Seven Sundays*; *The Stand*.

nizing with Robbins, and the duo have remained good friends ever since.

Robbins was another team member in *Top Gun* (as Merlin, Tom Cruise's co-pilot in the climactic dogfight), the biggest hit of 1986, and he then landed the human male lead in the same year's biggest flop – *Howard the Duck*. Robbins, looking absurdly young, was the geeky, bespectacled Phil Blumburtt (such a funny name), a would-be scientist who befriends the bird from outer space. Still, it was an experience.

It took two years and a number of worthy theatrical productions before Robbins would show his face on screen again. He reappeared, to good effect, opposite Jodie Foster and John Turturro in Tony Bill's excellent *Five Corners*, a gritty, atmospheric dramatic comedy. He was Harry, an earnest Bronx native caught up in the 1964 civil rights movement. For Robbins, it was the

Nightmares are made of this: Tim Robbins strapped down again – in Adrian Lyne's terrifying *Jacob's Ladder*

Robbins as the ruthless Hollywood executive Griffin Mill (with Greta Scacchi) in Robert Altman's acclaimed *The Player*

Robbins, a Greenwich Village folk singer (at one time his father was a member of The Highwaymen, who produced the No. 1 hit *Michael, Row the Boat Ashore*). Both his parents were staunch Democrats and dragged Tim and his siblings along to various Vietnam rallies and taught them about recycling before it became fashionable.

At the age of 12, Tim was already acting in experimental theatre and attended New York State University before transferring to the theatre course at the University of California, Los Angeles. Although he intended to move back to New York, he won an agent in Tinseltown and decided to make the most of it. He landed a string of cameos in some good TV shows, like *Hill Street Blues* and the first three episodes of *St Elsewhere*, and cornered the market playing psychos. 'I got to kill a lot of people,' the actor winced.

In 1981, he and a group of fellow UCLA students founded The Actor's Gang, for whom Robbins served as artistic director.

'We got together to buck the UCLA establishment,' Robbins explained. 'We wanted to do Surrealism, German Expressionism, a lot of strange shit. Anyway, not musicals or classical re-hashes. We

combined the discipline of Shakespeare with the vitality of rock 'n' roll.'

In 1984, Robbins was cast in the part of 'Ace' in *Toy Soldiers*, a reasonably well-tuned potboiler set in Latin America, starring Jason Miller and Cleavon Little. In the same year he found himself in Jerry Schatzberg's *No Small Affair*, way down the cast list below Jon Cryer and Demi Moore.

A year later he was 'one of the boys' in the execrable teen outing *Fraternity Vacation* (alongside, among others, Britt Ekland), and then had a good part – as Gary Cooper – in Rob Reiner's celebrated teenage romance *The Sure Thing*. The starring role went to John Cusack, but the latter was not above frater-

most important role of his film career to date.

Next, he teamed up with John Cusack in *Tapeheads*, in which they played a couple of security guards trying to make it in the LA music scene. The comedy was a little too hip for its own good, and although it attracted a small cult following, most dismissed it as too silly for words.

Then came *Bull Durham*. At the time (1988) the game of baseball was considered anathema in the hallowed halls of Hollywood. Nevertheless, Ron Shelton's wry, smartly calibrated *Bull Durham* gave the game a new sexual edge – and the movie became the sleeper hit of the US summer. Set in the dingy world of the minor league, the comedy submitted a trio of outstanding performances from three very hot actors. Kevin Costner was the world-weary catcher down on his luck, a spicy Susan Sarandon the fan who collected the sexual favours of players like trophies and Robbins the bull-headed pitcher with 'a megaton throw.' Of course, Costner and Sarandon were already well known outside the film community, but it was Robbins' naive, boastful Ebby Calvin 'Nuke' LaLoosh that captured the imagination of filmgoers. Who can forget the scene in which the rookie pitcher is tied to Sarandon's bed as she purrs Walt Whitman to him? Or the dream sequence in which he imagines himself on the field in nothing but a jock strap and garter belt.

Sarandon, although 12 years his senior, subsequently became the woman in Robbins's life, and mothered his two sons, Jack Henry and Miles Guthrie.

In 1989 Robbins joined Holly Hunter, Mary Steenburgen and Scott Glenn in the film version of Beth Henley's play *Miss Firecracker*, and continued his flirtation with comedy, playing Delmont 'Jughead' Williams, a loony who scrapes dogs off the highway for a living. He won the title role in another starry affair, Terry Jones's *Erik the Viking*, a very silly, Pythonesque romp that soured at the wickets. Explaining why he was attracted to the part, the actor asserted, 'basically, I feel I've been a Viking all my life. I have an affinity for the adventure. I like to take chances with my life and that takes a certain Viking spirit.'

Following a cameo in the would-be cult comedy *Twister*, Robbins ill-advisedly teamed up with Robin Williams in the manic *Cadillac Man*. A Feydeau farce crossed with a siege thriller, the melodrama featured Robbins as a demonically jealous husband who holds Williams hostage. Not a good move.

Adrian Lyne's psychological thriller *Jacob's Ladder* was considerably better, although it was a disturbing trip for the actor. At one point he wrote in his diary, 'the past two weeks have been nothing but horror. I find myself fraternizing less with the crew, taking refuge in my dressing room as much as I can ...' Five weeks later he confessed, 'I am getting lost in my role. My days are full of gut-wrenching emotional pain.' Robbins starred as Jacob Singer, a Vietnam vet haunted by demons in New York who imagines a terrible conspiracy. The film was not to everybody's taste, but overall it was a stylish, frightening and intellectually challenging addition to the horror genre.

Earlier, Robbins had had discussions with director Robert Altman about appearing in a

Tim Robbins as political candidate *Bob Roberts*, in the cult film he also wrote and directed and for which he sang his own songs

film called *Short Cuts*. When that project fell through, Altman turned to *The Player* and hired the actor to play the leading role of movie executive Griffin Mill. Till now, Robbins had played awkward, goofy, ingenuous men, at the mercy of those around him. Even when he was portraying arrogance (*Bull Durham*) or aggression (*Cadillac Man*), he was still one sandwich short of a picnic. With *The Player*, Altman was offering Robbins the chance to play a clever man, a knowingly callous manipulator to whom winning the game was everything. Yet, ruthless as Robbins' homicidal studio executive is, the actor still allows us to feel pity for him. Even as he beds his victim's girlfriend (Greta Scacchi), we feel for him. Yes, Tim Robbins had achieved the impossible: he had made a villain, if not likeable, at least sympathetic.

The Player proved to be both a critical success and a star-making platform for Robbins. He was now not only the lead of a hit movie, but his supporting cast was the stuff of legend. No fewer than 75 Hollywood names agreed to play themselves in the film, including Cher, Peter Gallagher, Jack Lemmon, Nick Nolte, Burt Reynolds, Julia Roberts, Susan Sarandon, Fred Ward, Bruce Willis and, of course, Tim's old pal John Cusack.

Cusack reappeared in *Bob Roberts*, Robbins's brilliant political satire about a

clean-cut, but decidedly corrupt candidate running for the US Senate (Robbins on icy good form). This, too, boasted its share of star cameos (Peter Gallagher, Alan Rickman, Susan Sarandon, James Spader, Fred Ward) – which just shows the sort of respect Tim Robbins commands in his profession. Even as *The Player* attacked the very gut of Hollywood, so every segment of its community wanted a piece of its action. And Tim Robbins, with a best actor prize on his mantel piece (and a Golden Globe nomination), was at the very centre of the frenzy.

He teamed up with Robert Altman again in *Short Cuts*, another ensemble piece, co-starring Robert Downey Jr, Peter Gallagher, Jennifer Jason Leigh, Jack Lemmon, Andie MacDowell, Matthew Modine, Lily Tomlin and Fred Ward, and then landed the lead in Joel and Ethan Coen's period industrial fantasy *The Hudsucker Proxy*, with Paul Newman, Jennifer Jason Leigh and Peter Gallagher in support.

FILMOGRAPHY

1984: *Toy Soldiers*; *No Small Affair*. 1985: *Fraternity Vacation*; *The Sure Thing*. 1986: *Top Gun*; *Howard the Duck*. 1988: *Five Corners*; *Tapeheads*; *Bull Durham*. 1989: *Miss Firecracker*; *Erik the Viking*; *Twister* (cameo). 1990: *Cadillac Man*; *Jacob's Ladder*. 1991: *Jungle Fever* (cameo). 1992: *The Player*; *Bob Roberts* (also wrote and directed). 1993: *Short Cuts*; *The Hudsucker Proxy*. 1994: *The Shawshank Redemption*; *Pret-a-Porter*; *I.Q.*.

Eric ROBERTS

Like a weed, Eric Anthony Roberts could spring up anywhere. He could be starring on Broadway in the highly-acclaimed *Burn This*, and then do an Italian TV mini-series, and then, on film, turn up opposite Cheech Marin in the hippy farce *Rude Awakening*. He is, in the vernacular of the business, 'a useful leading man', a committed actor who gives his all to his work, and is willing to try anything. With his sensuous, classical features, athletic grace and intense acting style, he has coloured many a monochromatic enterprise. And yet his career has so far failed to fulfil expectations.

He is at his best playing men on the edge. He turned in notable villains in *Star 80* and *Final Analysis*, and won an Oscar nomination for his role as an escaped convict in *Runaway Train*. He is a very good actor, but has been accused of over-doing the psychotic bit, while one viewer questioned in *Movieline* magazine opined, 'The creepiest thing about Eric Roberts is the way he talks. I mean, it sounds

like maybe he's on a low dose of some anti-psychotic drug and he has a spoonful of peanut butter stuck on the roof of his mouth.' He is also famous as the brother of Julia Roberts, an actress who made her film debut as his little sister in the costume melodrama *Blood Red*.

It was on 18 April 1956 when, he says, 'my mother was about to have me, and the airplane landed in Biloxi, Mississippi, and so I was born there.' The son of Walter Roberts, the blacklisted scriptwriter and founder of the Atlanta Actors and Writers Workshop, Eric was raised in Georgia and encouraged to act to cure his persistent stammer. 'My dad always found ways of making acting magical to me,' he recalls. 'He would wake me up in the middle of the night to see something special on TV. And I learned in grade school that if I memorized something, I wouldn't stutter, which made acting a cure.'

A young Eric Roberts in the 1978 *King of the Gypsies*

Roberts in an unlikely role as an ageing hippy – with Cheech Marin – in Aaron Russo's *Rude Awakening*

At seven, he was already appearing in such stage productions as *Charlie's Aunt*, *The Taming of the Shrew* and *A Member of the Wedding*, and at 15 won a place at RADA in London. That year he was also named America's national cross-country running champion. On his return from England, he enrolled at the American Academy of Dramatic Art in New York.

In 1977 he played Ted Bancroft in the long-running daytime soap *Another World*, and won the lead in his first film, *King of the Gypsies*, co-starring Sterling Hayden, Susan Sarandon and Brooke Shields. In the latter he played the title role, as the leader of a tribe of New York gypsies, and was nominated for a Golden Globe for his performance. The film's producer, Dino De Laurentiis, offered him a three-film contract, but the actor turned it down to concentrate on theatre. He also passed up a good part in Peter Yates's sleeper hit *Breaking Away*, afraid of being typecast as a juvenile lead. Instead, he waited three years until his next film, *Raggedy Man*, in which he starred opposite Sissy Spacek as Teddy, an enigmatic sailor who befriends her two kids and moves into her bed. When Teddy is banished from Spacek's life, the movie immediately lost its potency. *Raggedy Man* was not a commercial success, but critics noted Roberts's presence and versatility, although he almost lost the role. Shortly before he was due to make the film, he was involved in a car accident that put him in a coma for three days.

Again, he turned down a hit movie, *An Officer and a Gentleman*, waiting a further two years to play the thoroughly unstable Paul Snyder in Bob Fosse's gripping *Star 80*. Snyder was the real-life hustler who used Playmate of the Year Dorothy Stratten as his ticket to success, and who eventually murdered her. Roberts's chilling performance was the best in the film, and the actor won his second Golden Globe nomination.

A year later he was top-billed in Stuart Rosenberg's gritty drama *The Pope of Greenwich Village*, with Mickey Rourke and Daryl Hannah, as a loser who turns to crime, and then travelled to Australia to star in Dusan Makavejev's *The Coca Cola Kid*. The latter was a deliciously idiosyncratic comedy, in which Roberts played a narcissistic sales executive who tries to boost Coke sales Down Under. Greta Scacchi co-starred, but their relationship on set was strained (to say the least). 'The impression he gave me,' Scacchi confided, 'was that he didn't know I existed. He even ordered me off the set at one juncture.'

For *Runaway Train*, he put on 30 pounds

With Kim Basinger in Phil Joanou's cuticle-chewing thriller *Final Analysis*

and trained with weights to prepare for the character he described as, 'white trash, a man with no education, not very bright, but basically nice.' The film was a cuticle-chewing thriller, and earned Roberts and co-star Jon Voight Oscar nominations. He also became engaged at the time – to actress Dana Wheeler-Nicholson (but the liaison was short-lived).

And then his career nose-dived. *Slow Burn*, for TV, and the romantic comedy *Nobody's Fool*, with Rosanna Arquette, were both stillborn, although the actor did win good reviews for the TV movie *To Heal a Nation* (as real-life Vietnam vet Jan Scruggs). He had more luck on stage. When he took over from John Malkovich in Lanford Wilson's *Burn This*, he received the Theatre World Award.

Meanwhile, his films seemed to be a mixed bag of exploitation and TV movies, with few bright spots. Of the better entries, there was the surprisingly amusing and pertinent *Rude Awakening*, with Cheech Marin and Julie Hagerty. Roberts was on good form as a 1960s hippy who, after an absence of twenty years, returns to New York to find the world troubled by AIDS, acid rain and a depleted ozone layer. In the taut corkscrew thriller *Final Analysis*, he played a sleazy businessman married to Kim Basinger and gave the movie a nice edge of menace. Richard Gere, the film's star and executive producer, offered, 'Although Eric is probably a little younger than the character was conceived, he

brought something unexpected to the role. Eric is able to play the tough guy without making him a cliche. He is a very persuasive actor.' And then there was the exceptionally credible and gripping TV movie *Fugitive Among Us*, with Roberts as a sinister murder suspect hunted down by a Texan cop (Peter Strauss).

FILMOGRAPHY

1978: *King of the Gypsies*. 1980: *Paul's Case* (TV). 1981: *Raggedy Man*. 1983: *Star 80*; *Miss Lonelyhearts* (TV). 1984: *The Pope of Greenwich Village*; *The Coca Cola Kid*. 1985: *Runaway Train*. 1986: *Slow Burn* (TV); *Nobody's Fool*. 1987: *Dear America* (voice only). 1988: *To Heal a Nation* (TV); *Blood Red*. 1989: *Into Thin Air*; *Grandmother's House*; *Rude Awakening*; *Best of the Best*. 1990: *Fire Princess*; *The Lost Capone* (TV); *The Ambulance*; *Descending Angel* (TV). 1991: *By the Sword*; *Lonely Hearts*. 1992: *Final Analysis*; *Vendetta*; *Fugitive Among Us* (TV). 1993: *Mistress Cottage*; *Best of the Best II*; *Voyage*; *Love, Cheat and Steal*; *Free Fall*; *Love is a Gun*. 1994: *The Specialist*; *Babyfever*; *The Last Mafia Marriage*; *Heaven's Prisoners*.

Julia ROBERTS

In 1988 Julia Roberts was paid $50,000 to play one of the leading roles in *Mystic Pizza*. Four years later she was touted as the highest paid actress of all time, reportedly commanding $7 million a picture (one source quoted her price to be as high as $12m). In

four years she had accumulated six hits to her name, and audiences just couldn't get enough of her.

It was easy to see why. She had a smile that could run a nuclear power station, legs that went all the way to China and a naturalness that was just plain irresistible. She also possessed a sunny, dynamic beauty that gave entire streets of men neck ache. And yet she was the first to knock her own looks. Described as 'the lips of the 1990s', she owned up that, 'there was a time in high school when I felt a little grief because I had an unusual mouth, unlike the other girls who had perfect mouths with little heart-top lips. My mouth is crooked and I have a couple of little scars...' Equally, she has dismissed her luxuriant, spectacular hair as 'total straw'. She then caps her autobiographical assault with, 'I'm too tall to be a lady, and I never had enough dresses to be a lady, and I wouldn't call myself a woman. I'd say I'm somewhere between a chick and a broad.'

As an actress, she has elicited nothing but praise from her colleagues. Joel Schumacher, who directed her in *Flatliners* and *Dying Young*, feels, 'there's this wonderful dichotomy with Julia. There's this woman, this little girl, this shit-kicker, this very innocent lady. There's a *My Fair Lady* thing in there, and I think the reason she can pull it off is that all those

The Face That Launched a Thousand Stories: Julia Roberts

The film was then abandoned, putting an estimated 200 English technicians out of work. The native tabloids accused Roberts of single-handedly destroying the British film industry, while others applauded her guts and business sense.

She was also a leading contender for the role of Catwoman in *Batman Returns*. However, when the chosen one – Annette Bening – became pregnant, the part went to Michelle Pfeiffer. This in itself is ironic, as Pfeiffer had earlier been put on hold to play Tinkerbell in Steven Spielberg's *Hook* – following Roberts's hospitalization for nervous exhaustion. But Ms Roberts recovered, and played the mischievous elf in what turned out to be her seventh box-office hit. It seemed to be the story of her life. Everything was a battle, but the results paid dividends.

She was born Julie Roberts on 28 October 1967 in Smyrna, Georgia, the daughter of Walter Roberts, the blacklisted

Julia Roberts (*left*) in her first screen success, Donald Petrie's captivating, low-budget *Mystic Pizza* (with Lili Taylor)

Julia as the *Pretty Woman* who steals the heart of Richard Gere

people are in her.' Patrick Bergin, who played her brutal husband in *Sleeping With the Enemy*, believes, 'Julia just gives everything to what she's doing. She doesn't know any way of blocking that. In a sense, she's got no technique. If it's not happening, it's not happening.'

Of course, her leading men are famous for falling in love with her. For a while, she shared her life with Liam Neeson (who played her lover in *Satisfaction*), was briefly engaged to Dylan McDermott (her husband in *Steel Magnolias*), was linked to Richard Gere (*Pretty Woman*) and engaged to Kiefer Sutherland (*Flatliners*).

She was also much in demand from the studios who seemed to be endlessly publicizing new Julia Roberts movies that never materialized.

She was due to appear opposite Kiefer Sutherland in *Renegades*; was set to star with Tom Cruise in *The Princess of Mars*, for director John McTiernan; and was even announced to play the Amish wife of a 12-year-old Macaulay Culkin in the comedy *Holy Matrimony*. And then there was the *Shakespeare in Love* debacle.

In 1992, she was signed up to star in Universal's period romantic drama to be directed by Ed Zwick in England, from a screenplay by Tom Stoppard. She was to play a woman who disguises herself as an 'actor', triggering a hormonal rush from Shakespeare himself at a time when actresses were deemed unseemly. Daniel Day-Lewis was plugged as everybody's favourite Bard, but when he turned the project down, Roberts surveyed Universal's four replacements – Sean Bean, Ralph Fiennes, Colin Firth and Paul McGann – and passed on the project.

screenwriter who, with his wife, ran a local drama school. Her older brother is Eric Roberts, the actor who made his name in such pictures as *King of the Gypsies*, *Star 80* and *Runaway Train* – but, Julia declares, 'we're really different. He went to the Royal Academy of Dramatic Arts in London and I'm a kamikaze actress.' Their parents divorced when she was four, and their father died when she was nine. At first, she owns up, 'I said I wanted to be a veterinarian, but I was just afraid to admit that I wanted to be an actor.' As high school graduation approached, she gave herself three options. 'I could go to the University of Georgia, get married or move to New York. Nobody was asking me to get married, and I wasn't fond of higher education, so I moved to New York and began studying acting. I didn't know what else I could do.'

In New York she worked at a women's clothing store, did some brief modelling for the Click agency and changed her name after joining the Screen Actors Guild (to avoid confusion with another Julie Roberts). In 1986 Eric got her an acting job in the historical melodrama *Blood Red*, playing his younger sister. However, the film was deemed so bad that it failed to secure a release until the end of 1990, and even then it evaporated. She then had a bit on the TV cop series *Crime Story*, and had a decent role – as a man-devouring bass player – in the awful rock-'n'-roll caper *Satisfaction*. Next came the engaging HBO movie *Baja Oklahoma*, in which she played the plucky daughter of barmaid-songwriter Lesley Ann Warren, and then the role of Daisy Araju in *Mystic Pizza*. This was a vibrant, low-budget saga about three animated waitresses who work at Leona's Mystic Pizzeria in Connecticut, following their various adventures with the opposite sex. Superbly played by the three actresses – Roberts, Annabeth Gish and Lili Taylor – the film was a piquantly honest and touching tale that became the sleeper American hit of 1988.

When Daryl Hannah turned down the role of Shelby Eatenton Latcherie to play the less glamorous part of Annelle in *Steel Magnolias*, Julia Roberts was cast in her place and found herself up against the most impressive line-up of star actresses in recent history. Besides Hannah, there was Olympia Dukakis, Shirley MacLaine, Dolly Parton and Sally Field, and every one an Oscar contender. The film, based on the stage play by Robert Harling, gave everybody a chance to chew the Southern scenery, and they all did it sublimely – but it was Roberts's delicate, heart-breaking performance as Sally Field's tragic daughter that won the only Oscar nomination from the film. She also landed the Golden Globe Award, while the picture steamed off with $81 million at the US box-office, an extraordinary amount of money for a 'woman's film.'

Next, she was offered the role of Willem Dafoe's fiancee in the harrowing *Triumph of the Spirit*, based on a true story set in Auschwitz. She was required to shave her head for the part, and turned the offer down. As it happens, it was a prudent decision.

Disney were making a romantic comedy about a working-class hooker, and needed a very special actress to pull off the central role. According to one producer, 'there was no one else who could've played this part. What we needed was a *woman*. And few actresses today seem like women. There are a lot of beautiful *girls*, but Julia Roberts is a beautiful *woman*. You don't know how rare that is.'

Although a low-budget movie by Hollywood standards (costing less than $20m), *Three Thousand* (by which it was then known) was still a major picture and Roberts had the leading role. Ecstatic, she rang her mother. 'My mom works for the Catholic archdiocese of Atlanta,' the actress revealed. 'I mean, my mom's boss *baptized* me! So I called her at work, and it was like, "Hi, Mom. I got a job." She said, "You did? What'd you get?" And I said, "Oh, it's a Disney movie! I gotta go, Mom, I'll talk to you later."' Eventually, *Three Thousand* had its named changed to *Pretty Woman*, Richard Gere was brought in as the male lead, and the film grossed $170 million in the US, making it the second biggest hit of 1990 (after *Ghost*), beating out such box-office certainties as *Die Hard 2* and *Total Recall*.

We first see the eponymous prostitute, Vivian Ward, half naked in bed. The rump belonged to stand-in Shelley Michelle, but the fabulous 5'9" body striding down the sidewalk shortly afterwards was all Julia's: complete with blonde wig, thigh-high boots and an eight-inch blue leather skirt. She is the hooker from Heaven, fresh on the streets with a heart ready to be broken. When Prince Charming (Gere) turns up in his flash Lotus, takes her to his flash hotel and offers her a business proposition to be his escort for a week – for $3,000 – the film revved up into an MTV *Pygmalion*. Of course, this was strictly Mills & Boon stuff, but thanks to the to-die-for magnetism of the stars, particularly Julia's seductive, vulnerable and incredulous Vivian, the film was eight-piston entertainment, polished kitsch for audiences baying for unerring escapism. And, not only was Roberts's Vivian the model little-girl-lost, but the actresses's comic timing was perfect. Who can forget the scene, when at the races she is told, 'Edward's the most eligible bachelor. Everybody is trying to land him.', to which she breezily replied, 'Well, I'm not trying to land him. I'm just using him for sex.'? For her performance, she was nominated for her second Oscar (this time as best actress), and won her second Golden Globe. She was also voted NATO/ShoWest's Female Star of the Year, an accolade chosen by America's

As the battered wife of Patrick Bergin in Joseph Ruben's box-office triumph, *Sleeping With the Enemy*

cinema owners.

Next, she was in another hit – Joel Schumacher's MTV thriller *Flatliners* – in which she played Rachel Mannus, a private and intensely focused medical student severely into the concept of life-after-death. Thus, she volunteers for a clandestine experiment in which her heart is stopped under scientific supervision (courtesy of fellow students Kiefer Sutherland, Kevin Bacon and William Baldwin), and then revived moments later. 'Rachel is obsessed with the idea of death and making sure that, when you die, you're going to a good place,' the actress explained. The film grossed a flashy $10m in its opening week, and provoked reams of praise from the critics. *Rolling Stone* raved that Ms Roberts, 'combines beauty with a no-bull delivery that commands attention. Her private moments . . . have an emotional intensity that is more compelling than all the hokum in the lab,' while *Variety* volunteered that, 'the remarkably gifted Roberts is the film's true grace note.' This time she received the Movie Award for 'best actress in a drama'.

In Joseph Ruben's romantic thriller *Sleeping With the Enemy*, she played Laura Burney, who fakes her own death to escape her husband's brutality. The project had been kicking around for a while, and had been earmarked for Kim Basinger for more than a year. However, when Twentieth Century Fox couldn't come up with a leading man to fit Ms Basinger's taste, she left the project. Basinger wanted Kevin Costner or Harrison Ford, but Julia was happy with Patrick Bergin, an Irish actor with enough menacing presence to scare the lips off her. Indeed, the wife-battering sequences were harrowing in the extreme, causing the crew and director some alarm. It was, she admits, 'physically the biggest part I've had, and the most exhausting.' One scene involved her being beaten to the floor, and the actress's fall was so authentic that Ruben admitted, 'I almost stopped the take. I thought she had hurt herself. Instead, what it did was open up this outpouring of tears and fears and emotion. She went all the way – to the point where everybody who was there was horrified. But she was willing to do that to get to that place where she really needed to be.' Again, her combination of effervescence and fragility went straight to the heart, but the film was too one-dimensional and slick to fully engage the emotions. Nevertheless, it grossed over $100 million in America alone, and was still drawing sizeable audiences when *Dying Young* opened.

Insiders blamed the title. And, to be honest, '*Dying Young*' was hardly a name to attract swarms of cinemagoers looking for a good time. But the film was not much good either. Ms Roberts played another working class girl with great legs (yes, she wore a mini-skirt), who answers an ad to look after a wealthy, good-looking guy (Campbell Scott)

Julia with Campbell Scott in *Dying Young*, the flop that proved the actress could not overcome a lousy title

who is dying of leukemia. Inevitably, they fall in love, spout platitudes to beautiful music ('I have only one thing to give you – my heart') and discover that life is worth fighting for. It was all very lush and staged, and the film died young at the box-office with a disappointing $32m in the US bank.

Meanwhile, Julia had hooked up romantically with Kiefer Sutherland (who had left his wife and child for her) and the publicity machine had started grinding out news of The Wedding. The big day was set for 14 June 1991, but things looked dicey when Julia found out about Kiefer's fling with the stripper Amanda Rice. In May, she started work on Steven Spielberg's epic fantasy *Hook*, playing Tinkerbell to Robin Williams's Peter Pan and Dustin Hoffman's Captain. The budget was said to be in the $70 million range, and executives became nervous when Roberts was hospitalized. She was looking decidedly pale, took to wearing sun glasses and complained of severe headaches. In June, the week before the wedding, the actress cancelled the ceremony (estimated to cost $500,000) and, on the very hour she was due to voice her wedding vows, left for a week's holiday in Ireland – with the actor Jason Patric on her arm. The rumour machine went into overdrive; while the *Hook* executives were looking even more nervous. At least one newspaper suggested she had gone to Ireland to rekindle her affair with Liam Neeson, but the *National Enquirer* assured us that she 'RUNS AWAY WITH GROOM'S BEST FRIEND' – Patric (the two actors had worked together on Joel

Schumacher's *The Lost Boys*). In July, Julia had moved in with Patric and finished her chores on *Hook*, much to the relief of certain executives. She then went on another holiday with her new boyfriend, while the rumour mill suggested she was engaged and/or pregnant. In December 1991, *Hook* was savaged by the critics, most of whom seemed to miss the entire point of the film. Still, audiences loved its fresh approach to the J.M. Barrie classic, gobbled up the magical special effects and revelled in the guest cameos (Glenn Close, Phil Collins, rock star David Crosby). Julia was simply irresistible as the mutinous, ethereal Tinkerbell, and the picture went on to gross $250 worldwide.

She then took a well-earned rest, reassessed her career, and poked fun at herself (for free) in Robert Altman's *The Player*, one of the most highly acclaimed films of 1992. In the latter she played herself, who appears alongside Bruce Willis (as himself) in a fictitious film in which the latter bravely rescues her character from the electric chair. Meanwhile, she and Jason Patric had broken up, and she was seen in the company of various men, including her fitness trainer and an actor friend of her ex-lover. She finally put the lid on all the tabloid rumours when she married singer-actor Lyle Lovett, who played the cop-cum-suspect in *The Player*.

She then starred in Alan J. Pakula's highly efficient film version of John Grisham's best-selling legal thriller, *The Pelican Brief*, and joined Nick Nolte in the romantic comedy *I Love Trouble*, as a newspaper reporter. Then, for the phenomenal sum of $10 million (a record for an actress), she was signed to play the title role in Stephen Frears's *Mary Reilly*, as the chambermaid to Dr Jekyll.

FILMOGRAPHY

1988: *Blood Red*; *Satisfaction* (aka *Girls of Summer*); *Baja Oklahoma* (TV); *Mystic Pizza*. **1989:** *Steel Magnolias*. **1990:** *Pretty Woman*; *Flatliners*. **1991:** *Sleeping With the Enemy*; *Dying Young*; *Hook*. **1992:** *The Player*. **1993:** *The Pelican Brief*. **1994:** *I Love Trouble*; *Mary Reilly*; *Pret-a-Porter*; *Tracks*.

Meg RYAN

Meg Ryan was one of the most irresistible new stars of the late 1980s. She was cute, bubbly, bright as a button and very, very funny. She was also sexy, although she retaliates with: 'I never thought I was real sexy. I'm sexy sometimes, but I'm never going to be a glamourpuss.'

In a relatively short period, she stole a scene from Tom Cruise in *Top Gun* (her third

film), partnered the likes of John Candy, Dennis Quaid and Sean Connery, and then became a household name in *When Harry Met Sally ...* – all because of one sequence. You know the scene:

Harry Burns (Billy Crystal) and Sally Albright (Ryan) are enjoying a meal in a New York delicatessen. It's Manhattan, the clientele are predominantly Jewish and winter is in the air. Harry and Sally are just good friends, chatting about the great divide between the sexes. But Sally is getting a trifle annoyed by Harry's attitude. Harry, on the other hand, is attempting to be as casual as his masculinity will allow. Taking a large bite of her stacked sandwich Sally announces, 'You are a human affront to all women – and I am a woman.'

Taking the defence, Harry counters, 'Hey, I don't feel great about this, but I don't hear anybody complain.'

'Of course not. You're out of the door too fast.'

'I think they have an OK time.'

'How do you know?'

'Whadya mean "how do I know?" I know.'

'Because they ... ' Sally gesticulates with her left hand in a circular motion.

'Yes, because they ... ' Harry copies her, irritated.

Sally, repeating the motion, continues, 'How do you know that they're really ... ?'

Harry, clearly annoyed by now, speaks as if to a deaf child: 'What – are – you – saying? That – they – fake – orgasm?'

'It's possible.'

'Get out of here.'

'Why? Most women at one time or another have faked it.'

'Well, they haven't faked it with me.'

'How do you know?'

'Because, I ... '

'Oh. Right. That's right,' Sally declares firmly, screwing up her napkin. 'I forgot. You're a man.'

'What is that supposed to mean?'

'Nothing. It's just that all men are sure it never happens to them and most women at one time or another have done it. So you figure it out.'

Harry, amazed: 'You don't think that I could tell the difference?'

Sally, quietly: 'No.'

'Get out of here.'

Sally quietly surveys her partner. Her eyes burn with defiance. Her stare, unnoticed, declares war. Its message is clear: YOU – HAVE – GONE – TOO – FAR. It's the sort of chin-clenching expression of determination that can shrivel the apparatus of a Greek statue. Then it is gone.

Sally Albright lowers her eyes. For a split

Meg Ryan with Martin Short in Joe Dante's riotous sci-fi comedy *Innerspace*

second a smile plays at the corners of her gorgeous mouth. And then she slips out the first groan.

It was that scene in *When Harry Met Sally ...* that made Meg Ryan a star. It was a scene that became almost as famous as the movie itself. The Scene In Which Meg Ryan Fakes An Orgasm In A Crowded Delicatessen.

Considering the actress's shyness, it's amazing that Meg suggested the idea for the sequence in the first place. 'There are very few times in the movie where Sally one-ups Harry, so I thought it might as well be good,' the actress explains. 'The night before the scene I sat in my hotel room writing down every ooooh and aaaah so that I had a diagram of what I was going to do in my head. But when it came to the first take it was really hard. There I was in front of 150 New York extras, all listening. The worst thing was that nobody else was doing it with me. Usually you do a love scene and everybody fakes it, and it's on a closed set. Not in a restaurant. As we went on I was oooohing and aaaaahing off-camera as well as on. I did so many takes ... '

But it was worth every groan. The sequence became the most memorable in the movie. The film was a surprise hit, grossing over $91 million at the US box-office alone, and for her performance Meg Ryan was nominated for a Golden Globe award as best actress and actually won the American Comedy Award.

She was born on 19 November 1961 in

the Norman Rockwell town of Bethel, Fairfield County, in Connecticut. She had a comfortable upbringing, her parents were both teachers and young Meg strived to be an exemplary daughter. At school, she was voted homecoming queen ('the girl they chose first was suspended'), and endeavoured to be 'a do-gooder type.' Her parents divorced when she was 15 and her mother, who was active in amateur dramatics, dabbled in casting, sent Meg to audition for the role of Debby, Candice Bergen's daughter in *Rich and Famous*. She got it. She had ten lines but, because of an actors strike, it took her five months to complete her role. She found the experience, she says, 'too overwhelming. I didn't understand actors.' Still, acting seemed a profitable way to pay for night classes in journalism at New York University, and so Meg persevered. She won the role of Betsy Stewart Montgomery Andropoulos in the daytime soap *As The World Turns*, working 14-hour days for two years. 'I was kidnapped. I was pregnant. I was married to a psychotic paraplegic. But I learned how to act,' she recalls.

In 1984, she quit school and TV (Betsy was severely injured in a car accident), travelled to Europe, tried school again, and then decided on a full-time acting career. She played Callie Oaks, the owner of a newspaper, in Disney's Western TV series *Wildside* (it lasted a month), and then took a small role (Lisa) in *Amityville 3-D*, popped up in the TV movie *One of the Boys*, with Mickey Rooney, and then played Anthony Edwards's wife Carole in *Top Gun*. In the last named she had three scenes, filmed over three days, and stole each one of them. But the scene everyone remembers is the one in which

Meg with the man of her dreams, Dennis
Quaid, in the 1988 thriller *D.O.A.*

Edwards improvises 'Great Balls of Fire' on
the piano and Ryan screams to him, 'Hey,
Goose, you big stud. Take me to bed or lose
me forever!'

The film was a huge success (the biggest
that year) and Meg was in demand. She had
a good role in the derisory *Armed and
Dangerous*, and stole the film from John
Candy, and was then given the female lead in
the vastly entertaining fantasy *Innerspace*,
executive-produced by Steven Spielberg. She
played Lydia Maxwell, a feisty journalist in
search of ex-boyfriend Dennis Quaid, a
micro-sized astronaut injected into the rear
end of Martin Short. Short glowed at the
time, 'Meg's a phenomenal actress and she
has just enough self-doubt to make her even

Meg Ryan as Pamela Courson, Jim
Morrison's wife, in Oliver Stone's *The Doors*

Billy Crystal meets Meg Ryan in Rob Reiner's
magical *When Harry Met Sally . . .*

better. She takes a role that could be
something we've seen before and turns it
into something we've never seen.' Quaid, too,
was struck by his co-star: 'Meg has such great
range,' he marvelled, 'she's really a female
chameleon.'

Next, she took her most dramatic role to
date, playing a pink-haired drifter with
sexuality to burn, in the Robert Redford-
produced *Promised Land*, opposite Kiefer
Sutherland. She was re-teamed with Quaid in
the film noir thriller *D.O.A.* (a remake of the
1950 classic), playing an 18-year-old student

Meg Ryan in the huge 1993 box-office hit
Sleepless in Seattle

infatuated by her dying professor (Quaid). This time the sparks really flew, and Quaid and Ryan quietly became 'an item' (although the latter kept on her small apartment with the actress Daphne Zuniga).

In Peter Hyams's testosterone-packed *The Presidio*, she played Lt Col Sean Connery's spirited daughter (who falls for her father's old adversary, Mark Harmon), a role which she described as 'a hot vixen.' She was good, but, frankly, her part slowed down the action. She then lost the role of Tom Cruise's girlfriend in *Rain Man*, but her next picture more than made up.

This was Rob Reiner's *When Harry Met Sally . . .* , an effervescent, bittersweet New York comedy about a man and woman who meet, hate each other, become friends and do everything in their power not to become lovers. A stylish and engaging look at the battle of the sexes, the film highlighted Ryan's best performance to date, a plucky demonstration of a woman confused by love.

In the plodding, structurally sabotaged *Joe Vs the Volcano*, she played three roles, but failed to really shine in any of them. The film didn't seem to know what it wanted to be, and co-star Tom Hanks didn't seem to know what he was doing. Nevertheless, *Joe* clocked up $40 million in the States, so it wasn't a total failure. Neither was Ryan's personal life,

which saw her and Dennis Quaid finally tie the knot on St Valentine's Day (1991).

Again, she was wasted in Oliver Stone's ambitious *The Doors*, playing rock legend Jim Morrison's flower child wife, Pamela Courson. Still, who could turn down an opportunity to work with Stone? She did, however, turn down the lead in *The Butcher's Wife* which, although a box-office flop, was an enchanting romantic fantasy which might have been even better had Ryan played the role of the naive clairvoyant (in place of Demi Moore, who was miscast).

Still, Meg had an even more important production in the works – Jack Henry, who was born by caesarean section on 24 April, 1992. Three months later, the actress popped up in the romantic fantasy *Prelude To a Kiss*, playing the role originated by Mary-Louise Parker in the Broadway original. Alec Baldwin co-starred (recreating his stage performance), and the film received favourable reviews, but audiences failed to embrace the story of a love-struck beauty who ends up in the body of an old man.

She was re-teamed with Tom Hanks and director Nora Ephron (who had scripted *When Harry Met Sally . . .*) in the unusual romance *Sleepless in Seattle*, inspired by the 1957 tear-jerker *An Affair To Remember* (with Cary Grant and Deborah Kerr). Ryan played a young woman about to get married in Baltimore, but who's spiritually destined for Hanks, a mourning widower in Seattle. The joke is that they never meet until the end of the movie . . . It was one of the biggest hits of 1993.

She then joined Quaid for the third time, in Steve Kloves's *Flesh and Bone*, co-starring James Caan, and starred opposite Andy Garcia in the romantic drama *When a Man Loves a Woman*.

FILMOGRAPHY

1981: *Rich and Famous*. **1983**: *Amityville 3-D*. **1985**: *One of the Boys* (TV). **1986**: *Top Gun*; *Armed and Dangerous*. **1987**: *Innerspace*; *Promised Land*. **1988**: *D.O.A.* (UK: *Dead On Arrival*); *The Presidio*. **1989**: *When Harry Met Sally . . .* **1990**: *Joe Vs the Volcano*. **1991**: *The Doors*. **1992**: *Prelude To a Kiss*. **1993**: *Sleepless in Seattle*; *Flesh and Bone*. **1994**: *When a Man Loves a Woman*; *I.Q.*; *Restoration*.

Winona RYDER

The whole world was in love with Winona Ryder. At least, those who had seen her movies. Saddled with a very pretty face and an enviable body, Winona Ryder was also bright, well-read, outspoken and very funny.

And she could act the socks off her contemporaries.

Britain's *Telegraph Magazine* accused her of being 'the most exciting young actress in America'; *You* magazine echoed the phrase verbatim; and *Rolling Stone* called her 'the single most exciting actress of her generation.' Well, everybody was saying it, really. Tim Burton, who directed the actress in *Beetlejuice* and *Edward Scissorhands*, went one further: 'She's the best. She has something you can't even talk about. She's a throwback to movie stars throughout film history. There's something about her skin and her eyes and her ability and her gravity that you can't verbalize. Magical.'

Jim McBride, director of *Great Balls of Fire!*, is also a fan. 'It's amazing that Winona can be so sophisticated yet so unaffected. She's very sexy without seeming to be somebody who has a lot of sexual experience. She's just so charming and seductive, she's impossible to resist.'

Winona herself finds it hard to understand what all the fuss is about: 'My friend and her boyfriend had just seen *Mermaids*, and they were, like, saying, "You were *really* sexy in that." I was like "*What?*" That was, like, the most unsexy thing I've ever done.'

By the time she was 19, Winona Ryder had clocked up nine movies and had invariably received shining reviews. There were, however, a few dissenters. 'I did this press junket for *Mermaids*,' she recalls, 'and everyone there was saying, "Why are you always playing teenagers?" And, like, I'm 19, what am I supposed to do – play a judge?'

Besides her startling performances in some rather good films, she was also receiving publicity for her engagement to Johnny Depp. Depp, who made his name in the TV series *21 Jump Street*, had already been married to the musician Lori Anne Allison, five years his senior, and had subsequently been engaged to Sherilyn Fenn and Jennifer Grey. His was not a good track record. Depp and Winona first spotted each other at the premiere of *Great Balls of Fire!* ('It was a classic glance,' he says; she adding: 'It wasn't a long moment, but it was suspended.'). They finally dated months later, discovered a mutual obsession for J.D. Salinger, and to prove his undying love for her, he had 'Winona Forever' tattooed on his arm. For a while, they were the hottest couple in Hollywood. Later, tabloid numours paired her with Daniel Day-Lewis and other men, but whatever the invented fiction her engagement to Depp was off. In retrospect, she revealed about the break-up: 'I was just really young. I don't know what his excuse is, but that's mine.'

Winona Ryder with Jason Robards in *Square Dance*, her second film

Winona with Christian Slater in Michael Lehmann's revolutionary teen comedy *Heathers*

Born Winona Laura Horowitz on 29 October 1971, in Winona, Minnesota, the actress was the third of four children. Her father, Michael, was a bohemian intellectual and established a well-known bookshop, 'Flashback Books', in Petaluma, California, specializing in the Beat generation of the 1960s. Her mother, Cindy, headed her own video production company. Her godfather is the psychologist and LSD authority Timothy Leary.

As a child, she attended Black Flag and Agent Orange protests and spent a year travelling round South America. She admits that, 'I was a really weird kid', and enjoyed dressing up in boys' clothes while sporting a very short haircut. Once, she was mistaken for a 'faggot' and beaten up, but she brushes off the experience with a casual, 'It was sort of great. I felt like a real gangster or something.'

Recognizing the eccentricity of their child, Michael and Cindy Horowitz enrolled her at the American Conservatory Theatre in San Francisco. There, she was spotted in a school play by talent scout Deborah Lucchesi and

put forward for a screen test. The film was *Desert Bloom*, starring Jon Voight, but the role of Rose finally went to Annabeth Gish. Instead, Winona (or Noni, to her friends) won a good part (as a love-sick schoolgirl ignored by Corey Haim) in *Lucas*, opposite fellow unknown Charlie Sheen. She had also stumbled across a screenplay by Alan Hines, *Square Dance*, but, she says, 'thought the movie had already been made.' As it happens, the director Daniel Petrie had been scouring the countryside for a suitable female lead and was coming to the end of his tether. Winona auditioned, and a week later was starring in the movie.

Square Dance was the story of Gemma, a naive 13-year-old living with her grandfather (Jason Robards) on a Texas egg farm. Out of the blue, her mother (Jane Alexander) turns up to reclaim her, sending Gemma into shock. The girl refuses to accompany Mom back to Fort Worth, but after much soul-searching boards a bus to find her. Once in the big city, she falls for a retarded 21-year-old boy (Rob Lowe).

If nothing else, the picture was a platform for some exceptional acting. Rob Lowe was nominated for a Golden Globe for his turn, and Robards and Alexander were showered with praise. However, it was Winona who truly stole the movie, but was so good that nobody noticed she was acting.

It wasn't until her next picture, Tim Burton's colossal box-office hit *Beetlejuice*, that Hollywood sat up with a jolt. As the morgue-friendly Lydia Deetz, a pocket version of Morticia, she was an absolute scream. Veiled in black, she befriends ghosts Alec Baldwin and Geena Davis in favour of her own family and delivers her lines with the deadpan subtlety of an actress twice her age.

She took a step back with the meditative teen drama *1969* which, she admits she did 'because I was 16 years old, I was really bored, and I wanted to work. It was a big mistake.' Robert Downey Jr and Kiefer Sutherland shared the error.

However, she relished the role of Myra Gale, the 13-year-old child bride of Jerry Lee Lewis (Dennis Quaid) in *Great Balls of Fire!* Till now, this was the best dramatic work she had handled, and while Quaid played with his piano tops she quietly stole his thunder. It was an energetic, knockabout screen biography – and well-hyped – but was a disappointment at the box-office.

Much, much better was *Heathers*, a cunning black comedy that put *Blue Velvet* through high school. Winona played Veronica, a reluctant member of a bitch-riddled peer-pressure group, who mutinies when she teams up with a gun-toting Christian Slater. The actress enthuses, 'it turned out one of the best movies I've ever seen in my life.'

There was another treat in store with *Welcome Home, Roxy Carmichael*, a witty, off-beat comedy-drama about a 15-year-old misfit, Dinky Bossetti (Ryder), who imagines herself the daughter of the town's returning celebrity. Nicknamed 'Rosemary's Baby' by her legal mother, Dinky is a quirky cross

Winona with Gary Oldman in the box-office smash *Bram Stoker's Dracula*

Winona as 'Joan Arc' in Richard Benjamin's *Mermaids*

Winona in a dramatic shift of image for Jim Jarmusch's sublime *Night On Earth*

between Joan of Arc, Saint Clare and James Dean, and was winningly played by Winona at the top of her form. Unfortunately, the film was swallowed up in distribution hell and few were lucky enough to find it.

More successful was Richard Benjamin's *Mermaids* thanks, no doubt, to the stellar presence of Cher, Bob Hoskins and a top-selling soundtrack. Winona (who replaced Emily Lloyd) portrayed another 15-year-old, Charlotte, who dreams of being a nun and parades under the sobriquet of 'Joan Arc'. While Cher appeared ill-at-ease as Charlotte's man-devouring mother, and Bob Hoskins did his cheery American routine for the umpteenth time, Winona proved to be the only thing worth watching. Deservedly, she was voted best supporting actress by the National Board of Review.

On a roll, she starred in Tim Burton's exquisite modern fairy tale *Edward Scissorhands*. An updating of *The Beauty and the Beast*, the film featured Winona as a suburban teenager who falls for the misfit of the title (Johnny Depp), a gentle soul whose hands are replaced with metallic shears. Both a magical love story and a witty satire on

modern Americana, *Edward Scissorhands* should have been a much bigger hit than it was.

She was then signed up to play Mary Corleone – Al Pacino's daughter – in Francis Ford Coppola's long-awaited, final installment of *The Godfather* trilogy. Arriving in Rome on the back of three movies, Winona collapsed from a debilitating upper respiratory infection and retired from the picture. Coppola replaced her at the eleventh hour with his own daughter, Sofia.

After a much-needed rest, the actress appeared in Jim Jarmusch's inventive five-part omnibus film *Night On Earth*. Winona had asked her agent to arrange a meeting with Jarmusch, as she was an enormous fan of his work (*Stranger Than Paradise*, *Down by Law*, *Mystery Train*). It was a mutual admiration society. He says, 'When I met her I really liked her energy and enthusiasm, her interest in certain kinds of music, books and films; a lot of things. We just got along really well.' He suggested writing a part for her in his

next movie, and she was over the moon.

Jarmusch makes a habit of creating parts for people he likes, and he gave Winona a plum on a plate. She played a chain-smoking, down-to-earth LA taxi driver who is offered the chance to become a movie star (by casting director Gena Rowlands). But, in true Jarmusch fashion, she turns the offer down to pursue her dream of becoming a mechanic.

Meanwhile, Francis Coppola had been considering a script Winona had given him: James V. Hart's *Dracula – The Untold Story*. Based on Bram Stoker's original 1897 novel (as yet not translated faithfully to the screen),

the property fired Coppola's enthusiasm, both for its historical context and for its human allegory. 'I never thought he would even read it,' the actress recalls. 'I thought he would be too busy, or not interested.' On the contrary, Coppola had been a fan of the novel since reading it to a group of eight-and nine-year-old boys at summer camp.

Later, Winona discovered that she and Coppola, 'liked the same things about the script, which was very romantic and sensual and epic, a real love story that was very passionate. It's not really a vampire movie. To me, it's more about the man Dracula, the warrior, the prince.' Winona was cast both as the fiancee of Vlad the Impaler – in fifteenth century Transylvania – and as the nineteenth century English innocent, Mina Murray. Although her accent wasn't entirely consistent, her performance demonstrated a new dramatic range – and sexuality. The film, retitled *Bram Stoker's Dracula*, went on to become the most commercially successful the actress had appeared in.

During shooting, she was sitting in her trailer when the phone rang. It was Martin Scorsese. 'I was just, like, "Oh. Yes. Mr Scorsese. Hello." I was so caught off-guard.' He was offering her the role of May Welland in his adaptation of Edith Wharton's romantic drama *The Age of Innocence*. It just happened that Winona wrote about the novel in her final high school English report and won an 'A' for it. 'And he was going, "So we're going to do this, and it will be fun. Yeah. Looking forward to it." And I was, like, "OK." And then I kind of just flipped out in my trailer. Inside, I was, like, "Oh my God, I can't wait for three months from now."' Her co-stars were to be Daniel Day-Lewis and Michelle Pfeiffer, but it was Winona who eventually walked off with a Golden Globe for her performance.

After that, she joined another stellar cast – Meryl Streep, Glenn Close, Jeremy Irons, Antonio Banderas – for Bille August's *The House of the Spirits*. Based on the best-selling novel by Isabel Allende, the film followed the escapades of a family in Chile. Winona replaced the director's wife, Pernilla August, playing Meryl Streep's daughter, Blanca.

FILMOGRAPHY

1986: *Lucas*. 1987: *Square Dance*. 1988: *Beetlejuice*; *1969*. 1989: *Great Balls of Fire!*; *Heathers*. 1990: *Welcome Home, Roxy Carmichael*; *Mermaids*; *Edward Scissorhands*. 1991: *Night on Earth*. 1992: *Bram Stoker's Dracula*; *The Age of Innocence*. 1993: *The House of the Spirits*. 1994: *Reality Bites*; *Little Women*.

Annabella SCIORRA

The extraordinary thing about Annabella Sciorra is that she has been starring in progressively more successful movies, and yet has remained relatively unheard-of to the cinemagoing public. She was top-billed in her first movie, a critical triumph, and subsequently went on to play opposite Tim Robbins, Richard Gere, James Woods, Michael J. Fox, Wesley Snipes, Matt Dillon, Gary Oldman and Matthew Broderick – in a space of three years. The other extraordinary thing about Annabella Sciorra is that she is only one-quarter Italian. However, she seems to have cornered the market in playing hot-headed, olive-skinned beauties from the Bronx. 'In role after role, I find myself doing these parts,' she complains, 'but I don't even talk that way.' Indeed, her mother, a fashion stylist, is native French, while Annabella's father, a veterinarian, is half-Cuban as well as being half-Italian. And Annabella was born, not in the Bronx, but on Manhattan's Upper East Side.

That was in 1964 (although she's fiercely secretive about her age: 'When I walk into an audition and they ask how old I am, I like to say, "How old do you want me to be?" I'm an *actress*'). She was 13 when she enrolled at the prestigious HB Studio and later studied at the American Academy of Dramatic Arts. She says she 'grew up thinking acting was what I was supposed to do,' but first had to endure the obligatory support group – you know, that group of jobs that encompass waitressing, secretarial work, bartending . . .

At 20, she founded her own theatre company, The Brass Ring Theatre Co., and produced several productions. Four years later she badgered every agent she could find to play the role of Sophia Loren's daughter in the mini-series *Mario Puzo's 'The Fortunate Pilgrim'*, and was offered the part. She then won the lead in *True Love* by answering an ad in *Backstage* magazine. A low-budget comedy about the angst-ridden preparations of a Bronx wedding, *True Love* was a distinctive debut for director Nancy Savoca and boasted believable characters and plenty of memorable moments. Perhaps most unforgettable of all was the scene in which Donna (Sciorra) cannot face her new husband (newcomer Ron Eldard, coincidentally a good friend of the actress's) and, in full nuptial regalia, locks herself in a stall in the ladies' loo. The film attracted ecstatic reviews and walked off with the Grand Prize at the 1989 United States Film Festival in Park City, Utah. The actress recalls, 'it was, like, overnight – Boom! All of a sudden, here

were all these people calling me who wouldn't take my phone calls before.'

In Roger Donaldson's frantic comedy *Cadillac Man*, the actress played Tim Robbins's wayward wife, prompting the latter to lay siege to the car salesroom at which she works. Donaldson, who had previously directed the hits *No Way Out* and *Cocktail*,

Annabella Sciorra

Sciorra as the bride that wouldn't in *True Love*

thought 'Annabella was perfect. She has real range, real instincts, a real sort of fiery quality.' In Mike Figgis's *Internal Affairs* she was the trusting wife of rogue cop Richard Gere, but almost turned the part down. She told the director she thought the script was 'horrible', explaining, 'All I could do was be honest. I couldn't really hide that.' Figgis was impressed, shared her views, cast her and re-wrote the script. The film was a hit.

Next came the part of a young lawyer who becomes romantically involved with defence attorney Alan Dershowitz (Ron Silver) in *Reversal of Fortune*. Again, it was a supporting role in a film that cornered more than its fair share of attention (for starters, Jeremy Irons won the Oscar for it). Silver actually had the biggest part, and showered praise on his leading lady. 'There's an honesty about Annabella,' he revealed. 'She can't make a false move. She doesn't know how.' She was stuck in another 'girlfriend role' (belonging to James Woods, but admired by Michael J. Fox) in *The Hard Way*, a slam-bang comic-thriller. Fox agrees, '*The Hard Way* was a real guys' movie and there was no easy niche for her to fit in. But Annabella held up well; she created a terrific energy of her own.' Sciorra herself was more dismissive:

'I'm [just] the girl in the buddy movie. I think I giggle in very scene.'

She then landed her first lead in a major movie, as Angela Tucci, a working-class Italian-American woman coping with the stigma attached to her affair with a black middle-class architect (Wesley Snipes). The film was Spike Lee's *Jungle Fever*, which attracted acres of newsprint and landed on the cover of *Newsweek*, a sure sign of a picture making it as 'an event movie'. It was also a box-office success, but was nothing compared to Annabella's next outing, *The Hand That Rocks the Cradle*. Originally she was offered the role of the nanny from hell who takes over a middle-class Seattle family, but ended up playing the persecuted wife and mother instead. Still, she had top-billing, although Rebecca De Mornay, as the babysitter, had the flashier part. 'We screen-tested both ways,' Sciorra discloses. 'I don't know if Rebecca had real strong feelings either way, and I didn't either.' But, the actress admits, 'I think Rebecca was great.' The film touched a universal chord and had audiences reacting out loud. 'People were screaming all through the movie,' Sciorra recalls. 'The weird thing was, it was like they had already seen it. They knew a lot of the lines: "Don't go in the cellar, Claire!"'

The Hand That Rocks the Cradle knew which buttons to push and was arguably the year's most exciting thriller – but it wouldn't have been half as convincing if Sciorra hadn't produced a character to root for. There was

A mother scorned: Annabella Sciorra (with Madeline Zima) in the nail-biting *The Hand That Rocks the Cradle*

With Wesley Snipes in Spike Lee's tough romantic drama, *Jungle Fever*

another thriller, *Whispers In the Dark*, with the actress playing a psychiatrist who falls in love with a man whom she discovers was involved with a murdered patient. Again, Sciorra was top-billed, with Alan Alda and Jill Clayburgh in support, but the film barely caused a whisper at the box-office.

She then played Matt Dillon's ex-wife in *Mr Wonderful*, who is set up with a series of men (with a view to marry one of them) so that Dillon doesn't have to fork out his alimony payments. Then she played the wife of a corrupt New York cop (Gary Oldman) in Peter Medak's sexy black comedy *Romeo is Bleeding*, and joined the ensemble cast of *The Night We Never Met*, the story of a romantic mix-up in a New York apartment.

FILMOGRAPHY

1988: Mario Puzo's '*The Fortunate Pilgrim*' (TV). 1989: *True Love*. 1990: *Cadillac Man*; *Internal Affairs*; *Reversal of Fortune*. 1991: *The Hard Way*; *Jungle Fever*. 1992: *The Hand That Rocks the Cradle*; *Whispers In the Dark*. 1993: *Mr Wonderful*; *Romeo is Bleeding*; *The Night We Never Met*.

Ally SHEEDY

Vanity Fair described Ally Sheedy as 'pretty much' the *official* Brat Pack girlfriend. Of course, Diane Lane and Demi Moore were equally deserving of this dubious title, while Molly Ringwald may have been above such things (being a star in her own right). True, Ally Sheedy appeared in two seminal Brat Pack movies – *The Breakfast Club* and *St Elmo's Fire* – and buoyed such male stars as Sean Penn, Matthew Broderick, Rob Lowe and Judd Nelson (appearing with the latter on three occasions) before making it on her own in *Short Circuit*. But there's nothing official about Ally Sheedy.

Refreshingly unpretentious on screen, the actress displayed a sunny, forthright appeal, shot through with a mischievous twinkle. She was as American as apple pie and about as wholesome. She was also a talented actress, equally successful at playing dingbats, show ponies or tough professionals.

She was born Alexandria Sheedy on 13 June 1962, in New York City, the daughter of an advertising executive (father) and a literary agent/writer (mother). At six, she was performing at New York's Lincoln Centre with the American Ballet Theatre and at 12 published her first book, *She Was Nice To Mice*, the story of Queen Elizabeth's civility to rodents. The book was a best-seller (and later lent its title to the actress's own company, Nice to Mice Productions), and young Ally continued her precocity by writing a film review for the *Village Voice*, some children's stories for *The New York Times* and a feature (about her mother and herself) for *Ms Magazine*.

This, in turn, led to an appearance on TV's *Mike Douglas Show*, after which she was signed up by personal manager Breanna Benjamin. What spare time the 15-year-old had left, she spent developing a career doing TV ads and appearing off-off-Broadway. Following a commercial for Burger King, Sheedy embarked on a series of after-school 'specials,' television drama aimed at teenagers in which she played 'drug addicts, runaways, child prostitutes – the works!'

At 18, Ally moved to Los Angeles where she enrolled at the University of Southern California as a drama major. Not long after that, she appeared in her first TV movie, the well-received *The Best Little Girl In the World*, a disturbing drama about anorexia nervosa. This prompted a burst of activity in TV movies, culminating with her big-screen debut in *Bad Boys*. A tough, credible drama about juvenile delinquency, the film starred real-life bad boy Sean Penn, with Sheedy the one

Ally Sheedy

person who can cut through his machismo. Her next film, John Badham's *WarGames*, was a certified hit, starring Matthew Broderick as a computer whiz kid who thinks he's playing 'video games' with the US missile defence system. Sheedy was his feisty, pretty girlfriend and injected the film with an advantageous spark of humanity.

She joined Rob Lowe and Julian Sands for an enjoyable frolic at English university, courtesy of *Oxford Blues*; and then enrolled in detention class with Molly Ringwald, Emilio Estevez, Judd Nelson and Anthony Michael Hall in John Hughes's *The Breakfast Club*. Unrecognizable behind a mop of unruly hair, Sheedy was the resident weirdo and klepto-maniac ('an island unto herself'), making patterns with her dandruff and gleefully informing her schoolmates that she's a nymphomaniac. A considerable stretch from her previous bright-eyed, bushy-tailed beauties, this chipmunk of a girl almost stole the film from her co-stars. Hers was a

compelling, idiosyncratic and alluring performance.

St Elmo's Fire was another ensemble piece (Estevez, Rob Lowe, Demi Moore, etc) and again Sheedy shocked her critics by revealing yet another facet of her versatility. This time she played a recent college graduate and top-salaried architect living with Judd Nelson (but refusing to marry him). Until now saddled with characters considerably younger than her own age (23) it was a jolt to see her playing a self-assured adult.

She left the Pack to play Gene Hackman's daughter in the well-acted domestic drama *Twice in a Lifetime*, and she then joined Judd Nelson (yet again) for the hopeless revenge drama *Blue City*. After this she emerged with flying colours, and top-billing, in John Badham's wildly entertaining *Short Circuit*. The story of an amiable robot with an insatiable appetite for knowledge, the film was an engaging, fast-paced ride, helped no end by Sheedy's sassy performance as the machine's best friend. The film had 'hit' stamped all over it, and it went on to spawn a sequel.

Sheedy, meanwhile, was going through a difficult patch. Her subsequent films failed to

Ally Sheedy horsing around with Rob Lowe in the 1984 *Oxford Blues*

Ally as the tormented psychic Cayse Bridges in Rockne S. O'Bannon's *Fear*

capitalize on her recent success, and she retreated into alcoholism and bulimia. She entered a detox centre and later recalled her experience in poems published in her own anthology, *Yesterday I Saw the Sun*.

Since then, her career has consisted of supporting roles and TV movies, with one or two exceptions. She had the lead in *Fear*, an intriguing psychological thriller about a medium tormented by a clairvoyant serial killer, and she played John Candy's shy, dumpy girlfriend in the John Hughes-produced *Only the Lonely*, a minor success. She also had the lead in *Lethal Exposure*, the tale of a photojournalist who attempts to smash a Mafia ring, and was top-billed in *Man's Best Friend*, co-starring Lance Henriksen.

In 1992 she married the actor David Lansbury, nephew of Angela Lansbury.

FILMOGRAPHY

1981: *The Best Little Girl In the World* (TV); *The Day the Loving Stopped* (TV); *Splendor In the Grass* (TV); *The Violation of Sarah McDavid* (TV). 1983: *Deadly Lessons* (TV); *Bad Boys; WarGames.* 1984: *Oxford Blues; The Breakfast Club.* 1985: *St Elmo's Fire; Twice In a Lifetime.* 1986: *Blue City; Short Circuit.* 1987: *Maid To Order; We Are the Children* (TV). 1989: *Heart of Dixie.* 1990: *Fear; Betsy's Wedding; Seer* (TV); *The Lost Capone* (TV).

1991: *Only the Lonely.* 1992: *The Pickle; Kiss and Tell* (UK: *Tattle Tale*); *Home Alone 2: Lost in New York* (cameo). 1993: *Man's Best Friend; Lethal Exposure* (TV); *Chantilly Lace* (TV); *Before the Night; Parallel Lives.*

Charlie SHEEN

In a nutshell, Charlie Sheen was helped into the classroom by his father, made head prefect by Oliver Stone and saved from expulsion by his family. The son of the successful actor Martin Sheen, Charlie notes, 'a lot of people believe that, because of him, I was able to get a foot in the door. And that may be true on some level. But it's what you do once you get *behind* that door that really counts.' And yet an equally strong influence on Charlie's professional life was his older brother, Emilio Estevez. 'Watching Emilio work, seeing the life he had, made me think maybe I should try films, too.' In fact, after Emilio turned down the lead in Oliver Stone's *Platoon* (due to a prior commitment), Stone opted for Charlie to replace him. The movie was a box-office sensation, won four Oscars (including a statuette for best picture) and made Charlie Sheen a star. The following year Stone cast him as the Yuppie hero of *Wall Street*, another success, and Sheen was made. But – like his childhood friends Rob Lowe and Sean Penn – Sheen pushed his life to the brink and became a target of the press. He complained, 'I was angry when certain things were written about me, but I did all those things.' After the success of *Platoon*, 'I started assuming this role of the young movie star who's into money, wine, cars, women and partying all night,' he allows. Indeed, his womanizing became legend. He later admitted that he kept a list of all his dates numbered in order of preference, with star ratings beside their names. For a while he was devoted to the actress Charlotte Lewis (who had previously been linked with Eddie Murphy), and was engaged to Kelly Preston (who later married John Travolta).

'It got so I couldn't tell where the film world stopped and the real world started,' he confessed. And, worst of all, 'I realized I was an alcoholic.' But, in 1990, after a 32-day stint in a rehabilitation clinic, he cleaned up his act and faced the music. In 1991 he announced, 'I've cut out the booze. I've cut out the drugs. And I've settled down considerably. And it feels good.' Interestingly, his personal redemption coincided with the surprising success of *Hot Shots!*, an exhausted spoof of hit movies which grossed over $68 million in the States alone. Sheen – clean, keen and wiser – was back.

He was born Carlos Irwin Estevez on 3 September 1965 in New York City, the third of four children – all of whom went on to film careers with varying degrees of success. Emilio Estevez (born 1962), is an actor, writer and director; Ramon Estevez (born

directing Super-8 features with all-star casts (at least, stars of the future): brother Emilio, Sean and Christopher Penn, Rob and Chad Lowe . . .

At nine, he made his professional acting debut in the TV movie *The Execution of Private Slovik* starring his father, and a year later was an extra in *Apocalypse Now*. But when Sheen Sr suffered a heart attack during the making of the latter, Charlie swore off

Back then: Charlie Sheen (*right*) aged 19 in Penelope Spheeris's atmospheric, uncompromising *The Boys Next Door*, with Maxwell Caulfield

Charlie Sheen as Yuppie trader Bud Fox in Oliver Stone's giddy drama *Wall Street* – with Michael Douglas

Thanks to his father's influence, Charlie was spared a term in jail, but ran into more trouble when he was caught buying exam answers and, later, for assaulting a teacher. Such behaviour, and an intolerable attendance level, punctured Sheen's academic future and, consequently, his career as a baseball star.

Inevitably, he turned to acting. His father's manager circulated some publicity stills and Sheen ended up in a B-movie called *Grizzly II – The Predator*, which was never released. He was 19 when he starred in his first major film, *Red Dawn*, which united him with Patrick Swayze and C. Thomas Howell, his brother's co-stars from *The Outsiders*. The film, in which Sheen played a student on the run from a Russian invasion of the US, was a box-office success and something of a controversy. The same year he courted some controversy of his own when he fathered a daughter, Cassandra, and broke up with the child's mother before she was born.

He played Chad Lowe's best friend in the TV movie *Silence of the Heart*, and a killer in Penelope Spheeris's compelling drama *The Boys Next Door* (with Maxwell Caulfield), and then received top-billing for the first time in the sluggish *Three For the Road*, as a junior aide escorting his senator's daughter to a psychiatric clinic. However, it was a supporting role in the hit comedy *Ferris Bueller's Day Off* that made Sheen feel he had made it. 'The first time I really felt like people really knew who I was was when I picked up *MAD* magazine and they were doing a parody of *Ferris Bueller* and there I was in the artwork. Some artist interpreted the character I played in the film. I thought, "this is kind of cool." *MAD* magazine, a magazine I grew up worshipping, and they've got my ugly ass in there gracing the pages. Forget the Oscars, forget all the hoopla, that really stood out for me.'

Then came *Platoon*, Oliver Stone's outstanding, Oscar-winning Vietnam epic, with Sheen as Chris, the film's reluctant hero and narrator (much as his father was in *Apocalypse Now* which, coincidentally, was filmed not a hundred miles away from the same Philippines location). However, Sheen Jr brushed off the new acclaim, saying, 'It may be oversimplifying, but what was my role in *Platoon*, really? It was one every boy acts out as a kid, playing war.'

He found his part in Stone's *Wall Street* altogether more demanding, but he was left standing by Michael Douglas in his Oscar-winning role as the corrupt financial wizard Gordon Gekko. Sheen was Bud Fox, Gekko's callow fall guy and, quite frankly, wasn't up to

1963) is an actor, with such films as *Beverly Hills Brats* and *Common Ground* to his credit; and Renee Estevez (born 1966) is an actress who has appeared in *For Keeps*, *Heathers*, *Paper Hearts* and starred in *Marked For Murder*. Meanwhile, Janet Sheen, wife of Martin and mother of all, turned associate producer on the domestic satire *Beverly Hills Brats*, while even Uncle Joe Estevez jumped on the bandwagon, starring in *Soultaker*, *One Shot Sam* and *Double Blast*.

When Charlie was three, his father moved the family to Santa Monica, California, to pursue his film career, and made a point of taking his children on location with him. Soon Charlie was making movies of his own,

acting. Instead, he channelled his energies into baseball, and was good enough to win a college scholarship. But then Emilio started getting all the attention, making money, going places, influencing people (Charlie admitted, 'there was a lot of friction between us'). And while Emilio was making movies, his younger brother was making trouble. 'At 16,' Charlie owns up, 'I was arrested for possession of marijuana. Then I was arrested again – a year later – for this five-day crime spree. I went to the Beverly Hills Hotel and told people that I'd been a guest and had lost my term paper. They'd let me look through the trash, and I found all these credit card receipts and used the numbers to make phone orders.'

the demands of the part. He was better as a slick car thief in the stylish thriller *No Man's Land*, and then agreed to a supporting role – as Oscar 'Hap' Felsch – in the arty, baseball-themed *Eight Men Out*, which he took in order to play in a World Series on film and to work with the director John Sayles. However, the picture was a commercial flop (it *was* very boring), and due to a serious injury while making it, Sheen was forced to lose the lead in Ridley Scott's action-thriller *Johnny Utah*, a part the actor had been counting on (it was made three years later as *Point Break*, starring Keanu Reeves). With his career bumping downstairs, Sheen rang Emilio in desperation.

'I called Emilio and said, "This is really bad, I feel like shit." So he said, "Call Chris Cain [the director of *Young Guns*]. Dick Brewer has not been cast ... We can play bitter rivals on film."'

So, at the eleventh hour, Charlie was cast as Young Gun Brewer, but had to suffer the indignity of fourth-billing, behind Emilio, Kiefer Sutherland and Lou Diamond Phillips. Nevertheless, the film was a hit. He then took a cameo in *Never on a Tuesday* which

Charlie with brother Emilio in the latter's embarrassing *Men at Work*

he called, 'my most extreme character role to date,' in which he sported a menacing scar and a Southern accent. After that he had another hit, as Ricky Vaughn, the wild boy of the ill-fated Cleveland Indians' baseball team, in David S. Ward's riotous *Major League*. This time his baseball fanaticism paid off – with knobs on.

But then his career nose-dived. He was miscast as a pipe-smoking goatherd in a *Heidi* update – *Courage Mountain*; had a cameo as Jodie Foster's boyfriend in *Backtrack*; was a gung-ho commando in the awful *Navy SEALS*; was simply embarrassing as a garbage collector in the intolerable *Men at Work*, written, directed by and co-starring Emilio; and was unmemorable as Clint Eastwood's preppie, clean-cut partner in the routine cop thriller *The Rookie*, a dud. He was then directed by his father in the undistinguished *Cadence*, as a rebellious AWOL soldier incarcerated in a German stockade (with Sheen Sr as his warden).

His career in tatters, he was invited to his father's birthday party in Malibu, only to find his family had rallied around for a confrontation. 'They said, "Sit down. We're gonna talk." And we had it out.' It was Emilio's charitable words that turned Charlie's head, and at his brother's behest he checked himself into rehab. Charlie recalls, 'Emilio said, "If you kill yourself with drugs and alcohol, you're

Top Pun: Charlie as the heroic pilot 'Topper' Harley in Jim Abrahams's exhaustive spoof *Hot Shots!*

robbing the rest of the world of a very valuable talent."'

Then came *Hot Shots!*, Charlie's most successful film to date (that is, in which he had top-billing). He played Sean 'Topper' Harley, a renegade pilot who's turned his back on the Navy, preferring to spend time with the Indians and a wolf called Two Socks. But when an urgent mission brings him out of retirement, Topper proves himself as charismatic, dashing and horny as ever. A blatant spoof of *Top Gun*, with sidelong swipes at everything from *Gone With the Wind* to *The Fabulous Baker Boys*, Jim Abrahams' *Hot Shots!* was truly, in the words of the publicity, 'the Mother of all Movies.' Such was its success, that two years later a sequel appeared – *Hot Shots Part Deux* – taking on the legend of *Rambo*. Sheen then took a cameo (as a valet parking attendant) in *National Lampoon's Loaded Weapon 1*, starring Emilio; had the lead in the crime adventure *Fixing the Shadow*, unrecognizable as a long-haired, heavily bearded cop on the run from his past; and joined Nicolas Cage in *Deadfall*, a story of murder and deceit. He was due to star in Paramount's drama *Murder*

In the First, but when he was replaced by Christian Slater he teamed up with Chris O'Donnell and Kiefer Sutherland in Disney's *The Three Musketeers*. He was also announced as the star of *Frame by Frame*, an ecological mystery in which he was to play a fashion photographer who finds himself in Alaska.

FILMOGRAPHY

1974: *The Execution of Private Slovik* (bit; TV). 1979: *Apocalypse Now* (as extra). 1983: *Grizzly II – The Predator* (unreleased). 1984: *Red Dawn*; *Silence of the Heart* (TV). 1985: *The Boys Next Door*; *Three For the Road* (released 1987). 1986: *Lucas*; *The Wraith*; *Ferris Bueller's Day Off*; *Platoon*; *Wisdom*. 1987: *Wall Street*; *No Man's Land*. 1988: *Eight Men Out*; *Young Guns*; *Never on a Tuesday* (cameo). 1989: *Major League*; *Courage Mountain*; *Backtrack* (UK: *Catchfire*). 1990: *Navy SEALS*; *Men at Work*; *The Rookie*. 1991: *Cadence* (UK: *Stockade*); *Hot Shots!*. 1993: *National Lampoon's Loaded Weapon 1* (cameo); *Hot Shots Part Deux*; *Fixing the Shadow*; *Deadfall*; *The Three Musketeers*. 1994: *The Chase*; *Major League II*; *Terminal Velocity*; *Martin Eden*.

Ione SKYE

As a favour to a photographer, the 15-year-old Ione Skye Leitch agreed to pose for a fashion spread in *L.A. Weekly*. She had no intention of following the modelling career of her mother, Enid Karl, and had no aspirations to act. Her brother, the actor Donovan Leitch, was auditioning for a role in Tim Hunter's *River's Edge*, when the director recognized the family resemblance. He had seen Ione's pictures in *L.A. Weekly*, and was basing the 'look' of Clarissa in his film after her. With the help of Donovan (who didn't get his role), Hunter called in the actor's sister and cast her in the female lead.

River's Edge was not only a huge critical success, but a *cause célèbre*, and was allocated considerable space in the national press. The true story of a gang of teenagers who exhibit various degrees of apathy when one of them murders his girlfriend, the film was an authentic and disturbing study of alienated contemporary youth. In a cast that included Crispin Glover, Keanu Reeves and Dennis Hopper, Ione was surprisingly effective as perhaps the film's most anchored character, a young woman who calls on her own resources and becomes a stronger, wiser person for it. *Rolling Stone* magazine named her one of the year's hottest new talents.

Since then Ione Skye has made a career playing strong-willed, confident and alluring woman, invariably from moneyed backgrounds. She was Denise, the wealthy, promiscuous 'weekend date' of River Phoenix in *Jimmy Reardon*; the rich, popular Rachel in *The Rachel Papers*; the affluent, unattainable Diane Court, John Cusack's dream babe in *Say Anything*; and Rob Lowe's sexy, on-the-ball mistress in *Wayne's World*. Needless to say, Ione is bored of these 'girlfriend' roles, and we've all got a shock coming.

Ione Skye Leitch is probably most famous for being the daughter of Donovan (Leitch), the folk-rock singer who produced such 1960s hits as 'Sunshine Superman', 'Hurdy Gurdy Man' and 'Jennifer Juniper'. She was conceived in a remote farmhouse on the Scottish island of Skye and born in London on 4 September, 1970. However, her unmarried parents 'separated when I was in the embryonic stage,' she announced ruefully in 1989. 'When I was young I dreamt of meeting him, but not anymore. He's never been in touch with me. I listen to his music once in a while . . . ' (When she dropped the Leitch from her stage name, Donovan wrote to her mother to express his approval).

After London, Enid Karl moved her children to San Francisco and Connecticut before settling in Los Angeles, by which time Ione was seven. There, Ione attended the Immaculate Heart High School, excelling in

Ione Skye in her first film, *River's Edge*, with Keanu Reeves

As the perfect woman – Rachel – in Damian Harris's *The Rachel Papers*

history and science and writing short stories. By her own admission, she was 'very much a loner at school.' After *River's Edge*, she dropped her surname, dropped out of high school entirely (in tenth grade) and won top-billing in her second movie, *Stranded*, in which she and Maureen O'Sullivan are captured by aliens ('the film is so bad that I can't even describe it').

She was then one of River Phoenix's many girlfriends in *A Night in the Life of Jimmy Reardon*, and played Napoleon's promiscuous little sister, Pauline, in the ABC miniseries *Napoleon and Josephine* (starring Armand Assante and Jacqueline Bisset). After that she returned to London to play the object of Dexter Fletcher's desire in *The Rachel Papers* (based on Martin Amis's celebrated novel), with James Spader playing her boyfriend.

Then came Cameron Crowe's *Say Anything*, in which the actress played a high school 'show pony' who's obsessed with her father (John Mahoney). It takes John Cusack to shake her out of her comfortable tree and to see life a little more clearly. *Say Anything* was a tender, surprising and fresh addition to a time-worn genre, and permitted enough glimpses of truth to make its protagonists recognisable and interesting. Ione Skye was perfect.

In *The Color of Evening*, with Martin Landau, she was a small-town girl with her eye on Hollywood; and she had a supporting role – as Liv Ullmann's daughter – in the cerebral, talky *Mindwalk*, a sometimes fascinating 'ecological' drama – but, as it turned out, too intellectual for mass public consumption.

Ione with John Cusack in Cameron Crowe's wonderful *Say Anything*

Ione as the defiant and victimized Trudi in Allison Anders's outstanding *Gas Food Lodging*

In the quirky, well-acted comedy *Samantha*, she played Dermot Mulroney's violinist girlfriend, a meaty part she made the most of, and then won a starring role in Allison Anders's *Gas Food Lodging*. Not only was the latter one of the best independent American films of 1981, but it allowed Ione to stretch herself. Taking a sharp typecasting U-turn, she played Trudi Evans, a cheap, foul-mouthed slut, the victim of a gang rape in a backwater New Mexican town. Far from being the 'show pony' of yore, Ione's Trudi was both impoverished and unlikeable – at least, until we got to know her better. However, as big a jump as Trudi was from Ione's retinue of high school goddesses, the role did reflect some aspects of her own upbringing. Trudi is the eldest daughter of a single mother, and has never seen her father. To add further autobiographical flavour to the film, Donovan Leitch Jr played the best friend of her sister (Fairuza Balk).

Even with as sparse a career as Ione's, to have *River's Edge*, *Say Anything* and *Gas Food Lodging* in one's credits is credit indeed.

Next, she had a telling cameo in *Wayne's World* (as Elyse, who recognizes the commercial value of Wayne and Garth), and had another supporting turn in the low-budget *Guncrazy*, starring Drew Barrymore.

In 1989, Ione and her boyfriend, Anthony Kiedis – lead singer of the controversial rock group The Red Hot Chili Peppers – set up home together in West Hollywood. Two years later she married Adam Horovitz, lead singer of another controversial rock group – The Beastie Boys. The couple wed in California and honeymooned in Venice. To complete the fairy tale, Ione finally met her father and, schedules permitting, now sees him about once a month.

FILMOGRAPHY

1987: *River's Edge*; *Stranded* (aka *Shockwave*). 1988: *A Night In the Life of Jimmy Reardon.* 1989: *The Rachel Papers*; *Say Anything.* 1990: *Mindwalk.* 1991: *The Color of Evening*; *Samantha.* 1992: *Gas Food Lodging*; *Wayne's World*; *Guncrazy.* 1994: *Forever in Love.*

Christian SLATER

Christian Slater was the embodiment of teenage cool. He wasn't particularly handsome – like, say, Luke Perry. He wasn't wildly athletic – like Patrick Swayze. He didn't mumble in the tradition of Matt Dillon. And he wasn't as notorious as Rob Lowe. And, let's be honest, he wasn't as good an actor as Sean Penn or Eric Stoltz. But he had attitude. And that, in the 1990s, counted for a helluva lot. As the selling line for *Kuffs* proclaimed: 'When you have attitude – who needs experience?'

Had Christian Slater been born under another star sign, he could have been the film industry's pet nerd. But a combination of street savvy and a whacky charm kept him at the head of the class. There was also an arrogance, that even the timid, bookish Mark Hunter in *Pump Up the Volume* couldn't entirely camouflage. But likewise there was an honesty, a 'gee whiz' sensibility that endeared Slater to filmgoers. Thankfully, Christian Slater is still awe-struck by it all.

Allan Moyle, who directed the quintessentially hip *Pump Up the Volume*, noted, 'Christian has an ineffable blend of innocence and power that makes him thrilling to watch. He brings both wit and charisma to his role.'

Winona Ryder, who got to know the actor even better, volunteered, 'He's one of the funniest people I know. He has a style that's really his own. Forty years from now someone's going to write a book: *Slater – The Legend*.'

The son of stage actor Michael Hawkins and casting director Mary Jo Slater, the actor was born on 18 August 1969 in New York City. He confessed that his father was 'a little offbeat and strange,' while his mother was far from run-of-the-mill. As an example, she staged a rather unusual 20th birthday party for him. 'Yeh, she hired a stripper,' Slater confirms. 'I was sitting there in a chair, with all my friends watching, while a woman danced naked in front of me. That's a position I never want to be in again. This woman went on for, like, four or five songs. She did the entire soundtrack to *Last Tango in Paris*.' Slater also notes that, 'when I was a baby, my mother took me up on stage – I mean, it was like, *Roots*. She held me up above her head and said: "This is your life, my son." This is what she tells me. Of course, it could be a lie.'

He was seven when Mary Jo cast him in a small part in the daytime TV serial *One Life To Live*. 'Everybody applauded, and that was it,' he said. 'I was sold.' Two years later he was spotted on TV by the theatre director Michael Kidd and was signed up to play the cute, all-American Winthrop in a nine-month tour of *The Music Man*, starring Dick Van Dyke. 'In the beginning,' Slater recalls, 'I'd be onstage and start waving to my mother in the audience. I was just a young, excited kid. Then as the show went on I began to understand what it was all about.'

With typical candour he says, 'I'm all for nepotism,' and indeed, made the most of both his parents (who divorced when he was six). He played D.J. LaSalle in the daytime soap *Ryan's Hope*, in which his father was the original Frank Ryan, and, aged 14, had a small role in the well-received TV movie *Living Proof: The Hank Williams Jr Story* – starring Richard Thomas as the country singer. He had a big role – Binx – in *The Legend of Billy Jean*, opposite Keith Gordon and Helen Slater (no relation), but the film played to small audiences.

His breakthrough arrived with the young lead in *The Name of the Rose* which, especially in retrospect, seemed a bizarre casting choice. Slater says, 'When I first read the script, I thought, "There's no way I can play a medieval monk; there's just no chance." It was such an intense role, with this wild love scene, and I was just 16. I was surprised when the director, Jean-Jacques Annaud, cast me. I played Sean Connery's apprentice in the film, and our relationship on screen reflected real life. He was teaching me, and I was trying to take it all in.'

Christian Slater as JD, the ultimate rebel without a cause – in Michael Lehmann's *Heathers*

Christian Slater as DJ, the ultimate rebel with a cause – in Allan Moyle's *Pump Up the Volume*

Of course, Jean-Jacques Annaud is a Frenchman, and was little concerned that Connery, Slater and Michel Lonsdale all had competing accents – as long as they spoke English. The film's moody, Rembrandtian look was the order of the day, while Slater's deflowerment at the hands of the voluptuous Valentina Vargas was one of the most unexpectedly erotic moments of 1980s cinema.

He had the lead as a sadistic killer in the rather nasty *Twisted*, but the film wasn't released until 1992 when he was a name. He was then star-struck again in the company of Francis Ford Coppola and Jeff Bridges – as the latter's son – in the distinguished *Tucker: The Man and His Dream*, the stirring story of the persecuted auto genius Preston Tucker.

Slater then secured top-billing for the first time in the skate-boarding thriller *Gleaming the Cube*, in which he played a bad seed from Orange County – complete with spiked hair and earrings. 'I dyed my hair, let it grow long, pierced my ears, and practised on a skateboard for three months,' the actor recalls. 'Then a camera guy came over to me

A boy and his gun: Christian Slater as Regulator Dave Rudabaugh in *Young Guns II – Blaze of Glory*

Slater as a streetwise Will Scarlett in *Robin Hood: Prince of Thieves*

and said, "Jeez, you really sound like Jack Nicholson." At that point I hadn't seen any of his films; not really. Anyway, it was thrilling to hear that – especially as I had no idea I was doing it. Now I can't escape it. It's cool, but I gotta be me.'

He intentionally injected a dash of Nicholson – combined with a dollop of his father – in *Heathers*, the film that established him as the coolest dude on the Hollywood block. Ironically, he was advised against the project, but couldn't resist the temptation of playing J.D., the high school outsider who dishes out a terrible fate to three snotty princesses all called Heather. Slater's high school girlfriend Kim Walker played Heather Chandler; while his future (albeit brief) companion Winona Ryder co-starred as Veronica, an honorary Heather and Bonnie Parker to his Clyde Barrow. The film was as hip as tomorrow's catchphrase, and turned the teen comedy on its head with a satanic flourish. *Newsweek* hailed the picture as 'a

work of genuine audacity' and *GQ* called it 'the ultimate send-up of high school angst movies.' Slater was 20 years old.

By rights, he should have been an instant star, but his career failed to gather momentum. He had the lead in an unexceptional TV movie, *Desperate For Love*, loosely based on a real-life tragedy; took a supporting role in *Personal Choice*, a talky dud with Martin Sheen; was wasted as Fred Savage's older brother in the little-seen *The Wizard*; was insignificant in the omnibus horror film *Tales From the Darkside – The Movie*, as a college student menaced by a 3,000-year-old mummy; and was in another miss, *On the Prowl*, with Corey Haim.

If Slater's film career was going nowhere, his private life was even worse. He admits that he was, 'hitting an emotional and physical bottom,' and, in December of 1989, he was sentenced to ten days in jail after pleading no contest to his second Driving While Influenced charge within a year. His driving licence was withdrawn for 18 months, he was fined $1,400 and put on five years' probation. The 'incident' occurred when the actor, under the influence of illegal substances, exceeded the speed limit in LA

and resisted arrest. With the police in hot pursuit, he slammed his Saab 900 into a telephone pole and then hurled a cowboy boot at a highway patrolman as he scaled a chain-link fence.

'I did what a lot of people do at a certain age,' he explained ruefully. 'I went through a wild period, although I think I took it to an extreme. I know I could have been smarter. But I don't regret my past. I actually learned from the negative experiences.'

He ignored advice to turn down the lead in *Pump Up the Volume*, and returned with a professional bang as the shy high school student (Mark Hunter) who doubles as an underground DJ called Happy Harry Hard-On. This was his best performance yet, a tour-de-force in which his bespectacled recluse comes out at night to transform a sleepy Arizona suburb into a state of frenzy. Preaching rebellion and sexual honesty from the makeshift studio of his bedroom, Slater was nothing short of mesmerizing. Ironically, Allan Moyle's ultra-hip screenplay had been sitting around for years due to the fact that the filmmaker couldn't think of anybody who could carry off the dual demands of the role. Moyle marvelled that, 'When I met Christian Slater, I finally saw the character come alive.'

With his career back on track, the actor segued into the Hollywood mainstream. He was an outlaw with an inferiority complex in *Young Guns II – Blaze of Glory*, played Will Scarlett in the phenomenally successful *Robin Hood: Prince of Thieves* and, when Matt Dillon turned the role down, starred as the young Charles 'Lucky' Luciano in *Mobsters*. He said he took those roles, 'to protect myself in case I had to back things up. On the other hand, they were attractive projects because of the people involved.'

And because his mother was a *Star Trek* groupie, he found himself cast in a cameo in *Star Trek VI: The Undiscovered Country*, and then starred in the lightweight caper *Kuffs*, as a drop-out who inherits a police precinct when his brother is murdered. He supplied the voice of the hip wood nymph Pips in the animated feature *FernGully The Last Rainforest*, took a cameo as a social worker in *Where the Day Takes You* and then gave one of his very best performances in the sweet, touching romantic drama *Untamed Heart*. In the last named, he played Adam, a withdrawn orphan boy who believes he has the heart of a baboon, and who falls in love with an attractive, spirited waitress (Marisa Tomei). To her surprise, the waitress finds herself reciprocating his love, leading to a most unconventional and tender romance. The film had every right to drown in sentimentality, but artfully sidestepped mawkishness to become one of the year's most touching and surprisingly memorable films.

He then got his biggest break yet, top-billed in Tony Scott's gritty romantic comedy *True Romance*, in which he and Patricia Arquette attempt to find true happiness with a suitcase of Mafioso contraband. Based on a hot screenplay by Quentin Tarantino (*Reservoir Dogs*), the film co-starred Dennis Hopper, Gary Oldman, Brad Pitt, Val Kilmer and Christopher Walken. He then took over from Charlie Sheen in the role of a lawyer who befriends a criminal – in Paramount's *Murder In the First*.

FILMOGRAPHY

1983: *Living Proof: The Hank Williams Jr Story* (TV). 1985: *The Legend of Billy Jean*. 1986: *The Name of the Rose*; *Cry Wolf* (TV); *Twisted* (released 1992). 1988: *Tucker: The Man and His Dream*. 1989: *Gleaming the Cube*; *Heathers*; *Desperate For Love* (TV); *Personal Choice* (later *Beyond the Stars*); *The Wizard*. 1990: *Tales From the Darkside – The Movie*; *On the Prowl*; *Pump Up the Volume*; *Young Guns II – Blaze of Glory*. 1991: *Robin Hood: Prince of Thieves*; *Mobsters* (UK: *Mobsters – The Evil Empire*); *Star Trek VI: The Undiscovered Country* (cameo). 1992: *Kuffs*; *FernGully The Last Rainforest* (voice only); *Where the Day Takes You* (cameo). 1993: *Untamed Heart*; *True Romance*. 1994: *Jimmy Hollywood*; *Murder In the First*; *Interview With the Vampire*.

combat), he initially saw himself as a dancer, and possibly a singer, before deciding on drama. 'It was,' he noted, 'so easy.'

However, when in 1977 his family upped sticks and moved to Orlando, Florida, Snipes was devastated. So, as soon as he had completed high school in the Sunshine State, he returned to New York to attend SUNY-Purchase and graduated with a degree in theatre arts. In his early years he and a group of friends formed a puppet troupe called 'Struttin' Street Stuff' and toured for three years performing comedy, satire and drama at public parks and schools. 'We did everything from building sets to making the costumes,' he says. 'It was a lot of fun.' He also appeared on Broadway in a series of plays, including *Boys of Winter*, *Death and the King's Horsemen* and *Execution of Justice*. But he was still not ready to make it in films. In 1984 he auditioned for a role in the Harry Belafonte-produced musical *Beat Street*.

'Here's this piece about cats from the 'hood, and I'm enunciating my lines like a Shakespearean actor,' he recounts. 'Harry took one look and said, "That's enough, son. Go back to school."'

On television, he appeared in an episode of *Miami Vice*, and made his film debut in the Goldie Hawn comedy *Wildcats*, as a high school football player. In the same year he won third-billing in the routine *Streets of Gold*, playing an ambitious boxer trained by Klaus Maria Brandauer, and then had a minute part in the abysmal Richard Pryor comedy *Critical*

Wesley Snipes

Wesley Snipes, as Willie Mays Hayes, shakes James Gammon's hand in his first big role – in David S. Ward's baseball comedy *Major League*

Wesley SNIPES

When black cinema became box-office gold in the 1990s, a new star system was born. Suddenly, stand-up comedians like Robert Townsend and Damon Wayans and rap artists such as Ice-T and Ice Cube were being turned into movie stars. But the biggest name of all, who represented the new urban cool of Afro-American audiences, was a theatrically-trained actor. Looking for all the world like an accidental star, Wesley Snipes nevertheless excited critics and secured top-billing in extremely successful pictures. Maybe thanks to timing, or to good luck, or to sheer talent, Snipes became a box-office phenom-enon.

Born on 31 July 1963 and raised in the tough neighbourhood of the South Bronx, New York, Snipes enrolled at the High School for Performing Arts, the setting of Alan Parker's *Fame*. Naturally athletic (Snipes is a trained martial artist and student of the Afro-Brazilian Capoeria, a form of unarmed

Wesley as the ruthless druglord Nino Brown in Mario Van Peebles's *New Jack City*

Condition. But his breakthrough role arrived not on film nor on TV nor on stage, but in the 1987 music video for Michael Jackson's *Bad*. Martin Scorsese directed, and Snipes gave a performance of such aggressive power (as the gang leader who shoves Michael Jackson up against a wall) that, in the words of Spike Lee, 'he was so real, Michael Jackson must've been scared to death.'

Of course, *Bad* was no ordinary video, and its subsequent exposure got Snipes noticed. He turned down a part in Spike Lee's *Do the Right Thing* in order to play the showier role of Willie Mays Hayes in the hit baseball comedy *Major League*. It was a wise move. His high-octane comic performance deftly overshadowed his co-stars Tom Berenger, Charlie Sheen and Corbin Bernsen, and when the aforementioned all agreed to appear in *Major League II*, Snipes turned it down.

On TV, he played police officer Lou Barton in the pilot movie *H.E.L.P.* and appeared in the subsequent, short-lived series. Next, he starred in another series, HBO's *Vietnam War Stories*, and won the 1989 ACE Award as best actor for his performance. He then accepted Spike Lee's offer to play the ambitious, quick-tempered saxophonist Shadow Henderson in *Mo'*

Better Blues, rival to Denzel Washington. He also appeared in the hard-hitting, stylish thriller *King of New York*, as a New York cop trying to bust a nefarious crime ring.

He switched sides in *New Jack City*, winning top-billing as the gold-medallioned, super-smooth and ultra-vicious crime lord Nino Brown, a part specially written for him. His exercise in unremitting evil was nothing short of mesmerizing, epitomized by his heartless order to a henchman when his girlfriend wimps out on him: 'Cancel that bitch – I'll buy another.'

In a disastrous 1991 spring season, *New Jack City* was the only film in America to turn a profit, but it attracted more than just eager cinemagoers. The movie was criticized for glamourizing crime and, indeed, much violence and looting erupted around its release, leaving one murdered teenager in its wake. Snipes argues that young audiences 'can delineate between facts, fiction and naked reality,' adding that, 'the violence in the movie don't compare in no way, form or fashion to the violence that happens here in the streets. I've seen people get killed right in front of me.'

His next role, in Spike Lee's controversial *Jungle Fever*, was also written specifically for him. He played the middle-class architect Flipper Purify who conducts an affair with a white Italian woman (Annabella Sciorra) against the wishes of his community. The actor admits that, 'I was petrified. You couldn't find a person more unlike me. Everything I do is aggressive, spontaneous, and emotional. Whereas Flipper Purify is an

With Lonette McKee in Spike Lee's *Jungle Fever*

analytical, nonconfrontational character belonging to a yuppie business world I rarely spend time in. Basically, Flipper's a straight line. I'm a jagged edge.'

Nevertheless, Snipes was excellent in a powerful, engrossing drama that addressed some very pertinent issues with enormous style. The film was a huge critical triumph at Cannes and became an enormous talking point, landing the cover of *Newsweek*. Needless to say, it was another box-office success.

The actor took a supporting role in the affecting drama *The Waterdance*, playing a fast-talking, optimistic paraplegic in the process of losing his wife. The film was written and co-directed by Neil Jimenez, himself a paraplegic, whose insight provided *The Waterdance* with a conviction and dignity missing from most wheelchair dramas. It may now be a cliche to state that Snipes was the best thing in the movie, but his character was by far and away the most complex and interesting – although, to be fair, Eric Stoltz, William Forsythe and Helen Hunt were all superb.

He had another major hit on his hands with *White Men Can't Jump*, a richly entertaining, sharply written comedy (scripted and directed by Ron Shelton) set in the world of pick-up basketball. Snipes played Sidney Deane, an unscrupulous conman who meets his match when he's cheated by would-be nerd Woody Harrelson. They subsequently team up to make a formidable duo, betting sports-proud black men that they can't beat Harrelson. Again, Snipes proved to be compulsive viewing and his athletic grace was a huge asset to the basketball sequences. The film itself was a surprise success, knocking *Basic Instinct* off the top of the charts after only one week, and grossing

Wesley as terrorist tracker John Cutter in the exciting thriller *Passenger 57*

$70 million in less than three months.

Snipes was back at the number one slot half a year later in the action-packed, muscular thriller *Passenger 57*, playing a security expert who happens to be on board a jumbo jet when it is hijacked by an international terrorist (Bruce Payne). It was good to see a thriller of this size with a black man as hero (rather than sidekick), and Snipes gave *Passenger 57* his customary credibility and charisma, while showing off his martial arts skills into the bargain.

Next, he played a Treasury agent in *Boiling Point*, tracking down conman Dennis Hopper for killing his partner; and then teamed up with Sean Connery for Philip Kaufman's thriller *Rising Sun*. It was an indication of his new standing in the film community that he was now starring in pictures not specifically aimed at black audiences, and that he could hold his own against a cinematic giant like Connery. Indeed, Spike Lee complained that he could no longer afford Snipes, the latter receiving a polite $200,000 for his role in *Jungle Fever*. For *Sugar Hill*, the story of two brothers who build a drug empire in New York, Snipes was paid $2.25 million regardless of whether the film got made or not.

Snipes was also announced to play *The Black Panther*, Hollywood's first Afro-American comic-strip hero, a role Denzel Washington had begged for. He then appeared opposite Sylvester Stallone in *Demolition Man*, a big-budget futuristic thriller produced by Joel Silver (of *Die Hard* fame). For his contribution, Snipes received at least $4 million. For *Drop Zone* his fee escalated to $7m.

FILMOGRAPHY

1986: *Wildcats*; *Streets of Gold*. **1987**: *Critical Condition*. **1989**: *Major League*. **1990**: *H.E.L.P.* (TV); *Mo' Better Blues*; *King of New York*. **1991**: *New Jack City*; *Jungle Fever*. **1992**: *The Waterdance*; *White Men Can't Jump*; *Passenger 57*. **1993**: *Boiling Point*; *Rising Sun*; *Sugar Hill*; *Demolition Man*. **1994**: *Drop Zone*; *The Money Train*.

James SPADER

James Spader was the king bee at playing hot wasps. If a white, Anglo-Saxon professional snob was needed, Spader was there. He sneered his way through *Pretty In Pink*, slunk through *Mannequin* and positively leered a hole through *Less Than Zero*. And yet the actor seemed hurt when journalists suggested that he was typecast. 'I never clumped any of those roles together,' he accounted. 'They all seemed to be very different people to me. I thought I was telling different stories and doing different films. But maybe I wasn't.'

He was reluctant to accept the role of the impotent yuppie voyeur in *sex, lies, and videotape*, because, 'the humour was very hard to gauge. If it didn't work, I thought the film would be extremely self-indulgent and a huge bore.' As it happens, *sex, lies, and videotape* was one of the most original and daring films of the year, not because of the sex it revealed, but because of the psychology it exposed. Spader was sensational as the self-possessed stranger who ambles into the lives of a dysfunctional couple in Baton Rouge, opening the eyes of the sexually repressed Andie MacDowell. Neither Spader nor MacDowell were known as great actors, which made their triumph all the more sweet. MacDowell was voted best actress by the Los Angeles Film Critics' Circle, and Spader was honoured best actor at the 1989 Cannes Film Festival, while the film walked off with the coveted Palme d'Or.

Luis Mandoki, who directed Spader in *White Palace*, noted that he, 'has the ability that great actors have that makes you feel there's a character living inside, that they're not just saying the lines and feeling the feelings of the moment, but there's a whole background, the way we all have.'

The son of an English teacher, James Spader was born on 7 February 1960 in Boston and grew up on campus at Brooks School in Massachusetts. His mother was also a teacher, and his two older sisters became teachers later. But Jimmy Spader had his sights set on the theatre. Even at the prestigious Phillips Academy in Andover, Spader jettisoned academia in favour of drama, and made his stage debut (as a Chinaman) in a school production of Cole Porter's *Anything Goes*. At 17, he dropped out of school and moved to New York where he studied acting at the Michael Chekhov Studio and gained practical experience appearing in summer stock. To support himself, he endured a string of menial jobs, including the obligatory waiting on tables and the less routine shovelling of manure. On one occasion, he persuaded a health club to take him on as a yoga instructor, although his sole qualification was the handbook he had picked up at a supermarket. It was there that he met a fellow instructor, Victoria Kheel, whom he befriended, moved in with and married eight years later.

Another of Spader's humble positions was as janitor at a rehearsal studio in Times Square. One day his employer bent the rules and left the actor's photo on a casting agent's desk. Spader was duly called up to audition for a new film and in his excitement brought along his mother. He recalls, 'I was the only one to bring my mom.' But, the next day 'I flew to Chicago and started shooting. And the day after that I met Tom Cruise.' The movie was Franco Zeffirelli's *Endless Love*, and Spader had nailed the part of Brooke Shield's brother. Tom Cruise was likewise making his movie debut and found himself billed eleven places beneath 'Jimmy' Spader (as he was known in those days).

It was then time for TV movies and some high living. Spader was well known for his crazy antics, for drinking too much, frequenting strip venues, breaking the speed limit and driving cross-country for weeks on

the sons of Robert Mitchum, and were then re-teamed in Sean S. Cunningham's tepid thriller *The New Kids*, with Spader as head slimeball. He had the lead as a preppie Romeo in *Tuff Turf*, but the film was dated and unconvincing, and he had less luck in the TV outing *Starcrossed*, as a guy in love with a beautiful alien. He was reduced to fifth billing in his next film, but at least it was a hit. The movie was John Hughes's *Pretty in Pink*, and Spader marvelled at the writer-producer's 'incredible memory – visual, audio, emotional – of his own high school years.' Spader was at his smarmy best as the snobbish friend of

Andrew McCarthy (who looks down on the latter's liaison with poor girl Molly Ringwald), and the offers started flowing.

Next, he was in *Mannequin*, in which he portrayed the sleazy vice president of a department store, and volunteered, 'it was like some medieval torture sitting through that film.' In *Baby Boom*, he played Diane Keaton's assistant, a yuppie who is 'hungry, young, and fresh out of some training programme. I move in for the kill and take over her job.' Next, he was in the critically lambasted film version of Bret Easton Ellis's cult novel *Less Than Zero*, in which he played, 'someone who's into selling drugs and pimping and who handles it like a businessman.' As it happened, he was perfect in the role. He took a cut in billing in Oliver Stone's *Wall Street*, as a workaholic yuppie who takes to insider trading but, Spader says, 'I would have played a coffee filter in that movie. I really have got such respect for Oliver Stone.' Then, in *Jack's Back*, he was a dedicated doctor suspected of serial murder, and was sorely miscast. Salvation arrived with the role of Graham in *sex, lies, and videotape*, and Spader was in demand.

Meanwhile, he had portrayed a yuppie bore in the London-set *The Rachel Papers* (as Ione Skye's stuffy boyfriend), and next played the yuppie, drippy victim of Rob Lowe in Curtis Hanson's stylish thriller *Bad Influence*, in which he's videoed in flagrante delicto by the latter. During production, his wife gave birth to their first child, Sebastian. He was another yuppie in *White Palace*, who falls for

The breakthrough role: James Spader with Andie MacDowell in Steven Soderbergh's mesmerising *sex, lies and videotape*

Spader (*right*) with Rob Lowe in Curtis Hanson's stylish *Bad Influence*

end in his vintage Porsche. His friend Eric Stoltz recalls, 'We'd take road trips to the [Florida] Keys or up the coast, and he'd insist on having weapons in the trunk. He'd drive like a maniac – fast, with the music blaring – and I was always in fear that we'd be pulled over and some officer would find his crossbows, his lance, his 12-inch knife, his whip . . . ' But Stoltz is quick to point out that Spader is, 'a very peaceful man. He's the sweetest, nicest man in the world. He's just a tad eccentric.'

Work-wise, Spader and Stoltz had good roles in the TV movie *A Killer in the Family*, as

Just a gigolo: Spader with Susan Sarandon in the implausible *White Palace*

Susan Sarandon's working-class waitress, but it was hard to believe in their mutual attraction. He then played an upper-class employee of the Justice Department at odds with social climber John Cusack – but the outcome was predictable.

In *True Colors*, Cusack was campaigning for Congress, and in the melodramatic *Storyville*, Spader took over the task, although his political chances are marred when he is videotaped in the jacuzzi with Charlotte Lewis. Students of Spader's career would be forgiven for suspecting a recurring pattern. He was then back in the world of politics in the canny satire *Bob Roberts*, in which he was a news reader covering the campaign of Tim Robbins's two-faced senator (with Susan Sarandon as co-presenter).

Next, he changed tack dramatically, as a low-life drifter caught in a scam engineered by Charles Durning and Joel Grey – in the thoroughly enjoyable caper *The Music of Chance* – and played a young hunk looking for Ms Right in the dark, steamy romance *Dream Lover*. He then joined Jack Nicholson and Michelle Pfeiffer in Mike Nichols's lycanthropic *Wolf*, and starred opposite Kurt Russell in the $35 million sci-fi fantasy *Stargate*.

FILMOGRAPHY

1981: *Endless Love*. 1983: *Cocaine: One Man's Seduction* (TV); *A Killer in the Family* (TV). 1984: *Family Secrets* (TV). 1985: *The New Kids*; *Tuff Turf*; *Starcrossed* (TV). 1986: *Pretty in Pink*. 1987: *Mannequin*; *Baby Boom*; *Less Than Zero*; *Wall Street*. 1988: *Jack's Back*. 1989: *sex, lies, and videotape*; *The Rachel Papers*. 1990: *Bad Influence*; *White Palace*. 1991: *True Colors*. 1992: *Storyville*; *Bob Roberts*. 1993: *The Music of Chance*; *Dream Lover*; *Wolf*. 1994: *Stargate*.

Eric STOLTZ

Eric Stoltz defies categorization – you don't quite know where he'll pop up next. Take 1989. As the year started, Stoltz was on Broadway playing George Webb in Thornton Wilder's *Our Town*, for which he was nominated for a Tony award. Then, over the next four months he appeared in three films released in the US. In January he was seen in a supporting role in *Manifesto*, a Yugolsav sex romp directed by Dusan Makavejev. Looking positively out of place, Stoltz played a love-struck postal clerk opposite such British faces as Alfred Molina, Simon Callow and Lindsay Duncan.

In February he starred as the semi-human,

Eric Stoltz

half-insect son of Jeff Goldblum in *The Fly II*, a grisly, slick horror film. By way of explanation, the actor explained, 'these parts are very hard to find. I was attracted to the fact that my character gradually becomes an insect. I prepared for the role by watching a lot of TV specials, like *Life on Earth* and *National Geographic*.'

Two months after that he appeared in a very small role (19th-billed) – as Vahlere, 'the Key Master' – in Cameron Crowe's *Say Anything*. This declaration of modesty was no doubt a favour to Crowe, who scripted the actor's very first screen character, 'Stoner Bud' in *Fast Times at Ridgemont High*.

An ambidextrous, vegetarian Episcopalian, Stoltz admits that he 'thrives on insecurity,' which may account for his unusual career choices. Born in American Samoa (in the South Pacific) in 1961, the son of music teachers, Stoltz's upbringing was as unorthodox as everything else in his life. After Samoa the family moved to Paris, then London, then New York – before finally settling in Santa Barbara when Eric was eight.

Today, Stoltz is probably best known for anything but his face. Bearing a slight resemblance to Michael J. Fox, the actor spent five weeks playing Marty McFly in the first *Back to the Future* film – before director Robert Zemeckis fired him. Rumour has it that Steven Spielberg, the film's executive producer, thought Stoltz 'too intense' while, for the record, Zemeckis charitably declared, 'I found myself with a very good actor playing the wrong part.'

Eric Stoltz

for an actor who takes his craft so seriously (less generous critics denounced the film as production-line schlock). But then it's hard to predict what Stoltz will do next. Thumbing through his credits, you don't so much find a career as what looks like a potpourri of dramatic accidents.

In Amy Heckerling's seminal teen comedy *Fast Times at Ridgemont High* (scripted by Cameron Crowe from his own book), he

Stoltz as Martin Brundle, hero of *The Fly II*

Eric Stoltz as radio operator Danny Daly in *Memphis Belle*, directed by Michael Caton-Jones

played Sean Penn's surfer crony; in Franklin J. Schaffner's ill-fated Crusades epic, *Lionheart*, he played a 12th century knight; and in David Puttnam's gung-ho *Memphis Belle*, he was Danny Daly, the idealistic, Irish-American radio operator. And – in a departure daring even by Stoltz's standards – he played the romantic English poet Percy Shelley in Ivan Passer's artificial *Haunted Summer*.

Perhaps more significantly, Stoltz starred in one of the better teen romances around in the mid-1980s, *Some Kind of Wonderful*, produced and scripted by John Hughes. As Keith Nelson, the all-American high school student besotted with Lea Thompson and loved by Mary Stuart Masterson, Stoltz made a surprisingly agreeable leading man in the Michael J. Fox mould. On the surface, this

Stoltz, who explained that he wanted to act because it was 'a chance to reinvent myself,' made his name under a ton of make-up as Rocky Dennis in *Mask*, Peter Bogdanovich's moving, true-life drama made the same year as *Back to the Future*. Starring Cher as a tough and tender biker who lavished love on her disfigured son, the film featured an unrecognizable Stoltz, who – like John Hurt in *The Elephant Man* – managed to convey a humanity and warmth under several layers of latex (which took four hours a day to apply).

Mask was well-received, and won Cher the best actress prize at the 1985 Cannes Film Festival. Then there was *The Fly II*, which recruited its own following. *Film Review* magazine described it as 'a damn fine sequel ... Stoltz and ... Daphne Zuniga ... exude an affecting innocence that underscores the cutting edge of this *Beauty and the Beast* remake.' Stoltz himself saw it as the story of a 'character's quest for humanity. It's the heightened version of what everyone is on earth for: looking for a reason to justify our existence.'

The film also subjected the actor to another bout of make-up hell. As his character changed, so the latex increased, eventually leading to a daily five-hour cosmetic ordeal.

In spite of his intellectual reasoning, *The Fly II* would seem to have been a strange choice

Stoltz as the paraplegic writer Joel Garcia in *The Waterdance*

and Motion, starring his girlfriend Bridget Fonda. Described by the film's director, Michael Steinberg, as 'an existential romantic comedy,' it starred Fonda as the sensitive type who has an affair with a dope-smoking housepainter (Stoltz on excellent form) after her boyfriend (Tim Roth) has ditched her.

The actor then took a cameo (as an aggressive mime artist) in *Singles*, also with Ms Fonda, and starred in the TV movie *The Heart of Justice*, playing an entirely unlikeable, cocksure reporter covering the murder of a pulp novelist (Dennis Hopper). The latter was a slick, deftly-written Hitchcockian thriller with a good cast (Vincent Price, Jennifer Connelly, Dermot Mulroney), but failed to live up to the promise of its first half. He was also well-supported in *Naked in New York*, the story of an aspiring young playwright (Stoltz) who has to sacrifice love (to Mary-Louise Parker) for career. This time his co-stars included Timothy Dalton, Whoopi Goldberg, Tony Curtis, Ralph Macchio and Kathleen Turner. He then travelled to Paris to star in *Killing Zoe* for producer Quentin Tarantino.

FILMOGRAPHY

1982: *Paper Dolls* (TV); *Fast Times at Ridgemont High* (UK: *Fast Times*). 1983: *Thursday's Child* (TV); *A Killer In the Family* (TV). 1984: *Running Hot*; *Surf II*; *The Wild Life*. 1985: *Code Name: Emerald*; *Mask*; *The New Kids*. 1987: *Lionheart*; *Sister, Sister*; *Some Kind of Wonderful*. 1988: *Haunted Summer*; *Manifesto*. 1989: *The Fly II*; *Say Anything*. 1990: *Memphis Belle*. 1991: *The Widow Clare*; *The Waterdance*. 1992: *The Heart of Justice* (TV); *Singles*. 1993: *Bodies, Rest and Motion*; *Foreign Affairs* (TV); *Naked in New York*; *Killing Zoe*. 1994: *Sleep with Me*; *Roommates* (TV); *Pulp Fiction*; *Fluke*; *God's Army*; *Little Women*.

Sharon STONE

Not since Bo Derek emerged from the ocean in *10* had an actress so steamed up the pages of the tabloid press. Hers was not overnight stardom, but the velocity with which Sharon Stone hurtled from unknown to superstar was so potent that the effect was as giddying. The fuss was all about *Basic Instinct*.

The most controversial movie of 1992, *Basic Instinct* starred Michael Douglas as a San Francisco cop obsessed by a wealthy, bisexual novelist who may or may not be a serial killer. The story was nothing new (the device had been employed with some success in *Sea of Love*), but the film's patent homophobia had provided priceless publicity

Sharon Stone

while the film was still in production. After its scriptwriter Joe Eszterhas toned down the lesbian content, the film's notoriety dramatically changed direction. Audiences were now talking about *that* sequence in the police station. You know, the scene in which Sharon Stone is called in for questioning after the horrific murder of her lover.

Douglas: 'Did you ever engage in sadomasochistic activity?'

Stone: 'Exactly what did you have in mind'

Douglas: 'Did you ever tie him up?'

Stone: 'No. Johnny liked to use his hands too much. I like hands and fingers.'

She then uncrosses her legs to reveal an obvious lack of underwear, the first 'official' female flash in Hollywood history. Much has been written about how this came about. Michael Douglas has been quoted as saying that the film's director, Paul Verhoeven, tricked her, promising that her privacy would be concealed in shadow. In direct contrast, it was later revealed that Sharon removed her own 'crotch pad', saying: 'Let's stop pretending. I'm nude, we all know. Let's get on with it.' Later still, she refused to talk about it, terminating the subject with a cool, 'I don't want to talk about it. It's all resolved now – water under the bridge.'

may not seem too hard a task to accomplish, but as Nelson was actually a reprehensible snob, it took some acting skill on Stoltz's part to keep him even vaguely likeable and interesting.

The actor's other primary – and far more dramatic – role, was the paraplegic writer Joel Garcia in *The Waterdance*. Written and co-directed by Neal Jimenez, himself a paraplegic, the film was a cliché-free drama that genuinely got under the skin of what it must be like to be sexually impotent and dependent on others. Playing his role with a resigned, intellectual detachment, Stoltz wasn't so much aiming for the tear ducts as asking for a little understanding.

Beside his eclectic film work, the actor has done his share of television (*St Elsewhere* and various TV movies), theatre (including a stint at the Edinburgh Festival), and is a talented musician, having studied both the trumpet and piano from an early age. He also doubled as a production assistant on *Say Anything*, a job which entailed cueing extras and fetching the coffee. 'I figure if I do it at least once a year, it will keep me humble,' he explained. He didn't, and three years later was producing his own movie, *Bodies, Rest*

Sharon Stone with Richard Chamberlain in the 1985 version of H. Rider Haggard's *King Solomon's Mines*

Stone as Sara Toscani, wife of action hero Steven Seagal – in the 1988 action-thriller *Above the Law*

Whatever *really* happened, the scene was the talk of Hollywood and helped launch Sharon Stone into the forefront of Tinseltown's most visible ladies. British tabloids announced that she was to be paid $30 million for the sequel, a 'fact' which was discussed with some gravity in more serious newspapers. It was also disclosed that she was to get $7 million for her next film, *Sliver*, which was to make her the highest paid actress in the world. And this in the same year that Whoopi Goldberg, Julia Roberts and Sigourney Weaver were bestowed with the same distinction. A more realistic figure is that Ms Stone received $2.5m for *Sliver*, plus a hefty chunk of the gross profits. That's still an impressive pay cheque. And she may well get $7m for *Basic Instinct 2*.

In a remarkably short period of time, Sharon Stone had become the embodiment of men's primal fantasies. *Basic Instinct* became a talking point in newspaper articles, at dinner parties, at the bus stop ... Such was the power of the actress's performance as the hot-cold-hot siren Catherine Tramell, that many seemed to forget she had actually *acted* the part. It must be said that the star was equally adept at playing giggly damsels-in-

distress as well as predatory man-eaters. And let it not be forgotten that she had already made 17 movies and boasted an IQ of 154.

Still, Paul Verhoeven did find her, 'very seducing. She does a lot of flirting. One of the most threatening things about her is that she can change in a split second. I have hated her with all my heart, and I have loved her, too. She can be very clever with words and hit you with them right in front of the whole crew. And if you're not careful, she can be the victor.'

Joe Eszterhas, whose characters have been acted out by Glenn Close, Debra Winger and Jessica Lange, volunteered, 'Of the things I've done that have been made, no performance knocked me out more than what she

did in *Basic Instinct*.' He subsequently fashioned his screenplay of *Sliver* especially for her.

Sharon Stone was born on 10 March 1958 in the small town of Meadville, Pennsylvania, the daughter of a dye maker (her father) and book-keeper. One of four children, she was a bright kid and moved through school at the rate of knots before taking college courses at the precocious age of 15. Winning a writing scholarship to Edinboro State College, she excelled at science but took acting classes instead. After graduation, and encouraged by her track record of winning local beauty contests, she turned to modelling and was signed up by the prestigious Eileen Ford agency in New York. She also studied with an acting coach and appeared on TV endorsing the virtues of Charlie perfume, Clairol hair products and Diet Coke. At an extras' casting call for Woody Allen's *Stardust Memories*, she so impressed the director that he cast her in a small role in the film's opening scene – as the goddess who blows him a kiss from a passing train.

She had a good part in Wes Craven's Amish-esque thriller *Deadly Blessing*, starring Ernest Borgnine, and was a regular on the short-lived TV series *Bay City Blues*, about a minor-league baseball team (she played Patrick Cassidy's patient wife, Cathy St Marie). Next, she won the only good reviews going for her comic performance as a talentless starlet in *Irreconcilable Differences*, with Ryan O'Neal, joined Tom Skerritt and Robert Culp in the TV movie *Calendar Girl Murders* (a thriller set in the porn industry), and had the leading female role in the awful *The Vegas Strip Wars*, also for TV. However, the latter was vaguely notable for being Rock Hudson's last TV movie and, more importantly, for introducing Sharon to her future husband, the producer Michael Greenburg. She followed this with the TV mini-series *War and Remembrance*, from Herman Wouk's novel, and *King Solomon's Mines*, the first of two movies exploiting H. Rider Haggard stories to cash in (unsuccess-fully) on the *Indiana Jones* phenomenon. Still, the actress made a feisty heroine, and seemed to have more fun than Richard Chamberlain.

The sequel, *Allan Quatermain and the Lost City of Gold*, was filmed simultaneously, but wasn't released until 1987, the worst year of Sharon Stone's life. Never mind the film's failure – and the lack of artistic merit evinced by *Police Academy 4* and the crime drama *Cold Steel* – 1987 was a devastating year for personal reasons. For a start, Sharon's marriage came apart at the seams.

'Michael was a real straight guy and we had a sort of a squeaky-clean little relationship,' she confided. 'I wanted us to be the perfect couple. I wanted to be the perfect wife. Maybe I thought being perfect, being better, was being different from whom I actually was. It has taken me a long time to understand that who I am is enough.'

In December of that year, her school boyfriend Richard Baker Jr, a successful pilot, was found dead at the wheel of his car. He had shot himself in the head.

Career-wise, there was little to offer Sharon Stone solace. She continued steaming up a series of mediocre films, which invariably passed by in the night. She was the bad guy's innocent wife in *Action Jackson*; a love-struck American in the British home counties in the TV movie *Tears in the Rain*; Steven Seagal's missus in *Above the Law* (one of her worst performances); the Spanish *Blood and Sand* (which Ms Stone declares, 'was more like *Drunken Spanish Keystone Cops Make a Bad C Movie*); and the preachy, talky, virtually unheard of *Personal Choice*, in which she played the girlfriend of Robert Foxworth. The last named was bad even by Sharon Stone standards, but then Martin Sheen, Christian Slater and F. Murray Abraham were also in it, so who's to blame?

Salvation arrived with Paul Verhoeven's thrilling sci-fi extravaganza, *Total Recall*, with Stone slyly cast as Arnold Schwarzenegger's treacherous wife. The scene in which she and Arnie fight to the finish was a classic, capped by the muscleman blowing her away with the words, 'Consider that a divorce.' Ironically, Ms Stone almost turned the part down, saying, 'I've done every stupid action movie I'm gonna do. No thank you.' However, when she found out Verhoeven was directing, she changed her mind. The film was a colossal hit.

Unfortunately, more dross followed, namely the thriller *Scissors*, with Steve Railsback, and the romantic comedy *He Said, She Said*, starring Kevin Bacon. She was better in John Frankenheimer's *Year of the Gun*, as a tough frontline photographer, but the film was arguably Frankenheimer's worst.

When Ellen Barkin, Geena Davis, Michelle Pfeiffer and Julia Roberts turned down the central role of the temptress in *Basic Instinct*, Stone got a crack at the whip. She knew the part was big news, but she never dreamed they would give it to her – and refused to read the script. At first ... When she relented, she was stunned by the meatiness of the part and was determined to make it hers. She dressed up in the sexiest gear she could find and gave Verhoeven a run for his

As Stone looked in 1990, in Paul Verhoeven's *Total Recall*

money. After five nights of screen tests, his defences were crumbling. Carolco Pictures wanted a name actress for the role, but they also knew it would be difficult to find a star who was willing to meet the sexual demands of the script.

'Some very successful actors make very safe choices,' Stone conceded. 'That's not my way. To those actresses who didn't think that was their way, I'm incredibly indebted.'

Before *Basic Instinct* transformed Sharon Stone into a household name, she appeared in two more films: the low-budget thriller *Where Sleeping Dogs Lie*, in which she played an agent who encourages her client to write a novel about a serial killer (sound familiar?), and *Diary of a Hitman*, as the offensive sister of Sherilyn Fenn.

Once *Basic Instinct* opened, the scripts came pouring in. She was reportedly offered the female lead in *In the Line of Fire*, opposite Clint Eastwood, but turned it down because she considered Eastwood a has-been. Of course, this was before Eastwood's *Unforgiven* had opened to ecstatic reviews. Anyway, the part went to Rene Russo. Instead, Sharon took the starring role in *Sliver*, the story of a literary editor who, through an obsessive love affair, becomes involved in the murky

Romance with an ice-pick: Sharon Stone in Verhoeven's *Basic Instinct*

world of voyeurism and murder. Tom Berenger and William Baldwin co-starred.

According to the film's producer, Robert Evans, 'It's the first time that the subject matter, the taboo fantasy of voyeurism, has been explored without being exploitative. It's everyone's fantasy, but it's dealt with [here] in an intellectual way.'

She then took a cameo in *Last Action Hero*, and starred opposite Richard Gere in Mark Rydell's *Intersection*, an American re-make of the Michel Piccoli/Romy Schneider French film *The Things of Life*. She was also announced as the star of Paramount's *Lady Takes an Axe* and another Joe Eszterhas screenplay, *Original Sin*.

In 1992, Sharon Stone's private life picked up as well. For a while she dated the popular country singer Dwight Yoakim (but, according to press reports, he ditched her after the 'shock' of *Basic Instinct*), and was then seen escorting Chris Peters, son of movie mogul Jon Peters and actress Lesley Ann Warren. Later, she confessed, 'I'm too old for him,' and announced her engagement to *Sliver* producer William J. McDonald on national TV. Unfortunately, the liaison was short-lived.

FILMOGRAPHY

1980: *Stardust Memories*. 1981: *Deadly Blessing*; *Bolero*. 1984: *Irreconcilable Differences*; *Calendar Girl Murders* (released on video in 1993 as *Victimised*); *The Vegas Strip Wars* (TV). 1985: *King Solomon's Mines*. 1987: *Allan Quatermain and the Lost City of*

Gold (filmed in 1985); Police Academy 4: Citizens On Patrol; Cold Steel. 1988: Action Jackson; Tears In the Rain (TV); Above the Law (UK: Nico). 1989: Blood and Sand; Personal Choice. 1990: Total Recall. 1991: Scissors; Year of the Gun; He Said, She Said. 1992: Basic Instinct; Where Sleeping Dogs Lie; Diary of a Hitman. 1993: Sliver; Last Action Hero (cameo); Intersection. 1994: The Specialist; The Quick and the Dead.

Kiefer SUTHERLAND

When Kiefer Sutherland was good, he was a wimp. But when he was bad, he was great. It was almost as if he were two actors. When he was projecting a gentleness and vulnerability, his features would discernibly soften, but the end product was frequently bland. However, when Sutherland sunk his teeth into a villainous role, his lizard-like eyes would shine, his jaw would slip into a threatening angle, and his 5'10" frame would seem to stretch over six foot. He was mesmerizing.

After a mundane start as the gauche young lead in Daniel Petrie's prosaic The Bay Boy, the actor made a sizeable impression playing demonic bad guys in two hit movies: Stand By Me and The Lost Boys. In the former, he was the bully who antagonised River Phoenix, and in the latter was a sadistic biker and part-time vampire. Then came the

The face of innocence: Kiefer Sutherland in Promised Land, executive-produced by Robert Redford

starring role in the Robert Redford-produced Promised Land and a giddy attack of workaholism. In five-and-a-half years he clocked up 16 movies. He was 22.

Having established himself as a film star, Sutherland made the headlines via his stormy romance and engagement to Julia Roberts, which ended abruptly when she found out about his five-month affair with a stripper, Amanda Rice. Although their wedding was set for June 14, the invitations mailed and the whole thing due to cost a bank-breaking $500,000, the actress cancelled the event with four days' notice. She ran off to Ireland with Jason Patric (Kiefer's co-star from The Lost Boys); he was (reportedly) left in tears. Since then the actor's career has slowed down to a walking pace, stymied by the cancellation of Renegades (working title), a big-budget action adventure in which he was to have starred with Ms Roberts.

But if Kiefer Sutherland was not a model fiancé, he was a good actor. Michael J. Fox opined, 'he has a bizarre kind of energy all his own. He can get inside a role and mesh it with his own strange character.' While Meg Ryan reflected, 'two seconds before the camera rolls, the guy just clicks in faster than anyone I've ever seen. And he's one of the best-listening actors I've worked with.'

Kiefer Sutherland was born with grease-paint in his veins. The son of Donald Sutherland, the film star, and Shirley Douglas, a successful stage actress, Kiefer wanted to act for as long as he could remember. He was born Kiefer William Frederick Dempsey George Rufus Sutherland, in London, England, on 18 December 1966, the twin brother of Rachel. His first name was taken from the writer Warren David Kiefer, who scripted Donald's debut movie, Castle of the Living Dead. At four, Kiefer was transported to California, where his father's film career was flourishing, and where his mother was exercising her sixties' radicalism. She was blacklisted by the United States government, Donald protested against the Vietnam war with Jane Fonda, and they separated – for ever.

Kiefer says, 'I remember it all very well. I remember marching with my mother in Watts at the time of the Watts riots – I was five years old. I remember we had everybody at our house – Black Panthers, a rehab group for people coming out of San Quentin, bikers

Satanic Sutherland: Kiefer and his canines in Joel Schumacher's The Lost Boys

from all over . . . ' He remembers his father less clearly, who was busy starring in such movies as M*A*S*H, Klute and Don't Look Now.

In 1974, Kiefer moved again, to Canada, his parents' country of birth, and there sampled a number of private boarding schools. At 16, three years away from graduation, he dropped out and took the train from Ottawa to Toronto. There, he shacked up with a musician friend for eight months, until he won the title role in The Bay Boy and could afford to live on his own (previously, he had a walk-on in Max Dugan Returns, starring his father, Marsha Mason and Matthew Broderick). By international standards, The Bay Boy was nothing to write home about, but Kiefer won a Canadian Genie award nomination for his role as a teenager growing up in Nova Scotia in 1937.

In New York, he attended a number of auditions, but kept on returning to Canada to get work. Finally, he landed a lucrative jeans advertisement ('it paid $3,500') which enabled him to buy a car and drive to California. He was 17. In Los Angeles, he slept in his vehicle for six weeks to save money, before getting a role in the TV series Amazing Stories. His episode, The Mission, was

Promised Land and had another flashy supporting role – as a cocaine-sniffing yuppie – in *Bright Lights, Big City*, starring Michael J. Fox. In *1969* he was dropping out and dropping acid with Robert Downey Jr, and then buckled on his guns to join Emilio Estevez, Lou Diamond Phillips and Charlie Sheen in *Young Guns*, a stylish, ultra-violent western. He was then re-teamed with Phillips in Jack Sholder's slick thriller *Renegades*, playing an undercover cop in search of a mysterious Indian lance. Frankly, he looked entirely too young to play an officer of the law, moustache or no moustache, but was, nonetheless, surprisingly charismatic.

He was another cop in *Flashback*, escorting a 1960s fugitive (Dennis Hopper), and then travelled to England to play a homicidal GI in *Chicago Joe and the Showgirl*

Kiefer as cop in Jack Sholder's *Renegades*

Kiefer as Jeff Harriman in George Sluizer's *The Vanishing*

directed by Steven Spielberg, and was part of an omnibus released theatrically overseas (which also included segments starring Kevin Costner and Mary Stuart Masterson). He had a small role in *At Close Range*, with Sean Penn and Ms Masterson, and almost won the young lead in John Boorman's jungle epic *The Emerald Forest* – but the director found him too 'strange and quirky'. Then came his scene-stealing turn in Rob Reiner's *Stand By Me*, and the starring role – as an 'elective mute' – in an OK TV movie, *Trapped in Silence*, with Marsha Mason. He was also in an exploitative TV film called *The Brotherhood of Justice*, playing the good guy opposite Keanu Reeve's teenage vigilante.

He returned to Canada to star in *Crazy Moon*, as an alienated boyfriend of a deaf salesgirl, and then portrayed a psychotic murderer in *The Killing Time*, a low-budget thriller. The latter co-starred and was produced by a Puerto Rican-born beauty, Camelia Kath, 12 years Kiefer's senior. This age gap, and the fact that she had an 11-year-old daughter from a previous marriage (her husband had killed himself in a game of Russian roulette), failed to deter Kiefer's interest and the couple ended up living together before tying the knot.

In the meantime, Kiefer made a glamorous villain in Joel Schumacher's *The Lost Boys*, starred opposite Meg Ryan in the slow-moving, but well-intentioned romantic drama

203

(Emily Lloyd was the chirpy showgirl). The less said about the latter the better, except that it marked the break-up of Kiefer's short-lived marriage (which had produced one child, Sarah Jude – named after Kiefer's friend Sarah Jessica Parker). Romance flourished again when he starred opposite Julia Roberts in Joel Schumacher's *Flatliners*, an MTV look at death, in which he, she and Kevin Bacon played medical students experimenting with mortality. Kiefer's father himself had 'died', briefly, of acute meningitis, which lent a chilling air of authenticity to Kiefer's performance. The film was a hit, and with Kiefer top-billed, should have been an enormous career stepping stone. It wasn't.

There was a sequel, *Young Guns II*, followed by an all-star flop, *Article 99* (with Sutherland playing a materialistic medic), and then a walk-on in David Lynch's abysmal *Twin Peaks: Fire Walk With Me* (although Kiefer managed to convey exactly the right deadpan tone for his role as an FBI agent).

For his next film, Rob Reiner's *A Few Good Men*, he was reduced to fifth-billing, cast as a villainous Marine. With his hair shaved, his ears protuberant and his mouth fixed into a permanent sneer, he had never looked more like his father. And, like his father, he was beginning to excel in evil cameos.

However, he did have the lead in *The Vanishing*, an American re-make of the Dutch movie of the same name. Kiefer played Jeff, a man who becomes obsessed with his girlfriend (Sandra Bullock) after she suddenly and mysteriously disappears. 'To create an obsession on this level, you have to go through parts of your life,' Kiefer reasoned. 'You really have to figure out what you've ever been obsessed about, though I don't think I've ever been as obsessed as this character.' Jeff Bridges co-starred, but the film was a flop.

After that, he returned to the Brat Pack mode, joining Charlie Sheen and Chris O'Donnell as *The Three Musketeers*.

FILMOGRAPHY

1983: *Max Dugan Returns*. 1984: *The Bay Boy*. 1985: *Amazing Stories* (episode: *The Mission*) (TV; 1987 UK release); *At Close Range*. 1986: *Stand By Me*; *Trapped in Silence* (TV); *The Brotherhood of Justice* (TV); *Crazy Moon*. 1987: *The Killing Time*; *The Lost Boys*; *Promised Land*. 1988: *Bright Lights, Big City*; *1969*; *Young Guns*. 1989: *Renegades*. 1990: *Flashback*; *The Nutcracker Prince* (voice only); *Chicago Joe and the Showgirl*; *Flatliners*; *Young Guns II – Blaze of Glory*. 1991: *Article 99*. 1992: *Twin Peaks: Fire Walk With Me*; *A Few Good Men*; *The Vanishing*. 1993: *The Three Musketeers*; *Last Light* (TV) (also dir.). 1994: *The Cowboy Way*; *Teresa's Tattoo*.

Patrick SWAYZE

Patrick Swayze is the oldest star in this book, but his role as C. Thomas Howell and Rob Lowe's brother in *The Outsiders* sanctions his position as the patriarch of the Brat Pack. And he continued to appear in Brat Pack movies – *Grandview, USA*, again with Howell; *Red Dawn*, with Howell, Lea Thompson, Charlie Sheen and Jennifer Grey; and *Youngblood*, with Rob Lowe.

Today, Swayze is a star with a faithful following of female fans (and a few males ones) who is struggling hard to shed his image as hunk-of-the-month. In an attempt verging on desperation, he begged director Roland Joffe for the role of the tormented doctor working the slums of Calcutta in *City of Joy*.

Joffe, who had previously worked with such heavy-hitters as Paul Newman, Robert De Niro, John Malkovich and Jeremy Irons, was won over by Swayze's enthusiasm for the part. 'What I heard in his voice was not a man saying, "I want a leading role," or "I want to work with this calibre of director or this calibre of film." I heard a man saying, "I want to feel what this man feels – I feel it. I don't know if I'm a good actor, but I can feel it."'

'In my meeting with Roland, my emotions went all the way across the board,' Swayze admits. 'Because this man stimulated so many things in me. I cried, things came out of

Patrick Swayze

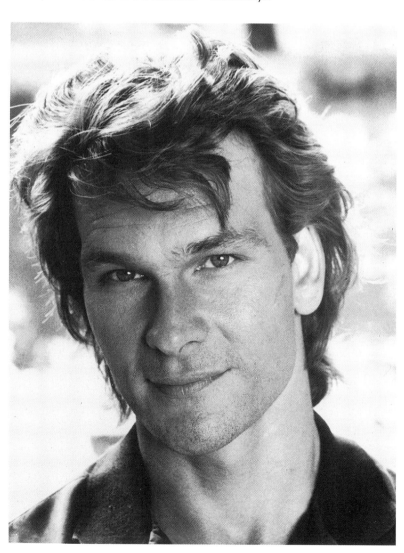

me . . . I came as close to begging for a role as I ever have in my life.'

Patrick Swayze's appeal – besides his sculptured good looks and athletic grace – is his straight-from-the-heart sincerity. He is unafraid to expose his emotions or to make a fool of himself. And that combination of sensitivity and catlike machismo is one helluva cocktail. Swayze is the sort of dream lover who can feed your fantasies, whisper sweet nothings *and* protect your home from outsize thugs. Some have accused the star of being unable to act, but even if that's the case – *boy* can he move.

'He's definitely got that *macho* edge,' volunteers his wife, actress Lisa Niemi. 'And he's good-looking, with that nice body. He fills that department very fine, thank you. But within all that masculinity, he's sensitive, caring, adores children. There's communication and understanding . . . all the attributes you associate with females. That's a pretty nifty combination. Aren't many men who have that.'

Swayze, who was branded the local sissy at school, is perfectly honest about his trigger-alarm sensitivity. 'I'm a sap for kittens and puppies,' he admits, 'and there's nothing – *nothing* – that beats a new-born foal. Just picking up that little thing in your arms . . . it brings tears to your eyes.'

Swayze's tears are now the stuff of legend. On an American chat show (hosted by Barbara Walters) he broke down while reminiscing about his late father, but he has the guts to be unashamed. He certainly boasts the credentials of a man with limitless self-confidence. Glancing quickly at his achievements it would be understandable to assume that whatever Swayze turned his hand to came easily to him. But the man has worked hard for his life. Besides being a popular movie star, Swayze earned the nickname 'Troph' at school for the number of sports trophies he won. He's also an accomplished carpenter and furniture maker, a successful singer (his single 'She's Like the Wind' made the American top-ten and got to number 17 in the British charts), a proficient archer, businessman, martial artist, playwright, stuntman, music publisher and composer. In his spare time he rides his Harley Davidson, paints, tends his farm, raises Egyptian-Arabian thoroughbreds, skates and studies Zen Buddhism. He has also toyed with est, *I Ching*, transcendental medicine, t'ai chi and collects spiritual crystals. And, of course, he regularly trips the light fantastic.

If anything else, Patrick Swayze was going to succeed as a dancer. Born on 18 August, 1952, in Houston, Texas, the son of a

Swayze as Sam Wheat, the sentimental spook, in *Ghost* – with Demi Moore

chemical plant engineer, he was dancing at the age of four under the instruction of his mother, Patsy, a Houston dance instructor and later a movie choreographer (*Urban Cowboy*). From the first grade Swayze was bullied for his love of ballet and eventually gave it up for gymnastics, diving, football, track and swimming, and became the school's star athlete. He won track and football scholarships to various universities, but attempted to make the national gymnastics squad instead. His short athletic career left its scars. To this day he still has a slight limp and at one time or another has broken his ribs, ankle, foot, all of his fingers, while his left knee alone has been shattered five times.

He made his showbusiness bow as Prince Charming in a year-long tour of 'Disney on Parade' and returned to Houston to take up a brief career as a professional ice skater. Finally, he moved to New York to pursue a career as a dancer. Then, as a member of the Feld Ballet, his ill-fated knee suffered a staph infection. Amputation was a serious consideration. 'My life was screwed at that moment,' he remembers. 'I thought it was all over. That's when I started smoking.' He also started acting, won a small role on Broadway in *Goodbye Charlie*, with Joel Grey, and then combined his acting, dancing and singing skills playing one of the lead roles in *Grease*. His performance was well received and Hollywood took note.

He had a smallish part (eighth-billed, as

Ace) in the forgettable *Skatetown USA* starring Scott Baio, but won one unforgettable review. Kevin Thomas, writing in *The Los Angeles Times*, enthused, 'Not since Valentino did his tango in *The Four Horsemen of the Apocalypse* has there been such a confident display of male sexuality. Patrick Swayze sizzles.' It was a perspicacious premonition. Meanwhile, the nascent Valentino segued into a series of TV movies before being signed up by Francis Coppola to play the oldest, and most heroic, of *The Outsiders*. As Darrel Curtis, the aggressive, volatile, but ultimately caring brother who fought for C. Thomas Howell's honour, Swayze gave a decent display of male sexuality. Besides flexing his (considerable) deltoids and throwing his fists, he also got to reveal his emotional side and – yes – cried on screen.

The cult following that built around *The Outsiders* failed to launch Swayze's career immediately, and for a while he was the sole cast member who didn't land a subsequent leading role. He *was* top-billed in the controversial *Red Dawn* (about the Russian and Cuban occupation of the US), but this was an ensemble picture in which the cast were largely swamped by the hardware and rural scenery. Fame, to some degree, arrived when Swayze landed the part of Orry Main in the 1985 TV miniseries *North and South*. A 12-part blockbuster about the American Civil War, the series starred Swayze as an officer and a gentleman on the side of the Confederates. It was followed by a sequel, *North and South Book II*, which co-starred James Stewart, Olivia De Havilland and Jean Simmons, among others.

'That blew the lid off things,' the star recalls. 'It was the first time I ever experienced getting off a plane and being mauled by thousands of people.'

But that was just the beginning. In 1987 he landed the lead role in a modest independent film with the somewhat provocative title of *Dirty Dancing*. Laughed off the screen by the critics, the picture's simple blend of romance, 1960s music and good-looking bodies hit all the right buttons and became one of the most visible hits of the year. Basically a *Romeo and Juliet* story set to the tunes of The Drifters, The Shirelles and co, *Dirty Dancing* transcended its clichés thanks to the chemistry discharged by Swayze (as a swaggering dance instructor) and Jennifer Grey as his up-market, holiday love. Ever since the film was released there has been talk of a sequel but, as yet, none has materialized.

The success of *Dirty Dancing*, unlike such hits as, say, *ET* or *Star Wars*, could be directly attributed to its human ingredient. And nobody could deny that Swayze's hulking, muscular presence was the star attraction. Baring his physique at the drop of a dance step, the actor strutted his stuff predominantly in tight jeans and a black cutaway T-shirt and became the most sought-after hunk in Hollywood. At least, for a while.

On one occasion, 300 fans discovered the whereabouts of his hotel and came looking

Swayze in villainous mood as Bodhi, in Kathryn Bigelow's hormonally-honed *Point Break*

for him. 'Just as they smashed down my door, I dived off the balcony from the third floor, into the shallow end of a swimming pool,' he recounts. 'I tell you, it was a narrow escape. Mass hysteria isn't a pretty sight, especially when it's your body they all want.'

However, the sex symbol's fidelity to his wife is well known. The couple met when Lisa, then 15, took dance lessons at Patsy Swayze's studio, when Patrick was 20. The story goes that he pinched her bottom, she protested and they married three years later. In 1987, the year he made *Dirty Dancing*, they made their first movie together, *Steel Dawn*. A futuristic variation on the western classic *Shane*, it was a box-office bomb, while Swayze's subsequent action films did little better.

The actor's main body of fans were women, and the violence displayed in *RoadHouse* and *Next of Kin* were definitely not for them. Swayze's attraction, whether he likes it or not, is as a romantic leading man. And the hard-core action fans who queued up to watch Schwarzenegger, Eastwood, Stallone and Steven Seagal, were just not interested.

If Patrick Swayze was to hold on to his stardom he had to act quick. When director Jerry Zucker was casting the male lead in *Ghost* he famously announced, 'over my dead body will Patrick Swayze get this role.' In Hollywood, the word on *Ghost* was hot, and grown actors found themselves begging for a piece of the action. Whoopi Goldberg fought for her role as the medium Oda Mae Brown, and Swayze certainly pleaded for his part, the film's romantic title role.

Swayze: 'I called Jerry and said, "Just give me a chance. I'll come in and I'll read for you. I'll do the whole script right in your office. The only thing I won't do is screen-test for it."' He got the part.

Only Demi Moore, it seemed – as Swayze's mourning wife – took the film in her stride. In fact, she almost turned it down. But, for her at least, Patrick Swayze was the perfect choice.

'I think Patrick did a good job,' she says. 'His haircut was bad news – he looks great when it's messy – but he's a sweet guy. He brought a tremendous sensitivity and a vulnerability to the role. Also, his physical attributes – and I don't mean his body – his talent to move served the film well. I don't

In the role of a lifetime: Swayze slums it in Calcutta in Roland Joffe's *City of Joy*

know if there is anybody else who could have done it. It's difficult acting opposite special effects. He had to do the whole fight scene alone.'

In spite of Jerry Zucker's initial misgivings and some unkind reviews, Swayze won the role of Sam Wheat and made it his own. His heart-felt chant of 'ditto' became a national catchphrase, the film grossed $201m in the States alone and was nominated for an Oscar as best picture. Swayze had won back his legion of fans.

He took a chance with his next film, *Point Break*, playing a supporting role to Keanu Reeves – and a villain at that. But then Swayze is not into career moves. For him, playing the gung-ho bank robber in *Point Break* allowed him to secure his licence as a sky diver and to surf some of the biggest waves in the world.

Ironically, the film was a hit and Swayze captured some of the best reviews of his career. He then sought to extend his range even more and played the emotionally tormented doctor Max Lowe in *City of Joy*, Roland Joffe's harrowing look at a leper colony in Calcutta. However, the film failed to generate much box-office heat. But, to be fair, even if Arnold Schwarzenegger had played an Indian slum medic, his fans would have thought twice about watching.

Still, Swayze was better than expected, and his innate likability was a welcome contrast to the horror of the ghetto. He says now that 'I would have done *City of Joy* for nothing. I would have paid *them* to do the movie.' It was a brave project for everybody concerned, and was incredibly arduous. Besides the inhumane filming conditions, the set was fire-bombed twice and two assistant directors were accused of murder. Under the circumstances, the final product is a miracle and a masterpiece. And Patrick Swayze was right – *City of Joy* is the best film of his career

FILMOGRAPHY

1979: *Skatetown USA*. 1980: *The Comeback Kid* (TV). 1981: *Return of the Rebels* (TV). 1982: *The Renegades* (TV). 1983: *The Outsiders*; *The New Season* (TV); *Uncommon Valor*. 1984: *Pigs vs Freaks/Off Sides* (TV); *Grandview USA*; *Red Dawn*. 1986: *Call to Action*; *Youngblood*. 1987: *In Love and War* (TV); *Dirty Dancing*; *Steel Dawn*; *Tiger Warsaw*. 1988: *RoadHouse*. 1989: *Next of Kin*. 1990: *Ghost*. 1991: *Point Break*. 1992: *The Player* (deleted from the final print); *City of Joy*. 1993: *Father Hood*. 1994: *Without a Word*; *A Tall Tale*.

D.B. SWEENEY

When the likes of Anthony Edwards or Andrew McCarthy weren't around, D.B. Sweeney was a decent substitute. Displaying a rough charm and good humour, Sweeney was actually better value than most of the roles he was offered. Best described as a young Jeff Bridges, he could be charming, gauche, rough or heroic – whatever the part called for. It goes without saying that he is also handsome and athletic.

Born Daniel Bernard Sweeney in 1961, in Shoreham, New York, the actor was something of a jock at school (in Long Island) and saw himself as a professional baseball player. However, following a debilitating motorcycle accident in 1980, Sweeney's crippled legs put an end to his dream. However, in his senior year he discovered drama and his future changed course.

'I had an English teacher who dared me to do it [drama],' he explains. 'I found acting to be similar to sports in that you get the same rush on stage that you do when the bases are loaded with two outs and the game is on the line.'

Three years after graduating from New York University, Sweeney had played Broadway and was a movie star. But he hung on to his love of baseball, and formed a New

D.B. Sweeney (*centre*) with James Caan and James Earl Jones in *Gardens of Stone*, the actor's big break

York team – The Skins – with some old schoolfriends. He also got to play the legendary outfielder 'Shoeless' Joe Jackson in John Sayles's critically revered baseball document *Eight Men Out*. Based on the notorious Black Sox scandal – when the Chicago White Sox threw the 1919 World Series for cash – the film was arguably the most accurate look at period baseball to date.

'The funny thing is, back in 1919, I probably would have been good enough to compete professionally,' the actor swears. 'It was a much more strategic game back then, less about raw athletic ability.'

To prepare for his role as Jackson,

D.B. (*left*) – as 'Shoeless' Joe Jackson – with Charlie Sheen in John Sayles' *Eight Men Out*

With Moira Kelly in Paul Michael Glaser's fairy tale romance, *The Cutting Edge*

D.B. Sweeney as Travis Walton in *Fire in the Sky*

Sweeney spent a summer touring with a minor-league baseball team (The Twins) and worked on hitting the ball left-handed (Jackson was a southpaw). Understandably, the actor is proud of his sporting savvy.

'As far as actors go, you're not going to find many ballplayers better than me,' he says. He prepares hard for his roles, he says, because 'it's just that I have respect for the people I'm playing. I'm playing hard-working people, and the people who will watch are hard-working people, too. There's a nobility to what they do, and you really ought to figure out how they do it before you go and play them. I don't want them to think I'm a Hollywood jerk.'

To prepare for his role as Dish Boggett in the epic western TV mini-series *Lonesome Dove*, Sweeney worked at cattle roping for a week on co-star Tommy Lee Jones's ranch. He also did as many of his own stunts as the production allowed. Indeed, Sweeney takes his craft very seriously.

He broke into showbusiness in a Broadway revival of *The Caine Mutiny Court Martial*, and then appeared in the highly acclaimed TV movie, *Out of the Darkness*, a real-life account of the investigation surrounding the serial killer 'Son of Sam.' A year later he made his large screen debut with one line in Sidney Lumet's starry

political thriller *Power*, and then got a decent part in *Fire With Fire*, ninth-billed.

His big break arrived with Francis Coppola's *Gardens of Stone*, in which he was cast (out of hundreds of hopefuls) as the young antidote to James Caan's grizzled, disillusioned Vietnam vet. As Private Jackie Willow, Sweeney was the idealistic and outspoken young recruit who injects a fresh hope into Caan's faded dreams. Set entirely on American soil (at Fort Myer, Virginia), the film shed a new light on the Vietnam conflict, as the war is felt through the endless funeral services held for the dead heroes sent home. Sweeney, who held his own against such experienced veterans as Caan, Anjelica Huston, James Earl Jones and Dean Stockwell, proved to be yet another discovery for Coppola, the director who unleashed the Brat Pack in his cult movies *The Outsiders* and *RumbleFish*.

'It was a great honour to work with Francis,' the actor declares. 'Francis is so very

open and supportive, and he treats his film as a true collaboration. In fact, I enjoyed working on *Gardens of Stone* so much that I dreaded the day it would end, knowing that I'd have to go on to work with a mortal "director" again.'

Next, he landed the starring role in *No Man's Land*, a muscular and absorbing crime thriller in which he played an undercover cop masquerading as a car thief. Befriending smooth operator Charlie Sheen, he gets

embroiled in a glamourous criminal world that he finds all too seductive. Although Sheen had the flashier role, at least Sweeney's innate likability made his cop a character to root for. The film was not a box-office success, but it did turn the actor into a leading man.

He teamed up with Charlie Sheen again in *Eight Men Out*, an ensemble piece, and was another team player in *Memphis Belle*, David Puttnam's glossy, surprisingly clichéd World War II melodrama. Sweeney was the hard-drinking, quick-witted navigator of the eponymous B-17 bomber, who is convinced he's going to die. Still, the film was a box-office hit.

After that he went on a working binge, appearing in a series of minor movies that saw very little light of day. An exception to the rule was *The Cutting Edge*, a calculated, sentimental Kleenex epic with an ice skating background. Sweeney was the rough diamond, a hockey player denied a crack at the Olympic Gold when he loses his peripheral vision. In desperation to get back on the ice, he agrees to partner a raging prima donna (Moira Kelly) as her figure skating beau – as nobody else will go near her. The outcome was shamelessly predictable, but the picture was skillful enough – and the ice-skating sequences thrilling enough (choreographed by Robin Cousins) – that it was immensely enjoyable pap.

Standing by the film, Sweeney nobly declared that, 'I was immediately struck by the sweetness of the relationship in the movie. They are both high-profile athletes who seem so together, yet underneath it all, there are some major things missing in their lives – trust, confidence, love ... I thought that was something to which the audience could really respond.'

Audiences did, too, and the film grossed a surprising $24 million – in America alone. After a dozen pictures, Sweeney had landed his first solo hit.

He then joined James Garner and Robert Patrick in *Fire in the Sky*, the 'true' story of an Arizona logger (Sweeney) who claimed he was abducted by a UFO.

FILMOGRAPHY

1985: *Out of the Darkness* (TV). 1986: *Power*; *Fire With Fire*. 1987: *Gardens of Stone*; *No Man's Land*. 1988: *Eight Men Out*. 1990: *Memphis Belle*; *Leather Jackets*. 1991: *Heaven is a Playground*; *Blue Desert* (UK: *Silent Victim*). 1992: *A Day in October* (aka *En Dag I Oktober*); *Sons*; *The Cutting Edge*; *Miss Rose White* (TV). 1993: *Fire In the Sky*; *Hear No Evil*. 1994: *Roommates*.

Lea THOMPSON

Lea Thompson was the silent partner of the Brat Pack. Although she appeared in a series of successful films, and frequently scored shining reviews, she remained for the most part outside of the public eye. And this in spite of such leading men as Tom Cruise, Patrick Swayze, C. Thomas Howell, Charlie Sheen, Michael J. Fox, Tim Robbins, Eric Stoltz, Emilio Estevez, Ray Liotta and Kiefer Sutherland. She was even once engaged to Dennis Quaid, no less, with whom she lived for almost five years.

Indisputably pretty, in a girl-next-door sort of way, Lea Thompson usually provided more depth to her characters than they deserved. She landed her big break – and top-billing for the first time – in George Lucas's big-budget *Howard the Duck*, only to watch the film become an historical benchmark for celluloid catastrophe. When Bruce Willis's *Hudson Hawk* met a similar fate in 1991, the media instantly dubbed it *Hudson the Duck*. That's a tough stigma to shake.

'I'd never seen the press go after something like that before,' she recalls with rancour. 'I was in such shock. I wasn't prepared. You can say anything about the movie – I'm not defending it – but you have to realize how much work it was, six months, every single day. I was so committed to that duck; I had to fall in love with a mechanical ILM effect, and in order to do that you have to believe. So, yeah, it was really disappointing.'

Lea Thompson began her acting career younger than most. Her mother, Barbara Barry Hanson, was an amateur actress of some commitment. 'My mom was pregnant with me while she was doing *Kiss Me Kate*,' Lea explains. 'You know that research about how babies can be affected by sounds they hear in the womb? Well, my mom swears that when I was seven months old, she was rehearsing in our house and I began singing 'Too Darn Hot,' from *Kiss Me Kate*, on pitch, in baby words, in my crib.'

The youngest of five children (her brother Barry is also an actor), Lea was born in Rochester, Minnesota, on 31 May 1962. Her parents divorced when she was seven and, at 16, Lea took a Greyhound bus to Philadelphia to start a career with the Pennsylvania Ballet. At 19, she changed her

mind and moved to New York to try her luck at acting, landing a total of 22 Burger King commercials. That, in turn, led to her film debut as the survivor of a shark attack in the abysmal *Jaws 3-D*, when she met and fell in love with the film's star, Dennis Quaid.

In *All the Right Moves* she won the role of Lisa, Tom Cruise's 17-year-old girlfriend. Serenading her leading man with the sax and sharing a tender but explicit love scene with him, Lea won the attention of the critics and public alike. The film was a success in America, although it was unreleased in Britain. She had another hit with the controversial *Red Dawn*, co-starring Patrick Swayze, C. Thomas Howell and Charlie Sheen, in which she played a teenage guerrilla fighting off the Commies.

Her next film, *The Wild Life*, was a tired rehash of *Fast Times at Ridgemont High*, and then she was cast as both the teenage *and* 47-year-old mother of Marty McFly (Michael J. Fox) in *Back To The Future*. This delightful time-travelling fantasy turned out to be the highest grossing picture of 1985. Sequels inevitably followed (two of them, filmed back-to-back) and Lea proved to many millions of cinemagoers that she was more than just a pretty face.

'What makes the *Back To The Future* films so wonderful for an actress,' she says, 'is that the filmmakers didn't try to cast someone who just looked like us in the older versions of our characters. When I read the script to the first film, I thought the story was terrific. When they told me I would be playing both the young and old Lorraine, I knew it would be a tremendous challenge.'

In the sequel, Thompson was not only required to play Lorraine McFly at 47, but at 77 as well! In the third instalment, banishing vanity to the wind, she also played Marty's great-great grandmother, Maggie McFly. Needless to say, both sequels were colossal box-office hits.

In between this ample exposure there were two duds – the *Duck* and *SpaceCamp* – and then the fine teen romance *Some Kind of Wonderful*. In the last-named, she played the preppie, beautiful Amanda Jones, the object of Eric Stoltz's romantic fantasies. In the end, after she has ditched her unprincipled boyfriend (Craig Sheffer), Stoltz runs off with his true love Mary Stuart Masterson – leaving Lea on her lonesome. Still, she found her own happy ending when the film's director, Howard Deutch, walked off with her into the sunset. They married a year later.

Since then, Lea Thompson's career has taken a rocky path. Having shaken off her

Lea Thompson in her most famous role – as the eventual mother of Michael J. Fox – in *Back to the Future*

209

image as the cute, eternal 17-year-old, she starred in a daring feminist comedy called *Casual Sex?* – which only did casual business. Nevertheless, the director of the picture, Genevieve Robert, was impressed with her star's performance.

'There's something interesting about this young girl,' Ms Robert volunteered. 'She lets her instincts float out. I never, never found it boring to watch her . . . Other young women – they are so boring, you want to go home and recast.'

Again, Thompson exercised her skills as a character actress, playing the mentally unstable aunt of Lukas Haas in the intimate World War II drama *The Wizard of Loneliness*. After that she did a couple of TV movies: *Nightbreaker*, a highly acclaimed Cold

War thriller, playing a scientific assistant and girlfriend of Emilio Estevez; and *Montana*, a contemporary Western starring Gena Rowlands and Richard Crenna (she was their daughter, Peg). She then played a rebellious medic in husband Howard Deutch's melodramatic black comedy *Article 99*, and joined Walter Matthau and Christopher Lloyd in the long-awaited screen version of Hank Ketchman's comic strip *Dennis the Menace* – for producer John Hughes. Next, she turned up in the long-awaited film version of the old favourite TV show, *The Beverly Hillbillies*.

FILMOGRAPHY

1983: *Jaws 3-D*; *All the Right Moves*. **1984:** *Going Undercover* (aka *Yellow Pages*); *Red Dawn*; *The Wild Life*. **1985:** *Back to the Future*. **1986:** *Howard the Duck* (UK: *Howard . . . A New Breed of Hero*); *SpaceCamp*. **1987:** *Some Kind of Wonderful*. **1988:** *Casual Sex?*; *The Wizard of Loneliness*. **1989:** *Nightbreaker* (TV); *Back to the Future Part II*. **1990:** *Montana* (TV); *Back To the Future Part III*. **1992:** *Article 99*. **1993:** *Stolen Babies* (TV); *Dennis the Menace* (UK: *Dennis*); *The Beverly Hillbillies*. **1994:** *The Substitute Wife* (TV).

A middle-aged Lea Thompson and Crispin Glover in *Back to the Future*

With Thomas F. Wilson in *Back to the Future – Part II*

Uma THURMAN

She has the face of a Renaissance beauty and the smouldering sex appeal of something out of a pre-war Berlin nightclub. She can convey a virginal innocence and yet exude a sexual mystery that promises forbidden fruit. Although she is American, there is nothing remotely apple pie about her – more a hint of oranges in Grand Marnier. Even her name – Uma Karuna Thurman – conjures up an exotic taste. And just to give her a further Bohemian, rebellious edge, for a time she was married to that most anarchic of English actors, Gary Oldman.

John Malkovich, who played her seducer in *Dangerous Liaisons*, when she was just 18, offered, 'Normally, I can't talk to a girl under 30 for more than five minutes. They have nothing to say. But Uma's amazing for a girl her age. She's bright, instinctive, generous. She's a natural.'

Uma Thurman was born not in Stockholm or Copenhagen, but in Boston, Massachusetts – on 29 April 1970. Her father was a college professor, her mother a psychotherapist. But, dig a little deeper, and the exotica begins to surface. Her mother was born in Sweden, and her father taught comparative literature and Buddhism at Columbia University. To this day, Uma has a keen interest in the religion. When she was 12, her father moved the family to India, where they returned on several occasions. It was an appropriate change of locale, for a girl christened after a Hindu deity.

At 15, she moved to New York determined to make it as an actress. After attending The Professional Children's School, she spent time as a dishwasher and fashion model, before landing her first film, *Kiss Daddy Good Night*. However, she is not overly proud of this movie, a nondescript, melodramatic thriller, but Uma did have the starring role – as a crazy vamp who lured men back to her New York apartment, drugged them and then robbed them.

Her second film, *Johnny Be Good*, was no better. A scatological, obnoxious comedy about a high school quarterback unscrupulously courted by various colleges, the picture was an embarrassment for all concerned. Ms Thurman was the jock's steady girlfriend, with Anthony Michael Hall and Robert Downey Jr top-billed.

The good news arrived with Terry Gilliam's ambitious, epic fantasy, *The Adventures of Baron Munchausen*. Although a much-publicized financial disaster (some reports put the film's budget as high as $52 million), it provided the actress with a scene-stealing turn. As Venus, the goddess of love, she emerged virtually naked from a giant clam (courtesy of Botticelli), and transfixed the eponymous Baron on the spot. 'She looks as though she floated down from the clouds,' Gilliam marvelled. 'When I learned that "Uma" was a goddess in Hindu mythology, I thought, "This is too good to be true." Because of this beautiful, long creature, I changed the concept of Venus and created a sense of someone who almost doesn't know her own power.'

In *Dangerous Liaisons*, she played the virginal, angelic Cecile de Volanges, who is seduced by Malkovich's conniving Vicomte de Valmont. Cast for her fresh-faced innocence and European beauty, Uma clocked up another endorsement for scene-stealing. The director, Stephen Frears, was overawed. 'She's shocking in the scene where Valmont tricks her, deflowers her – she sobs and suffers. And ten minutes later she's jubilant. Shocking!' The production was a critical

Uma Thurman as the radiant Rose in Terry Gilliam's extraordinary *The Adventures of Baron Munchausen*

Uma Thurman (*right*) with Glenn Close in Stephen Frears's *Dangerous Liaisons*

triumph, and waltzed off with a trio of Oscars.

Bouncing from one English director to the next, Uma turned up in modern dress in John Boorman's sumptuous, bizarre comedy *Where the Heart Is*. The story of a Capraesque family attempting to come to terms with the 1990s, the film was killed off by the critics, robbing the public of one of the year's more unusual, most charming cinematic treats.

More visible was Philip Kaufman's controversial screen adaptation of Anaïs Nin's diaries, *Henry & June*. Uma Thurman co-starred as June, the wife of the notorious novelist Henry Miller (Fred Ward), and for the first time played a character of depth, complexity and intelligence – and sexual awareness. The film itself leaned towards artistic pretension, but was beautifully acted and particularly well photographed. However, *Henry & June* will be best remembered for stirring up so much dust that the Motion Picture Association of America was forced to invent a new certificate – the NC-17 – so as to distinguish between 'art' and pornography.

She was back in costume – as a spirited, tomboyish Maid Marian – in John Irving's lively TV movie *Robin Hood* (released theatrically outside of America), and then joined her husband Gary Oldman in *Dylan*, a TV movie about the tragic Welsh poet Dylan Thomas (she was Caitlian, the poet's wife). Next, she portrayed Kim Basinger's duplicitous sister in *Final Analysis*. This was a high-concept, pulse-accelerating, corkscrew thriller with Thurman the wacko patient (who is 'ambivalent about her phallic fantasies') of psychiatrist Richard Gere. Nobody was who they seemed, and until the film ran into one U-turn too many, the audience was kept entirely out of breath.

In Bruce Robinson's intelligent, atmospheric thriller *Jennifer Eight*, she played a rather sweet, wise-beyond-her-years blind girl, terrorized by an unseen attacker. Although treading on territory already explored in *Wait Until Dark* and *Blind Terror*, the film introduced a fresh reality to the condition of blindness, with Thurman bringing both acuity and vulnerability to her character.

In John McNaughton's seductive, edgy *Mad Dog and Glory* she played Glory, a gorgeous

the part for Uma. The cast also included Keanu Reeves, Rain Phoenix (sister of River), Angie Dickinson and John Hurt.

FILMOGRAPHY

1987: *Kiss Daddy Good Night*. 1988: *Johnny Be Good*; *The Adventures of Baron Munchausen*; *Dangerous Liaisons*. 1990: *Where the Heart Is*; *Henry & June*. 1991: *Robin Hood* (TV; UK theatical release); *Dylan*; *Final Analysis*. 1992: *Jennifer Eight*; *Mad Dog and Glory*. 1993: *Even Cowgirls Get the Blues*. 1994: *Pulp Fiction*.

bartender who is presented to a shy forensic detective – Mad Dog (Robert De Niro) – as a gift from loan shark Bill Murray. Reports from the set indicated that all was not well, as Thurman found the nude scenes particularly daunting. One source revealed that the crew was kept waiting six hours as she summoned up the courage to disrobe. This came as a surprise to some, as the actress had revealed her splendid form to the camera on several previous occasions. Eventually she came round, tearing off her cosmetic body shields, and launched into the scene. McNaughton was understanding. 'You don't think of her as being so young,' he allowed, 'except once in a while she'll say something, and you go, "Ummaaa! Oh, yeah, that's right, you're 21."'

She then landed the biggest role of her career – playing Sissy, the central character in Gus Van Sant Jr's long-awaited *Even Cowgirls Get the Blues*. Based on Tom Robbins's cult novel, the film follows the exploits of Sissy and friends on a 'beauty ranch,' where the cowgirls rebel and attempt to take the place over. Madonna was originally signed up to star, but on a project-ditching binge vacated

Uma as June and Fred Ward as Henry Miller in Philip Kaufman's controversial *Henry & June*

With Robert De Niro in John McNaughton's *Mad Dog and Glory*

Uma as Maid Marian in the TV version of *Robin Hood*

Jean-Claude VAN DAMME

Whatever Jean-Claude Van Damme may tell you to the contrary, he is not a great actor. He has charm, he has grace and he has wonderful pectorals, but he is no actor. And, let's be honest, his innumerable fans don't check out his videos to watch Chekhov. What the name Van Damme promises is action, some spectacular martial arts and a great body. For some years insiders have been predicting that the Belgian karate champion was the Next Big Thing, and to listen to him talk one might agree. 'I fight long,' he says in his makeshift English. 'I'm so flexible, smooth, a dancer, and I never get hurt. Look at my face – it's smooth, like a baby. Feel my arms. I don't believe in luck. By having a conviction, everything is possible if you train or push yourself.' He has, however (he swears), 'got a talent to act. No matter what any newspaper says about me, I am one of the most sensitive human beings on earth – and I know it.' Maybe his fans do, too. After all, he has been known to receive 3,000 fan letters a month.

The second of two children, he was born Jean-Claude Van Varenberg on 1 April 1961 in Brussels, Belgium, where his accountant father and mother ran a florist shop. A weak and skinny child, hampered by poor sight and thick spectacles, he was taken to a karate class by his father and instantly fell in love with the art. 'I was nine years old,' he recalls. 'My father encouraged me to take karate because I was very small for my age and got picked on a lot. He is a very, very smart man. He knew that karate was not only physical – it also builds your mental attitude. But I also wanted to get bigger and stronger, so I started training with weights.' A few years later he added ballet class to his curriculum and was offered a position in a Paris company, but turned the offer down. His vision was to become a movie star – in Hollywood. 'It was a dream as a young child to do movies. I love movies. You can escape. Belgium is a beautiful but sad country. It is always raining and grey.'

After earning a black belt in *shotokan* (a Japanese style of karate), he turned professional and less than a year later won the European Professional Karate Association's middleweight championship. At 17, he quit school and established his own gymnasium – which he christened the California Gym – and which was soon bringing in $15,000 a month. 'I was making tons of money, but I was not happy.' He was still not a movie star.

He won the part of a villain in the French film *Rue Barbar*, but walked out after an argument with the director. Instead, he did some modelling in Hong Kong, sold his gym and, in 1981, headed for Hollywood. Behind him, he left his Venezuelan wife, Maria Rodriguez, seven years his senior. Unable to speak English, let alone American, Jean-Claude slept in a rented car for his first week in the States, and then worked as a bouncer, carpet layer and limo driver, and eventually began teaching martial arts. Meanwhile, he distributed his photo all over the place, occasionally winning work as a film extra. The only problem was that he didn't have a work permit, nor permission to stay in America for longer than six months (necessitating bi-annual trips across the Mexican border). He also changed his name: 'It's better in America, Van Damme, than Van Varenberg: Van Damage, Hot Damme, Damme Good, Wham Bamme Thank You Van Damme . . . '

In 1985, he landed his first film, playing the Russian villain Ivan in the unbelievably bad martial arts dud *No Retreat, No Surrender*, in which he gets beaten up by a kid (Kurt McKinney – *who?*). The same year he married his second wife, Cynthia Derderian, and left her after twelve months. But he had already set his sights on his true love – the bodybuilder and fitness model Gladys Portugues. 'I was in love with her since I was 19,' he confessed. 'For many years I saw her picture in the magazines.' When he discovered that she was doing a photo shoot in Mexico for *Muscle and Fitness*, he telephoned the publisher and offered to pay his own way to appear alongside her. The publisher agreed and the rest is legend. The Belgian relates, 'I see Gladys and I say, "I've come for you. I'm Van Damme, the karate champion." A month later, she moves from New York to LA to be with me.' Shortly after that they were married, and today have two children, Kristopher and Bianca. 'I do everything fast. Life is so short.'

His stay on the Arnold Schwarzenegger blockbuster *Predator* was certainly short, as he was replaced mid-shoot by Kevin Peter Hall. Van Damme was cast in the title role, but felt constricted by his costume ('the director, John McTiernan, asked me to run and jump and make all these animalistic moves. Then they put me in a body cast. It was disgusting. They covered everything, even my face, with mud. It was very dangerous; I knew I was going to break something'). Still, he got his SAG card, and Kevin Peter Hall was provided with a new outfit (incidentally, Hall is 7'2", compared to Van Damme's 5'10").

When he bumped into the movie mogul Menahem Golan in a Beverly Hills restaurant, he threw a karate kick over Golan's head,

Jean-Claude Van Damme

Jean-Claude in action in *Lionheart*

different'). He was very different as a Royal Canadian Mountie with a strange accent in *Death Warrant*, but was more credible as a soldier of the French Foreign Legion who goes *AWOL* to avenge his brother's death (at the hands of drug dealers) in LA. He then tried very hard to act in *Double Impact*, playing twin brothers who reluctantly team up to avenge their father's death in Hong Kong (Chad Wagner smiled a lot, Alex Wagner snarled). Still, the Stanislavsky effort paid off, and the film grossed $128 million worldwide. For *Universal Soldier*, his best film, he was paid $1.35 million to play a Vietnam corpse resurrected as a robotic soldier-of-fortune. The problem is, the soldier starts remembering the good old days, not least his on-going feud with fellow stiff Dolph Lundgren. The film was actually a terrific action adventure, augmented by some spectacular set pieces, state-of-the-art technology and an agreeable self-mocking humour. Worldwide, it grossed over $100m.

Next, he was paid $3.5m to star in *Nowhere to Run*, furnished with a script by the estimable Joe Eszterhas (*Basic Instinct*, *Music Box*) and a leading lady of the calibre of Rosanna Arquette. Unfortunately, it was as dumb as his earlier movies, with the corn as high as an elephant's eye. For the record, Van Damme played a bank robber on the run, who shacks up with a farmer's widow (Arquette), and then fights for her property against an evil land developer (Joss Ackland). Not surprisingly, the film was a box-office disappointment.

Still, the muscles from Brussels was booked up to the eyeballs with movies, and next starred in *Hard Target*, under the direction of the controversial Hong Kong filmmaker John Woo. 'Lots of movie star want Woo now,' the star explained. 'But he wants to do Van Damme. It will be a beautiful action film.' Promises, promises. Then, at the 1993 Cannes Film Festival, the Belgian announced his plans to direct a historical epic called *The Quest*. He pledged, 'I believe it's going to be the *Ben Hur* of martial arts. It has a great philosophical message.' He also announced his engagement to Darcy La Pier, a former Hawaiian beauty queen.

Two for the price of one: Jean-Claude as Chad and his brother, Alex, in *Double Impact*

JC as the robot with a human memory in Roland Emmerich's thrilling *Universal Soldier*

and was invited to the tycoon's office for the following day. There, he waited six hours before he was seen, and then performed a spectacular split while suspended between two chairs. According to Van Damme, 'Menahem stepped back. He said, "Bring me *Bloodsport*. You want to be a star? I'm gonna make you a star!"'

In *Bloodsport*, shot in five weeks for less than $2 million, he played the real-life American (!) commando Frank Dux, who was the first westerner to win the illegal martial arts competition ('the Kumite'), held every five years in Hong Kong. Van Damme finally got the chance to prove he couldn't act, but his admirable kickboxing skills helped the film to become a popular success, first in France and Asia, and later in America.

His subsequent films gathered momentum at the box-office, their irresistible blend of bone-snapping violence, effortless plots and balletic karate appealing to a growing legion

of fans. He was another Russian villain in *Black Eagle*, also starring Sho Kosugi; was the hero in the post-apocalyptic *Cyborg*; and in *Kickboxer*, in which he sought to avenge the crippling of his brother, he illustrated his strength by kicking down a tree (Van Damme admits, 'I was really hurt, but I wanted to show something on the camera that was

FILMOGRAPHY

1980: *Monaco Forever*. 1986: *No Retreat, No Surrender*. 1987: *Predator; Bloodsport*. 1988: *Black Eagle*. 1989: *Cyborg; Kickboxer*. 1990: *Death Warrant*. 1991: *Lionheart* (aka *AWOL – Absent Without Leave/Wrong Bet*); *Double Impact*. 1992: *Universal Soldier*. 1993: *Nowhere To Run; Hard Target; Last Action Hero* (cameo). 1994: *TIMECOP; Street Fighter*.

Damon WAYANS

The fourth of ten children, Damon Wayans emerged from a family bursting with showbusiness acumen. In order to gain attention he honed his comedy down to a fine art and thus made his way in the world as a stand-out, stand-up comic. He was funny alright, but his comedy eventually became fuelled by rage.

'I get so angry,' he acknowledged, 'but you can't straighten what's crooked, and the system is crooked. I have to find humour in that, so that I don't end up on top of some roof with a gun.' On stage he played the angry comedian, opening his act: 'Good evening. A funny thing happened on my way here. I killed three white people.' His idol was Richard Pryor, but was disappointed when Pryor sold out. Wayans intends to keep *his* edge intact. It is ironic then, when Richard Pryor was not up to voicing the black kid, Eddie, in *Look Who's Talking Too*, that it was Wayans who was called on to replace him.

Like fellow comic Dudley Moore, Damon Wayans was born with a club foot. Unlike Dudley Moore, he was born in 1960 and raised in a six-room apartment on a black housing project in New York. His father, Howell, was a supermarket manager and a devout Jehovah's Witness – and was not above chastising his children with the occasional beating. His disciplined children included Damon, Keenen Ivory, Kim, Shawn, Duane and Marlon, all of whom went on to act with some success in showbusiness.

But life was hard for the Wayans family, and Damon suffered his share of hard knocks. While working for a credit card company, aged 21, he 'borrowed' some plastic for his own use. 'I got caught,' he confesses, 'and was charged with a felony. But I think I ended up turning a negative into a positive.' Indeed, Damon used the experience for his screenplay of *Mo' Money*, the 1992 hit which he also executive-produced and starred in.

As a child, he idolized his older brother, Keenen, who started doing stand-up comedy when Damon was still in his teens. Damon even wrote jokes for him – in between stints at McDonald's. Egged on by his wife, Lisa, he eventually went out on his own. But things didn't take off immediately.

Keenen's old friend Robert Townsend (later the star and director of *Hollywood Shuffle*) helped out when Damon moved to Los Angeles. So did Eddie Murphy, who cast him as the camp hotel employee in his 1984 hit *Beverly Hills Cop* (it was Damon who slipped Axel Foley the bananas from his fruit stall).

A year later Damon found himself on the team of the cult TV series *Saturday Night Live*, alongside Robert Downey Jr, Anthony Michael Hall and Jon Lovitz. However, it was not a successful season and Wayans fell foul of the series' producer and creator, Lorne Michaels, when he ad-libbed a sketch out of the blue.

According to Michaels, 'at dress rehearsal Damon did one thing and then on the air he did something else. He did a sort of caricature gay voice. It was a funny voice, but it was completely inappropriate for the scene. More importantly, it threw the other two actors in the scene, who had no idea what he was doing. I fired him after that – a mistake on my part, but it was a bigger mistake on his.'

In 1987 he appeared alongside brother Keenen and Townsend in *Hollywood Shuffle*, which the latter duo also scripted, and he then had a flashy role as a gang member in Dennis Hopper's controversial *Colors*. But it was Damon's stand-up comedy that was getting him noticed.

On HBO he had a half-hour special, *One Night Stand*, and he then co-starred in both episodes of *Take No Prisoners: Robert Townsend & His Partners In Crime*. He had a bigger part in the 1988 film *I'm Gonna Git You Sucka*, a parody of 1970s blaxploitation movies starring, written and directed by Keenen, with an impressive line-up of former black idols making fun of themselves (Isaac Hayes, Jim Brown, Steve James). Then Keenen came to the rescue again with his innovative, hard-edged TV sitcom *In Living*

Damon Wayans in 1992

Damon Wayans with Halle Berry in Tony Scott's outrageous *The Last Boy Scout*

Damon (*right*) with little bro' Marlon Wayans in *Mo' Money*

Forest WHITAKER

Due to an excess of weight (260 pounds), a lethargic left eyelid and painful shyness, Forest Whitaker is not exactly leading man material. He does, however, exude an engaging innocence that makes him a mouth-watering foil for any star. Invariably good-humoured, and often brainy, Whitaker's screen image became useful to the point of indispensable. Then Clint Eastwood cast him in the title role of *Bird*, as Charlie Parker, the legendary bebop saxophonist. No longer the friendly, gentle giant, Whitaker turned in a performance of enormous anger, pain and complexity, getting to grips with a suicidal genius who abused his body with heroin. The actor proved more than able to meet the demands of the part and stormed off with the best actor award at the 1988 Cannes Film Festival.

Nevertheless, 'after winning the prize at Cannes, it was a search to find a part,' the actor revealed. However, the action director Walter Hill was at the festival and was in the middle of casting *Johnny Handsome*, a crime thriller. He still needed an actor to play the elderly, Southern plastic surgeon who transforms Mickey Rourke's face, and Hill altered the role to fit Whitaker in. On reflection, the actor notes, 'maybe that prize brought focus on *Bird*. The role allowed me to do a lot of different things and show my work.'

Still, his character in *Johnny Handsome* was only a supporting one, and the film was a flop. He took second-billing to Anthony Edwards in *Downtown*, a crime melodrama and another dud, and then landed the lead in the made-for-cable-movie, *Criminal Justice*. In the latter, Whitaker played an ex-con and single parent jailed for attacking a crack addict (Rosie Perez), and his sense of hurt and indignity was almost unbearable to watch. The film never made it clear whether or not Whitaker was innocent, but his performance spoke volumes and made him a hugely sympathetic victim of circumstance.

The actor then bounced from critical acclaim to the most showy role of his career: the naive hero of *A Rage in Harlem*. The actor not only produced *Harlem* himself, but surrounded himself with an impressive cast, not least Robin Givens, Danny Glover and Gregory Hines. The picture should have made him a certified star, but it was not the success it could've been, and he took another supporting role (as a cardio-vascular surgeon) in another flop, *Article 99*. He then played a contract killer in *Diary of a Hit Man*, co-starring Sharon Stone, James Belushi and

Color, which he created and starred in, with Damon and Kim Wayans in support. Damon also wrote a lot of the material. The show was an enormous success, in particular Damon's recurring creation of Homey D. Clown, a bitter, bilious funnyman. The show made him a star and he walked away with two Emmy nominations.

He got his big-screen break when he was given equal billing to Bruce Willis (above the title) in *The Last Boy Scout*. A hard-hitting, highly entertaining action-comedy, the film received shaky reviews in the States but went on to amass a solid $60 million at the US box-office, reviving Willis's career and upping Wayans's ante.

The latter played a not-so-tough, poorly educated erstwhile football hero fighting a cocaine habit and a frame-up. When his girlfriend is murdered, he teams up with private eye Willis to uncover a plot involving blackmail, extortion and inconceivable corruption. Wayans relied on the film's cracking script to spit out the laughs, playing down his dumb, wise-cracking anti-hero with admirable restraint. It was the film's throw-away humour, amplified by the violence erupting around it, that made *The Last Boy Scout* such an enjoyable, *Man's Own* cocktail. This was not *48 HRS* – this was *Die Hard* meets the World Series. *The Last Boy Scout*

gave Wayans the clout to make his own movies, and he subsequently took up the mantle of executive producer on his own screenplay, *Mo' Money*, in which he and little bro' Marlon played a pair of obnoxious small-time conmen. Damon would have directed, too, if he'd had the time. *Mo' Money* grossed $17 million in its first week, adding credence to the media's label of Wayans as 'the next Eddie Murphy.'

However, 'I don't want to be the *next* anything,' he retorted. 'And I don't want to be the number one star. I'd rather just be number 16 and say and do what I feel like.'

However, the blend of jokes, foul language, mugging and gratuitous violence in *Mo' Money* didn't help separate Wayans from the Murphy image. Here were the familiar funny voices, the courting of the unattainable babe (as in *Boomerang*) and the quick-fire sketches. The only difference was that Eddie Murphy did this sort of thing much better.

Next, Wayans starred in his own screenplay of *Blankman*, a project that teamed him opposite Keenen, on which Damon also served as producer.

FILMOGRAPHY

1984: *Beverly Hills Cop*. 1987: *Roxanne*; *Hollywood Shuffle*. 1988: *Colors*; *Punchline*; *I'm Gonna Git You Sucka*. 1989: *Earth Girls Are Easy*. 1990: *Look Who's Talking Too* (voice only). 1991: *The Last Boy Scout*. 1992: *Mo' Money*. 1993: *Last Action Hero* (cameo). 1994: *Blankman*; *The Private War of Major Benson*.

Sherilyn Fenn. Again, all the credentials were there for a very popular film, but it wasn't, and the would-be star returned to supporting roles. At the end of the day it is clear that Forest Whitaker makes a better actor than a leading man.

Born on 15 July 1961, in Longview, Texas, Forest was the son of an insurance salesman (his father) and a teacher (his mother). Soon after his birth, his family moved to Los Angeles, where Forest grew up on the tough streets of Compton. Big enough to handle himself (he's 6' 2''), Forest resisted joining the local gangs and concentrated on his love of music and painting. He escaped the grim reality of LA's South Central by becoming a football star at Palisades High, consequently winning scholarships from UCLA, Hawaii, Utah State and Arizona. 'But there was a problem,' he explains. 'I didn't live in the school zone. I should have been at Compton High, but my mother wanted me to go to a good school.' At this point the Palisades High football team was undefeated. But Forest was reported by a snitch and to save his team forfeiting all their games, he had to back out of a major match: subsequently, his team lost for the first time. Devastated, Forest

Forest Whitaker as Charlie 'Bird' Parker – courtesy of Clint Eastwood

Whitaker as the good doctor Steven Resher, with Morgan Freeman, in Walter Hill's Johnny Handsome

accepted a football scholarship to Pomona College and concentrated on studying music.

At Pomona he took a speech class for singing, and was asked to audition for a university production of Under Milk Wood. He won the role of the narrator in the play, and then transferred to the University of Southern California to study opera and drama. Ironically, his first professional part was in The Beggar's Opera.

Other local stage work followed, and then numerous bits in TV and film. On the small screen he turned up in Hill Street Blues, Cagney and Lacey and The Fall Guy, and made his film debut in the high school thriller Tag: The Assassination Game, starring Robert Carradine and Linda Hamilton. He landed his first decent role – as the school football star – in Amy Heckerling's Fast Times at Ridgemont High, alongside fellow debutees Eric Stoltz and Anthony Edwards.

As a pool shark, he humiliated Paul

With Stephen Rea in the award-winning *The Crying Game*

Robin WRIGHT

Although Texan by birth, Robin Wright radiated a beauty of European grace and delicacy, topped by a sheaf of glowing strawberry-blond hair and a subtle smattering of freckles. She would be as perfect playing a Thomas Hardy heroine (Bathsheba Everdene, say) as any Dorset-bred graduate of RADA. And she had talent to spare.

After displaying her breath-catching loveliness in *The Princess Bride*, Ms Wright illustrated her acting mettle in the gritty realism of *State of Grace*, playing the strong-willed sister of Irish gangster Gary Oldman. And yet, in spite of her attention-seizing roles, the actress's films were decidedly few and far between.

'Good roles come along only once or twice a year, and if I can't get one of them, I'd rather not work,' she has said. 'It will probably hurt me, or so I hear, but I don't care. If you do a movie you don't really want to do and you sell yourself out, you get old, you burn out your facets.'

Robin Wright was born in Dallas, Texas, in 1966. She and her brother were raised by their mother, a cosmetics sales rep, and when Robin was four, 'we all got into the car and just kept driving till we hit the ocean.' The ocean was the Pacific, and Robin grew up in San Diego, California, becoming a model at the age of 14, working both in Paris and Japan. This, in turn, led to a series of commercials in California paving the way for acting auditions.

In 1984 she landed a small part in the dramatic TV series *The Yellow Rose*, starring Cybill Shepherd and David Soul, and then made her name playing Kelly Capwell in the daytime soap *Santa Barbara*, for which she was twice nominated for an Emmy.

In 1987 she was one of hundreds of hopefuls who auditioned for the title role in *The Princess Bride*, Rob Reiner's magical, comic romance. Reiner, who has an unerring nose for talent, cast Robin on the spot. 'She is stunningly beautiful', he asserted. 'Two sentences out of her mouth, and I knew she was the girl I wanted.'

The film, a romping, playful parody of the traditional fairy tale, was one of the year's most enjoyable surprises. Robin Wright was perfect as the demure Buttercup, awaiting rescue from her prince charming (a dashing Cary Elwes) before being married to the dastardly Count Rugen (Christopher Guest on excellent form). Part swashbuckling adventure and part spoof, the film was also a touching love story and appealed to audiences of all ages and persuasion.

Newman in Martin Scorsese's *The Color of Money*, and then worked for Oliver Stone on *Platoon*, playing 'Big Harold.' He was a cop in *Stakeout*, playing pranks on Richard Dreyfuss and Emilio Estevez, and was another officer of the law – in Hong Kong – in *Bloodsport*, with Jean-Claude Van Damme. In *Good Morning, Vietnam* he won second-billing to Robin Williams, as the latter's bewildered chauffeur, and then came Clint Eastwood's *Bird*.

Eastwood defended his decision to cast an unknown as Charlie 'Yardbird' Parker. 'If you had a name player, people would have had to do a lot of deciphering. I'd seen Parker play in Oakland, where I grew up in the Forties, and he had a tremendously sympathetic character even when he was being a bad boy. Forest seems like that. He has those qualities.'

In 1992, in Neil Jordan's provocative *The Crying Game*, Whitaker played a British soldier held hostage in Northern Ireland, causing much protest from Anglo-African actors. Nevertheless, the star – who had never worked outside of the States before – showed an uncanny knack for a Cockney accent, and never intruded on the gritty realism of the film. The director defended his casting choice by saying, 'I couldn't find another actor who could equal the power and the quality of Forest's work. He has that particular sense of innocence, and is possessed of all the emotions and methods of research that American actors bring with

them to a role. He was great.' So was the film, which ended up on many critics' top ten lists and scored powerfully at the US box-office, becoming one of the most successful British films ever made. In the last week of 1992 *The Crying Game* was making more money per cinema in America than any other movie. Two months later it stormed off with six Oscar nominations, including an unexpected (but deserved) nod for best film.

He had a supporting role, as a Southern private detective, in Alan J. Pakula's daft, glossy thriller *Consenting Adults*, a flop, and then co-starred in *Body Snatchers*, the 1992 remake of Don Siegel's sci-fi classic. He also trained extensively and shed considerable weight to prepare for the title role in *The Brown Bomber*, the long-awaited biography of heavyweight boxer Joe Louis.

When he's not acting, Forest enjoys painting ('an art critic would probably call my paintings primitive, aggressive, off-kilter realism'). In 1993 he made his debut as a film director with *Strapped*, an indictment of guns in New York.

FILMOGRAPHY

1982: *Tag: The Assassination Game; Fast Times at Ridgemont High.* 1985: *VisionQuest.* 1986: *The Color of Money; Platoon.* 1987: *Hands of a Stranger* (TV); *Stakeout; Bloodsport; Good Morning, Vietnam.* 1988: *Bird.* 1989: *Johnny Handsome.* 1990: *Downtown; Criminal Justice* (TV). 1991: *A Rage in Harlem.* 1992: *Article 99; Diary of a Hit Man; The Crying Game; Consenting Adults.* 1993: *Body Snatchers; Last Light* (TV); *Strapped* (dir. only); *Lush Life; Jason's Lyric; Bank Robber.* 1994: *Blown Away; The Gold Cup; The Number Four* (dir. only); *Pret-a-Porter; Smoke.*

Robin Wright as *The Princess Bride*

At the time, the beauty was living with former *Santa Barbara* co-star Dane Witherspoon, planning to marry him in April of 1988, followed by a honeymoon in Africa. Instead, thanks to the success of *The Princess Bride*, she won the starring role in *Loon*, playing a young woman trapped in flashback hell as she moped after erstwhile love Jason Patric. The film was not good, and resurfaced three years later on video under the title *Denial*.

A year later Robin skewered the female lead in the aggressively male *State of Grace*, the violent story of a gang of Irish-American thugs spreading fear across the streets of New York's Hell's Kitchen. Robin played Kathleen Flannery, childhood sweetheart of local boy Sean Penn, the latter returning to the neighbourhood after an absence of some years. In amongst the bloodshed, Robin lent the film considerable nobility as the strong-willed Irish woman who is not afraid to speak her mind.

'The female lead in these types of films is often a thankless role,' explained the movie's director Phil Joanou. 'It was one of the things on which we worked very hard. Kathleen is the character who ultimately stands up to the men, head to head, with self-respect and dignity.'

Although Robin Wright had met Sean Penn before, the couple warmed to each after during the shooting (in both senses of the word), and after the film's completion started seeing a lot of each other. She was offered the role of Maid Marian in Hollywood's $50 million *Robin Hood: Prince of Thieves*, opposite Kevin Costner, but had to back out when she became pregnant with Sean's baby. Mary Elizabeth Mastrantonio stepped into her part at the eleventh hour and the film became the second highest-grossing sensation of 1991.

Following the birth of her daughter, Dylan Frances, the actress got her own back on Hollywood by winning the best role of her career. Annette Bening was signed up to play the headstrong Tara Maguire in *The Playboys*, when she walked – followed by a law suit. Robin Wright stepped in, and was promptly joined by Albert Finney and Aidan Quinn as her leading men.

Set in an isolated Irish village in 1957, *The Playboys* was a drama of considerable emotional strength and beauty, capped by a stirring performance from Ms Wright. As a single mother who refuses to name the father of her child, she was passionate, seductive and sympathetic in an exceptionally demanding role. She also obliterated all traces of her American accent, opening up avenues for her seemingly endless talent.

In Barry Levinson's long-awaited *Toys*, she played Gwen, Robin Williams's romantic interest, and revealed a hitherto unrealised sense of the wacky. In the memorable scene in which she and Williams fall for each other in a factory canteen, she displayed a delightful spontaneity – pulling faces, laughing and acting as both a romantic and a comic foil to Williams. Although her role was a supporting one (she received fourth billing), it is obvious why she took it, as it allowed her to shed her image as 'an intense beauty'. It also allowed her to use her own Texas accent on screen, which must have come as a shock to most of her fans. And even if the film was a critical and commercial bomb, Wright's zany, comic and delightful performance still left a sweet taste in the mouth.

Next, she teamed up with Tom Hanks and Sally Field in the romantic comedy *Forrest Gump* – directed by Robert Zemeckis – and in August of 1993 gave birth to her second child, Hopper Jack. Then, in January of 1994, she began work on *The Crossing Guard*, alongside Jack Nicholson and Anjelica Huston, with Sean Penn behind the camera.

FILMOGRAPHY

1986: *Hollywood Vice Squad*. **1987**: *The Princess Bride*. **1990**: *State of Grace*. **1991**: *Denial* (aka *Loon*; filmed in 1988). **1992**: *The Playboys*; *Toys*. **1994**: *Forrest Gump*; *The Crossing Guard*.

Robin as the defiant Kathleen Flannery in Phil Joanou's *State of Grace*

As the stubborn Tara Maguire in Gillies Mackinnon's *The Playboys*

Sean YOUNG

To be honest, notoriety and Sean Young are inseparable. Thanks to a series of highly publicized incidents, the actress has become more famous than her films and continues to be God's gift to the tabloids. Much has been reported on her wild behaviour, most of which she denies. On screen, she is not adverse to shedding her clothes, can be both sexy and funny, has shown some talent as a serious actress, and yet, equally, has turned in some frankly embarrassing performances. Her co-stars seem to either love her or hate her, while, to the press, she has appeared alternately aloof, cold, disarmingly honest and whacky. In short, Ms Young is an enigma.

After a promising start in the comedy hit *Stripes*, Sean Young landed the female lead in Ridley Scott's rightfully revered *Blade Runner* and then caused a sensation in *No Way Out*, seducing Kevin Costner in the back of a limousine. Then came the troubles.

While she was filming Oliver Stone's *Wall Street*, co-star Charlie Sheen stuck a note on her back that proclaimed her 'the biggest c**t in the world.' Charitably, she says, 'you have to understand, Charlie is so young.' But

when she arrived on set to find Daryl Hannah delivering one of her lines, she had a blazing row with the director and left the film. That is *her* story. Others suggested that she was fired. Anyway, most of her part ended up on the cutting room floor.

Next, she landed the female lead opposite James Woods in the searing drug drama *The Boost*. Besides stories of her flashing the crew (minus underwear), reports filtered out that she and Woods were conducting an affair – in spite of the latter's engagement to one Sarah Owen. Later, Woods called the film's production 'a nightmare' and slapped a $2 million harassment lawsuit on Young for 'intentional infliction of emotional distress' on him and Owens. The suit accused the actress of sending 'photographs and graphic representations of violent acts, deceased persons, dead animals, gore, mutilation and other images specifically designed to cause Woods and Owen great emotional distress.' The final straw was a doll found on the actor's doorstep which had its throat slashed, with iodine splashed over it to represent blood (reportedly to remind Woods of his fiancée's abortion). Anyway, this episode in the Sean Young soap opera ended with a settlement in the actress's favour, complete with a cheque to cover her legal costs. And, a year later, Woods and Owen started divorce proceedings.

At times reluctant to discuss this spell in her public life, the actress can also enter into the spirit of the absurdity of it all. 'The story supposedly was that ten years ago [scriptwriter] James Dearden and I were lovers and he based *Fatal Attraction* on me.' Oh, how the gossip mongers love Ms Young.

Following the 1988 *Boost* to her career, Sean was signed up to play Vicki Vale to Michael Keaton's *Batman* – which promised to be the most visible female role of the year. But, no sooner had rehearsals started than Young broke her collarbone in a riding accident and was replaced at the eleventh hour by Kim Basinger. She was also announced to appear in Woody Allen's *Crimes and Misdemeanours*, but was nowhere to be seen in the finished film (although Daryl Hannah turned up in an unbilled cameo).

Still, although Sean didn't get *Batman*, she *was* signed up to play Tess Trueheart, the female lead in *Dick Tracy*, the big-budget comic-book extravaganza starring Warren Beatty. But . . . 'Artistic differences' was the

Sean with Michael McKean in Garry Marshall's *Young Doctors in Love*

term used to describe Sean's departure from that film (she was replaced by Glenne Headley at the final hour) – or, as she puts it, 'Warren didn't know how to deal with the fact that he looked more like my dad than my boyfriend.'

Still, Sean knew that she had the coveted part of Catwoman sewn up for *Batman Returns*. Early on she revealed to one journalist: 'I'm going to kidnap Kim Basinger and Batman's gonna have to follow me to get her back. I'm gonna *torture* her.' However, in the now-familiar tradition of irony, Warren Beatty's girlfriend, Annette Bening, was cast as Catwoman instead. But Sean Young had the next laugh, when Bening had to back out of the picture after conceiving Beatty's baby. It was then open season at Warner Brothers. Cher, Michelle Pfeiffer – hell, even *Julia Roberts* – were all up for the role, while Sean Young donned feline mask and cape and roamed the Warner lot in search of director Tim Burton (who reportedly hid in the loo). So determined was she to get the part that she even went on *The Joan Rivers Show* on TV in full cat regalia. But, as history relates, Burton went straight from the wash room to Michelle Pfeiffer's agent . . .

Next to her role in the tabloids, Sean

Sean Young as she looked in 1982

Young's film career seemed almost inconsequential. But, for the record, she was born in Louisville, Kentucky, on 20 November 1959, the youngest of three children, her parents both involved in journalism. Growing up in Cleveland, she was prey to bullies and decided on a career as a ballerina. She attended the Interlochen Arts Academy in Michigan and, after graduating in 1978, headed for New York to take up dance. Instead, she turned to modelling, and through her mother's literary agent met a talent scout who landed her her first film role, in James Ivory's *Jane Austen in Manhattan*. This led to the part of Harold Ramis's army girlfriend in *Stripes*, and the role of the serene android Rachel in *Blade Runner* (with Daryl Hannah in support as another android). She was the ingenue in the sporadically funny *Young Doctors in Love*, and played the beautiful heroine, Chani, in David Lynch's epic translation of Frank Herbert's cult sci-fi novel *Dune*.

On TV, she portrayed two F. Scott

With Kevin Costner in the box-office hit *No Way Out*

Sean and James Woods in a typical pose – from *The Boost*

Then she starred opposite Michael Caine in the romantic thriller *Blue Ice*, playing a sexy, mysterious American in London. Caine was a fan: 'When I heard that they had cast her, I thought, "Oh, shit." But she's the easiest actress I've ever worked with. Easy as pie – and totally cooperative; a sweetheart.' The film was a bomb. She then joined Armand Assante in Carl Reiner's detective spoof *Fatal Instinct*, and was announced to star in a film called *The Black Cat*. Maybe her test run as Catwoman might have paid off after all.

FILMOGRAPHY

1980: *Jane Austen in Manhattan*. 1981: *Stripes*. 1982: *Blade Runner; Young Doctors in Love*. 1984: *Dune; Baby . . . Secret of the Lost Legend*. 1985: *Under the Biltmore Clock* (TV). 1987: *No Way Out; Wall Street*. 1988: *The Boost*. 1989: *Cousins*. 1990: *Fire Birds* (UK: *Wings of the Apache*). 1991: *A Kiss Before Dying; Once Upon a Crime; Love Crimes*. 1992: *Forever; Sketch Artist; Hold Me, Thrill Me, Kiss Me; Blue Ice*. 1993: *Even Cowgirls Get the Blues; Fatal Instinct*. 1994: *Ace Ventura: Pet Detective; Witness to the Execution* (TV); *Model by Day* (TV); *Dr Jekyll and Ms Hyde*.

Fitzgerald heroines – in the BBC miniseries *Tender is the Night*, and in the critically lambasted movie *Under the Biltmore Clock* – and also co-starred in the CBS mini-series *Blood and Orchids*.

She was better as Ted Danson's unfaithful wife in *Cousins*, a tender, witty remake of the French comedy *Cousin Cousine*, but her subsequent films – *Fire Birds, A Kiss Before Dying, Once Upon a Crime* and *Love Crimes* –

were all flops. In 1992 she played the ghost of a Hollywood goddess (who shacks up with music video whizkid Keith Coogan) in the lamentable *Forever*, but was better served by the intriguing mystery thriller *Sketch Artist*, as Jeff Fahey's wife – who may or may not be a murderess. She was also memorable in the bizarre romantic comedy *Hold Me, Thrill Me, Kiss Me* in which she sent up her public persona rotten.

Z

Billy ZANE

The comparisons with Brando are inevitable and constant. There is the same etched bone structure, the fleshy mouth, the straight nose and that brooding, smouldering stare. At times, the similarity is uncanny. Billy Zane knows he has the physical presence to become a major star, but downplays his looks by constantly referring to his Brandoesque features as 'the mug'. "'The mug'", he says, 'is a tool. To have looks is the bonus on top of what motivates me to be an actor. Not to realize they're an asset would be counterproductive to the cause – they serve the common good.'

To prove he was not just a pretty face, Zane followed early roles as a deranged psychotic and as a serial killer with the part of a dashing bombardier, and then expanded his repertoire to include the complex portrayal of a government assassin wrestling with his conscience. He then adds that, 'a musical would be interesting. I'd love to be remembered for tap dancing and catching a pie in the face.'

The son of dedicated theatregoers and amateur actors, Billy Zane was born in 1966 and raised in Chicago, where he attended Lincoln Park's Francis Parker High School. His parents' enthusiasm for the stage fired his professional interest, as it did his sister's, the latter (Lisa Zane) going on to a successful screen career herself (she had leading parts in *Bad Influence* and *Freddie's Dead: The Final Nightmare*). During his high school summers, Billy cut his acting teeth on such musicals as *Oklahoma!* and *Guys and Dolls* and, in 1982, studied writing and acting at the American School in Switzerland.

In 1984 he moved to Hollywood,

Billy Zane as the menacing imposter in Phillip Noyce's gripping *Dead Calm*

Billy Zane with Tom Berenger in *Sniper*

promising his father that if he didn't make it as an actor within the year he would return to college. Three weeks later he landed the role of 'Match' – one of Biff's bullying sidekicks – in *Back to the Future*, shortly followed by a good role in the jokey horror film *Critters* (which spawned three sequels). He also flexed his thespian talents on stage, performing with the Second Theater Company (in *American Music*) and with Tim Robbins's experimental group, The Actors' Gang (in *The Boys in the Backroom*). On TV, he was memorable in the movie *The Brotherhood of Justice*, as Les, a hip, gum-chewing and ultimately dangerous high school vigilante at odds with Keanu Reeves and Kiefer Sutherland – and then came his Big Break.

In April of 1987, the Australian director Phillip Noyce called on Zane to audition for the role of Hughie Warriner, the psychotic survivor of a sinking ship in *Dead Calm*. By Australian standards, the film was a big-budget production and Noyce had his pick of stars to choose from. But besides casting the reasonably well-known New Zealand actor Sam Neill (in the film's third biggest part), the director opted for two newcomers – Nicole Kidman and Billy Zane. 'We had our choice of any number of young, fairly well-known up-and-coming male actors, both from America and other countries,' Noyce noted. 'But we made a conscious decision to go with an unknown. This way, he comes into the audiences' lives as a real stranger.'

After wading through a sea of publicity stills, the director zeroed in on 40 actors to audition for the part of Warriner. Zane was his man. 'He gave us something that was totally fascinating,' Noyce swears, ' – without being neurotic or "strange". Billy's acting is always on the edge, always surprising in his choices of how to play a scene. He's entirely spontaneous; totally fresh.'

In the film, Hughie Warriner is rescued by a surgeon (Neill) and his beautiful young wife (Kidman), and is given hospitality aboard their luxury yacht. He explains that his companions have died of food poisoning, but while he sleeps the surgeon rows off to investigate the sinking schooner. There, he finds Warriner's shipmates brutally murdered, but as he frantically rows back to his yacht, Warriner wakes, sets sail and makes himself acquainted with Ms Kidman ... *Dead Calm* was a nail-biting thriller in the traditional sense, beautiful to look at, superbly directed by Noyce and backed by powerhouse performances from Kidman and Zane. It was both a commercial and critical success.

Not only did *Dead Calm* turn Billy Zane's

Zane as the American adventurer
Shelmerdine, with Tilda Swinton in Sally
Potter's *Orlando*

Billy Zane laying on the sex appeal in the
dismal *Lake Consequence*

career around, but it introduced him to his
wife, the Australian actress Lisa Collins.
Although she was only a model for a
photograph in the film (as one of Warriner's
shipmates spotted in a logbook), it was love
at first sight. Since, she's changed her name
to Rachel to avoid confusion with Billy's sister
Lisa.

After *Dead Calm*, Billy Zane dallied in
more evil, playing a serial killer in the TV
movie *The Case of the Hillside Stranglers*, with
Richard Crenna; returned as 'Match' in *Back
to the Future Part II*; and then won top-billing
for the first time in the intriguing sci-fi thriller
Megaville, on good form as an idealistic cop

Zane as the corrupt Colonel Graham – with Mario Van Peebles – in *Posse*

in a futuristic fascist state. He was all swaggering charm and teeth – as bombardier Val Kozlowski – in the hit World War II flying adventure *Memphis Belle*, and conjured up favourable memories of Clark Gable.

On TV, he joined David Lynch's cult series *Twin Peaks*, as John Justice Wheeler, the environmentalist with the hots for Audrey Horn (Sherilyn Fenn), and then returned to the big screen in the stylish comic-romantic thriller *Blood and Concrete*, with Jennifer Beals. He described the latter, in which he played a car thief and reformed drug dealer, as 'a send-up of LA archetypes – from pseudo-

beat poetry junkies to Santa Monica bad boys.' In Italy, he starred in Carlo Vanzina's *Miliardi*, as the ruthless heir to a family fortune – with supermodel Carol Alt – and then joined his sister (and Colin Firth) in the silly psychological drama *Femme Fatale*.

In the jungle-set thriller *Sniper*, he was a smarmy, irritating government agent assigned to oversee veteran assassin Tom Berenger, but the film fell foul of its own pretensions. Both actors created some compelling, uneasy electricity, but the script's psychological belly-aching tripped up a perfectly decent action-thriller. It was, however, a mild box-office success.

He then took a supporting role in the bizarre English film *Orlando*, as a hunky American 'in the pursuit of liberty,' who is first seen riding out of the mist following the caption '1850 – SEX'. Next, he starred opposite Joan Severance in *Lake*

Consequence, an erotic drama from Zalman King, the producer of *9 1/2 Weeks*, and then played a colonel of the Spanish-American war who tracks down a gang of deserters – in Mario Van Peebles's *Posse*.

Besides acting, Billy Zane spends his time making comedy shorts, has directed a music video for Robbie Nevil ('Back on Holiday') and wrote a screenplay, *Gargoyle*.

FILMOGRAPHY

1985: *Back to the Future*. 1986: *Critters*; *The Brotherhood of Justice* (TV). 1988: *Dead Calm*. 1989: *The Case of the Hillside Stranglers* (aka *The Hillside Stranglers*) (TV); *Back to the Future Part II*. 1990: *Megaville*; *Memphis Belle*. 1991: *Blood and Concrete, A Love Story*; *Miliardi* (aka *Billions/Millions*); *Femme Fatale*. 1993: *Sniper*; *Orlando*; *Lake Consequence*; *Posse*; *Cyborg Agent*. 1994: *Silence of the Hams*; *Tombstone*; *Just in Time*; *Flash Fire*.